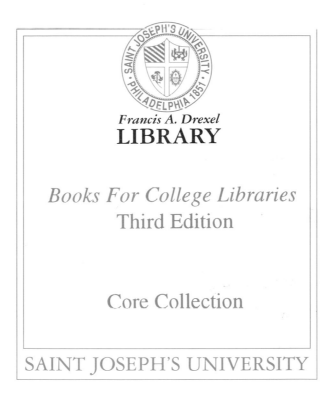

Francis A. Drexel
LIBRARY

Books For College Libraries
Third Edition

Core Collection

SAINT JOSEPH'S UNIVERSITY

EDUCATING

EXCEPTIONAL

CHILDREN

HOUGHTON MIFFLIN COMPANY

BOSTON

New York

Atlanta

Geneva, Illinois

Dallas

Palo Alto

EDUCATING

EXCEPTIONAL

CHILDREN

SECOND EDITION

SAMUEL A. KIRK

Professor of

Special Education,

University of

Arizona

Library of Congress Catalog Card Number: 73–158210

ISBN: 0–395–12599–5

To the memory of
Ray Graham,
humanitarian and friend,
whose dynamic and effective
leadership in Illinois
and in the nation
has left a lasting imprint
on all who labor to make
life more meaningful
to children who are
in some way "different."

. . . Of a good leader
who talks little
When his work is done,
his aim fulfilled,
They will say,
"We did this ourselves."

Lao-tzu

CONTENTS

Classification and Prevalence of Speech Disorders / Articulatory Disorders / Vocal Disorders / Stuttering / Delayed Speech / Speech Defects Associated with Hearing Loss / Speech Defects Associated with Cleft Palate / Speech Disorders Associated with Cerebral Palsy / Public School Speech Correction Programs / Summary / References

FOURTEEN 421
ADMINISTRATIVE ORGANIZATIONS

The Role of the Federal Government / The Role of State Agencies / The Role of Local Administration / Summary

LIST

OF

FIGURES

LIST

OF

TABLES

PREFACE

The first edition of *Educating Exceptional Children* is ten years old. During those ten years much has transpired in the field of exceptional children. Greater emphasis has been placed on educating both the handicapped and the gifted. Public concern has demanded significant changes, and governmental interest at local, state, and national levels has expanded. This is evidenced by the fact that in 1970 the newly created Bureau of Education for the Handicapped administered or monitored over 170 million dollars' worth of Federal funds as contrasted with less than 5 million in 1962. These changes, together with major advances in theory and practice, have made it necessary to update the original book.

There probably is no such thing as a perfect textbook. Undoubtedly, this book is no exception even in its second edition. But ever since 1935, when I taught my first courses about exceptional children, I have felt the need for an integrated and unified text in this field. At that time I had been asked to teach two consecutive courses. The first was entitled "The Psychology of Exceptional Children," and it was followed by a course in "The Education of Exceptional Children." I soon found from the available literature that the title of the psychology course was a misnomer, since the content included biology, physiology, and sociology, as well as psychology. To describe the characteristics of the children it was necessary to describe them in physical, psychological, and social terms. Similarly, the course in the education of exceptional children could not be taught in a vacuum. It was necessary to review the characteristics of the children for whom educational modifications were to be made. Subdividing the subject matter on exceptional children into the various academic disciplines of a university may simplify the writing of books, but it does not provide a unified approach to the necessary learnings of a student.

The field of exceptional children is so extensive that it is difficult for one person to be sufficiently versed in all areas to write a comprehensive text. The tendency has been to prepare such a text through multiple authorship, which of course, has the advantage of utilizing experts in each field. Having prepared and edited *The Education of Exceptional Children* (the Forty-ninth Yearbook of the National Society for the Study of Education), I am also aware of the difficulties involved in working with a number of authors, who have different styles and different philosophies, and who are inclined to present overlapping content.

This book is intended to be the basis for an introductory course in exceptional children. Customarily, students enrolled in such a course will have had introductory courses in psychology or educational psychology and in education. An attempt is made here to avoid content which would overlap with that of other courses and to include only information specific to this field.

In attempting to provide an integrated and unified book on exceptional children I have relied heavily on the concept of intraindividual differences or discrepancies in growth within the exceptional child. I have found that this approach clarifies and unifies the concept of exceptional children. By applying it to the various kinds of deviating children we supply an integrating element which gives meaning to both the deviating characteristics of the children and the resulting suitable modifications of educational practice. Instead of entitling the first chapter "Introduction" I have called it "Intraindividual Differences: Discrepancies in Growth and Development." This application of the concept of discrepancies I consider to be the main contribution of the book.

The preparation of this revised text required professional advice and assistance from various sources. Many of the chapters were submitted to pertinent specialists for criticisms and suggestions. My colleagues have been most gracious in critically evaluating the chapters and in making constructive suggestions for improvement. I am highly indebted to the constructive criticisms and suggestions from Professors Natalie Barraga, Betty Hannah, Alice Streng, Elizabeth Sharp, Herbert Quay, Loyd Wright, Walter Olson, John Irwin, Alice Mason, and Francis Lord. Each of these individuals devoted considerable time in evaluating and in suggesting new ideas, new facts, and new approaches to the education of exceptional children. Any errors or omissions, however, I claim as my own.

I especially wish to acknowledge the professional and technical assistance of my wife, Winifred D. Kirk, whose contributions deserve more than this acknowledgement provides. The valuable assistance of LaMartha Wallace, graduate assistant, and Graciela Osterberg Mason, stenographer, are gratefully acknowledged.

Samuel A. Kirk

EDUCATING

EXCEPTIONAL

CHILDREN

ONE

INTRAINDIVIDUAL

DIFFERENCES:

DISCREPANCIES

IN GROWTH

AND

DEVELOPMENT

Education in any society tends to reflect the political philosophy of that society. Under a democracy as practiced in the United States, where the state is believed to exist for the welfare of the individual, education must be organized primarily to achieve this end. "All men are created equal" has become trite, but it still has important meaning for education in a democratic society. Although it was used by the founding fathers to denote equality before the law, it has also been interpreted to mean equality of opportunity. This implies educational opportunity for *all* children—the right of each child to receive help in learning to the limits of his capacity, whether that capacity be small or great.

It is consistent with a democratic philosophy that all children be given the opportunity to learn, whether they are average, bright, dull, retarded, blind, deaf, crippled, delinquent, emotionally disturbed, or otherwise limited or deviant in their capacities to learn. Our schools have evolved, therefore, numerous modifications of regular school programs to adapt instruction to children who deviate from the average and who cannot profit substantially from the regular program. These modified programs have been designated as programs for exceptional children.

The programs for exceptional children in school systems have been found to benefit not only the deviant child but also other children. Handicapped or gifted children in a regular classroom sometimes require individual attention. It is inevitable that if a regular classroom teacher devotes adequate time to a deviant child he must curtail the attention which he ordinarily gives the other children. But when special services are offered the deviant child, the normal pupils benefit by having more of the regular teacher's time.

A second contribution which has been made to all children has come indirectly from studies of handicapped and gifted children. Today, for example, mental and educational tests are used throughout school systems as guidance aids for all children. The development of individual psychological testing began about 1900 when the French government assigned Binet the task of devising an objective means of identifying mentally retarded children. The Binet-Simon intelligence test, with various modifications, is still being used extensively all over the world with all types of children.

Similar contributions have been made in instruction and curriculums. Programs for exceptional children have served as laboratories for developing methods and procedures which in some cases have a universal application. Just as we learn about the normal from the abnormal, so we can learn about teaching in general from programs of teaching exceptional children.

Who Is the Exceptional Child?

There have been various attempts to define the term "exceptional child," and all need considerable elaboration before they can be understood. Some use it when referring to the particularly bright child or the child with unusual talent. Others use it when they refer to any atypical or deviant child. The term has been generally accepted, however, to include both the handicapped and the gifted child. For the present purposes the exceptional child is defined as *the child who deviates from the average or normal child (1) in mental characteristics, (2) in sensory abilities, (3) in neuromuscular or physical characteristics, (4) in social or emotional behavior, (5) in communication abilities, or (6) in multiple handicaps to such an extent that he requires a modification of school practices, or special educational services, in order to develop to his maximum capacity.*

But this is a very general definition and raises many questions. "What is average or normal?" "How extensive must the deviation be to require special education?" "What is special education?"

To complicate the picture further, the exceptional or deviating child has been studied by various disciplines—psychology, sociology, physiology, medicine, and education—and thus from varying points of view. If we define an exceptional child as one who deviates from the norm of his group, then we have many kinds of exceptionalities. A redheaded child in a class becomes an exceptional child because he differs from the norm of his group. A child with a defective or missing thumb becomes exceptional. Actually, such deviations, although of possible importance to physicians, psychologists, geneticists, or others, are of little concern to the teacher. A redheaded child is not an exceptional child, educationally speaking, because the educational program of the class does not have to be modified to serve his needs. A child is considered educationally exceptional only when it is necessary to alter the educational program to meet his needs. Hence, the use of "exceptional children" in education may differ from its use in biology, psychology, or other disciplines and professions. A child is *educationally exceptional* if his deviation is of such kind and degree that it interferes with his development under ordinary classroom procedures and necessitates special education, either in conjunction with the regular class or in a special class or school, for his maximum development.

A general breakdown of the major deviations as organized in this text is as follows:

1. *Communication disorders,* including children with (a) learning disabilities and (b) speech handicaps;
2. *Mental deviations,* including children who are (a) intellectually gifted and (b) mentally retarded;
3. *Sensory handicaps,* including children with (a) auditory handicaps and (b) visual handicaps;
4. *Neurologic, orthopedic, and other health impaired;*
5. *Behavior disorders.*

History and Philosophy of the Education of Exceptional Children

As we look back into history we find that the entire concept of educating each child to the limits of his ability is relatively new. The current use of the term "exceptional" is itself a reflection of radical changes in society's view of those who deviate. We have come a long way from the Spartans' practice of killing the deviant or malformed infant, but the journey was by slow stages. Exploitation of the handicapped in the role of court jester several hundred years ago can still be found in today's circus side shows. But certainly, on the whole, tremendous changes have taken place in society's attitude toward the exceptional person.

And this change is still going on; for example, the mentally gifted have moved upward in the American value system as a result of Russia's Sputnik.

Historically, three stages in the development of attitudes toward the handicapped child can be recognized (Frampton and Gall, 1955). First, during the pre-Christian era the handicapped were persecuted, neglected, and mistreated. Second, during the spread of Christianity they were protected and pitied. Third, in very recent years there has been a movement toward accepting the handicapped and integrating them into society to the fullest extent possible. In education, *integration* denotes a trend toward educating the exceptional child with his normal peers to whatever extent is compatible with his fullest potential development.

The three stages in the development of attitudes toward the deviant can be seen in the educational history of our own country. Prior to the 1800's there were few educational provisions for the handicapped child. The mentally subnormal individual was generally relegated to an attic or to the role of village idiot. In the first decades of the nineteenth century such leaders as Horace Mann, Samuel Gridley Howe, and Dorothea Dix gave impetus to the movement by establishing residential schools for the blind, deaf, retarded, epileptic, orphaned, and others, as was being done in Europe. These schools offered training, but equally important was the protective environment, often covering the life span of the individual.

Interestingly, however, as early as 1871 Samuel Gridley Howe, according to Irwin (1955), was able to predict future educational provisions for the exceptional child. He was speaking particularly of the blind, but his interests and insights extended to other areas of special education. He felt that a sure trend in the education of exceptional children would be toward integrating them into the "common" schools with "common" classmates in all areas possible. He also saw a decrease in the extent to which residential schools would be utilized with some forms of exceptionality.

The public school movement began slowly at the turn of the century. Since then it has spread in various forms until now almost all types and degrees of exceptionality can be found in public school programs.

The student, noting the several million children classed as exceptional today and the proliferation of programs and provisions for them, may well ask why these deviations were not a source of concern much earlier. The notion of free and compulsory education for all who are educable is slightly more than 100 years old. The changing economy of our country has affected the role, function, and scope of education for all our citizens, the exceptional included. The area of individual differences has been of scientific concern for less than 100 years. It is well known that Wundt, who is considered the father of modern psychology, established the first laboratory for psychological studies in Leipzig in 1879, but it is perhaps not so well known that he ruled out individual differences as a legitimate field of interest for psychologists. He felt that psychology ought to be concerned with the "generalized human mind." Thus children, psychotics, and animals were excluded from psychology, as was the study of individual differences. Only with the advent of the mental testing movement in the early 1900's did refined techniques for assessing individual differences in areas other than the physical begin to be developed. With these diagnostic methods came ideas and concepts which made the modern programs of education for exceptional children possible.

Today in the United States, as well as in Western European countries and the Soviet Union, provisions for the education of exceptional children are relatively universal. Practically all countries who have established universal and compulsory education have found that general programs for the ordinary child are not suitable for the exceptional child.

Inter- and Intraindividual Differences

Education has long recognized that grouping children in grades according to chronological age does not assure homogeneity of grouping in other characteristics. Within every grade in every school, children differ from one another to some extent. Two boys of the same age and height may differ in weight; two children of the same age and mental level may differ in their reading or spelling ability. Every classroom teacher must organize his instructional methods and assignments to meet the needs of children who vary one to three grades above or below the grade in which they are placed.

The concept of individual differences (meaning that in some respects Johnny is different from—more advanced or less advanced than—Billy in the same grade) is only one of the factors to be taken into account in considering the characteristics of the exceptional child. He does differ from the average child in class. He may be intellectually superior or inferior, he may not see or hear as well, he may not have the mobility of the average child, he may not have the degree of language or speech of the average child, or he may be a deviant in interpersonal relations (Wright, 1960).

This is the concept of *interindividual* differences; namely, that one child is significantly different from another child. It is the basis upon which most tests are constructed, i.e., to determine children's relative abilities on a particular characteristic—height, weight, intelligence, reading ability, and so forth.

Another concept of individual differences refers to a comparison of the child's abilities and skills with his disabilities. A comparison of the child's abilities and disabilities within himself determines *intraindividual* differences. This meaning of individual difference is actually the major one to be considered in planning an educational program for the exceptional child. The exceptional child has *intraindividual differences* or *discrepancies in growth.* This has led many to say that the exceptional child is a normal child who has exceptionalities or deviations only in some characteristics. In other words, they feel that the similarities in characteristics between the exceptional child and the average child far exceed the differences.

In general, the concept of *interindividual differences* is used for classification and for grouping children into special classes or ability groups. The concept of *intraindividual differences,* on the other hand, is used to organize an instructional program for a particular child in conformity with his abilities and disabilities, without regard to how he compares to other children.

To illustrate (1) how the exceptional child differs from the average and (2) how the exceptional child grows unevenly, the following pages will present the major types of exceptional children in the form of profiles as well as descriptive material. In subsequent chapters each of these types of exceptional children will be discussed in greater detail with suggested educational programs adapted to the discrepancies in growth. This chapter gives a very brief overview of discrepancies in each area of deviation.

Mental Deviates—the Intellectually Gifted and the Mentally Retarded

Intellectually gifted and mentally retarded children represent the upper and lower groups on the intelligence scale. In Figure 1–1, which represents the distribution of IQ's as found by Terman, the lower left-hand part of the curve shows that children with an IQ below 70 constitute 2.63 percent of the population studied and represents the group Terman has labeled mentally retarded or mentally deficient. The right-hand portion of the curve shows children with IQ's above 140 and represents 1.33 percent of the population. These children are labeled very superior or gifted. Similarly, another 5.6 percent of the population are borderline deficient and 14.5 percent are low average, according to Terman. The 46.5 percent of the population at the center of the curve are considered average or normal. Above this, Terman has designated IQ's between 110 and 120 (18.1 percent) as high average and IQ's between 120 and 140 (11.3 percent) as superior.

It is with the two extreme groups, the intellectually gifted and the mentally retarded, that we are at present concerned. Their unique characteristics and educational programs will be discussed in later chapters. Here it is well to take a look at a picture of the development of these two kinds of exceptional children to see how they deviate in growth from the normal (*interindividual differences*) and how they are affected by deviations within themselves (*intraindividual differences*).

Figure 1–2 shows the discrepancies in growth of an *intellectually gifted child* and of a *mentally retarded child*. Both children are 10 years of age; both are in a fifth-grade class; both have normal hearing and vision. But the similarities stop here. They differ markedly from the average child in many characteristics and, in addition, have variations in growth within themselves. The history and status of these two children, typical of their types of exceptionality, can best be illustrated by a description of their characteristics and development and by the profile in Figure 1–2.

John, the gifted child, was the older of two children. His father was employed

FIGURE 1–1

Distribution of composite IQ's (Form L-M)

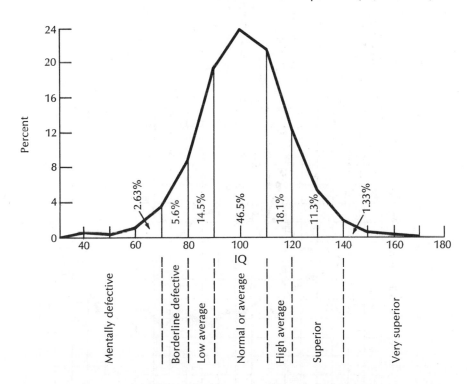

Source: Adapted from Lewis M. Terman and Maud A. Merrill, *Stanford-Binet Intelligence Scale, Manual for the Third Revision Form L-M* (Boston: Houghton Mifflin Company, 1960), p. 18.

as a teacher in the local high school. John's developmental history showed that he learned to talk at an earlier age than most children and that he walked at the age of 10 months. He became interested in books, and at the age of 5½ was reading some books and simple picture stories.

Upon entering school at the age of 6, he quickly learned to read and by the end of the year he was a fluent reader in third-grade material. He was not allowed to advance in school beyond his age group and by the age of 10 he was in the fifth grade. At this time a series of examinations was administered to him.

FIGURE 1–2

Profiles of a gifted and a retarded child

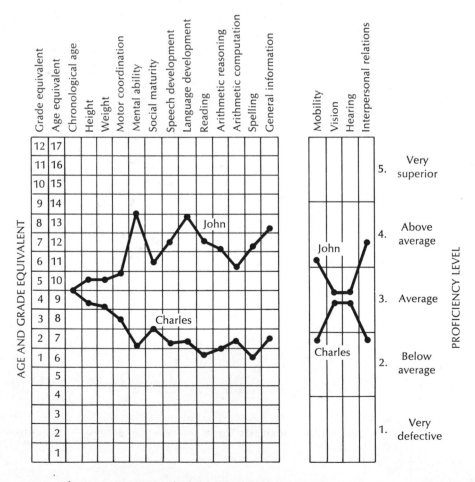

Test results are given in various forms. For example, John had an IQ of 140 and a mental age of 14 years. His height was 4 feet, 6½ inches (54.5 inches). This can be translated into a height age of 10–8, meaning that his height was similar to that of an average boy of 10 years and 8 months, even though John was only 10 years of age (10–0). On a reading test his score was Grade 7–7, meaning that his reading level was similar to the average of children in the seventh month of the seventh grade, even though John was in the fifth grade. His reading score, when translated into an age score, was 12 years, 7 months (12–7).

There are other characteristics of an individual that cannot be stated in terms of precise age. For example, vision and hearing are either normal or defective. John's vision and hearing were normal. Interpersonal relations do not necessarily increase with age; hence, there are no age norms. In the profile these characteristics are represented on a five-point scale: (1) very superior, (2) above average, (3) average, (4) below average, and (5) very defective.

On the various tests given to John the scores were translated into ages or points on a scale so that they could be readily compared. His scores were as follows:

Chronological age	10–0
Height age	10–8
Weight age	10–8
Motor coordination age	10–11
Mental age	14–0
Social age	11–6
Speech development age	12–8
Language age	13–10
Reading age	12–7
Arithmetic reasoning age	12–2
Arithmetic computation age	11–4
Spelling age	12–4
General information age	13–2
Mobility	above average
Vision	average
Hearing	average
Interpersonal relations	above average

Figure 1–2 shows John's growth patterns at the life age of 10. Note that there are some points on the profile showing John to be like other children of his age. In vision and hearing he is like other children with normal sense organs, neither superior nor inferior. His height, weight, and motor coordination are slightly superior to those of most children, but not abnormally so. His mental age, however, deviates very markedly from the average of other 10-year-olds and is 4 years beyond his age and grade placement. His social age is not as advanced as

his mental age, being only a year and one-half accelerated. His achievements in school vary but in general are more accelerated than the physical factors, though not as far as is the mental-age level. Note that general information, language, speech, and reading are more advanced than arithmetic computation. This is a quite common finding among intellectually advanced children.

On the scaled portion of the profile, John shows above average mobility, average hearing and vision, and above average interpersonal relations. He presents a developmental picture different from that of a child who is average in all respects. On this scale an average child would show only minor deviations from a straight line.

Not only does John differ from the average child in many characteristics, but he also varies within himself in some characteristics. In this respect he is said to have *discrepancies in growth,* or more precisely, *intraindividual differences.* Because of these deviations, he will require certain adaptations of educational practices—to be described in later chapters.

Charles, the mentally retarded child in Figure 1–2, shows a markedly different profile from that of John, the gifted child. The profiles are very nearly mirror counterparts of each other. Charles was the second child in a family of four children. His father worked as a machinist. During infancy Charles was a sickly child and at the age of 1 year had a very high fever, diagnosed as encephalitis and later assumed to have had neurological effects fundamental to his slow mental development. Charles developed at a slower rate than the other children. He walked at 16 months but did not talk in sentences until he was 3 years of age. (On the average, children begin to talk in sentences at 2 years of age.) He was admitted to the first grade at the age of 6 and in spite of his inability to learn was promoted year by year until at the age of 10 he, like John, was in the fifth grade. The school system in which he was enrolled believed that children should be neither held back in school nor accelerated. The philosophy of the school held that the teacher should adapt her instruction to wide individual differences among children.

In the fifth grade Charles was given a series of examinations. He obtained the following ratings:

Chronological age	10–0
Height age	9–2
Weight age	9–1
Motor coordination age	8–5
Mental age	7–2
Social age	8–0
Speech development age	7–3
Language age	7–4
Reading age	6–8
Arithmetic reasoning age	7–0

Arithmetic computation age	7–5
Spelling age	6–6
General information age	7–6
Mobility	below average
Vision	average
Hearing	average
Interpersonal relations	below average

When these age scores and ratings are plotted in Figure 1–2 we find that Charles, with an IQ of 72, presents a reversal of the picture shown by John. Although both boys are 10 years old and have normal hearing and vision, their growth patterns in other characteristics are very different.

As with most mentally retarded children, Charles's profile indicates that he can be considered normal or near normal in height, weight, mobility, motor coordination, and in vision and hearing. But he is exceptional in other areas of development. He differs from the average child in social, mental, and educational growth, and he differs from his own physical levels in these developmental characteristics. His mental age is 7–2 and in the academic subjects of reading, spelling, and arithmetic, he tests at educational ages of 6–8, 6–6, 7–0, and 7–5; that is, after four years in school his educational accomplishments are at the first- and beginning second-grade level. His deviation from the majority of children in the fifth grade in mental, social, and academic abilities, in spite of his similarity to the other children in physical characteristics, again requires a special adaptation of school practices, which will be discussed in later chapters.

The Auditorily Handicapped Child

Figure 1–3 shows the developmental pattern of Tony, a 10-year-old deaf child. Auditorily handicapped children may be totally deaf or only hard of hearing. They may have been born deaf or they may have acquired deafness after learning language and speech. Tony was born deaf. He does not have sufficient hearing even with the use of a hearing aid to develop language and speech through the sense of hearing.

Tony's profile shows that he is average in height, weight, and vision. He is slightly below other 10-year-olds in mobility, motor coordination, and mental age but is considered within the average range in these characteristics. The lowest point is, of course, his hearing, which is rated as very defective. In Tony's case this defect is irremediable. He will have to live with it all his life. The question here is how deafness affects his other traits. First of all, we notice that it affects speech development most. Even with special instruction his speech is no better than that of a 2-year-old child. His next lowest points are in language,

FIGURE 1–3

Profile of an auditorily handicapped child

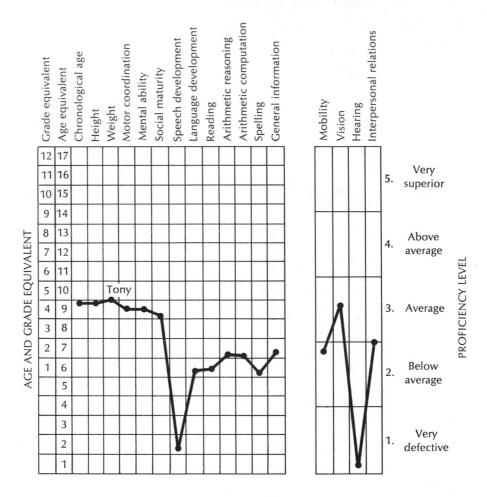

reading, and spelling. Although he is average in mental development, his achievement in language, reading, and spelling is similar to that of a first-grade child. The hearing defect has interfered with his development in these areas. Furthermore, his difficulty with communication skills has created problems in interpersonal relations and prevented normal social maturity.

Thus Tony, who is normal in many ways, differs from the average child in his response to the usual school program. He has greater discrepancies in growth; he differs within himself in many characteristics. An educational program must take into consideration his deviations from the average and the deviations within himself. It must organize instruction so as to circumvent the irremediable deafness. For Tony's adequate development, special education must use channels of communication other than hearing.

The hard-of-hearing child is not as retarded as the deaf child in speech, language, and school subjects. The less the disability, the less special education is usually needed. But whether such a child is mildly or severely hard of hearing, his retardation below average children and below his other abilities is considerably less than that of a deaf child. In most instances he remains in the regular classroom but receives special instruction in speech and auditory training to assist him in coping with the regular school curriculum. While the deaf child requires a great deal of teaching in a special class and by a skilled teacher, the hard-of-hearing child requires only extra consideration and some specialized education. How much of the latter he needs is dependent upon the discrepancies in his growth. This total program will be discussed in greater detail in Chapters 8 and 9.

The Visually Handicapped Child

Children with visual handicaps fall into several categories for educational purposes. In the first group are those whose visual defects can be corrected through medical treatment or optical aids. Such children are not regarded as exceptional since with corrective devices they are considered normal and can be educated without modification of school practices.

In the second group are children whose vision is quite defective even after correction. They have difficulty in the regular grades and need instructional compensations for their defects. They utilize their eyes in learning, but to a lesser degree than does the average child. They are referred to as "visually impaired children." Since they can use their residual vision in learning, they are not considered blind.

In the third group are the blind. These children, like the deaf, require instruction primarily through other senses.

Figure 1–4 shows the developmental pattern of Sarah, a blind 10-year-old. Vision is her lowest point on the profile. Associated with blindness are retarded mobility, restricted interpersonal relations, and lowered school achievement. Because Sarah cannot see to learn to read, she learns reading through the tactile sense by means of braille. The process is generally more time-consuming than learning to read through the use of the eyes and for this reason Sarah is slightly retarded educationally.

Another profile could show the growth patterns of a visually impaired child. In general, the educational retardation would not be as great. The differences between the average child and the visually impaired child are fewer. The dis-

FIGURE 1–4

Profile of a blind child

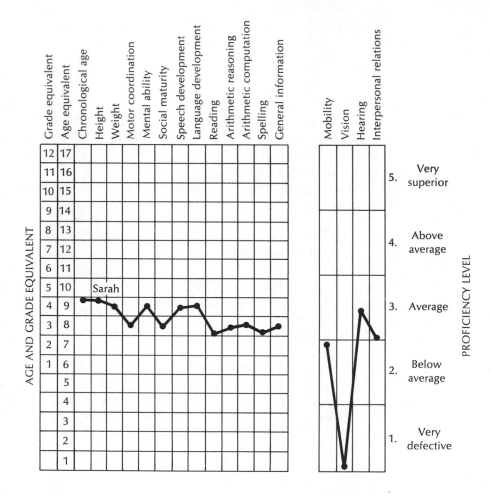

crepancies in growth within the child are also fewer. Hence, the modifications of school practice and the adaptations of instructional material are not as radical or as great as they are for the blind child.

The Speech-Defective Child

Speech is one of the major characteristics differentiating man from the lower animals. Much communication among people is dependent upon their ability

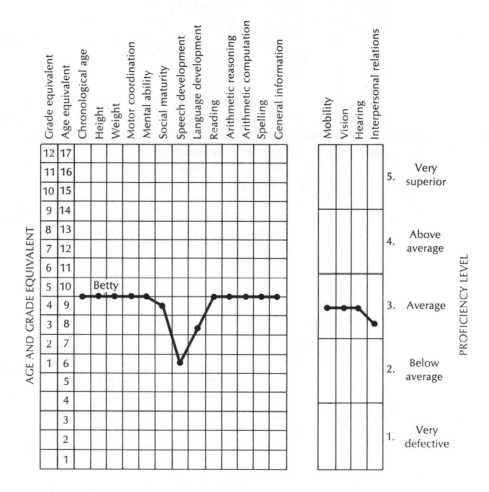

FIGURE 1–5

Profile of a speech-defective child

to speak and to understand the spoken word. Any defect in one's speaking ability is likely to interfere with his interpersonal relations.

There are many forms of speech disorders, ranging from complete inability to speak to minor articulatory defects. There are also many causes for speech difficulties. This deviation is sometimes associated with other handicapping conditions, such as deafness, mental retardation, or cerebral palsy, as will be discussed in subsequent chapters.

Figure 1–5 shows the developmental pattern of a speech-defective child of 10 years. Betty's profile differs markedly from that of the gifted or mentally retarded or deaf child. She is, for educational purposes, normal except that speech and, to a lesser extent, language development are below average. No very extensive educational adaptations have to be made for her in the regular grades. Special classes are not usually organized for this type of handicapped child. Betty was left in the regular grades with other children, but an itinerant speech teacher gives Betty corrective lessons several times a week. With this help and that of the regular classroom teacher Betty's difficulties can probably be removed.

Thus, the speech-defective child with an otherwise average developmental pattern does not differ from the normal, nor does he differ within himself except for the one specific difficulty, speech. He does not have widely varying discrepancies in growth. His educational program is like that of other children. Special education is provided for him on a part-time basis by an itinerant speech correctionist while he is being educated in the regular grades.

As will be discussed in Chapter 3, speech-handicapped children often have other handicaps. A cerebral-palsied child may have a motor handicap, speech handicap, and visual handicap. In such cases a special class instead of only an itinerant teacher may be required.

The Orthopedically Handicapped Child

The orthopedically handicapped child is one who is disabled in motor abilities. A simple example would be a child who, through an accident, had lost the use of both legs. It is necessary for him to use a wheel chair. The growth pattern of such a child, according to the profile of Mark (Figure 1–6), shows deficiencies in mobility, motor coordination, social age, and interpersonal relations. There is no retardation in educational subjects. The motor disability does not affect his educational achievements in school although consequent emotional problems may. He learns to read, write, and spell by the same methods as do other children in the class. The school adapts to his disability primarily by providing physical facilities which he needs because of the use of the wheel chair. His lack of mobility tends to interfere with his social development and his interpersonal relations.

Not all orthopedically handicapped children show similar profiles. Motor handicaps can result from brain injuries, such as those found in cerebral-palsied children, in which case they are often associated with speech defects, mental retardation, and/or other handicapping conditions. These conditions, of course, complicate the educational picture, for the more disabling the mental and physical circumstance, the more special education is necessary. The cerebral-palsied child is discussed in greater detail in Chapter 12, but no profile is given here because the individuals show no consistent pattern.

FIGURE 1–6

Profile of an orthopedically handicapped child

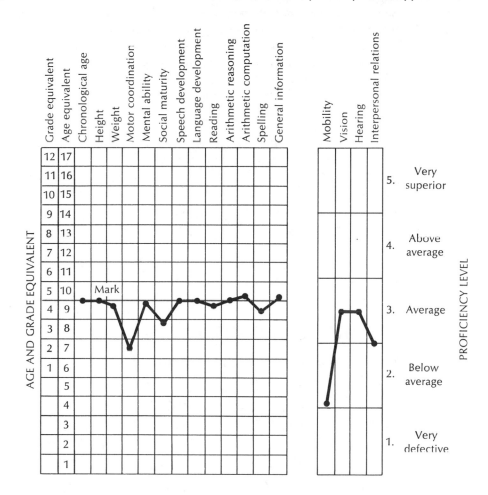

The Child with Behavior Disorders

Behavior disorders may take a variety of forms and stem from a variety of causes. There may be hostility and aggression or withdrawal and restraint. There may be a high or low IQ. There may or may not be physical concomitants. There may be academic success but more often failure in at least some school subjects. The category of those with behavior disorders may include psychotic and neurotic children, children with lesser emotional difficulties, and delinquent children.

The child represented in Figure 1–7 was a rebellious truant ten years old. As can be seen by reading his profile, Steve was normal mentally and physically but, in addition to his low scores in interpersonal relations and social adjustment, he showed retardation of a year or two in most school subjects. A series of unfortunate family experiences had left Steve with hostile attitudes and no interest in school. With many absences and much failure he had no motivation to succeed and was dropping farther and farther behind in his academic subjects.

Such a child needs specific help in alleviating some of the underlying causes of his maladjustment, including counseling and guidance by professional work-

FIGURE 1–7

Profile of a child with a behavior disorder

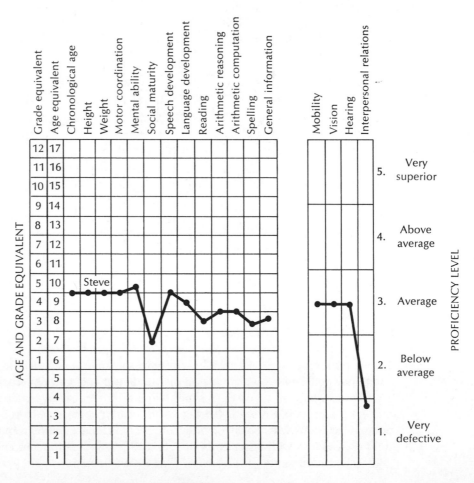

ers at home and at school. In addition, there will have to be some adaptation of the school program. Steve, for example, may need some individual tutoring and certainly modified materials since he is educationally unable to function at a fourth-grade level. Only for more extreme cases are there special classes or special schools. If Steve's problems bring him into too great a conflict with society, he may even require institutionalization.

The Child with Specific Learning Disabilities

Specific learning disabilities is a relatively new category in the education of exceptional children. Its gradual evolvement resulted from the recognition that handicapped children do not always fit into neat, well-defined categories with uniform characteristics. Special educators have found that there are a number of children who are not deaf, but cannot understand language; who are not blind but cannot perceive visually; or who are not mentally retarded but cannot learn under ordinary school instruction.

Children listed under the caption of "specific learning disabilities" are children who cannot be grouped under the traditional categories of exceptional children, but who show significant retardation in learning to talk, or who do not develop normal visual or auditory perception, or who have great difficulty in learning to read, to spell, to write, or to make arithmetic calculations.

Although these children form a heterogenous group and fail to learn for diverse reasons, they have one thing in common; namely, developmental discrepancies (intraindividual differences in growth). Figure 1–8 presents the profile of Julius at the age of 10–0. He was the first-born child of parents who were both teachers. His development was normal physically and mentally, he had no motor problems, and his visual and hearing acuity were normal. On the WISC (Wechsler Intelligence Scale for Children) he obtained a total IQ of 130, with no marked discrepancies between his verbal or performance IQ. Yet, after four years of school he was unable to learn to read. Because of his general knowledge and his ability in arithmetic he had been socially promoted to the fourth grade. It will be noted from the profile that in his case discrepancies in growth are quite marked. He is unable to read or spell in spite of regular school attendance, adequate instruction, and adequate family background. His retardation in reading and spelling cannot be accounted for as a result of mental retardation, sensory handicap, emotional disturbance, or environmental deprivation. He has a specific learning disability in the form of deficient visual sequential memory, deficient sound blending ability, and deficient ability in visual closure. These specific learning disabilities will have to be remedied before he will be able to learn to read.

FIGURE 1–8

Profile of a child with a specific learning disability

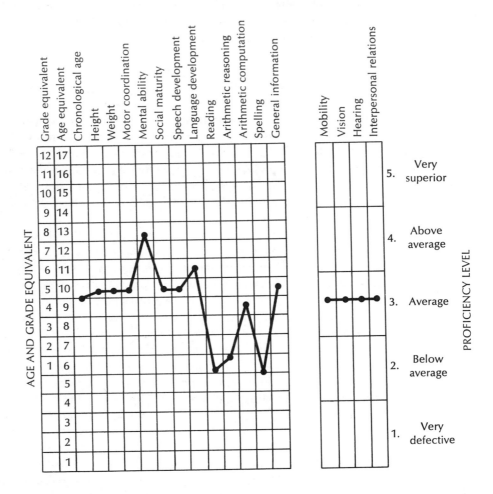

Other Handicapping Conditions

There are other types of handicapping conditions which make modification of school practices necessary. Most of these are health problems. A tuberculous child, for example, needs an opportunity for rest during the school day. Children with cardiac disabilities may find the regular class too strenuous. For many of these children, however, the educational program is not altered. Only the physical arrangements are varied from those for the average child.

In many instances we find *multiple handicaps* (Wolf and Anderson, 1969) or other combinations of divergences from the normal. A crippled child may be gifted. A deaf child may be blind. A cerebral-palsied child may have many deviations; he may be visually impaired, hard of hearing, mentally retarded (or gifted), and defective in speech. Sometimes two handicaps are so severe that the child cannot adapt to a special class for either one. In such cases other arrangements must be made, using itinerant teachers, homebound education, or more specifically adapted special classes. In other cases the child can be placed in a class designed to take into account his major disability.

The preceding profiles representing discrepancies in growth of different kinds of exceptional children were specific to the conditions discussed. For any particular child, such discrepancies may be less or greater than was represented. In all of these cases, however, educational adaptations are needed for the maximum development of the child. The differences in growth and development will be discussed in greater detail in the subsequent chapters which deal separately with each kind of exceptional child.

Prevalence of Exceptional Children

Various attempts have been made to determine the prevalence of handicapped and gifted children in the population. These attempts have yielded such diverse results that investigators hesitate to give a definite figure for each type of exceptional child. Much of this difficulty stems from the fact that the line of demarcation between a normal and an exceptional child is not agreed upon. For example, some define a gifted child as one having an IQ of 120 and above on an individual intelligence test. Others use a criterion of 135 IQ and above, or 140 and above. Still others use an achievement criterion in addition to an intelligence test, such as 130 IQ and an acceleration in school achievement of two or more years. It is obvious that with these different criteria there will be different percentage figures. In the field of speech correction the estimates vary from 2 percent to 20 percent, depending on what is meant by a speech defect. In addition to differences in criteria, communities themselves differ. For example, a national figure of 2 percent mentally retarded does not apply to all communities. Some areas may have 3 or 4 percent, others less than 2 percent, even though they all use the same criteria.

Despite these difficulties in determining the prevalence of exceptional children in school, various writers have been able to hazard guesses based on different studies. The U.S. Office of Education has from time to time issued estimates of the frequency of exceptional children in the school population. In 1944 it estimated that 12.4 percent of all school children (or 4,000,000) required special services (Martens, 1944). In a later report from the U.S. Office of Education, Mackie and Dunn (1954) estimated that the percentage of exceptional children in the schools of the United States stood at 12.7, roughly the same as the earlier estimate.

Because of new Federal legislation enacted since 1964 and the creation of a Bureau of Education for the Handicapped within the Office of Education in 1967, new approaches to the acquisition of prevalence figures have been used. To obtain state funds under Federal regulations, states have been required to submit reports on the number of handicapped children in their state and a statement of the number being served.

The planning and evaluation staff of the Bureau of Education for the Handicapped estimates that as of July 1, 1968, "There were approximately 75,000,000 children in the United States from birth to 19 years of age of which an estimated 7,083,500 are handicapped" (Bureau of Education for the Handicapped, August, 1970). This figure includes preschool children and indicates that slightly over 10 percent are handicapped. The difference between this estimate and the 1944 and 1954 estimates of around 12.5 percent is due in part to the deletion of the gifted from the statistics for exceptional children. The Bureau's estimate of percentages of school-age children according to categories of handicaps is:

Speech Impaired	3.5%
Emotionally Disturbed	2.0
Mentally Retarded	2.3
Learning Disabled	1.0
Hard of Hearing	0.5
Deaf	0.075
Crippled or other health impaired	0.5
Visually Impaired	0.1
Multihandicapped	0.06
TOTAL	10.035% of school-age children from 5 to 19 years

The estimated number of handicapped children in school in the various categories is presented in Table 1–1. This is the composite of data reported to the U.S. Office of Education by the 50 state departments of education for the successive years of 1968 and 1969 (Bureau of Education for the Handicapped, 1969, 1970). These are probably minimal estimates, since complete information cannot be obtained without a national survey of greater magnitude.

It will be noted from Table 1–1, as well as from the prevalence percentages presented above from the Bureau of Education for the Handicapped, that the most common type of handicap in the schools is speech impairment; the next most common is mental retardation. In 1968 the third place is held by the emotionally disturbed. In the figures for 1969, however, the third place is

TABLE 1–1

*Number of handicapped children
as reported by states*

Type of Handicap	Fiscal year 1968	Fiscal year 1969
Mentally retarded	1,503,000	1,360,737
Hard of hearing and deaf	286,200	316,456
Speech impaired	2,141,600	2,180,589
Visually handicapped	75,800	66,679
Emotionally disturbed	800,000	767,108
Crippled	305,400	192,662
Other health impaired (including learning disabilities)	759,900	1,089,817
Multihandicapped	89,100	35,918
National total	5,961,000	6,009,966

Source: Bureau of Education for the Handicapped, 1969, 1970.

held by "Other Health Impaired (including Learning Disabilities)." Figures are not available for children with learning disabilities as a separate category, but it is very probable that children with specific learning disabilities make up the bulk of this category. With the recent impetus of work in this field it is possible that when the area becomes more clearly defined the category of specific learning disabilities will contain a larger number of children. This assumption is made because many children now listed under mental retardation, speech impairment, and emotional disturbance could be reclassified as children with specific learning disabilities. It will also be noted from Table 1–1 that visual and auditory impairments are among the least frequent handicaps among school children. Their handicap is such, however, that special arrangements and special training are indispensable.

A less accurate but easier approach to determining the prevalence of handicapped children is derived from the number of exceptional children being served in the community. This is obtained from enrollment statistics in special schools and classes. The U.S. Office of Education has obtained these data over many years. The first survey, conducted in 1922, consisted of a questionnaire to local school systems. This type of survey was conducted every five to eight years between 1922 and 1958. Since then such statistics have been derived from annual reports from state departments of education, beginning in 1967–1968.

Table 1–2 presents the enrollment figures for special schools and classes in public school systems for 1922–1958, and also more inclusive information obtained in 1969. Great care should be taken in drawing conclusions from this table. The 1969 figures include enrollment in both public and private schools and also in residential institutions, whereas the earlier figures did not consistently include private schools or residential institutions. It should also be borne in mind that the figures for the period of 1922 to 1958 are not necessarily complete since the information was obtained from questionnaires to local school systems, and the return of questionnaires is notoriously inadequate. Note should also be made of figures being influenced from period to period by changing definitions, changing conditions, and changing cut-off points.

Some tentative conclusions may be drawn, however, from the data in Table 1–2, for the figures seem to reflect certain historical facts:

1. Although there were marked increases in most categories from 1932 to 1940, it will be noted that the period from 1940 to 1948 showed little increase in enrollment and even decreases for some of the groups of exceptional children. This may reflect a lack of emphasis on the education of exceptional children during World War II, as well as the shortage of teachers, facilities, and funds at that time.

2. Since the war, classes for the crippled made a marked gain in enrollment in 1958; this growth probably reflects the inclusion of cerebral palsied children and the strong parent movement during the 1950's to provide more adequate care for these children. The increase in the 1969 figure for the number of crippled children now being served cannot be compared with the 1948 figure unless we combine the figures for crippled and special health problems which are included in the 1969 figure. Comparing these combined figures shows that three times the former number of children were being served in 1969.

3. Over the years there has been a drop in the percentage of children in classes for special health problems, due to medical advances. Epileptic seizures, for example, can now be controlled to such an extent that most epileptic children attend regular classes. Likewise, tuberculosis has responded so well to antibiotics that such children are only occasionally found in special classes. Such mild handicaps have been absorbed by the regular classes.

4. The most phenomenal rise in enrollment has been in classes for the gifted where these figures suggest that there were nearly thirty times as many children in such classes in 1958 as in 1932. (The figures for 1969 are not included in statistics from the Bureau of Education for the Handicapped.) Even this phenomenal rise may not adequately reflect the status of education for the gifted, since enrichment in the regular classes and acceleration of some children to higher grades are not reported as special provisions.

TABLE 1–2

Enrollments in public special schools and classes, 1922–1969

Type	1922[a]	1932[a]	1940[a]	1948[b]	1952[c]	1958[c]	1969[d]
Mentally retarded	23,252	75,099	98,416	87,030	113,565	213,402	703,800
Speech-defective	no data	22,735	126,146	182,308	306,747	474,643	1,122,200
Crippled	no data	16,166	25,784	14,510	17,813	28,355	109,000
Deaf and hard of hearing	2,911	4,434	13,478	13,959	15,867	19,199	65,200
Blind and partially seeing	no data	5,308	8,875	8,185	8,853	11,008	22,700
Special health problems	no data	24,020	27,291	19,579	11,455	21,714	under crippled
Gifted	no data	1,834	3,255	20,712	22,916	52,005	no data
Socially maladjusted	no data	14,354	10,477	15,340	no data	27,447	99,400
Learning disabilities	no data	no data	no data	no data	no data	no data	120,000

Sources: [a] *Statistics of Special Schools and Classes for Exceptional Children, Biennial Survey of Education in the United States, 1946–48* (Washington, D.C.: Federal Security Agency, Office of Education, 1948), p. 10.
[b] *Statistics of Special Education for Exceptional Children, Biennial Survey of Education in the United States, 1952–54* (Washington, D.C.: U.S. Department of Health, Education and Welfare, Office of Education, 1954), p. 15.
[c] Romaine P. Mackie and Patricia P. Robbins, "Exceptional Children in Local Public Schools," *School Life* 43 (November, 1960), p. 15.
[d] *Handicapped Children in the United States and Special Education Personnel Required, 1968–1969* (est.) (Washington, D.C., Bureau of Education for the Handicapped, U.S. Office of Education, 1970).

The figures reflect only enrollment in special classes and special schools, programs not always approved by educators. In spite of these qualifications, the statistics reveal several interesting trends. It will be noted that there were two periods in which there was a marked acceleration in enrollment in classes for the gifted. The first was during World War II when many categories of exceptional children showed a drop in enrollment. In classes for the gifted, however, there were over six times as many children served in 1948 as in 1940. This probably reflects the rising awareness of the need during a war period for high level leadership and technological training. A second increase occurs in the 1958 figures, which more than doubled the 1952 number. This increase could be attributed to a greater interest in special provisions for the gifted in response to the Soviet advances in technical and scientific education and the launching of Sputnik during that period.

5. Beginning with the 1940 figures, the largest number of exceptional children served has been in the area of speech correction. These children are generally being educated in the regular grades receiving speech correction two or three times a week for short periods. One speech correctionist can carry a load of up to 100 children. This area of special education differs from most other areas in that the other areas require special classrooms for every five to fifteen children. The last thirty-five years has seen a very rapid rise in the services offered speech-impaired children.

6. In classes for the mentally retarded there has also been a marked increase in enrollment, the number receiving special help being second only to the number of speech-defective children being served. This probably reflects the increased awareness of the problem of mental retardation in our society resulting partly from the organization of state and national parents' groups which have vigorously brought the problem to the attention of the general public, school administrators, and legislators. It will be noted that the most rapid rate of increase has been since 1952 when the efforts of parents' groups were just beginning to materialize. It should also be noted that the recent increase in enrollment in classes for the mentally retarded includes the children in classes for the trainable mentally retarded—classes which were rare in the 30's and 40's.

7. Classes for the deaf and hard of hearing made a rapid increase before 1940 but only a gradual gain in enrollment since then. The higher figure indicated for 1969 reflects the figures for private schools and institutions.

8. There is historical significance in the figures for children in classes for the blind and visually impaired. The enrollment here remained fairly constant up to 1958 when there was a sudden jump in enrollment. In large part, this increase can be explained by (a) the influx of six-year-old children suffering from a new eye malady known as retrolental fibroplasia (which will be discussed in Chapter 10) and (b) an increased interest in educating blind children in public schools rather than in residential institutions.

The above figures and tentative conclusions refer to the number of children who were being served regardless of the total number available. Table 1–3 relates similar data to the total by giving the percent of all handicapped children being served and the percent not being served. This is national information for 1969 derived from material reported by state departments of education. From this table it will be noted that:

TABLE 1–3

Handicapped children receiving and not receiving special educational services in 1969

Type of handicap	Number of handicapped children	Receiving services	Not receiving services
Mentally retarded	1,360,737	52%	48%
Hard of hearing and deaf	316,456	21%	79%
Speech impaired	2,180,589	51%	49%
Visually handicapped	66,679	34%	66%
Emotionally disturbed	767,108	13%	87%
Crippled	192,662	33%	67%
Other health impaired	1,089,817	15%	85%
Multihandicapped	35,918	26%	74%
National totals	6,009,966	38% 2,258,395	62% 3,751,571

Source: Bureau of Education for the Handicapped, 1970.

1. Approximately one-half of the children with mental retardation and one-half of the children with speech impairment were being offered special educational services.

2. Approximately one-third of the crippled and one-third of the visually handicapped were being served.

3. Less than one-quarter of the children who were deaf and hard of hearing, or who were emotionally disturbed, or those who had other health handicaps (including specific learning disabilities) were being served.

4. Of the estimated number of all handicapped children combined, only 38 percent or three-eighths were being offered special education services in 1969.

How Exceptional Children Are Educated

The large majority of exceptional children are educated in public school systems. Some exceptional children are educated in public and private residential schools. To provide for these children and their different disabilities and abilities, various kinds of organizations have evolved to meet their unique needs.

Reynolds (1962) has presented a hierarchy of services that can be offered to exceptional children. Figure 1–9 presents Reynolds's triangle of services, showing types of services arranged from "less severe to more severe," i.e., from those included in the regular grades to those treated in hospitals and treatment centers. The minor problems, which constitute the largest number, are in the regular grades, while the severe handicaps, which constitute the smallest number, are in the hospital program. Not all of these services are needed or available for all types of exceptional children, but the general plan is usable in whole or in part. The major offerings of: (a) itinerant service, (b) special class and resource rooms, (c) special schools, (d) residential schools, and (e) hospitals are discussed below.

ITINERANT PERSONNEL

Speech correctionists, social workers, school psychologists, remedial reading teachers, learning disability specialists and other special educational personnel may deal with exceptional children on an itinerant basis. They may serve several schools and travel over a considerable area, visiting the exceptional child and his teacher at regular intervals or whenever necessary. Thus, the youngster spends the major part of his time in the regular classroom and is taken out of the room only for short periods. A speech correctionist, for example, may work with the speech-defective child several times a week for short periods, while an itinerant teacher for the visually impaired child might visit only once a month

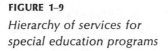

FIGURE 1–9

*Hierarchy of services for
special education programs*

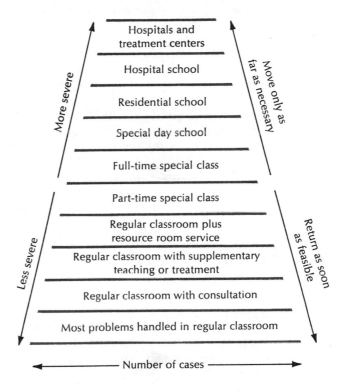

Hospitals and
treatment centers

Hospital school

Residential school

Special day school

Full-time special class

Part-time special class

Regular classroom plus
resource room service

Regular classroom with supplementary
teaching or treatment

Regular classroom with consultation

Most problems handled in regular classroom

More severe

Less severe

Move only as far as necessary

Return as soon as feasible

◄──── Number of cases ────►

Source: M. C. Reynolds, 1962, p. 368.

to bring special materials and to confer with the regular teacher. In both cases the primary responsibility for the general education of the exceptional child rests with the regular classroom teacher.

The school social worker and psychologist may interview and confer with a child, his parents, and his teacher and generally assist in the adjustment of the behaviorally disturbed child in the home and school. They may counsel a child consistently over an extended period of time or only occasionally.

The itinerant special-teacher type of program is particularly valuable in rural areas where the exceptional children are few and scattered over a wide area. Thus one teacher may serve several schools. This program is also well suited to certain types of exceptionality such as defective speech or partial vision which require limited services or materials. Often one of the itinerant teacher's primary roles will be that of a consultant or resource person for the classroom teacher. Itinerant teachers also provide homebound and hospital services, as described later.

SPECIAL CLASS AND RESOURCE ROOM

Classrooms for mentally retarded, gifted, deaf, blind, visually impaired, auditorily handicapped, or crippled children may be organized within a school system. If the exceptional child is enrolled in such a class with a specially trained teacher, and spends most of the day there, it is usually referred to as a *special class*. If, on the other hand, the exceptional child is enrolled in the regular classroom and goes to the special room only for specialized instruction, it is usually called a *resource room*. There may be many gradations of these two programs, the difference in terminology usually being dependent upon the amount of time spent in the special room. Deaf children, for example, usually are assigned to a special class of six to eight youngsters and spend the entire day in it. A program for the gifted, however, may be organized so that the gifted child spends a half-day in the regular room and the other half-day in a special room. A mentally handicapped child may spend nearly half of the time with normal children in physical education, art, music, homemaking, and so forth, and yet be a member of the special class. Often a blind child goes to the resource room only for brief periods of braille instruction, sometimes spending the entire day in the regular classroom. We may think of these two types of organization as being roughly at opposite ends of a continuum with various degrees of activity in the special rooms.

The special class teacher or resource teacher is trained in methods not used by the regular teacher. She also has access to special equipment not available in a regular classroom.

Advantages of the special class or resource room over residential schools or special day schools include the fact that the youngster remains in his own community and in close association with normal children and yet has the benefits of individualized and specialized training.

Disadvantages often pointed out include the possibility of a youngster's having to travel a considerable distance to the school which houses the special class. This may separate him from his neighborhood friends. It is also possible that, although a special class is physically integrated in a school system, it may simultaneously be socially isolated and so unduly emphasize the exceptional child's deviation.

The general tendency is to move away from a self-contained special class to a resource room organization, especially for the milder forms of handicaps. For these children, who constitute the larger number of handicapped children, it is preferable to enroll them in the regular grades and to provide special education for their specific disabilities on an individual tutoring basis or in small groups in a resource room. For the more severe handicaps like deafness or severe mental retardation, the discrepancy between the handicapped child's performance and that of his normal peers is so large that self-contained special classes may be necessary.

SPECIAL SCHOOLS

Some school systems have organized special day schools for different kinds of exceptional children, especially the emotionally disturbed, crippled, trainable mentally retarded, and multiply handicapped. In general, however, there is a trend toward organizing special class programs within neighborhood schools and reducing the number of special schools, at least for certain types of handicapping conditions. Physically handicapped and mentally handicapped children, for example, can make appreciable adjustment with normal children. Likewise, it is felt that contact with average children provides the gifted with a better preparation for future life. There are still, however, many special day schools, especially for the child with severe behavior disorders and for the trainable mentally retarded.

RESIDENTIAL SCHOOLS

All the states of the union have residential schools or institutions for various types of handicapped children, including the mentally retarded, delinquent, blind, deaf, crippled, and emotionally disturbed. These institutions are sometimes privately administered, but they are usually administered by a state agency. Historically, residential schools are the oldest educational provision for exceptional children. They tended to be built away from population centers and to become too often segregated, sheltered asylums with little community contact. In recent years this fault has been recognized and to an extent remedied. Disadvantages of a residential school include removal of the child from home and neighborhood, emphasis on the handicap, and rigidity of institutional life. This is not to say, however, that such a program no longer meets the needs of some exceptional children, for it does indeed. In a sparsely populated area no other provision may be feasible, especially for a condition, like deafness, which requires extensive equipment and special training on the part of the teacher. In some cases the defect itself demands professional attention for more than a few hours a day. Often with young deaf-blind children specialized treatment, stimulation, and education are carried out in the dormitory or cottage of the residential school on a twenty-four-hour-a-day basis. There may be situations within the child's home which require that for the welfare of the family and the child he must be placed in a residential school, at least for a time.

There is no reason to believe that any of the types of programs discussed will disappear in the immediate future; they will continue to supplement each other. A changing role may, however, be seen for many residential schools. As public school special education programs expand and enroll more of the most able exceptional children, the residential schools may emphasize programs for the severely and multiply handicapped children.

HOSPITAL AND HOMEBOUND SERVICES

Sometimes physically handicapped children are confined to hospitals or to their homes for long periods of time. To avoid educational retardation, itinerant teachers especially prepared to teach the homebound tutor these children during their convalescence in the hospital or at home. Usually the local school system assigns these teachers of the homebound to help such children for an hour or more a day if the youngster's condition permits. The teacher's case load varies according to the type of disabilities she is handling and the academic help needed. In larger children's hospitals these classes are manned by full-time teachers.

In some cities two-way telephone communication can be established between the child's home and the classroom so that the child can listen in to the class discussion and make his contribution. In Los Angeles a more highly developed system—Teleteach—has been established whereby the teacher can communicate with a group of homebound children and monitor each child, while each child is in constant communication with the teacher and with the other children.

Special Education—Its Meaning and Philosophy

The term "special education" has been used to denote those aspects of education which are applied to handicapped and gifted children but not usually used with the majority of average children. "Special" is defined by Webster as "distinguished by some unusual quality; uncommon; noteworthy; extraordinary; additional to the regular; extra; utilized or employed for a certain purpose in addition to the ordinary." These definitions are certainly applicable to special education, which consists of the modifications of, or additions to, school practices intended for the ordinary child—practices that are unique, uncommon, of unusual quality, and in particular are in addition to the organization and instructional procedures used with the majority of children.

It should be pointed out that special education is not a total program which is entirely different from the education of the ordinary child. It refers only to those aspects of education which are unique and/or in addition to the regular program for all children. For example, the general educational program for a child with a speech defect is carried out in all phases by his regular classroom teacher. The *special* part of his education is the correction of his speech defect by a speech correctionist. This may be carried on for only two hours a week out of a possible thirty hours in the regular classroom. The ordinary child does not receive this additional help, which we call special education, because he does not need it. On the other hand, a deaf child is usually assigned to a special class for the deaf for the whole day. His teacher for the regular portions of his education is the same teacher who ministers to his special needs, which in the case of the deaf are speech reading, speech development, special techniques of language training, and so forth. What the deaf child receives as special education is, of course, a great deal more *special* than that received by a child with a minor speech handicap.

The amount and kind of special education which is needed by an exceptional child depends upon many factors, among them the degree of discrepancy between his development and the development of the ordinary child (the greater the degree of discrepancy, the greater the extent to which special education is needed); the discrepancies in development within the child himself; the effects of the disability on other areas of achievement. Various areas of special education will be described in subsequent chapters. It suffices at this point to say that special education, its quality, kind, and amount, is dependent upon the growth pattern of the child in relation to his peers and the discrepancies in growth within himself.

The need for special education can be recognized in the problem faced by a regular teacher. In many schools a teacher has a class of thirty-five children, one of whom is gifted and one of whom is mentally retarded. She also has one child who stutters and one who is a behavior problem. Asked to organize an educational program for a fifth-grade class, she must adapt instruction for the mentally retarded child who reads barely at the second-grade level, for the gifted child, who reads at nearly the eighth-grade level, for the speech defective, for the problem child, and for the other thirty-one children in her class, who also deviate, but not to the extent of those mentioned. Because of the difficulty of this task, special education programs have evolved in a large number of school systems. They are designed not only to help the exceptional child but also to help the regular teacher with her responsibility, so that she can devote most of the class time to a more homogeneous group of children. The organization of special education, then, benefits the average child in the regular grade as well as the exceptional child.

Education often begins where medicine stops. For example, fitting a visually impaired child with glasses or a hard-of-hearing youngster with a hearing aid is a medical concern. But teaching the child to use what vision and hearing he has most effectively and aiding him in using his other senses compensatorily is a special education function.

If a hearing loss, for example, can be corrected, this problem is solely a medical, not an educational, concern. If it cannot be corrected, it must be ameliorated to whatever extent is possible by decreasing its effects. Hearing aids, auditory training, and speech reading are directly geared to strengthening the ability to function auditorily and are considered amelioration, not cure.

In the case of total blindness for which medicine offers no remedy or improvement, the problem becomes solely an educational concern. Instruction in braille, provision of special braille materials, mobility training, and counseling are but a few of the aspects of a special education program.

One of the general aims of special education is first to ameliorate the deficit by medicine, training, or whatever means are feasible, and then to compensate for the residual deficit by strengthening other abilities and providing specially adapted materials.

The emphasis on the exceptional child in the public schools has had its advocates and also its opponents. Some feel that the support of programs for exceptional children is detracting from the major purpose of the public school— the education of the normal or average child. This point of view has been presented in the following verse:

> Johnny Jones has lost a leg,
> Fanny's deaf and dumb,
> Marie has epileptic fits,
> Tom's eyes are on the bum.
> Sadie stutters when she talks,
> Mabel has T.B.
> Morris is a splendid case
> Of imbecility.
> Billy Brown's a truant,
> And Harold is a thief,
> Teddy's parents gave him dope
> And so he came to grief.
> Gwendolin's a millionaire,
> Gerald is a fool;
> So every one of these darned kids
> Goes to a special school.
> They've specially nice teachers,
> And special things to wear,
> And special time to play in,
> And a special kind of air.

They've special lunches right in school,
While I—it makes me wild!—
I haven't any specialties;
I'm just a normal child.   (Scheideman, 1931)

SUMMARY

Inherent in the philosophy of a democracy is the right of all children to develop to their maximum. This philosophy has led to the organization of programs for exceptional children within the public schools. We have considered the following concepts:

1. Exceptional children have been defined as those children who deviate from the average in (a) mental, (b) physical and neuromotor, (c) sensory, (d) behavior, and (e) communication characteristics to such an extent that they require a modification of school practices and services in order to develop to their maximum.
2. Individual differences are viewed as having two components: (a) *interindividual differences,* or the difference between one child and another, and (b) *intraindividual differences,* a term which refers to the discrepancies in development within the child himself. The concept of interindividual differences is used in the classification or grouping of children, while the concept of intraindividual differences is used for designing the instructional program for a particular child without reference to his rank with other children. Discrepancies in physical, social, intellectual, and educational achievement have been presented in the form of profiles. The profiles show typical assets and deficits which necessitate different educational methods and programs for various types of deviant children: the gifted, the mentally retarded, the auditorily and visually impaired, learning disabled, those with physical and neuromotor handicaps, the behaviorally disordered, speech-defective, and the multiply handicapped.
3. Special education has been defined as that additional service, over and above the regular school program, that is provided for an exceptional child to assist in the development of his potentialities and/or in the amelioration of his disabilities.
4. The prevalence of exceptional children has been estimated conservatively at about 12.5 percent of the school population. Approximately 38 percent of handicapped children, or two and one-quarter million, in the United States in 1969 were being offered special services in public and private schools and residential institutions.
5. The educational facilities developed for exceptional children include itinerant personnel, special classes and resource rooms, special schools, residential schools, and hospitals and homebound service.

REFERENCES

Bureau of Education for the Handicapped. *Better Education for the Handicapped.* Annual Reports FY 1968 and FY 1969. Washington, D.C.: 1969, p. 4; 1970, p. 4.
Frampton, Merle E., and Gall, Elena D. (eds.) 1955. *Special Education for the Exceptional,* 3 vols. Boston: Porter Sargent.

Irwin, R. 1955. *As I Saw It.* New York: American Foundation for the Blind.

Mackie, Romaine P., and Dunn, L. M. 1954. *College and University Programs for the Preparation of Teachers of Exceptional Children,* U.S. Office of Education, Bulletin No. 13. Washington, D.C.: U.S. Government Printing Office.

Martens, Elise H. 1944. *Needs of Exceptional Children,* U.S. Office of Education, Leaflet No. 74. Washington, D.C.: Government Printing Press.

Reynolds, M. C. 1962. A Framework for Considering Some Issues in Special Education. *Exceptional Children* 7 (March, 28):367–370.

Scheideman, N. V. 1931. *The Psychology of Exceptional Children,* 2 vols. Boston: Houghton Mifflin.

Wolf, J. M., and Anderson, R. M. (eds.). 1969. *The Multiply Handicapped Child.* Springfield, Illinois: Charles C. Thomas.

Wright, Beatrice A. 1960. *Physical Disability: A Psychological Approach.* New York: Harper & Brothers.

ADDITIONAL REFERENCES

Association of Secondary School Principals. 1955. The Education of Handicapped and Gifted Pupils in the Secondary Schools. *Bulletin of the National Association of Secondary School Principals* 39 (No. 207).

Baker, H. J. 1959. *Introduction to Exceptional Children,* 3rd ed. New York: Macmillan.

Barker, R. C.; Wright, Beatrice; Meyerson, L.; and Gornick, Mollie. 1953. *Adjustment to Physical Handicap and Illness: A Survey of the Social Psychology of Physique and Disability.* New York: Social Science Research Council.

Brotemarkle, R. A., ed. 1931. *Clinical Psychology: Studies in Honor of Lightner Witmer.* Philadelphia: University of Pennsylvania Press.

Cruickshank, W. M., ed. 1963. *Psychology of Exceptional Children and Youth* (rev. ed.). Englewood Cliffs, New Jersey: Prentice-Hall.

Cruickshank. W. M., and Johnson, G. O., eds. 1967. *Education of Exceptional Children and Youth.* Englewood Cliffs, New Jersey: Prentice-Hall.

Dunn, L. M., ed. 1963. *Exceptional Children in the Schools.* New York: Holt, Rinehart, and Winston.

Garrison, K. C., and Dewey, G. F., Jr. 1959. *The Psychology of Exceptional Children,* 3rd ed. New York: Ronald Press.

Goodenough, Florence L. 1956. *Exceptional Children.* New York: Appleton-Century-Crofts.

Haring, N. G., and Schiefelbusch, R. L. (eds.). 1967. *Methods in Special Education.* New York: McGraw-Hill.

Heck, A. O. 1953. *The Education of Exceptional Children: Its Challenge to Teachers, Parents, and Laymen,* 2nd ed. New York: McGraw-Hill.

Horn, J. L. 1924. *The Education of Exceptional Children: A Consideration of Public School Problems and Policies in the Field of Differentiated Education.* New York: Century.

Jenks, W. F. 1954. *The Atypical Child.* Washington, D.C.: Catholic University of America Press.

Johnson, G. O., and Blank, Harriet D. 1968. *Exceptional Children Research Review.* Arlington, Virginia: The Council for Exceptional Children.

Jones, L. 1971. *Problems and Issues in the Education of Exceptional Children*. Boston: Houghton Mifflin.

Jordon, T. E. 1962. *The Exceptional Child*. Columbus, Ohio: Charles E. Merrill.

Kirk, S. A., Chairman. 1950. *The Education of Exceptional Children, Forty-ninth Yearbook of the National Society for the Study of Education*, Part II. Chicago: University of Chicago Press.

Kirk, S. A., and Wiener, B. 1963 (eds.). *Behavioral Research on Exceptional Children*. Arlington, Virginia: Council for Exceptional Children.

Louttit, C. M. 1957. *Clinical Psychology of Exceptional Children*, 3rd ed. New York: Harper & Brothers.

Magary, J. F., and Eichorn, J. R. 1960. *The Exceptional Child: A Book of Readings*. New York: Holt, Rinehart and Winston.

Magnifico, L. X. *Education for the Exceptional Child*. 1958. New York: Longmans, Green and Company.

Pintner, R.; Eisenson, J.; and Stanton, Mildred. 1941. *The Psychology of the Physically Handicapped*. New York: Appleton-Century-Crofts.

Taylor, W. W., and Taylor, Isabelle W. 1960. *Special Education of Physically Handicapped Children in Western Europe*. New York: International Society for the Rehabilitation of the Disabled.

Telford, C. W., and Sawrey, J. M. 1967. *The Exceptional Individual*. Englewood Cliffs, New Jersey: Prentice-Hall.

Van Sickle, J. H.; Witmer, L.; and Ayres, L. P. 1911. *Provision for Exceptional Children in Public Schools*. U.S. Bureau of Education, Bulletin No. 14. Washington, D.C.: Government Printing Office.

Wallin, J. E. W. 1949. *Children with Mental and Physical Handicaps*. New York: Prentice-Hall.

———. 1924. *The Education of Handicapped Children*. Boston: Houghton Mifflin.

White House Conference on Child Health and Protection. 1931. *Special Education: The Handicapped and the Gifted*. New York: Century.

———. 1932. *Organization for the Care of Handicapped Children: National, State and Local*. New York: Century.

———. 1933. *The Handicapped Child*. New York: Appleton-Century.

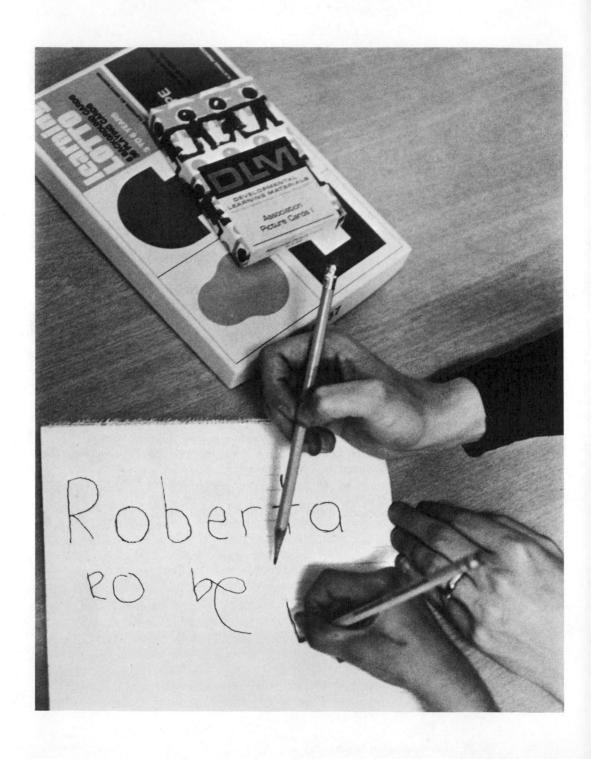

TWO

SPECIFIC

LEARNING

DISABILITIES

One of the areas in which intraindividual differences are most dramatic and most relevant is that of learning disabilities. Here we find children who often appear quite normal in most respects but have marked disabilities in one area or another. We also find children who appear mentally retarded but have normal abilities in some areas. They may be delayed in learning to talk or in understanding spatial relations or in comprehending what is said to them.

Traditional school programs for handicapped children tend to identify and classify children according to each one's major handicap. These classifications result from an assessment of the child and lead to placement in one of the existing programs for mentally retarded, deaf, crippled, speech defective, emotionally disturbed, or subcategories of these, such as visually impaired, or hard-of-hearing.

Educational authorities have recognized for some time that handicapped children do not always fit into neat, well-defined categories with uniform characteristics. They have recognized that mentally retarded children, even with a narrow IQ range, are not homogeneous in characteristics, and that not all deaf children learn at the same rate. One deaf child might learn speech reading, while another unfortunately does not. One child may be classified as cerebral-palsied but may also be mentally retarded, while another cerebral-palsied child may learn adequately in school or may become a college student. To make matters worse there is a number of children who are not deaf, not blind, not mentally retarded, but who are unable to learn under ordinary school instruction. This is the group that has come under the heading of "specific learning disabilities."

Definitions

The concept of learning disabilities has recently evolved to encompass the heterogeneous group of children not fitting neatly into the traditional categories of handicapped children. There is a substantial number of children who show retardation in learning to talk, or who do not develop language facility, or who do not develop normal visual or auditory perception, or who have great difficulty in learning to read, to spell, to write, or to make arithmetic calculations. Some of them are not receptive to language but are not deaf, some are not able to perceive visually but are not blind, and some cannot learn by ordinary methods of instruction but are not mentally retarded. Although these children form a heterogeneous group and fail to learn for diverse reasons, they have one thing in common: developmental discrepancies in abilities.

Because of the heterogeneous nature of this group of children, the concept of specific learning disability has been hard to define. Numerous definitive labels have been used, employing such terms as "minimal brain dysfunction," or "central processing dysfunction," or "perceptually handicapped children." Specific disabilities have been labeled "dyslexia" for severe reading disabilities, or "aphasia" for children who are delayed in learning to talk. Because the field of learning disabilities is of interest to psychiatrists, neurophysiologists, psychologists, speech pathologists, and educators, the problem has been viewed from these various perspectives. In general, however, the definitions fall into two broad categories: (a) those definitions involving functions of the central nervous system as they relate to the learning disability and (b) those definitions placing an emphasis on the behavior or learning disorder without specific reference to central nervous system etiology (cause).

An example of the first type of definition is presented by Clements (1966):

The term "minimal brain dysfunction syndrome" refers to children of near average, average, or above average general intelligence with certain learning or behavioral disabilities ranging from mild to severe, which are associated with deviations of function of the central nervous system. These deviations may manifest themselves by various combinations of impairments in perception, conceptualization, language, memory, and control of attention, impulse, or motor function. (p. 9–10)

Another definition that gives reference to the central nervous system is proposed by Myklebust (1963). He states:

We use the term "psychoneurological learning disorders" to include deficits in learning, at any age, which are caused by deviations in the central nervous system and which are not due to mental deficiency, sensory impairment, or psychogenicity. The etiology might be disease and accident, or it might be developmental. (p. 27)

These two definitions and the terms used were designed to emphasize that, although the disability results in behavior aberrations, the cause of the deviant behavior is deviant neurological functioning.

In the second category of definitions, stress is laid on behavioral characteristics without reference to brain dysfunction or etiology. The authors of such definitions feel that since all behavior, normal or abnormal, is related to brain function, it is of no benefit educationally to infer brain dysfunction from behavior. It is difficult to find the dysfunction in the brain, and even if it is found, little can be done about it. For pragmatic purposes, the task is to delineate within a child the basic behavior disability or disabilities and to organize a remedial program for the amelioration or correction of the disability.

Chalfant and Scheffelin (1969), in a review of research on learning disabilities, use the term "central processing dysfunctions." After reviewing a number of definitions they report a variety of descriptive characteristics:

Characteristics which are often mentioned include disorders in one or more of the processes of thinking, conceptualization, learning, memory, speech, language, attention, perception, emotional behavior, neuromuscular or motor coordination, reading, writing, arithmetic, discrepancies between intellectual achievement potential and achievement level, and developmental disparity in the psychological processes related to education. (p. 1)

In a discussion of learning disabilities, Kirk (1968) states that:

A learning disability refers to a specific retardation or disorder in one or more of the processes of speech, language, perception, behavior, reading, spelling, writing, or arithmetic. (p. 398)

Because of national interest in the problem and because states and the Federal Government were engaged in passing legislation, the National Advisory Committee on Handicapped Children of the U.S. Office of Education proposed a definition (1968) which was used in the Congressional bill entitled "The Learning Disabilities Act of 1969." This definition states:

Children with special (specific) learning disabilities exhibit a disorder in one or more of the basic psychological processes involved in understanding or in using spoken or written language. These may be manifested in disorders of listening, thinking, talking, reading, writing, spelling, or arithmetic. They include conditions which have been referred to as perceptual handicaps, brain injury, minimal brain dysfunction, dyslexia, developmental aphasia, etc. They *do not* include learning problems which are due primarily to visual, hearing, or motor handicaps, to mental retardation, emotional disturbance, or to environmental disadvantage. (p. 14)

To some, the term "learning disabilities" is confusing since mentally retarded children also have difficulty learning, but it should be noted that their disability is a general difficulty in learning rather than difficulty in a more limited area. It is for this reason that the word "specific" was added to indicate that we are not dealing with general problems in learning but rather with a specific developmental problem. Hence, the term "specific learning disabilities" refers to severe handicaps in central processes which inhibit the child's normal development in such specific areas as talking, thinking, perceiving, reading, writing, and spelling.

All of the definitions have a common core even though their emphases on the central nervous system may be different. The common areas of agreement among different authors are:

1. The learning problem should be specific and not a correlate of such other primary handicapping conditions as general mental retardation, sensory handicaps, emotional disturbance, and environmental disadvantage.

2. The children must have discrepancies in their own growth (intraindividual differences) with abilities as well as disabilities.

3. The deficits found in a child must be of a behavioral nature such as thinking, conceptualization, memory, speech, language, perception, reading, writing, spelling, arithmetic, and related abilities.

4. The primary focus of identification should be psychoeducational.

Prevalence

How many children with learning disabilities are there in a given population? This is a question that has been raised by school officials and by legislators. Because of the difficulty of defining learning disabilities, most statements of prevalence are based on estimates or even "guesstimates" derived from meager empirical information.

Few comprehensive studies have been conducted on the prevalence of learning disabilities in a school population. Myklebust and Boshes (1969) made an extensive study of learning disabilities in four school systems. By administering psychological and educational tests to a large group of third- and fourth-grade school children, they were able to identify what they termed children with learning disabilities and those without. They then proceeded to examine both groups medically, neurologically, ophthalmologically, etc. to determine the differences between these two groups. Their research asked such questions as: Does a pediatric examination or an EEG identify the same children as do the psychoeducational tests?

To establish criteria for learning disabilities, Myklebust and Boshes derived a learning quotient (LQ) for each of seven psychoeducational tests by dividing the age score by the chronological age. Using an LQ of 90 as the cut-off point, they defined as learning disabled those children who scored an LQ below 90 on any one of the seven tests. Using this criterion, Myklebust and Boshes found 15 percent functioning as underachievers. When additional tests were given and a criterion of 85 or below on any one test was used, the percentage of children labeled as learning disabled dropped to 7 percent. Since the prevalence issue was not the major purpose of Myklebust and Boshes's study, further data was not presented to show what percentage of children attained LQ's below 80 or 75 or 70.

In perusing the data of Myklebust and Boshes's study, it appears that the children from third- and fourth-grade classes who were identified as learning disabled were performing in reading, spelling, and arithmetic on a third-grade level. Hence, the children classified as learning disabled were, on the average, only one year retarded educationally as compared to their chronological ages. To some, these children do not constitute the hard core learning-disability children, but only the minor ones.

The National Advisory Committee on Handicapped Children (1968) of the U.S. Office of Education states:

The total number of children involved cannot be accurately determined until more adequate diagnostic procedures and criteria have been developed. The disorders may range in degree from mild to severe. While the milder degrees of learning difficulties may be corrected by the classroom teacher, the more severe cases require special remedial procedures. A conservative estimate of the latter group would include from 1 to 3 percent of the school population. (p. 14)

At the present time it is difficult to estimate the percentage of children who require special remedial education for the correction or amelioration of specific learning disabilities. With further research it may be possible to determine the specific kinds of learning disabilities found in children and the prevalence of each. At the present time the best guess is that from 1 to 3 percent at the least, and possibly 7 percent at the most, of the school population require special remedial education.

Approaches to the Concept of Learning Disabilities

It would be simple if there were only one kind of specific learning disability. In this case the task would be to identify it, determine the extent of the disability, and apply one effective remedial program. Unfortunately, this is not the case. There are diverse problems, correlates, and remedial methods. One remedial procedure may be appropriate for one type of disability and completely inappropriate for another type of disability. For example, a remedial method that may be appropriate for a child with a visual perception problem would be inappropriate for a child whose visual perception is intact but who has a severe auditory perception disability. Both of these children may be classified as having a specific learning disability, but the procedures for assessment and remediation are different.

Only since 1963 has the term "specific learning disability" generally replaced many of the terms that utilize biological concepts such as brain injury, or such special disabilities as aphasia, perceptual handicaps, and dyslexia. Although recent emphasis on detecting and remediating specific learning disabilities in children is relatively new, the recognition of disorders in language, in reading, and in perception has existed for some time.

In order to put current concepts of learning disabilities in perspective, it would be well to summarize some historical viewpoints and current theories. The next few pages, therefore, will present (1) some historical neurological approaches, (2) some perceptual-motor approaches, (3) a visual perception approach, (4) three multisensory approaches, and (5) several remedial reading approaches.

NEUROLOGICAL APPROACHES

Over the centuries reports have been made about individuals who have lost the ability to understand language, or to speak, or to read, as a result of an injury to the brain. These cases led neurologists to investigate the relation between brain function and communication.

Hughlings Jackson (Taylor, 1932), although not the first neurologist who contributed to knowledge in this area, is probably the best known. The theory of cerebral dominance as related to speech and other behavioral disorders had its true beginning with Jackson. In 1868 Jackson pointed out that there are various degrees of aphasia (loss of the ability to speak), and that aphasia, agraphia (loss of the ability to write), and alexia (loss of the ability to read), are defects in utilizing symbols, i.e., thinking. He alleged that writing was affected, not as a separate "faculty" but as a part of the failure to proposition in words. He formulated his brain theories on studies of brain-damaged adults and epileptics. His writings and case descriptions had a marked influence on the later work of Henry Head in England and Samuel T. Orton in the United States. Henry Head (1926), following the lead and theories of Hughlings Jackson, published two volumes on aphasia.

Much of the early work on language disorders was conducted on adults who lost the ability to speak, read, or write as a result of damage to the brain. Little work was done with children who did not develop language ability or who did not learn to read. The belief about these children was that, although they did not have known brain damage similar to that in adult cases, they must have had an early damage before, during, or shortly after birth; hence their inability to learn.

A good example of the inferences from adult brain damage to that of children is found in the work of Hinshelwood (1917). As an ophthalmologist, Hinshelwood had referred to him for visual examinations, children who were having difficulty in learning to read. Teachers in England at that time believed that, since reading is accomplished through vision, those who failed to learn must have a visual defect. Upon examination of these children, Hinshelwood found that very few of the children referred to him as reading failures had visual defects. At the time Hinshelwood was pondering this problem, he received a patient who, through an accident, had a brain concussion. This man desired a visual examination because after the brain concussion he was unable to read. Upon examination Hinshelwood found that, although the man was unable to read, his visual acuity was intact. Hinshelwood diagnosed this problem as "alexia." Although before the accident the man had been a good reader, he was now unable to recognize words or phrases. An attempt to teach him to recognize words as wholes failed, but he was able to learn isolated letters. Hinshelwood then proceeded to teach him to read successfully by the spelling method.

Several years later the patient contracted pneumonia and died. By previous agreement Hinshelwood was able to procure the brain and to study the extent of the damage. In this patient he found a lesion in the angular gyrus of the left hemisphere. As a result of this case and others, Hinshelwood postulated that the reading center was in the angular gyrus of the left hemisphere and that lesions in this area would produce alexia. He further postulated that children who have difficulty in learning to read must have had an injury or underdevelopment of the left angular gyrus which produces what he called "word blindness." Thus Hinshelwood differentiated between adults who lost the ability to read as "acquired word blindness" (alexia) and children who were unable or had difficulty in learning to read as "congenital word blindness," sometimes referred to as "dyslexia."

In the United States Samuel T. Orton (1928) questioned Hinshelwood's concept of congenital word blindness and its localization in the left angular gyrus. He proposed instead a theory of cerebral dominance which could account for a child's stuttering or inability to read. Orton postulated that when neither of the two cerebral hemispheres was dominant over the other, the child began twisting symbols and seeing *no* as *on,* or *saw* as *was.* He called it the theory of "strephosymbolia" (twisted symbols). Orton's associates, Marion Monroe (1932), Gillingham (1936), and others followed his theories by developing diagnostic procedures and phonic remedial methods for children diagnosed as dyslexics or as having strephosymbolia.

PERCEPTUAL MOTOR APPROACHES

During the post–World War II period, Strauss and Lehtinen (1947) generated wide-spread interest in the problem of specific learning disabilities by focusing attention on brain-injured children. Strauss was a German physician and neurologist who migrated to the United States in the late 1930's. The specialty which he brought with him was the education of children who showed abnormal development and who were suspected of having brain damage. In collaboration with Hans Werner, a child psychologist, and Laura Lehtinen, a teacher, he conducted research and organized programs for children thought to have suffered brain damage. The publication in 1947 of *Psychopathology and Education of the Brain-Injured Child* (Strauss and Lehtinen, 1947) describing the authors' research, theories, and educational methods stimulated national interest in children with learning disabilities.

Strauss's main thesis was that children with brain injuries incurred before, during, or after birth are subject to major disorders in (1) perception, (2) thinking, and (3) behavior, and that these disorders affect the child's ability to learn to read, write, spell, or calculate using arithmetic symbols. The diagnosis of brain injury was reached primarily from the presence of behavioral manifestations or disorders, and was not based solely on traditional neurological diagnosis. His educational methods consisted of instructional procedures and environmental changes that would correct or ameliorate the disturbances in perception, thinking, and behavior, integrating these techniques with procedures in teaching reading, writing, spelling, or arithmetic.

Although Strauss's concept of brain-damaged children and the procedures in assessment that led to such a diagnosis have been challenged, the educational procedures for remediation of the behavioral symptoms have not been seriously questioned. Many subsequent developments in learning disabilities were stimulated by Strauss and Lehtinen's work. Among these developments are the perceptual motor approaches of (1) William Cruickshank, (2) Newell Kephart, (3) Raymond Barsch, and (4) Gerald Getman.

1. *Cruickshank* and his associates working with cerebral-palsied and hyperactive children have adopted and extended the philosophy and procedures of

Strauss and Lehtinen. This group states that the majority of children with known brain damage have the behavioral characteristics pointed out by Strauss, namely:

a. motor disinhibition (inability to refrain from a response);

b. disassociation (the tendency to respond to pieces [elements] of a stimulus);

c. figure-ground disturbance (confusing a figure with its background);

d. perseveration (difficulty in shifting from one psychological task to another); and

e. absence of a well-developed self-concept and body image.

Cruickshank et al (1961) tested the Strauss hypothesis that a nonstimulating (barren) classroom with specially designed instructional materials will improve the functioning of these children. Forty hyperactive children, all of whom fitted the behavioral criteria for brain-damaged children (although not all of them showed neurological signs of brain damage), were divided into four equal groups of ten each. Two of the groups were given the nonstimulating classroom special program, while the other two groups were placed in special classes with a traditional program.

The general plan for the education of these hyperactive children in the non-stimulating classrooms included:

a. reducing the environmental stimuli;

b. reducing to a minimum the space in which the child works;

c. providing a structured school program simplified so that the child does not have too many choices to make; and

d. maximizing the stimulus value of the materials to which the child is asked to attend.

The four groups in the Cruickshank experiment (two experimental groups and two control groups) were examined with a series of posttests after one year of training and again after a follow-up year with no special training. The comparison results did not show a superiority of the two experimental nonstimulating classes. For both the experimental and control groups the Stanford-Binet IQ's of approximately 80 did not change on the posttest after one year and on the follow-up tests after a second year. Similar results with no statistically significant differences were also obtained on the Goodenough Draw-a-Man Test and on the Vineland Social Maturity Scale. On educational achievement tests all four groups showed statistically significant academic progress, but there was no significant difference in final achievement on posttests and follow-up tests between the experimental and control groups.

On several scoring categories of the Bender-Gestalt Test and on the Syracuse Visual Figure-Ground Test, the experimental groups made temporary gains in comparison to the control groups, but on the follow-up test a year later, the experimental groups had lost the temporary gains.

This experiment by Cruickshank et al, as well as other less extensive experiments (Rost, 1967; Burnett, 1962), did not demonstrate that hyperactive or distractible children can profit more significantly, either intellectually or academically, from a nonstimulating classroom environment than from a special class organized along more traditional lines. The experiment did show, however, that special education with or without the nonstimulating class environment can produce academic progress in such children. It may also be true that for some individual children who are hyperactive, the procedure of decreasing the environmental stimuli is very beneficial. Group results, as cited above, do not always determine what is most beneficial for a particular child.

2. *Kephart,* a well-known contributor to the field of learning disabilities, also worked with Strauss, first in research, and later as a co-author (Strauss and Kephart, 1955). Kephart (1960) later evolved a system of diagnosis and remediation along somewhat different theoretical lines, relying less on brain dysfunction and more upon developmental psychology, which was more in keeping with his own background in child psychology.

Kephart's basic thesis is that the child's first encounter with his environment is through motor activities and that this muscular behavior is a prerequisite for later learnings. In normal development the child acquires patterns of movement from which he develops motor generalizations. On the basis of these motor generalizations a perceptual-cognitive structure is organized. Kephart (1964) has defined four major motor generalizations or groupings of movement patterns, as follows: (1) posture and the maintenance of balance through which the child learns to resist the force of gravity in order to right himself, and to play one set of muscles against an antagonistic set of muscles in order to maintain balance; (2) contact, including the experience of reaching, grasping, and releasing through which the child develops contact patterns which lead to new generalizations; (3) locomotion, in which the child generalizes his patterns of walking so as to adapt to rough surfaces, intervening objects, and restraining clothes; (4) receipt and propulsion, which are elaborations of an integrated body schema and are dependent primarily upon an awareness of self. As the child matures, Kephart postulates, he is able to generalize and objectify the relationships of objects in time and space without using himself as the focal point.

Kephart emphasizes the hierarchy of these motor generalizations in developing space and time perception. Without the generalizations of posture and balance the child cannot explore his environment and develop the generalizations of contact and locomotion. Without the generalizations achieved through contact and locomotion, the child does not have the tactual-kinesthetic information to be integrated with other sensory input into a perceptual configuration. Thus, through proprioceptive and exteroceptive experiences the child develops a perceptual world that matches his motor world. Kephart emphasizes the importance of this perceptual-motor match in which what the child perceives must be matched to his motor awareness in order to have meaning. This perceptual-motor match is developed through a feedback system in which the child receives information from his own output, thereby monitoring the correctness or incorrectness of his own perceptions and actions.

The Purdue Perceptual Motor Survey was developed by Kephart (1960) as an aid in diagnosing the child's level of perceptual-motor development prior to instituting a training program. It evaluates: (1) balance and postural flexibility, (2) body image and differentiation, (3) perceptual-motor match, (4) ocular control, and (5) form perception.

Kephart's approach to remediation of these problems attempts to fill in the gaps in the sequence of generalizations which allow the child to integrate and manipulate the information he receives from his environment, such as an understanding of form and space and rhythm. Kephart emphasizes process-oriented, rather than task-oriented, procedures; i.e., the basic motor generalizations and perceptual motor skills should be developed before you can expect the child to progress academically. He therefore provides various training activities such as: (1) sensory-motor training using walking boards, trampolines, making "angels-in-the-snow," and various games to teach variations in movement, rhythm, and bilateral as well as unilateral abilities; (2) chalkboard activities designed to develop movement patterns and matching visual perceptions; (3) ocular motor training to help the child match his visual control to the motor and kinesthetic patterns he has learned; and (4) form perception exercises such as peg boards, stick figures, and puzzles.

Although there has not been any controlled research to determine the efficacy of this approach, it has been widely accepted, and beneficial results have been reported. This approach is applicable to certain children with specific perceptual-motor problems, but it is not claimed that the procedures are beneficial for all children with specific learning disabilities. Children who do not have visual-motor perceptual problems but who have retardation in auditory, vocal, and language disorders may require different kinds of remediation.

3. *Barsch* (1965, 1967), who also worked with Strauss, has developed what he terms a "movigenic" curriculum. He postulates that man is a moving being in a spatial world. Learning difficulties that children have are deficits in movement efficiency. The movigenic curriculum is, therefore, designed to facilitate move-

ment efficiency. This program of training movement efficiency is, in a sense, the end in itself. Barsch does not relate this development to deficits in learning to talk, or in learning to read—deficits which usually are associated with the concept of learning disabilities.

4. Getman (1965, 1968), an optometrist who is another contributor to this field, has applied his knowledge of vision to children with learning disabilities. He has developed a learning-readiness program designed to prepare the child for school learning. Like Kephart, he uses motor and visual perception exercises to accomplish his goals.

Comment. The thread of similarity among the preceding approaches is quite apparent. All involve the importance of perceptual-motor diagnosis and subsequent remediation through sensory-motor activities.

It is interesting to note that a century and a quarter ago Edward Seguin (1846) emphasized sensory-motor training of the mentally retarded. He introduced a physiological method of training the mentally retarded, and his work had some impact on Alfred Strauss. Seguin's work is heavily reflected in the methods of Kephart and Barsch. His treatise on physiological education for the mentally retarded was primarily sensory-motor. His aim, like that of Strauss and Kephart and partly like that of Barsch and Getman, was from motor or muscular training to sensory-motor training, and from sensory-motor training to abstract thought. Seguin's use of the trampoline to develop balance, or the game of "statue" to develop attention, or perceptual motor training to develop cognition are similar in aim and practice to those of the current perceptual-motor emphasis. It is indeed interesting that a system developed in the middle of the nineteenth century for the mentally retarded should crop up in the middle of the twentieth century in somewhat the same form for children with learning disabilities. It is also interesting that Strauss, Barsch, and Kephart developed their theories and procedures with mentally retarded or slow-learning children and then applied them to children with learning disabilities.

A VISUAL PERCEPTION APPROACH

Another approach to modifying certain kinds of learning disabilities was developed by Marianne Frostig at the Frostig Center of Educational Therapy in Los Angeles. Her hypothesis is that children with disabilities in visual perception will have difficulty learning in school and that remediation of these disabilities will prevent future school failures.

Frostig et al's *Developmental Test of Visual Perception* (1964) measures the child's developmental level of ability in various tasks involving visual perception. Recognizing that evaluating a single facet of visual perception does not give a true picture, Frostig developed tests in five different areas of perceptual skill.

These five areas are: (1) *eye-hand coordination* (the child draws between increasingly narrower boundaries); (2) *figure-ground discrimination* (the child traces figures on increasingly complex backgrounds); (3) *constancy of shape* (the child recognizes geometric figures presented in different sizes, contexts, or positions); (4) *position in space* (the child discriminates reversals and rotations of figures); and (5) *spatial relations* (the child perceives space relations between simple forms and parts of a pattern and their relationship to himself).

The scores on the Frostig tests (which can be used as group tests) can be translated into a Perceptual Age (PA), Perceptual Quotient (PQ), and Scaled Scores for the test as a whole and for each of the five subtests. The scores can be represented on a profile showing a comparison of abilities and disabilities among the five visual perceptual skills.

A program for remediation has been developed by Frostig and Horne (1964). The materials consist of work sheets for the children, supplemented by other related remedial techniques and suggestions for physical exercises and for three-dimensional activities. These exercises are designed to develop skills in the five areas tested by the Developmental Test of Visual Perception. The materials have been used with kindergarten and first-grade children to develop readiness for later academic achievement as well as with children diagnosed as having visual-motor handicaps.

It should be pointed out that the description of the tests and the remedial procedures of Frostig do not imply that she excludes other approaches. On the contrary, she uses an eclectic method in both diagnosis and remediation. She uses many instruments including the Wechsler Intelligence Scale for Children (WISC) and the Illinois Test of Psycholinguistic Abilities (ITPA) as well as her Developmental Test of Visual Perception. By such an analysis she determines the abilities and disabilities of children and creates appropriate remedial instruction.

Research on the efficacy of the Frostig-Horne program is not clear cut. In a review of the studies conducted on the materials, Myers and Hammill (1969) report contradictory results. In general, using the Frostig materials with heterogeneous groups of children increases the scores on the Developmental Test of Visual Perception, but whether or not these children show accelerated reading achievement later is still a question. Similar research on children with disabilities is not available.

MULTISENSORY APPROACHES

This section will discuss briefly the diagnostic and remedial procedures of (1) Myklebust and his colleagues, (2) Kirk and his colleagues, and (3) Friedus.

1. *Myklebust's* original interest was in the psychology and education of the deaf. Since deaf children have as their basic functional deficit the acquisition of language, Myklebust's interest also included language disorders and learning

disorders in reading, writing, and other school subjects. Although his earlier publications were primarily in the field of the deaf, his later publications, notably with Johnson (1967) dealt with learning disabilities.

The Johnson-Myklebust approach to the remediation of learning disabilities is to some extent an eclectic approach rather than a unique diagnostic remedial system. Although theoretically it emphasizes neurological relationships as explanations, in practice it is a behavioral approach with an emphasis on psycho-educational diagnosis of specific disabilities followed by remediation of the disabled behavioral responses. The emphasis is also on auditory-vocal disabilities as basic to other disabilities in school-age children.

Myklebust prefers the term "psychoneurological learning disabilities." Although his assessment of children's problems is primarily at a behavioral level, he feels that disorders of function are related to lack of integrity of the central nervous system and that the term more adequately relates the brain to behavior.

In an early publication, Myklebust (1960) presented a hierarchical scheme by which language develops. He stated that a child first gains experience, then develops by stages through (1) development of inner language or meaning, (2) comprehending the spoken word, or auditory receptive language, (3) speaking, or auditory expressive language, (4) reading, or visual receptive language, and (5) writing, or visual expressive language. Thus, auditory language comes first, and when a child is learning to read and write, he superimposes the visual language on the already acquired auditory language.

Myklebust refers to psychoneurological learning disabilities as the result of deficits in one of the language development levels. He also recognizes nonverbal learning in addition to verbal language learning. While difficulties in verbal learning are concerned with verbal symbolization and conceptualization, the nonverbal learning disabilities are in visual perception and imagery. In a sense, these correspond to, but are not identical with, perceptual-motor learning, body image, spatial orientation, visual perception, and functions at the automatic level of the ITPA.

In the book by Johnson and Myklebust (1967) emphasis is placed on the diagnosis of learning disability by first asking "what disability?" The analysis of the problem in a child requires neurological, psychological, and educational assessment. When the specific disability is isolated, remediation is organized to correct the deficit. Johnson and Myklebust concentrate on several disorders in children including: (1) disorders of auditory learning, (2) disorders of reading, (3) disorders of written language, (4) disorders of arithmetic, and (5) nonverbal disorders of learning. The reader is referred to the original source for details. No especially designed tests or workbooks are provided but remedial techniques are outlined in their book.

2. *Kirk* and his colleagues developed the *Illinois Test of Psycholinguistic*

Abilities (ITPA) (Kirk, McCarthy, and Kirk, 1968) after many years of research and clinical experience with mentally retarded children and learning deficits. This test evaluates various aspects of the process of communication, including memory and cognitive, associative, and expressive abilities.

During his work with preschool mentally retarded children, Kirk (1958) observed marked deviations in ability within certain individual children. This led to the concept of intraindividual differences, the relationship of abilities and disabilities in the same child. In an effort to diagnose these intraindividual differences, Kirk recognized the need for a diagnostic test which would pinpoint linguistic, cognitive, and perceptual abilities so that appropriate remedial methods could be instituted to ameliorate the deficits.

The ITPA was designed to assess the abilities and disabilities of children between the ages of three and ten. Based on a theoretical psycholinguistic model, it evaluates three dimensions of the communication process. The abilities measured by the twelve subtests include:

a. the ability to receive and understand what is seen and heard;
b. the ability to make associations and understand interrelationships of what is seen and heard;
c. the ability to express oneself by verbal and motor responses;
d. the ability to grasp automatically the whole of a visual pattern or verbal expression when only part of it is presented; and
e. the ability to remember and repeat visual and auditory sequences of material.

The scores on the twelve subtests can be placed on a profile, as in Figure 2–1. This is a profile of the abilities of a six-year-old child of average intelligence. It will be noted that the three developmental ages represented on the left section of the profile show no differences. This would suggest normal growth. The ITPA scores, however, show a different picture. The child shows some abilities above his CA (in auditory association and verbal expression at the representational level and in grammatic closure and auditory sequential memory at the automatic level). He shows disabilities of different degrees in visual reception, visual association, and manual expression at the representational level, and deficits in visual closure and visual sequential memory at the automatic level. The intraindividual difference between the visual-motor channel and the auditory-vocal channel is quite marked, indicating that this child has a visual channel disability. Remedial work would focus on the improvement of this disability so that the child can begin to function equally in all areas.

In remediation, Kirk advocates that intensive training be given in the area of disability rather than allowing these areas to deteriorate still further by avoiding

FIGURE 2–1

*Profile of psycholinguistic ages for a child
with a visual channel disability*

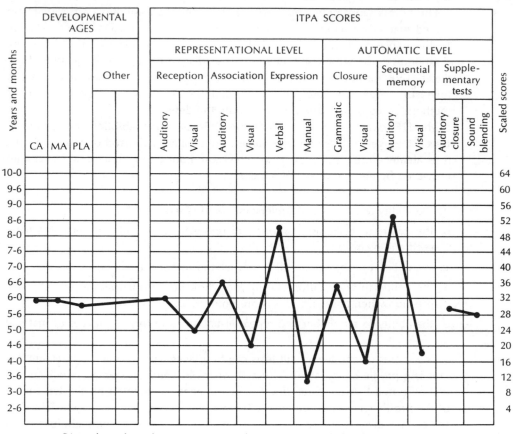

CA = chronological age; MA = mental age; PLA = psycholinguistic age

them and only compensating with the areas of strength. Remediation of disabilities indicated by the subtests of the ITPA is dealt with in *Psycholinguistic Learning Disabilities: Diagnosis and Remediation* (Kirk and Kirk, 1971), in which a finer analysis has been made of the tasks required for each of the functions tapped by the ITPA. A summary of this breakdown of abilities is presented in Table 2–1.

Following the publication of the experimental edition of the ITPA in 1961, a number of experiments evaluated the results of remediation based on the model of the ITPA. Smith (1962) conducted an experiment on the training of psycho-linguistic functions with educable mentally retarded children. His positive results led him and Dunn to prepare the widely used Peabody Language Development Kits (Dunn and Smith, 1967, 1968, 1969). Wiseman (1964) and Hart (1963) also demonstrated improvements in the achievement of groups receiving training as compared to those in classes under traditional programs. Kirk (1966) has presented results of training individual children over a period of several years. These are case studies rather than a controlled experiment, but the children were given pre- and posttesting as well as follow-up testing after the termination of remediation. Karnes (1969) has reported positive results from training specific ITPA functions with disadvantaged preschool children.

3. *Friedus* (1964) was influenced by Strauss and Lehtinen in developing her remedial procedures, but she recognizes that no one method applies to all types of learning disabilities. As a general principle in teaching, she likens the child to a computer in which the child must (a) attend to and (b) receive information through the senses, then (c) integrate this information with other information, (d) organize the perceptual with the motor activities, and (e) produce an adequate response.

Friedus emphasizes materials and methods that give feedback and that will allow the child to monitor his own response. In teaching arithmetic the child is given instructions to check his own work through concrete aids. Her teaching approach is applied to special disabilities as well as to the teaching of academic subjects such as arithmetic.

REMEDIAL READING APPROACHES

Many learning disabilities are not detected until the child begins to fail academically in school. Failure in reading is the most common point of detection and one of the most frequent kinds of learning disabilities with which the school is concerned.

All children are exposed to reading programs, sometimes these begin at home, sometimes in kindergarten, but most commonly when they are admitted to the first grade. Reading instruction may proceed on any one of three different levels: (1) developmental reading, (2) corrective reading, and (3) remedial reading.

1. *Developmental reading* refers to the various systems of teaching reading in the classroom and provides a sequential development of the skills of reading;

2. *Corrective reading* refers to the methods used to change minor incorrect habits or gaps in knowledge acquired in the course of a developmental reading program. Because even normal children differ in their abilities to acquire reading skills, it is not uncommon, under our system of mass education, to find some children in nearly every class who need special help. Absenteeism, inattention, poor health, emotional disturbance, lack of background experience, inap-

TABLE 2-1

Task analysis of ITPA functions

Representational level

AUDITORY CHANNEL	VISUAL CHANNEL
Auditory reception: The child may not have adequate auditory discrimination. The child may not recognize and identify sounds in his environment. The child may not have developed a listening attitude. The child may have difficulty attaching meaning to words. The child may not understand consecutive speech.	*Visual reception:* The child may lack basic skills of visual-motor perception. The child may lack knowledge and experience. The child may not observe things within his visual field. The child may not attach meaning to visual symbols. The child may not utilize visual imagery.
Auditory association: The child may have difficulty holding two or more concepts in mind and considering them in relation to each other. The child may have difficulty identifying and verbalizing first-order relationships (directly relating two verbal concepts). The child may have difficulty identifying and verbalizing second-order relationships (finding a specific relationship to match one already given). The child may have difficulty learning to classify or categorize concepts. The child may have difficulty finding and evaluating alternative solutions to a problem.	*Visual association:* The child may have difficulty holding two or more concepts in mind and considering them in relation to each other. The child may have difficulty identifying first-order relationships (directly relating two visual concepts). The child may have difficulty identifying second-order relationships (finding a specific relationship to match one already given). The child may have difficulty classifying or categorizing visual concepts. The child may have difficulty finding and evaluating alternative solutions to a problem.
Verbal expression: The child may lack basic vocal skills. The child may lack adequate vocabulary. The child may not express ideas spontaneously (difficulty in retrieval of words or ideas). The child may lack automatic grammatic skills. The child may lack adequate interpersonal communication.	*Manual motor expression:* The child may lack prerequisite perceptual skills. The child may lack ideas leading to motor expression. The child may not make ideas operational.

propriate content, poor teaching, frequent changes of school—any of these and other reasons can cause gaps in the child's growth in ,reading ability; but such delay in learning to read need not imply that the child has a specific learning disability. He does, however, need help from a corrective reading teacher or a classroom teacher who can spot his difficulties and correct them. He may need help in word recognition skills, in vocabulary understanding, in phonics, or in

Automatic level

AUDITORY CHANNEL	VISUAL CHANNEL
Auditory closure and grammatic closure: The child may not have had sufficient exposure to the material being presented. The child may lack adequate short-term auditory memory. The child may not reactivate what he hears, either vocally or subvocally. The child may not learn readily even when experiences have been repeated many times. The child may have difficulty synthesizing isolated sounds into words (sound blending).	*Visual closure:* The child may lack prerequisite perceptual skills. The child may lack the ability to visualize. The child may lack the ability to organize a disparate visual field into a unified percept. The child may lack adequate speed of perception.
Auditory sequential memory: The child may have difficulty attending to the details of auditory stimuli. The child may have difficulty remembering and repeating what he has heard and attended to. The child may have difficulty storing and retrieving information.	*Visual sequential memory:* The child may show physical correlates inhibiting development of visual sequential memory. The child may have difficulty attending to visual details. The child may have difficulty remembering what he has seen and attended to. The child may be unable to read and spell due to a visual sequential memory deficit. The child may have difficulty storing and retrieving information once learned.

Source: Kirk and Kirk, 1971.

speed of reading. This has been called "corrective reading" since the habits, not the basic processes of the child's thinking, need correcting.

3. *Remedial reading* refers to the procedures used with children whose reading skills are still not developed after exposure to developmental reading and corrective reading. These children have special disabilities within themselves that require remediation before the child will learn to read. These children are said to have learning disabilities.

There have developed a large number of remedial reading methods for children with learning disabilities. Included in this section will be brief descriptions of (1) the kinesthetic method, and (2) phonic methods.

1. *The kinesthetic method* was developed by Grace Fernald, a psychologist who became interested in children who had difficulty in learning to read or

spell. Her method involves four developmental stages: (1) In stage one the child traces the form of a known word while saying it, then writes it from memory, comparing each trial with the original model. (2) In stage two he just looks at the word or phrase while saying it, then tries to write it from memory, comparing his result with the model until he is successful. (3) In stage three he writes the word without vocalizing it until he is successful. (4) In stage four he begins to generalize and reads new words on the basis of his experience with previously learned words.

The Fernald kinesthetic method of teaching disabled readers (Fernald and Keller, 1921) has withstood the test of time, since it has been used in various forms by many teachers. Fernald (1943) describes in case studies the progress made by severe reading disability cases following training by the kinesthetic method.

Kirk (1933) compared the manual tracing method with the look-and-say method using six subnormal boys, with each boy serving as his own control. The boys learned 5 words a day for 30 days, alternating between the two methods. He found no difference between the tracing method and the look-and-say method in number of trials in learning, but retention of the words over a 24-hour period was significantly superior for words learned by the tracing method.

Hirsch (1963) gave a series of visual sequential memory tests to 16 subjects and trained 8 of them on unknown words by the kinesthetic method. The group that had learned by the kinesthetic method scored higher on the visual memory retests than did the control group, suggesting that the kinesthetic method may train visual sequential memory.

The Fernald kinesthetic method has been beneficial to certain children with certain kinds of reading disabilities because the procedure encompasses important variables in learning. First, by writing and using a motor movement, *attention* is focused upon the visual task. Second, although the method has been called "kinesthetic," its more important function may be that of training *visual sequential memory,* or visualization ability, since the emphasis of the method is to write the words from memory. Third, the method has a built-in feedback system. The child can write the word, check it with the original word, and if incorrect, write it from memory again. It can be self-correctional.

2. *Phonic methods.* Many phonic methods have been developed, but only three of the most commonly used phonic remedial methods will be briefly described here.

The *phonic-grapho-vocal method* of Hegge, Kirk, and Kirk (1936) was developed while the authors were working with high-grade mentally retarded children who were also classified as disabled readers. The Hegge, Kirk, and Kirk *Remedial Reading Drills* is a programmed phonic system that emphasizes sound blending and incorporates much kinesthetic experience.

The procedure begins by giving the child auditory training in sound blending and grapho-vocal practice in writing and vocalizing letter sounds, running them together as he sounds them. When sound blending has been achieved, the child is presented with two- and three-letter words in which the child sounds each element separately and then blends the sounds into a word. Supplementary to the printed lessons, the grapho-vocal method is used by asking the child to write words as he pronounces the separate components and blends them into a word.

Remedial Reading Drills contains a series of short programmed lessons, each lesson incorporating only one new sound with the sounds which have been previously learned. The presentation follows the same principles found valuable in programmed learning: (1) the principle of minimal change, (2) overlearning through many repetitions of each new sound in a variety of settings, plus frequent review drills, (3) prompting and confirmation, (4) only one response taught for each symbol, and (5) the child is provided with immediate knowledge of his success by social reinforcement given by the tutor.

The method has been found effective with disabled readers of both normal and subnormal intelligence (Kirk, 1934, 1940). It reflects the influence of Fernald and also of Marion Monroe (1932) who developed one of the early analytic tests for reading disability and who emphasized a phonic approach during a period when phonics was in disrepute among educators.

The *VAK (Visual-Auditory-Kinesthetic) Method* of Gillingham and Stillman (1936, 1965) is a phonic system for the remediation of reading disabilities. In this method the children learn both the names of the letters, and the sounds of the letters. Sounding is used for reading, but letter names are used for spelling. A systematic procedure is followed in which the child is told the names of a letter, then the sound. The child then says the sound and traces it or writes it from memory. After he has learned some consonants and vowels he is required to sound each letter and blend the sounds into a word. After the child has learned to sound, write, and read three-letter words, these words are made into stories and the child reads them silently, then orally.

The procedures are developed by stages from the names of the letters to the sounds, to the associations, to the reading of words, sentences, stories, and finally to reading books. The Gillingham VAK system is an association system, since the theoretical approach is to associate visual, kinesthetic, and auditory sense inputs. Many who follow the Gillingham method feel it produces results with normal children who have been unable to learn by the "whole word method" and thus require a more atomistic approach through letter sounds and letter names. Like the Hegge-Kirk-Kirk *Remedial Reading Drills,* it has been used for over thirty years including the period during which the use of phonics was severely criticized.

The Spalding Method is a phonic system presented in *The Writing Road to Reading* (1957). It was not originally devised for children with reading disabilities but as a classroom method for all children in the first through third grades. It can readily be individualized for remedial work.

This method begins with sounds the child hears and uses in speaking. He learns to say and to write the sounds of a series of phonograms (single letters and letter combinations) shown separately on cards. As soon as the child can recognize the symbols, pronounce the sounds, and write them, he is asked to write words from a word list presented auditorily. He repeats the word sound by sound as he writes the corresponding symbols. Thus, he learns sound blending analytically rather than synthetically, breaking the word into its separate sounds as he writes. The letter names are never used, and nonphonetic words are learned by memory as configurations. As soon as the child becomes adept in writing what he hears, he is presented with visual material to read. The Spalding method is based on Orton's theory of cerebral dominance in which writing the sounds is an attempt to establish laterality in writing.

It will be noted that all three phonic methods discussed here utilize the learning of single sounds associated with written symbols and blending them into words. All three phonic methods also involve writing the words as does the Fernald kinesthetic method, which teaches words as wholes without phonics. All three methods rely on auditory cues and on the child's success in developing an independent method of word recognition.

Psychoeducational Diagnostic Procedures

To assess a child's specific learning disability and to organize an appropriate remedial method for the amelioration of the disability it is necessary to follow a systematic procedure in diagnosis. A diagnostic process that leads to a program of remediation was originally described by Kirk in the first edition of *Educating Exceptional Children* (1962) and later by Kirk and Kirk (1971). This diagnostic process generally proceeds in five stages, namely: (1) determining whether the child's learning problem is specific, general, or spurious; (2) analyzing the behavior manifestations which are descriptive of the specific problem; (3) discovering the physical, environmental, and psychological correlates of the disability; (4) evolving a diagnostic inference (hypothesis) on the basis of the behavior manifestations and the correlates; and (5) organizing a systematic remedial program based on the diagnostic inference.

The application of these five steps can be best understood if applied to a specific child. Miss Jones, a third-grade teacher, had an 8-year-old child in her class who was unable to read even at the primer level. After working with him for four months without success, she decided there was something drastically wrong with the boy because he seemed not to learn readily nor to remember what he had learned from one day to the next. She referred him to a child-study clinic.

1. *The first step taken at the clinic was to determine whether the learning problem was specific, general, or spurious.* To this end a general intelligence test was administered to find out if the child had the mental capacity to be expected to learn to read. If this 8-year-old boy should be found to have an IQ of 50, one would not expect him to be able to read. In this case, however, Miss Jones's boy was found to have an IQ of 104 on the Stanford-Binet Intelligence Scale. He also scored at a second-grade level on an arithmetic computation test, although, as Miss Jones had predicted, he scored at a first-grade level (6 years, 3 months) on a series of reading tests. The psychologist analyzing the problem now had the following information:

Chronological Age	8–4
Mental Age	8–10
Arithmetic Computational Age	7–8
Reading Age	6–3

There was a discrepancy between the chronological age, mental age, and arithmetic achievement age on the one hand, and the level of reading on the other hand. The child had attended school with fair regularity, had had adequate teaching for two years, and still had not learned to read. It was clear that a problem did exist, and that it was specific, not general. The boy could not read although the apparent capacity was there.

2. *The second step taken at the clinic was to analyze the behavior manifestations which were descriptive of the specific problem.* It was necessary to specify the exact nature of the problem, to delineate in greater detail just what the child could and could not do in the reading process. It was necessary to know more than the *level* of reading. It was necessary to know *how* the child read. What faulty habits did he display in reading? How did he attack new words? What kinds of words did he confuse? What kinds of errors did he make? How fast did he try to read? A skilled diagnostician can answer some of these questions by observing the child read, but diagnostic tests are more objective. In the case at hand it was found on a diagnostic reading test that the child did not make use of phonics. Although he could tell the sounds of the different letters in isolation, he sounded only the first letter or two of a word. It was also noted that he had had difficulty learning to write his name and found it difficult to reproduce short words from memory. He guessed at many words from context or from interpreting the pictures in the book. He knew a few sight words but often confused similar words such as *that* and *what, the* and *ten, see* and *she.*

3. *The next step taken was to discover the physical, environmental, and psychological correlates of the disability.* The clinic staff knew that there are many reasons why children fail to learn to read. Did this boy have poor school attendance? Was there an abnormal home background? Was he culturally deprived? An investigation of these factors proved negative. No such conditions were found that could explain his reading retardation. A medical examination revealed no abnormalities. Visual acuity was normal, and on an audiometric test the boy appeared to have normal hearing. His inability to learn to read was therefore not the result of visual or hearing impairment. Should the boy's condition merely be labeled "dyslexia"? Should it be assumed that the boy must be brain-injured? The staff knew that these designations would be of little help to the teacher since they would only be substituting the word "dyslexia," a medical term, for the term "severe reading disability," an educational term. To say that the boy was brain-injured when the neurologist could not find evidence of brain injury was not very helpful since they would be inferring brain function from behavior observation.

There was one other handicap the clinic had not investigated. Was it possible that the child was so emotionally disturbed that he was unable to concentrate and learn? The teacher reported that he could not concentrate on the reading work books she gave him; that his attention to reading materials was very short; and that he resisted pressure to read. A psychiatric examination did not confirm the hypothesis of emotional disturbance since the boy appeared normal in interpersonal relations and did concentrate on other tasks not involving reading and spelling. His concentration on arithmetic lessons, for example, was adequate. The psychiatrist concluded that the inability to learn to read was not the result of an emotional condition.

In the past, much emphasis has been placed on finding the cause of a malady, but with learning-disabled children the cause is frequently nebulous, often unknown and usually irremediable. If a child's aberrant functioning is the result of brain damage (which may or may not show up on an electroencephalogram), it helps little in designing remediation to know that a birth injury affected certain neurons. When the cause is irremediable, it is the behavior which must be remediated.

It is for this reason that the term "correlates" is used instead of "causes," since the emphasis here will be primarily on educational correlates, or factors relating to the functional behavior of the child. A child who is unable to learn words may have a sound-blending disability. This is considered a correlate of inability to learn to read and leads to a remedial program which will include training the child to blend sounds in relation to teaching him to read.

The search for correlates of a learning disability is a search for related factors within the child or his environment which have been found to occur frequently with the disability under consideration and which need correction or amelioration. These correlates may be (a) physical factors, (b) environmental factors, or (c) psychological factors, such as the following:

Physical Correlates	Environmental Correlates	Psychological Correlates
Visual defects	Traumatic experiences	Poor visual or auditory perception and discrimination
Auditory defects	Conditioned avoidance reactions	
Confused spatial orientation	Undue family pressures	Slow understanding and interpretation of concepts
Mixed laterality	Bilingualism	
Hyperkinesis	Sensory deprivation	Poor organizing and generalizing ability
Poor body image	Lack of school experience	
Undernourishment		Inability to express concepts vocally or manually
		Minimal motor and verbal skills
		Defective short-term memory
		Poor closure and sound blending

In the case of Miss Jones's boy, the physical and the environmental correlates mentioned above had been ruled out. In the search for correlates which might explain the reading difficulty and at the same time be the springboard for remediation, the clinic psychologist administered the ITPA which might show some psychological correlates. The test did show marked intraindividual differences in the boy's perceptual and cognitive abilities. Although functioning at or above his chronological age in all of the subtests at the representational level, this boy was very deficient in visual sequential memory (the ability to remember a sequence of figures or letters), auditory closure, and auditory synthesis (sound blending). These were deficiencies quite commonly associated (together or in isolation) with poor reading.

4. *The next step taken was to find a diagnostic hypothesis (inference) based on the behavior manifestations and the correlates observed in steps two and three.* The diagnostic inference is one of the most important factors in diagnosis. It involves specifying the relationship among symptoms and the correlates that have inhibited a child's learning to talk, read, write, spell. It requires experienced clinicians who can use the relevant tests, select the relevant facts, and put the pieces together in organized form so as to explain the child's inability to learn.

The diagnostic hypothesis must select the relevant variables in the case and pinpoint the specific disabilities upon which the remedial program can be organized.

For Miss Jones's boy two working hypotheses were evolved from the information at hand. (1) Having observed that the boy did not sound more than the initial letter of a word although he knew the sounds of all of them in isolation, it was conjectured that he had not learned the skill of sound blending. This was verified by the child's low score on the sound-blending test of the ITPA. This would explain why he had so little success trying to use phonics in deciphering unknown words. (2) The second inference came from the low score on the visual sequential memory subtest of the ITPA coupled with the fact that our boy had learned very few sight words and showed confusion and uncertainty on many of the ones he thought he knew. The hypothesis was that the boy's inability to remember a sequence of figures made it difficult for him to identify sight words because he had poor memory of what the complete word was supposed to look like. This hypothesis was corroborated by his difficulty in learning to write his name and to reproduce short words from memory. The two handicaps, (1) inability to use a phonic approach in identifying words and (2) inability to use a sight-word approach, gave this boy no usable technique for decoding the printed page.

5. *The final step in any diagnosis is organizing a systematic remedial program based on the diagnostic hypothesis.* The crux of a diagnosis is the effectiveness of the remedial program it generates. It should be based on the inferences made in step four and attempt to alleviate the symptoms and, if possible, the correlated factors observed. In the present case, recommendations were given for improving the visual sequential memory, suggesting particularly the use of the kinesthetic method in learning new words and thus training the use of visual imagery and visual sequential memory. Likewise, specific suggestions were made for developing sound-blending ability which in most cases is rather easily acquired once the knack is understood. The remedial program began by teaching the boy words and phrases by the kinesthetic method (to develop visualization ability) and later introduced exercises in sound blending and phonics. Through this approach the child learned to read.

Organization of Remedial Programs

One of the problems facing schools is how to best organize programs for the remediation of learning disabilities. It is obvious that children with learning disabilities constitute a very heterogeneous group, and unless children with the same type and level of disability are grouped together, a self-contained class would be difficult to manage. Several types of organization within a school system have evolved. The more common ones are discussed below.

THE ITINERANT DIAGNOSTIC REMEDIAL SPECIALIST

A highly trained itinerant teacher, one who can diagnose the disability and organize a remedial program, is probably the preferred type of personnel. Such a teacher, sometimes termed a diagnostic remedial specialist, deals with one child at a time. For the minor cases the itinerant diagnostic remedial specialist identifies the basic disability in the child, develops remedial instruction through clinical work with the child to determine which procedures are successful, and then transfers the procedures and materials to the classroom teacher. In such a situation the classroom teacher is given itinerant help with the child and may be able to remediate the disability within the classroom setting. The diagnostic remedial specialist supervises the progress. For more severe cases this specialist works with the child himself on an individual basis. He can thus serve approximately four or five such children a day, but can also help with five or ten other children within the classroom organization. He can also move from school to school in cases where there are not enough children in any one school needing his attention.

THE RESOURCE ROOM

A common type of service to children with learning disabilities is provided through the organization of a resource room. In this type of organization a diagnostic remedial specialist mans a small classroom to which individuals or small groups of children are assigned for one or more periods of the day. In the resource room the diagnostic remedial specialist evaluates the abilities and disabilities of each child sent to him and offers remedial instruction to one child at a time or to two or three children if their disabilities are compatible. He may also assist the regular teacher in the adaptation of instruction for the learning-disabled child in the regular classroom. The resource room organization has the advantage of housing adequate materials and equipment and instructional aids in one room and of providing adequate space for tutoring and self-instruction through programmed materials and equipment which can be used for more than one child. The room can usually schedule 8 to 20 children, each for part of the day. The resource room organization is not applicable to a small school.

THE SELF-CONTAINED CLASSROOM

The self-contained classroom for children with learning disabilities may be the least satisfactory. An exception to this statement is the case in which the special class program is so organized that each child in the class will receive individual instruction for a part of the day. This is accomplished in one of two ways. The first procedure is to enroll only five to seven children in the class. The diagnostic remedial teacher organizes the class in such a way that she can provide at least thirty minutes of remedial instruction on an individual basis for each child in the class. The usual procedure is to tutor one child, then give him assignments he can do at his seat while she tutors another child. A part of the day is devoted to group activities. Another procedure is to have a larger class but to assign two teachers to the class. In this way one of the teachers devotes her time to individual instruction of the children, while the other conducts group activities.

CLINICS

Another procedure is to establish a learning disability clinic to which the children are assigned for a part of the day. This involves transportation of the children to and from their regular schools. It is used primarily in universities that have available students who can tutor the children in the clinic. In this situation it may be more economical to transport the children than to transport the university students to schools that may or may not have available the remedial materials or space for tutoring.

SUMMARY

1. Children with specific learning disabilities constitute a heterogeneous group of children who do not fit into the traditional categories of exceptional children, but who have significant intraindividual differences, i.e., discrepancies in growth that require special remediation.
2. Although the concept of learning disabilities has been difficult to define objectively, it generally refers to the problems of children who, although normal in sensory, emotional, and intellectual abilities, exhibit disorders in spoken and written language, including disorders in perception, listening, thinking, talking, reading, writing, spelling, or arithmetic.
3. It is estimated that approximately 1 to 3 percent of children have specific learning disabilities.
4. Early work on what is now known as learning disabilities stemmed from a neurological interest in brain damage and abnormalities in communication in adults.
5. Remedial methods for children with learning disabilities include (a) perceptual motor strategies, (b) visual perception training, (c) multisensory strategies, and (d) remedial reading.
6. Two basic remedial methods have been used with children who have severe reading disabilities. They are (a) the kinesthetic method and (b) the phonic method.
7. A diagnostic procedure involves (a) determining whether a specific problem exists, (b) analyzing the behavioral manifestations of the disability, (c) discovering the physical,

environmental, or psychological correlates, (d) evolving a diagnostic hypothesis, and (e) organizing an appropriate remedial program.

REFERENCES

Barsch, R. 1967. *Achieving Perceptual Motor Efficiency: A Space-Oriented Approach to Learning*. Seattle, Washington: Special Child Publications.

———. 1965. *A Movigenic Curriculum*. Madison, Wisconsin: Wisconsin State Department of Public Instruction.

Burnett, E. 1962. *Influence of Classroom Environment on Word Learning of Retarded with High and Low Activity Level*. Unpublished doctoral dissertation, George Peabody College for Teachers.

Chalfant, J. D., and Scheffelin, Margaret A. 1969. *Central Processing Dysfunctions in Children: A Review of Research*. Washington, D.C.: U.S. Government Printing Office.

Clements, S. D. 1966. *Minimal Brain Dysfunction in Children*. Public Health Service Publications, No. 415. Washington, D.C.: U.S. Department of Health, Education, and Welfare.

Cruickshank, W.; Bentzen, F. A.; Ratzeburg, F. H.; and Tannhauser, Miriam. 1961. *A Teaching Method for Brain-Injured and Hyperactive Children*. New York: Syracuse University Press.

Dunn, L. M., and Smith J. O. 1967, 1968, 1969. *Peabody Language Development Kits*. Levels I, II, III. Circle Pines, Minnesota: American Guidance Service.

Fernald, Grace M. 1943. *Remedial Techniques in Basic School Subjects*. New York: McGraw-Hill.

Fernald, Grace M., and Keller, H. 1921. The Effect of Kinesthetic Factors in the Development of Word Recognition in the Case of Non-Readers. *Journal of Educational Research* 4.

Friedus, Elizabeth. 1964. Methodology for the Classroom Teacher. In Hellmuth, J. (ed.), *The Special Child in Century 21*. Seattle, Washington: Special Child Publications.

Frostig, Marianne, and Horne, D. 1964. *The Frostig Program for the Development of Visual Perception*. Chicago: Follett.

Frostig, Marianne; Maslow, Phyllis; Lefever, D. W.; and Whittlesey, J. R. B. 1964. *The Marianne Frostig Developmental Test of Visual Perception*, 1963 Standardization. Palo Alto, California: Consulting Psychologists Press.

Getman, G. H. 1965. The Visuo-Motor Complex in the Acquisition of Learning Skills. In Straub, B. and Hellmuth, J. (eds). *Learning Disorders*, Vol. 1. Seattle, Washington: Special Child Publications.

Getman, G. H.; Kane, E. R.; Halgren, M.; and McKee, G. W. 1968. *Developing Learning Readiness*. Manchester, Missouri: Webster Division, McGraw-Hill.

Gillingham, A., and Stillman, B. 1965. *Remedial Training for Children with Specific Disability in Reading, Spelling, and Penmanship*, 5th ed. Cambridge, Massachusetts: Educators Publishing Service.

———. 1936. *Remedial Work for Reading, Spelling, and Penmanship*. New York: Hackett and Wilhelms.

Hart, N. W. M. 1963. The Differential Diagnosis of the Psycholinguistic Abilities of the Cerebral-Palsied Child and Effective Remedial Procedures. *Special School Bulletin 2:* Brisbane, Australia.

Head, H. 1926. *Aphasia and Kindred Disorders of Speech.* Vols. I and II. New York: Macmillan.

Hegge, T. G.; Kirk, S. A.; and Kirk, Winifred D. 1936. *Remedial Reading Drills.* Ann Arbor, Michigan: George Wahr.

Hinshelwood, J. 1917. *Congenital Word Blindness.* London: H. K. Lewis.

Hirsch, Esther. 1963. *Training of Visualizing Ability by the Kinesthetic Method of Teaching Reading.* Unpublished master's thesis, University of Illinois.

Johnson, Doris J., and Myklebust, H. R. 1967. *Learning Disabilities: Educational Principles and Practices.* New York: Grune and Stratton.

Karnes, Merle B. 1969. *Research and Development Program on Preschool Disadvantaged Children, Final Report,* Vol. 1, Project No. 1181. Washington, D.C.: U.S. Office of Education, Bureau of Research.

Kephart, N. C. 1964. Perceptual-Motor Aspects of Learning Disabilities. *Exceptional Children* 31 (December): 201–206.

———. 1960. *The Slow Learner in the Classroom.* Columbus, Ohio: Charles E. Merrill.

Kirk, S. A. 1968. The Illinois Test of Psycholinguistic Abilities: Its Origin and Implications. In Hellmuth, J. (ed.), *Learning Disorders,* Vol. 3. Seattle, Washington: Special Child Publications.

———. 1966. *The Diagnosis and Remediation of Psycholinguistic Disabilities.* Urbana, Illinois: University of Illinois Press.

———. 1962. *Educating Exceptional Children,* Boston: Houghton Mifflin.

———. 1958. *Early Education of the Mentally Retarded: An Experimental Study.* Urbana, Illinois: University of Illinois Press.

———. 1940. *Teaching Reading to Slow-Learning Children.* Boston: Houghton Mifflin.

———. 1936. *Manual of Directions for Use with the Hegge, Kirk, and Kirk Remedial Reading Drills.* Ann Arbor, Michigan: George Wahr.

———. 1934. The Effects of Remedial Reading on the Educational Progress and Personality Adjustment of High Grade Mentally Deficient Problem Children: Ten Case Studies. *Journal of Juvenile Research* 18 (July): 140–162.

———. 1933. The Influence of Manual Tracing on the Learning of Simple Words in the Case of Subnormal Boys. *Journal of Educational Psychology* 24 (October): 525–533.

Kirk, S. A., and Kirk, Winifred D. 1971. *Psycholinguistic Learning Disabilities: Diagnosis and Remediation.* Urbana, Illinois: University of Illinois Press.

Kirk, S. A.; McCarthy, J. J.; and Kirk, Winifred D. 1968. *The Illinois Test of Psycholinguistic Abilities,* revised edition. Urbana, Illinois: University of Illinois Press.

Monroe, Marian. 1932. *Children Who Cannot Read.* Chicago: University of Chicago Press.

Myers, Patricia T., and Hammill, D. D. 1969. *Methods for Learning Disabilities.* New York: John Wiley.

Myklebust, H. R. 1960. *The Psychology of Deafness.* New York: Grune & Stratton.

———. 1963. Psychoneurological Learning Disorders in Children. In Kirk, S. A. and Becker, W. (eds.), *Conference on Children with Minimal Brain Impairment.* Urbana, Illinois: University of Illinois.

Myklebust, H. R., and Boshes, B. 1969. *Minimal Brain Damage in Children*. Final Report, Contract 108–65–142, Neurological and Sensory Disease Control Program, Washington, D.C.: Department of Health, Education, and Welfare.

National Advisory Committee on Handicapped Children. 1968. *First Annual Report, Subcommittee on Education of the Committee on Labor and Public Welfare, U.S. Senate*. Washington, D.C.: U.S. Government Printing Office.

Orton, Samuel T. 1928. Specific Reading Disability—Strephosymbolia. *The Journal of the American Medical Association* 90 (April).

Rost, K. J. 1967. Academic Achievement of Brain-Injured Children in Isolation. *Exceptional Children* 34 (October): 125–126.

Seguin, E. 1846. *Traitement moral, hygiene, et éducation des idiots et des autres enfants arrières*. Paris: J. B. Balliere.

Smith, J. O. 1962. Effects of a Group Language Development Program Upon Psycholinguistic Abilities of Educable Mentally Retarded Children. *Special Education Monograph* 1. Nashville, Tennessee: George Peabody College.

Spalding, R. B., and Spalding, W. T. 1957. *The Writing Road to Reading*. New York: Morrow.

Strauss, A. A., and Kephart, N. 1955. *Psychopathology and Education of the Brain-Injured Child*, Vol. II. New York: Grune and Stratton.

Strauss, A. A., and Lehtinen, Laura. 1947. *Psychopathology of the Brain-Injured Child*. New York: Grune and Stratton.

Taylor, J. (ed.). 1932. *Selected Writings of Hughlings Jackson*. London: Hodden and Stroughton.

Wiseman, D. E. 1964. Program Planning for Retarded Children with Psycholinguistic Abilities. *Selected Convention Papers,* 42nd Annual CEC Convention. Arlington, Virginia: Council for Exceptional Children, NEA.

THREE

SPEECH-

HANDICAPPED

CHILDREN

Speech involves more than the ability to articulate sounds. It calls for the assimilation of sounds into words, then the combination of these words into units that convey meaningful utterances. In essence, it may be defined as the vocal (as opposed to written) representation of the symbols of a formalized language, and its aim is to achieve the mutual exchange of ideas.

When speech is seriously deficient, the expression of these ideas can be impaired. The effect of speech deficits will be mentioned in the discussions on the mentally retarded, the auditorily handicapped, and the cerebral palsied. But speech defects are found in all groups of children, including otherwise normal children and even in the intellectually gifted.

Many seriously speech-handicapped children also exhibit language defects. They are confused about how to form words and put them in the right order and they cannot properly employ language symbols as tools to assist in organizing and expressing their visual, auditory, tactile-kinesthetic and other sensory experiences. These deficits have been partially explained in the preceding chapter on learning disabilities.

In the development of speech and language in children, organic factors such as sensory impairment, structural abnormalities, or problems of muscular incoordination may produce a speech defect. Often defective speech and language are correlates of a developmental lag or of nonorganic factors such as psychological, cultural, or environmental problems. It is with these problems that we are concerned in this chapter.

Definition of Defective Speech

It is generally accepted that any speech which draws unfavorable attention to itself, whether through unpleasant sound, inappropriateness to the age level, or interference with communication, may be classified as defective. Speech which contributes to feelings of self-consciousness or inadequacy in the speaker himself is also regarded as deviant. For example, the stuttering child may grow so reticent that the casual listener may not be aware of the extent to which the problem has affected him. When speech shows any of these characteristics, its user is in need of speech correction. To be normal, speech should permit the undistracted interchange of verbal language, free from grimaces, phonemic misarticulations, unnatural and unusual voice qualities, speaking rates, and rhythms. Vocabulary and sound usage should be adequate and appropriate for the age level, and speech should be delivered in logical, syntactical order.

Speech inadequacy, of course, may vary to some extent in different locales. The southern drawl, the eastern twang, and the midwestern nasality might be considered unpleasant in other areas, but the persons living in these environs would not be candidates for speech correction because of these characteristics. Into this group would fall the student from a foreign country. Even though his spoken English contains the phonemic and intonational peculiarities of his native tongue, it generally is not regarded as defective. For him, approximating and not perfecting is a more realistic goal.

Relation of Speech Defects to Other Disabilities

In the previous discussion of learning disabilities, it was pointed out that disabilities in the communication processes may be in speech, language, reading, writing, or spelling. Sometimes a learning disability in one function is correlated with retardation in other areas; in other cases the learning disability is specific to one area only. Of interest to investigators has been the question of the relation of a speech defect to other facets of development.

Since the child with defective speech may be found in any group of exceptional or otherwise normal children, he may have a high or a low IQ; he may be severely handicapped in motor skills or have good coordination; he may hear exceptionally well or be hard of hearing; he may be well-adjusted emotionally and socially or be emotionally disturbed; he may have normal vision or he may be blind; he may have a well-built body or suffer from multiple physical handicaps; he may be energetic or lazy; he may come from a professional home or from a laborer's home. Most frequently, articulation difficulties are encountered in the cerebral-palsied, in the deaf and hard of hearing, and in the mentally retarded. In addition, children who are not exceptional in any other characteristic sometimes have speech difficulties as the sole deficiency in their development, as represented in Chapter 1, Figure 1–5.

A direct relationship between speech defects and lack of educational achievement has not been clearly established. In a review of the literature dealing with speech and reading difficulties, Artley (1948) concludes that there appeared to be a relationship between speech difficulties and reading deficiencies but no agreement as to the extent of this relationship. On the whole, studies indicate that speech defects might be the "cause of reading defects, the result of reading defects, or the two may exist as a result of some common factor." Jackson (1944), studying various differences between 300 advanced readers and 300 retarded readers in Grades 2 through 4, found 23 percent of the retarded readers had speech defects in comparison with 10 percent within the advanced group. Monroe (1932) found that among 415 reading defectives 27 percent had speech defects, compared to 8 percent of a control group of 101 normal readers. Robinson (1946) found, however, that when speech difficulties which appeared to be caused by retarded reading were removed, the reading did not improve.

Weaver, Furbee, and Everhart (1960) believe that research has not found an underlying variable which can account for both adequate speech and reading. They feel, however, that if there is a causal relationship between poor speech and poor reading it could be accounted for in one of the following ways:

1. Poor speech habits may generalize to silent reading.
2. The reader, intent on his speech, may ignore the meaning.
3. Speech defects may interfere with rate and phrasing.
4. Articulatory disorders may result in misunderstanding of words.
5. Speech defects may cause reading to be unpleasant and result in less practice.

Eisenson (1963) states: "(1) the two disabilities have a common cause; (2) speech disability may cause reading disability, especially when reading is taught by the oral method; and (3) reading disability may cause speech deficiency" (p. 200).

Development of Speech and Language

Children in all cultures develop the speech and language of their culture. How speech and language develop in children has been of long-standing interest to psychologists, linguists, and speech pathologists. For a time, each of these disciplines tended to study different aspects of the problem. The psychologist studied speech and language learning, the linguist studied the properties of natural language, and the speech pathologist concentrated on deviations or disorders of speech and language. In recent years these disciplines have attempted to integrate their knowledge into systems that employ research findings from all disciplines.

The process by which a child learns speech and language has been explained by different authorities in different ways. Skinner (1957), a behaviorist psychologist, tended to explain the development of verbal behavior on the basis of principles of learning, i.e., stimulus, response, reinforcement. Some linguists, on the other hand, do not accept the acquisition of speech as wholly learned but tend to explain the development of speech and language on the basis of an inherent disposition similar to walking. Lennenberg (1964) states:

Just as we can say with assurance that no man inherits a propensity for French, we can also and with equal confidence say that all men are endowed with an innate propensity for a type of behavior that develops automatically into language and that this propensity is so deeply ingrained that language-like behavior develops even under the most unfavorable conditions of peripheral and even central nervous system impairments. (p. 589)

Although the quote from Lennenberg applies to language, it could also apply to speech production. The maturational cycle for the development of verbal behavior has been described by Berry (1969), as follows:

Prelinguistic Vocalization. An infant cries, utters sounds of various kinds.

Babbling. Babbling follows early vocalization, but may not be clearly differentiated from early vocalization and may not relate to later speech. It probably serves as a tuning-up period for the speech organs, which are later used in the production of speech.

Imitation. At this stage, usually between the fourth and sixth month, the child "oohs" and "ahs," imitating his own speech production and responding in some vocal fashion to the speech of others.

First words. It is difficult to establish an age level for first intelligible and meaningful words. Nevertheless, by 18 to 20 months most children may be saying "mama" and "daddy" and a few other words.

Two-word Sentences. At about 2 years of age most children are using two-word sentences—"more milk," "shoe off," and so forth.

Development of Syntax. After age 2 to 3 the child begins to develop his own grammatic system, explores his own use of grammar, noun-phrases, subject-predicate sentences, and so forth.

Templin (1957) made a study of the phonemic development of 480 children between the ages of 3 and 8 and has tabulated the phonemes of each age level. At the age of 3 years children enunciated the sounds of all the vowels and the consonants /m/, /n/, /ng/, /p/, /t/, /b/, /d/, /g/, /f/. At 4 years they also produced /k/, /b/, /g/, /s/, /sh/, /v/, /j/, /r/, /l/, some double and triple consonants, e.g., /pl/, /mp/, and /mpt/. The years of 5 and 6 added more difficult consonants, double consonants, and triple consonants.

Somewhere along the line, a minimum of 5 percent of the future school population will not reach the efficiency in speech which is considered normal or adequate for the age level. Some children will not be talking at 4 and 5 years, some will start to speak normally but because of some trauma will stop talking, some will develop their own lingo (prevalent among twin members, who devise their own code, called idiopathic speech), some will have difficulty with sounds for a number of reasons, some will stutter, some will have unintelligible speech, some will show laryngeal nodes due to crying and yelling, and a few will even have a laryngeal web. Although a speech impairment is associated often with a physical or psychological disorder or as one of multiple handicaps, there is a preponderance, as far as percentage is concerned, of speech difficulties with the outgoing, normally participating child. If the speech difficulty exists as a single handicap, it may vary from one which gives a slight degree of annoyance to one which promotes frustrating experiences, causing withdrawal from speech attempts and insecurity in social experiences.

Identification and Diagnosis

In many school systems the procedure in establishing a speech correction program follows three stages: (1) screening children in the grades to identify those requiring further diagnosis, (2) diagnosing those selected from the initial screening tests, and (3) choosing those children who require and can benefit from speech correction.

SCREENING PROCEDURES

Preparatory to diagnostic testing, the speech clinician[1] will screen certain grades each year, depending on the routine established within the school system. Those

[1] Those specialists who assess and remediate speech handicaps in school children have been referred to as "speech clinicians," "speech correctionists," or "speech specialists." "Speech pathologists" and "speech therapists" are terms used more frequently in medically oriented clinics. The labels "speech clinician" and "speech correctionist" will be used synonymously in this chapter for those whose major function is in the school. The title preferred by the professor, however, is *speech clinician* (Friebe and Johnson, 1969).

who indicate some speech deficiency—articulatory, vocal, rhythmical, linguistic —are called back at a later time for diagnostic testing. In screening, most speech correctionists use a picture type of test, such as the Deep Test of Articulation (McDonald, 1964), and the Goldman-Friscoe Test of Articulation (1969). Some use their own picture test cards for convenience, even though they have not been standardized. The Templin-Darley Tests of Articulation (1960) provide a total of 176 items, 50 of which may be used for screening purposes. Previous research by Templin (1952) on the development of articulation in children provides test items and norms. In addition to the validated test material, objects are sometimes used to stimulate conversation for identification of other than articulatory disorders.

DIAGNOSIS

Children who are referred by teachers or parents for speech correction and those who have been identified through the screening procedure require a diagnosis of their specific problems before correction can be started. The procedure in the diagnosis includes steps similar to those described in Chapter 2 "Learning Disabilities." These include the following:

Intellectual Assessment. The first assessment to be made of a child with a speech defect is his intellectual development. In some cases psychological tests of a performance (nonverbal) type are administered, in order to determine whether the child's delay in speech or the articulatory defects are due to severe mental retardation. Inasmuch as many children referred for speech correction have a history and a record of normal intellectual development, psychometric evaluations may not be necessary in such cases. Screening tests such as the Peabody Picture Vocabulary Test (1965) are frequently used.

Assessment of Defect. A speech correctionist attempts to ascertain the defect or defects by (1) obtaining spontaneous vocal responses from the child by showing him pictures to be named, (2) asking the child to repeat after the examiner certain words which will identify the articulation defect, (3) asking the child to repeat sounds in nonsense formation, and (4) obtaining samples of his habitual conversation. Each of these procedures—spontaneous speech, imitation, nonsense syllable routine and habitual conversation—has its place in helping the clinician determine the type of speech defect. From this initial assessment he obtains clues to further diagnosis and recommendations for remediation.

Determining Causal Factors and Correlated Defects. If a child has delayed speech or a defect in articulation, voice, or rhythm, the next question is, Why? What factors are responsible for or associated with this difficulty? In the examination, the speech diagnostician will assess critically tongue movements and position, alignment and irregularities of teeth, occlusion of jaws, and palate intactness to note their role, if any, in causing the defect. He will survey the home environment to find whether or not factors there may be responsible for the defect. He will consider other possibilities, including hearing impairment, cleft palate, or cerebral dysfunction. The symptoms or syndromes observed will indicate the necessity for referral to other specialists, such as audiologists or neurologists, for further diagnosis.

Ordinarily, the initial assessment suggests the initial remedial procedures. Assessment, however, is an ongoing procedure since many aspects of the child's difficulty will come to light during the process of remediation. The major purpose of the diagnosis is to assess the special defects and so lead to a program for correction. The speech correction sessions which follow will depend in each case on the assessment of the speech defect, the severity of the defect, and the motivational factors involved.

Classification and Prevalence of Speech Disorders

The classifications of speech disorders are various, depending to some extent on whether the category is to be used in a public school system, a clinical organization within a hospital, or a speech and hearing clinic. Thus far no one has been successful in finding a classification in which the terminology is consistently logical—that is, one which is arranged totally according to etiology or one which indicates only the phenomenology or description of the speech deficiency.

CATEGORIES OF SPEECH DISORDERS

In most texts on speech disorders the grouping of speech defects has been narrowed for practical rather than logical reasons to include (1) disorders of articulation, (2) disorders of voice, (3) stuttering, (4) retarded speech development, (5) cleft palate, (6) cerebral palsy, (7) impaired hearing, and (8) aphasia and related disorders. This type of grouping may give the impression that there is a speech disorder called "cerebral palsy" or "cleft palate speech" or "mentally retarded speech." Although this terminology is used by the speech correctionist, the practice is unfortunate. Some who have cerebral palsy may have adequate speech, some no speech. The lack of speech may be due to mental retardation, to hearing impairment, to congenital aphasia, or to the cerebral dysfunction which caused the neuromuscular handicap. It is more accurate to speak of a speech disorder *associated with* hearing loss, cleft palate, mental retardation, or cerebral palsy rather than designating the speech defect as a distinct characteristic of another handicap.

In 1952 the Midcentury White House Conference report on "Speech Disorders and Speech Correction," basing its data on an assumed total population of 40,000,000 children between the ages of 5 and 21 years, estimated that 5 percent are handicapped by speech difficulties. The committee reports, however, that the figures are the "lowest defensible estimates" and "leave out of account an estimated additional 5 percent, or 2,000,000 children, who have relatively minor speech and voice defects, unimportant for most practical purposes but serious in their effects on personal and social adjustment in some cases, and obviously significant for children destined for fields of work, such as teaching, requiring good speech." Statistics on prevalence in each of the categories of speech defects are listed in Table 3–1.

TABLE 3–1

Estimate of incidence of speech defects among children in the United States between the ages of 5 and 21 years, based on an assumed total population of 40,000,000

(Gross estimates for all age levels, based on an assumed total population of 150,000,000, and on the same percentages, are also shown.)

Type of defect	Ages 5–21 years		All ages
	Percent	Number	Number
Functional articulatory	3.0	1,200,000	4,500,000
Stuttering	.7	280,000	1,050,000
Voice	.2	80,000	300,000
Cleft palate speech	.1	40,000	150,000
Cerebral palsy speech	.2	80,000	300,000
Retarded speech development	.3	120,000	450,000
Impaired hearing (with speech defect)	.5	200,000	750,000
Total	5.0	2,000,000	7,500,000

Source: American Speech and Hearing Association, Committee on the Midcentury White House Conference, "Speech Disorders and Speech Correction," *Journal of Speech and Hearing Disorders* 17 (June, 1952), p. 130. Reproduced by permission of the Association.

Another study was sponsored by the American Speech and Hearing Association committee to study the facilities and organization of public school speech and hearing services in the United States. In an effort to find the prevalence of various speech disorders in the speech correctionist's case load, the classification of disorders presented in Table 3–2 was sent to speech correctionists in five

TABLE 3–2

Percentage of defects in speech-handicapped groups in public schools

Type of defect	Percent
Articulation	81.0%
Stuttering	6.5%
Delayed speech	4.5%
Hard of hearing	2.5%
Voice problems	2.3%
Cleft palate	1.5%
Cerebral palsy	1.0%
Bilingual Mentally retarded Aphasia	0.7%

Source: American Speech and Hearing Association, "Public School and Hearing Services," *Journal of Speech and Hearing Disorders, Monograph Supplement 8* (Danville, Illinois: Interstate Printers and Publishers, 1961), p. 38. Reproduced by permission of the Association.

geographic areas. Data were tabulated according to the percentage of defects found within the speech-handicapped group.

According to the U.S. Office of Education (see Chapter 1, p. 25) there were 2,180,589 speech-impaired children in the United States in 1969 who required special instruction. This is an estimate of approximately 3.5 percent of school-age children. Inasmuch as most school systems probably are using a classification similar to those in Tables 3–1 and 3–2, it may prove helpful to follow the briefer list (Table 3–1) in this chapter, noting that mental retardation and aphasia will be classified under delayed speech.

One of the major difficulties in classification of speech disorders is the overlapping of categories. Articulatory defects, in which the formation, blending, and enunciation of sounds for intelligibility are involved, may be present without an associated handicap. They occur also in cerebral palsy, in mental retardation, in cleft palate disorders, and with other associated handicaps. Deviations of the vocal aspect of speech (which involves the phonation of speech sounds, as well as their intensity, resonance, and pitch) occur in hearing-impaired children, the cerebral palsied, and others. With these overlapping defects in mind, the subsequent discussions will be organized around (1) articulatory disorders, (2) vocal disorders, (3) stuttering, (4) delayed speech, (5) speech defects associated with hearing loss, (6) speech defects associated with cleft palate, and (7) speech defects associated with cerebral palsy.

Articulatory Disorders

Articulatory disorders are those deviations which involve substitutions, omissions, distortions, and additions of phonemes. These difficulties may occur as the articulators (tongue, teeth, lips, palates, jaws) modify the flow of air-sound from the larynx by changing their positions and contacts. Learning to direct the air flow and to make rapid shifts in the position of the articulators in order to emit intelligible sounds and sound sequences is largely imitative and associative, utilizing visual perception, kinesthetic awareness, memory, touch, and auditory discrimination.

ARTICULATORY MECHANISM

The articulatory mechanism is part of an intricate speaking system, any part of which may show abnormalities of structure or function. It includes (1) a breathing apparatus to assist in the production, formation, and direction of sounds through various resonating cavities; (2) two vocal cords housed in the larynx to vibrate for the phonation of sounds; (3) an auditory mechanism for discrimination between sounds; (4) an intact brain and nervous system; (5) swallowing musculature, involving tongue and pharynx; and (6) oral mechanism, including tongue, lips, teeth, hard and soft palates, and jaws, which can be utilized in modifying the sounds coming from the larynx.

Malfunctioning of any of these parts may cause speech difficulty. In the mouth alone, for example, there are many parts which have to function properly. But it should be noted that many persons have malocclusions of the teeth, missing teeth, abnormal tongues, high and narrow hard palates, and various other structural malformations and still have good speech. Even with these deviations, adjustments are possible without any particular effort for many persons and exceedingly difficult for others. Often there are misarticulations with no apparent structural defect. These disorders of functional origin have been attributed to varied influences, including impoverished environment, infantile perseveration, bilingualism, emotional problems, slow maturation, and over-indulgence in the home. There are times when the diagnostic finger apparently

tory, visual, and kinesthetic senses in the production of speech. At times speech correction is conducted in collaboration with physiotherapy.

5. Children do not speak unless they are motivated to speak. One of the problems with cerebral-palsied children is how to create a need in them for improving their speech. Their own efforts in exercises to correct inappropriate tongue and jaw movements or breathing require concentrated attention on their part. How to supply the necessary motivation is one of the major concerns of a speech clinician.

6. Finally, it will be necessary for a speech clinician to help the child manage his tongue movements, control the synergic movements of swallowing, control facial movements (grimaces, tics), and control breathing, inflection, and intonations of voice.

Public School Speech Correction Programs

Speech correction is conducted in hospital clinics, speech and hearing centers, college and university training programs, and in elementary and secondary schools. The largest number of speech clinicians are employed in school systems, and the largest number of children are being served in the schools.

In 1969 there were over one million speech-handicapped children receiving services in elementary and secondary schools in the United States. These were being served by 13,749 teachers of speech-defective children (U.S. Office of Education, 1970). These children are remediated individually or in small groups by itinerant speech clinicians who serve one or more schools.

The speech clinician is responsible for the assessment and selection of children needing speech correction. The large proportion of children selected and served are in kindergarten and the primary grades. Articulatory disorders constitute the largest group of children in the case load of a speech clinician, which is generally about one hundred children a week. Speech correction is generally offered once or twice a week to speech-handicapped children. Attempts are being made in some school systems to reduce the case load so that the speech clinician can serve, more intensively, children with severe speech and language problems.

SUMMARY

1. Speech is considered defective when its deviation from average speech draws unfavorable attention to the speaker.
2. Approximately 3 to 5 percent of school children exhibit deviations in speech requiring correction.

3. Speech defects are the result of (a) organic factors, such as hearing losses, cleft palate, and cerebral dysfunction, and (b) environmental and emotional factors.
4. Speech defects are classified into (a) articulatory disorders, (b) vocal disorders, (c) stuttering, (d) delayed speech, (e) speech disorders associated with hearing impairment, cleft palate, or cerebral palsy.
5. Approximately 80 percent of speech cases in schools display functional articulation disorders.
6. Schools employ the largest number of speech clinicians and serve the largest number of children.
7. In general, speech correction in public schools serves young children. Over three-fourths of the case load of speech clinicians is in the kindergarten and first and second grades.
8. Speech clinicians currently deal with speech and language problems and related communication disorders.

REFERENCES

American Public Health Association. 1955. *Services for Children with Cleft Lip and Cleft Palate.* New York: The Association.

Artley, A. S. 1948. A Study of Certain Factors Presumed to be Associated with Reading and Speech Difficulties. *Journal of Speech and Hearing Disorders* 13 (December): 351–360.

Bender, Lauretta. 1958. Psychiatric Aspects. In *Symposium on the Concept of Congenital Aphasia from the Standpoint of Dynamic Differential Diagnosis.* pp. 15–20. Washington, D.C.: American Speech and Hearing Association.

Berry, Mildred F. 1969. *Language Disorders of Children: The Basis and Diagnosis.* New York: Appleton-Century-Crofts.

Bloodstein, O., and Bruitten, E. J. 1966. Stuttering Problems. In Rieber, R. W. and R. S. Brubaker (eds.), *Speech Pathology,* pp. 354–402. Philadelphia: J. B. Lippincott.

Denhoff, E., and Robinault, Isabel. 1960. *Cerebral Palsy and Related Disorders.* New York: McGraw-Hill.

Eisenson, J. 1963. The Nature of Defective Speech. In Cruickshank, W. M. (ed.), *Psychology of Exceptional Children and Youth,* 2nd. ed. Englewood Cliffs, New Jersey: Prentice-Hall.

————. 1958. *Stuttering: A Symposium.* New York: Harper and Brothers.

Fairbanks, G. 1960. *Voice and Articulation Drillbook,* 2nd. ed. New York: Harper and Row.

Fiedler, Miriam F. 1949. Teacher Problems with Hard of Hearing Children. *Journal of Educational Research* 42: 618–622.

Fogh-Anderson, P. 1942. *Inheritance of Harelip and Cleft Palate.* Copenhagen: Nyt Nordisk Forlag, Arnold Busck.

Freibe, J. E., and Johnson, K. O. 1969. Personnel Incomes in the Speech and Hearing Profession: Elementary and Secondary School Personnel. *Journal of the American Speech and Hearing Association* 2 (No. 6). 267–271.

Goldiamond, I. 1968. Stuttering and Fluency as Manipulative Operant Response Class. In Sloan, H. N., and Macauley, B. D. (eds.), *Operant Procedures in Remedial Speech and Language*, pp. 348–407. Boston: Houghton Mifflin.

Goldman, F., and Fristoe, M. 1969. *Test of Articulation*. Circle Pines, Minnesota: American Guidance Testing Service, Inc.

Jackson, J. A. 1944. A Survey of Psychological, Social, and Environmental Differences Between Advanced and Retarded Readers. *Journal of Genetic Psychology* 65 (September): 113–131.

Johnson, Doris J., and Myklebust, H. R. 1967. *Learning Disabilities: Educational Principles and Practices*. New York: Grune and Stratton.

Johnson, W. 1956. *Speech Handicapped School Children*. New York: Harper and Brothers.

Kendall, D. C. 1966. Language Problems in Children. In Rieber, R. W., and Brubaker, R. S. (eds.), *Speech Pathology*, pp. 285–298. Philadelphia: J. B. Lippincott.

Kirk, S. A., and Kirk, Winifred D. 1971. *Psycholinguistic Learning Disabilities: Diagnosis and Remediation*. Urbana, Illinois: University of Illinois Press.

Kisatsky, T. J. 1967. The Prognostic Value of the Carter-Buck Tests in Measuring Articulation Skills of Selected Kindergarten Children. *Exceptional Children* 34 (October): 81–86.

Lennenberg, E. H. 1964. The Capacity for Language Acquisition. In Fodor, J. P., and Katz, J. J. (eds.), *The Structure of Language*. Englewood Cliffs, New Jersey: Prentice-Hall.

Martin, R. 1968. The Experimental Manipulation of Stuttering Behaviors. In Sloan, H. N., and Macauley, B. D., *Operant Procedures in Remedial Speech and Language*, pp. 325–347. Boston: Houghton Mifflin.

Mase, D. J. 1946. *Etiology of Articulatory Speech Defects*. Teachers College Contributions to Education. New York: Teachers College, Columbia University.

McDonald, E. 1969. *A Deep Test of Articulation (Picture and Sentence Forms)*. Pittsburgh: Stanwix House.

McGinnis, M. 1963. Aphasic Children. *Volta Review*. Washington, D. C.

Midcentury White House Conference, 1952. Speech Disorders and Speech Correction. *Journal of Speech and Hearing Disorders* 17 (June): 129–137.

Monroe, Marion. 1932. *Children Who Cannot Read*. Chicago: University of Chicago Press.

Myklebust, H. R. 1954. *Auditory Disorders in Children*. New York: Grune and Stratton.

Peabody Picture Vocabulary Test. 1965. Minneapolis: Minnesota Test Bureau.

Peacher, W. G. 1950. The Etiology and Differential Diagnosis of Dysarthria. *Journal of Speech and Hearing Disorders* 15 (September): 252.

Perkins, W. H. 1970. Physiological Studies. In Sheehan, J. G. (ed.), *Stuttering Research and Therapy*, pp. 190–222. New York: Harper and Row.

Robinson, Helen. 1946. *Why Pupils Fail in Reading*. Chicago: University of Chicago Press.

Sheehan, J. G. (ed.). 1970. *Stuttering Research and Therapy*. New York: Harper and Row.

Skinner, B. F. 1957. *Verbal Behavior*. New York: Appleton-Century-Crofts.

Spreistersbach, D. C., and Sherman, Dorothy, 1968. *Cleft Palate and Communication*. New York: Academic Press.

Sullivan, E. M. 1944. Auditory Acuity and Its Relation to Defective Speech. *Journal of Speech Disorders* 9: 127–130.

Templin, Mildred. 1957. *Certain Language Skills in Children*. Minneapolis: University of Minnesota Press.

Templin, Mildred, and Darley, F. 1960. *The Templin-Darley Tests of Articulation.* Iowa City, Iowa: Bureau of Educational Research, State University of Iowa.

Travis, L. E. (ed.). 1931. *Speech Pathology.* New York: Appleton-Century-Crofts.

U.S. Office of Education. 1970. *Better Education for the Handicapped.* Annual Report, 1970. Washington, D.C.: Government Printing Office.

Van Riper, C. 1970a. Historical Approaches. In Sheehan, J. G. (ed.), *Stuttering Research and Therapy.* New York: Harper and Row.

————. 1970b. *Behavior Modification: An Overview in Conditioning in Stuttering Therapy.* Memphis, Tennessee: Speech Foundation of America.

————. 1963. *Speech Correction Principles and Methods,* 4th. ed. rev. Englewood Cliffs, New Jersey: Prentice-Hall, Inc.

————. 1957. Symptomatic Therapy for Stuttering. In Travis, L. E. (ed.), *Handbook of Speech Pathology.* New York: Appleton-Century-Crofts.

Van Riper, C., and Irwin, J. V. 1958. *Voice and Articulation.* New York: Prentice-Hall.

Weaver, C. H.; Furbee, Catherine; and Everhart, R. W. 1960. Articulatory Competence and Reading Readiness. *Journal of Speech and Hearing Research,* 3 (June) pp. 174–180.

West, R. 1966. A Historical Review of the American Literature in Speech Pathology. In Rieber, R. W. and Brubaker, R. S. (eds.) *Speech Pathology.* Philadelphia: J. B. Lippincott Co., pp. 25–41.

————. 1958. An Agnostic Speculation About Stuttering. In Eisenson, J. (ed.), *Stuttering: A Symposium.* New York: Harper and Brothers.

Wolfe, W. G. 1950. A Comprehensive Evaluation of Fifty Cases of Cerebral Palsy. *Journal of Speech and Hearing Disorders,* 15 (September) pp. 234–251.

Wood, Nancy E. 1959. *Language Disorders in Children.* Chicago: National Society for Crippled Children and Adults.

FOUR

THE

INTELLECTUALLY

GIFTED

CHILD

During the 1950's, interest in the education of gifted children in the United States intensified. This interest, of course, is not new; throughout the centuries various cultures have attempted to develop those individuals who were of superior intelligence. Concern for the gifted, like that for many other exceptional children, arises from the needs and social and political philosophy of the society and the times.

In ancient Greece, over 2,000 years ago, Plato advocated that children with superior intellect be selected at an early age and offered a specialized form of instruction in science, philosophy, and metaphysics. The most intelligent and knowledgeable would then become the leaders of the state. Plato felt that the survival of Greek democracy was contingent upon its ability to educate the superior citizens for leadership positions in that society.

In the sixteenth century, Suleiman the Magnificent made special efforts to identify the gifted Christian youth throughout the Turkish Empire and provide them with education in the Moslem faith and in war, art, science, and philosophy (Sumption and Luecking, 1960). His talent scouts, who surveyed the population at regular intervals, were able to select and educate a large group of superior individuals. Thus, within a generation after this system of education began, the Ottoman Empire became a great power in art, science, culture, and war, and even attempted to conquer the whole of Europe.

During the nineteenth and twentieth centuries little organized effort was made in Europe to select gifted children or to offer them special education. This was not felt to be necessary since secondary schools and universities were in general keyed to the education of those in the higher social strata, from which it was believed the more intelligent leadership would come. In many countries in Europe a small proportion of the population of children is selected at the fourth or sixth grade and assigned to academic secondary schools, while the masses continue in the common schools and learn a trade. Traditionally, this selection was made according to the social class and influence of the family, but there is a growing tendency for the selection to be made according to the interests and academic achievement of the child. The percentage of children who attend secondary schools or universities is much smaller in most European countries than the percentage who attend such schools in the United States. Even in Russia, where great emphasis is placed on developing the intellectual potential of its youth, only 12 percent of people over 15 years of age in 1959 had completed secondary school and 2.5 percent had completed college, whereas in the United States the comparable figures were 26.4 percent and 6.8 percent (Hildreth, 1966).

In the United States the concentration of effort in public education has been on the education of "all of the children of all of the people," generally by mass education procedures. With a few exceptions, opportunities for education under public auspices have been offered all children without differentiation. It is as if we had implicit faith that all men are created with equal potential and that education is the avenue through which this equality could express itself. A noted behaviorist psychologist, John B. Watson, bolstered this point of view when he stated that he could take any well-formed, healthy baby and make of it what he pleased—"rich man, poor man, beggar man, thief."

In spite of the efforts of some individuals who advocated special provisions (over and above the regular school programs) and even of some school systems which initiated special classes or special programs for the gifted, until recently these programs did not receive wide public support. The rationale of those who opposed special education for the gifted was that we were already offering diversified curriculums in the secondary schools—commercial courses, vocational and trades courses, and others of a less academic nature, as well as college preparatory curriculums. This multiple-track plan was believed to be the most suitable for enriching the programs for brighter children. Furthermore, colleges and universities were originally organized for the superior students; hence it could be argued that the public has been providing extended education for those of superior intellect.

The argument that American society has supplied colleges and universities for the most able did not take into consideration that not all superior students were economically able to attend college. In a study during the depression years of 1930 to 1940, Goetsch (1940) presented an alarming picture of the waste of human resources resulting from economic factors. Ninety percent of the superior high school graduates who came from families in the higher-income groups were able to attend college, but less than 20 percent of superior high school graduates from the lower-income groups attended college. According to this study, American society was providing higher education only for superior students who were economically able to attend college.

One of the effects of World War II was the creation of the G.I. Bill, which offered stipends to veterans for higher education. This bill, to some extent, and for a limited time, tended to offset the implications of the Goetsch study, since it provided the opportunity to go to college for many young men and women who otherwise could not have afforded it. In addition, the increasing number of scholarships and fellowships offered to college students, and particularly to graduate students, has decreased the economic deterrents.

The recent public interest in the special education of the gifted child in the United States (not only at the college level but at the elementary and secondary levels as well) stems from a number of national and international situations. Gallagher (1960) has given some of the major reasons for this acceleration of interest:

This sharp conflict of ideology between world powers has given a new sense of urgency to the complaints about the role of the gifted child in the American educational system. A casual reading of the literature will reveal that the same complaints—low standards for gifted children, unimaginative teaching and planning, and inadequate stimulation of their mental potential—that have been given such wide publicity today were being made in the 1920's and 1930's by educators and psychologists such as Hollingworth, Terman, and Pressey. Apparently the culture was not yet ready at that time to respond to their challenge.

A direct conflict between two great world powers has undeniable dramatic implications. There is reason to believe, however, that there are other changes taking place in the world culture which may, in the long run, cause more attention to be directed to the educational opportunities for intellectually superior children. There has been much talk of the "Population Explosion" in recent years. Not much has been said about the "Knowledge Explosion." . . . Only a half-century ago, many fields and professions that are important to our lives were nonexistent. Entire areas of inquiry and work such as economics, sociology, group dynamics, atomic physics, radiology, electronics, servo-mechanisms, jet propulsion, and many others were either unthought of or in their infancy. In some of these fields today books sometimes become outdated before they come off the presses. (pp. 1–2)

Who Are the Gifted?

There are many kinds of talented and gifted children, and no real agreement as to who is a gifted child. The major reason for disagreement is that among the many kinds of talents there are various degrees of talents. Guilford (1959) in analyzing the structure of intellect, postulates as many as 120 different intellectual abilities. Thus, if a person is facile in one set of abilities, he may be talented along one line; if facile in a different set of abilities, he may show quite different talents. Some authorities use the term "gifted" to refer only to those highly capable in a wide variety of abilities, whereas others use it to mean anyone highly competent in any one area. Some think of giftedness only in terms of a high IQ or a high degree of abstract and symbolic learning ability; others include facility in music, art, mechanics, or creativity.

One definition of giftedness is presented in a 1958 yearbook of the National Society for the Study of Education: "A talented or gifted child is one who shows consistently remarkable performance in any worth-while line of endeavor. Thus, we shall include not only the intellectually gifted but also those who show promise in music, the graphic arts, creative writing, dramatics, mechanical skills, and social leadership" (Education for the Gifted, 1958, p. 19).

This definition not only allows a very narrow ability to qualify for giftedness but relies solely on performance rather than potentiality for development. It does not include the underachieving gifted child or the child who has not made use of his abilities in socially acceptable channels. A child with an IQ of 150 who does not perform in school or along socially acceptable lines would not be considered gifted. A potentially gifted child with an underprivileged or foreign background might easily be overlooked because he does not appear to perform well.

Sumption and Luecking (1960) define the gifted as "Those who possess a superior central nervous system characterized by the potential to perform tasks requiring a comparatively high degree of intellectual abstraction or creative imagination or both." Fliegler and Bish (1959) use the following definition: ". . . the term *gifted* encompasses those children who possess a superior intellectual potential and functional ability to achieve academically in the top 15 to 20 percent of the school population; and/or talent of a high order in such special areas as mathematics, mechanics, science, expressive arts, creative writing, music, and social leadership; and a unique creative ability to deal with their environment" (p. 409).

Lucito (1963) has suggested a definition including creativity as defined by Guilford (1959). Lucito proposes such criteria as productive thinking and evaluative thinking:

The gifted are those students whose potential intellectual powers are at such a high ideational level in both productive and evaluative thinking that it can be reasonably assumed they could be the future problem solvers, innovators, and evaluators of the culture if adequate educational experiences are provided. (p. 184)

It will be noted that this definition includes both divergent thinking and convergent thinking under the term of "productive thinking" and that "evaluative thinking" is also included, thus eliminating the child who is high in divergent thinking but low in evaluative thinking and who therefore produces bizarre, unrealistic responses without adequate evaluation.

In defining giftedness there is a current effort to avoid depending too heavily on the IQ, but when it comes to identifying or selecting gifted children most schools and research workers rely on a standardized intelligence test, partly because there are few other measuring devices. Perhaps some of the current attempts to measure creativity as another facet of intelligence may bear fruit.

Another reason the IQ has been depended upon is that it does tap a wide variety of abilities. In order to obtain a high IQ a child has to show either considerable ability in many areas or tremendous ability in more limited areas. It is possible, however, that present measures of intelligence leave some areas untapped.

When the IQ has been used to define intelligence, there has been a wide divergence in determining the cutoff point above which a child is considered gifted. Various authorities for various purposes have used anywhere from 115 IQ to 180 IQ as the dividing line.

Gloss and Jones (1968) report that of 159 school districts in a midwestern state, 7 percent accept children with IQ's below 114 as gifted, another 7 percent accept 114 to 119, and only one district required IQ's of 140 and above.

DeHaan and Havighurst (1957) have divided the intellectually gifted into two groups for educational purposes. The highest one-tenth of one percent they call "first-order" or extremely gifted and the remaining upper 10 percent "second-order" gifted. The extremely gifted are very rare and may require a different kind of education from that given the second-order gifted.

With giftedness showing itself in so many different ways perhaps we can think of it in more general terms for practical purposes as *superior ability to deal with facts, ideas, or relationships,* whether this ability comes from a high IQ or a less well-defined creativity. We can then refer to those with special aptitudes in more specific fields as talented, such as:

the socially talented
the mechanically talented
the artistically talented
the musically talented
the physically talented
the linguistically talented
the academically talented

Obviously there is much overlapping. The intellectually gifted may also be socially talented; the musically talented may also be intellectually and mathematically gifted. The academically talented are usually intellectually gifted, although not all intellectually gifted are academically talented. Usually a high degree of talent in one or more areas is accompanied by intellectual giftedness. DeHaan and Havighurst (1957) in trying to identify the top 10 percent in each of several areas of talent, found so much overlapping that in the end they found that these groups constituted only 15 percent of the high school population. This gives support to the use of general intelligence measures as criteria for defining giftedness.

To be highly endowed in an intellectual field requires a gifted intellect, but the direction which that intellect follows is dependent on many other factors such as experience, motivation, interest, emotional stability, hero worship, parental urgings, and even chance. Many an intellectually gifted individual might also have been successful in another area had his interests and training been in that direction.

Usually the very talented are also intellectually gifted but there are cases of special talents of a nonintellectual nature or abilities narrow in range in which the individual is not able to handle ideas and relationships outside a very limited field.

Admitting that superior intelligence is only one factor in determining success, achievement, or contribution to society, it still remains a basic ingredient of what we call giftedness. Other qualities are necessary for successful accomplishment, but our major concern here is with cognitive and reasoning abilities. By trying to include in a definition of giftedness those other factors which are commendable (such as social leadership, performance, worth-whileness) we are confusing the concept of giftedness with our goals for gifted children. We do have so-called gifted children who are not performing because of emotional, motivational, or circumstantial factors; we do have so-called gifted children who are not outstanding in creativity; we do have so-called gifted children who are using their talents in socially unacceptable ways. But the common denominator is intellectual superiority.

Finding Gifted Children

Salvaging our wasted high-level manpower is more than a problem of establishing classes or other measures for developing gifted children. Before these children can be helped they must be found—and not just the obvious ones who have already achieved must be found but also those who are "hiding their light under a bushel." In every generation many gifted children pass through school unidentified and uncultivated. Children from low socioeconomic or foreign cultures whose lack of verbal ability conceals their merit, those who have to drop out of school for economic reasons, those from minority groups, and those with emotional problems are often not detected as potentially gifted.

The man on the street expects that of course the teacher will spot these children and do something for them, but various studies have shown that teachers do not do a very good job of recognizing the gifted child; in fact they fail to identify from 10 to 50 percent of their gifted. Pegnato and Birch (1959) for example, in evaluating various methods of identifying gifted children found that teachers were not able to select such children at all accurately. They picked many children (31.4 percent of their choices) who were not gifted and missed more than half of the really gifted children in their classes. At the kindergarten level the record is even worse. Kirk (1966) found that kindergarten teachers fail to take CA (chronological age) into account and tend to select older children as being bright. Seventy percent of the children selected as bright were mistakenly identified and had a mean IQ of only 102.5. The teachers failed to identify 68 percent of the children with IQ's of 116 and above. When the teachers were given guidelines for selection and an adjustment was made for CA differences, twice as many correct identifications were made and the teachers missed only 30 percent of the eligible children. The mean of those missed was only 118, just above the cutoff which was used.

Children who are successful academically, who have a high degree of social leadership, who have a cultivated ability in dramatics or the arts, or who have successful achievement in some other line of endeavor are readily identified as probably gifted. But the child who is not achieving in school, or who is inhibited and lacking in outgoing personality traits, or who is nonconforming in habits, interests, and attitudes may have potentialities which are easily overlooked.

However, if given some guidance in making observations, teachers can provide much significant information. In fact, their observations probably provide the greatest single resource (other than objective tests) in identifying gifted children. Kough and DeHaan (1955) have developed a *Teacher's Guidance Handbook* providing observational methods for discovering special abilities and disabilities. (It can be used for maladjusted and handicapped children as well as the gifted.) It provides a list of identifying characteristics in the areas of intellectual ability, scientific abilities, talents in the fine arts, social leadership ability, mechanical skills, and physical skills. For example, the following distinguishing characteristics are to be checked in the area of intellectual ability:

1. Learns rapidly and easily.
2. Uses a lot of common sense and practical knowledge.
3. Reasons things out, thinks clearly, recognizes relationships, comprehends meanings.
4. Retains what he has heard or read without much rote drill.
5. Knows about many things of which other children are unaware.
6. Uses a large number of words easily and accurately.
7. Can read books that are one to two years in advance of the rest of the class.
8. Performs difficult mental tasks.
9. Asks many questions. Is interested in a wide range of things.
10. Does some academic work one to two years in advance of the class.
11. Is original, uses good but unusual methods or ideas.
12. Is alert, keenly observant, responds quickly. (p. 44)

Subjective evaluation, such as teacher or parent referral, needs to be checked by more objective measures of ability such as standardized tests. Any program for identifying the gifted children in a school system should include both subjective and objective methods of evaluation. Some types of behavior are best observed informally, some by a more controlled method. Classroom behavior, for example, may point up a child's ability in organizing and utilizing material and interpreting it to other people better than a test can, whereas a class situation seldom taxes an accelerated child to the limit of his ability, as can be done in a test situation. Many aspects of creativity and verbal fluency are also best observed in a classroom or in informal experiences.

Most schools have some test scores available from group intelligence tests or group achievement tests. Although these are not sufficient in and of themselves they serve as a starting point in selecting candidates for a special program. Certain pitfalls are widely recognized in utilizing this material: (1) group intelligence tests are not as reliable as individual tests; (2) they seldom differentiate abilities at the upper limits; (3) some children do not function adequately in a timed test situation. Group intelligence tests, however, are practical for screening purposes, since it is financially prohibitive to expect all children to be given individual examinations. Those children who are near the cutoff point or for whom it is felt the group test is not representative are usually given individual tests.

Achievement tests are even less discriminating; the same criticisms hold, and in addition they detect only children who are achieving academically. Emotional disturbance, family problems, peer-group standards of mediocrity, poor study habits, a foreign-language background, and many other factors may affect a child's ability to perform academically. In the opposite direction, there are some children who because of family pressures, good study habits, or intense motivation achieve at a higher educational level than is consistent with their other abilities or their apparent mental level.

Gallagher (1959) has summarized the limitations of various techniques of identifying gifted children:

SUMMARY OF METHODS OF IDENTIFYING GIFTED CHILDREN

Method	Limitations
Individual intelligence test	The best method, but expensive in use of professional time and service. Not practical as general screening tool in schools with limited psychological services.
Group intelligence test	Generally good for screening. May not identify those with reading difficulties and emotional or motivational problems.
Achievement test batteries	Will not identify underachieving gifted children. In addition, same limitations as group intelligence test.
Teacher observation	May miss underachievers, motivational problems, emotional problems, and children with belligerent or apathetic attitude toward the school program. Definitely needs supplementing with standardized tests of intelligence and achievement. (p. 9)

How Many Gifted Children Are There?

The question of prevalence of gifted children in a particular school population depends to a large extent on two factors: (1) the criterion for identifying them and (2) the type of community being studied.

If the criterion used is an IQ, the number of gifted in a given community depends on the IQ cutoff point. Leta Hollingworth (1942), for example, studied children with IQ's above 180. With this high a criterion of giftedness probably only one child in a million would be considered gifted. If we used an IQ of 115 and above on the Stanford-Binet test as the criterion, we would find 15 to 20 percent of most school populations in this category. Using varying cutoff points, we could divide the group of high-IQ children according to degree of ability into (1) superior children, with IQ's of 116 to 132; (2) very superior children, with IQ's of 132 to 148; and (3) gifted children, with IQ's above 148. Programs of education for these children would probably differ somewhat.

The intellectual and cultural level of a community also influences the number of gifted children found. Communities composed largely of professional people show a higher percentage of gifted children than do communities of a lower intellectual and occupational status.

The early experiences of the children from higher socioeconomic and educational levels are probably much more conducive to the development of reasoning ability, seeing relationships, understanding abstract concepts, and other abilities usually considered indicative of intellectual capacity. If so, society could do much more than it now does to develop and cultivate giftedness. Pressey (1960) calls attention to the greater frequency of certain types of genius during particular periods of history when emphasis was placed on them. Pointing up the importance of early training and stimulation, he postulates that ". . . a practicing genius is produced by giving a precocious, able youngster early encouragement, intensive instruction, continuing opportunity as he advances, a congruent stimulating social life, and cumulative success experiences" (p. 14).

The greater frequency with which gifted children are found in communities of a higher cultural and socioeconomic level suggests that had children from other communities had the same experiences we would have more high-level manpower. This is the group which should receive extra attention in trying to locate the potentially gifted, the more so since their true ability is less likely to be spotted by our predominantly verbal and abstract intelligence tests.

Gallagher (1959) has formulated an estimate of gifted children in various IQ categories and in two different socioeconomic groups, as presented in Table 4–1; there may be less than 1 per 100 school children (taking the IQ of 140 and above in an average community) to over 45 in 100 (taking the lowest IQ of 115 in a superior socioeconomic community). Actually, the only way to find out in a particular community is to examine the whole school population, and then the percentage will be relatively accurate for only that community.

Case Studies of the Intellectually Gifted

To illustrate the achievements of individuals who are considered intellectually gifted, two types of illustrations follow: (1) life sketches of a few great men and (2) profiles of gifted children in the elementary school.

HISTORIES OF GREAT MEN

The term "genius" has been applied to outstanding individuals who have attained eminence in some field of intellectual or creative endeavor. Sometimes the individual is recognized as a child prodigy at a young age; sometimes he is not recognized as "great" until he has become known for a unique contribution at a later stage of his life or in some instances after his death.

John Stuart Mill (1806–1873). John Stuart Mill is considered one of the greatest philosophers of the nineteenth century. He was the son of an English author and

TABLE 4–1

*Approximate proportions of school
populations at various intellectual levels*

Stanford-Binet intellectual levels	Percent of school population		Educational expectations
	Average community	*Superior socioeconomic community*	
IQ above 140	.5 to 1%	2 to 3%	Graduate college
IQ above 130	2 to 4	6 to 12	(medicine, law,
IQ above 125	5 to 7	15 to 20	Ph.D. programs in physical and social sciences)
IQ above 120	10 to 12	30 to 40	Undergraduate
IQ above 115	16 to 20	45 to 60	college

Source: James J. Gallagher, *The Gifted Child in the Elementary School (What Research Says to the Teacher,* No. 17, 1st ed.) (Washington, D.C.: American Educational Research Association, N.E.A., Association of Classroom Teachers, 1959), p. 5. Reproduced with the permission of the publisher.

philosopher who had himself been self-educated. His life history and education have been reported by Cox (1926) and in his own writings (1924). According to Mill's own report, "My father's scheme of education could not have been accomplished if he had not carefully kept me from having any great amount of intercourse with other boys" (p. 24). His father kept him out of school and away from other children to avoid the "contagion of vulgar modes of thought and feeling." He educated John Stuart at home until the boy was 14 years of age. John Stuart began the study of Greek at the age of 3, and geometry and algebra at the age of 8. When he was 12 he began to study philosophy and logic. It is reported that he wrote a history of Rome at the age of 6½. His productive professional career began at age 17. Cox estimated his IQ to be between 190 and 200.

The reactions of John Stuart Mill to his education by the tutorial system of his father (out of school and with little influence of a society of his peers) can best be expressed by direct quotations from his own writings. "I consequently remained long, and in a less degree have always remained, inexpert in anything requiring manual dexterity. . . . The education which my father gave me, was in itself much more fitted for training me to *know* than to *do*" (pp. 25–26).

The history and accomplishments of John Stuart Mill raise a number of questions. First, is it necessary to segregate very superior children from their childhood peers in order to educate them for a scholarly career? Second, can such an education be accomplished in a school situation? And third, is such achievement the result of a tutorial system which can begin at an early age, uncontaminated by a school curriculum and grade placement?

Norbert Wiener (1894–1964). Norbert Wiener (1953) is one of the great men of our present age, known for his theories of cybernetics from which have been developed the "electronic brains" of various forms, including the high-speed digital computers.

Wiener's father was a German intellectual who migrated to the United States. He, like Mill's father, devoted a great deal of time to tutoring his son at home but, unlike Mill, allowed the boy to attend school. Thus Norbert obtained a combination of home tutoring and a somewhat erratic school career.

Norbert Wiener began to read at the age of 3½ and read *Alice in Wonderland* and *The Arabian Nights* when he was 4. Refused admission to school because he was not yet 6, he attended a one-room country school for a time. At the age of 7 he entered a city school and was placed in the third grade. Soon he was accelerated to the fourth grade but was then taken out of school until the age of 9, when he was admitted to a high school. He graduated from high school at the age of 11 and entered Harvard College the next year. He obtained his Ph.D. in mathematics at age 18. Wiener states that his father tutored him at home, but at times he was tutored in certain subjects by others. His father was a perfectionist and a "task master" and in a sense reproduced a similar educational program for Norbert as was given to John Stuart Mill, with the exception of additional school and college attendance. Wiener's adjustment to college at such a young age was not made without great difficulty.

In view of Wiener's distinction in theoretical mathematics, it is interesting to note that in school he counted on his fingers long after this method was acceptable. In spite of the fact that he had great difficulty in learning by rote the addition combinations and the multiplication tables, he had an understanding of complicated operations in mathematics at an early age. He stated: "My understanding of the subject was too fast for my manipulation, and on the other hand, my demands in the nature of the fundamentals went too far for the explanations of a book devoted to manipulation" (p. 46).

Wiener's achievements and educational career also raise numerous questions. We can state that his early educational acceleration was not the result of the program of the schools he attended. Was it the result of inherent mental abilities that would have led to inevitable achievement, or was it the result of home tutoring by a parent who insisted on perfect learning, thinking, and achieving at a high theoretical level?

Albert Einstein (1879–1955). The education and early history of Albert Einstein differ markedly from the early education of Mill or Wiener. Reiser (1930) reported that Einstein was retiring in personality and slow in learning to talk, and that his parents believed him retarded in development. The father was a merchant conducting an electrical business in Munich, Germany. He was without theoretical training but had abilities in technical matters. Einstein's school experiences were not happy ones nor did they necessarily contribute to his basic interest in physics and mathematics. Actually he attended the Luifold Gymnasium in Munich, where the basic studies were in the humanities—Latin, Greek, and ancient history. He was bored with school and recalls only one instructor who inspired interest in the classical world.

Einstein's interest in mathematics was aroused by his uncle, his father's partner in the factory. After he had learned the essentials of algebra and heard about the Pythagorean theorem, he studied mathematics on his own and outside of school. At the age of 14 he had mastered the essentials of higher mathematics, which his school did not teach. He continued to be mediocre in school as a language student.

At the age of 15 he left school to go to his parents, who had moved to Milan. Later he failed the entrance examination of the Polytechnic Academy at Zurich. He returned to the secondary school and later was admitted to the Zurich Technical Academy. He became interested in physics, but even here school was not inspiring. He missed classes to read in a wide range of fields, including physics. He completed his work at the University of Zurich, then obtained positions, once as teacher and once in a patent office. In 1909 he procured a professorship at Zurich. He later held professorships in Austria and finally became Director of the Kaiser Wilhelm Institute for Theoretical Physics in Berlin. Einstein's theory of relativity became famous after World War I when its implications began to be understood by the scientists of the world. His life after 1933 was spent at Princeton University in the Institute of Advanced Study.

Einstein was never conceited and never requested from society more than a meager livelihood. Although by nature a pacifist, he wrote to President Roosevelt in 1939 suggesting the possibilities of developing an atomic bomb. In spite of his greatness, he retained a kind, humble nature. It should be recalled that Mill was kept away from children and school so that he would not develop conceit because of his superiority, and Wiener's father was careful not to allow Norbert to recognize his superiority.

The story of Einstein indicates that he did not show precocity at an early age, that he did not come from a family of high educational attainments, and that his early school years did not contribute materially to his later accomplishments in physics and mathematics.

Wernher Von Braun (1912–   ). Von Braun is known for his invention of the

German V-2 rocket during World War II and his leading role in America's present missile and space program.

Von Braun was the middle son of Baron Magnus Von Braun, a local state administrator in eastern Germany. His mother was an enthusiastic amateur astronomer, who pointed out to her son the planets and constellations. About this experience Wernher stated, "For my confirmation I didn't get a watch and my first pair of long pants, like must Lutheran boys. I got a telescope. My mother thought it would make the best gift" (*Time,* Feb. 17, 1958).

Aside from his mother's interest in astronomy, Wernher did not receive extraordinary tutoring during his childhood. He attended the regular schools in Germany and received his Ph.D. at the age of 22. In his early teens he obtained a book on interplanetary rockets and found that it contained considerable mathematics, which he disliked and in which he had done poorly in school. This motivated him to learn mathematics and physics, which he later taught to his classmates.

Beginning at the age of 20, he was the top civilian specialist for the German army rocket program. He continued to be recognized as such until he was captured by the American army in 1944 and brought to the United States. He elected to remain in the United States after the war and to work for the American government on missile and space programs.

The experiences of Von Braun indicate that accomplishment is possible without the tutorial systems used with Mill and Wiener. It should be pointed out, however, that his interest and accomplishments in rocketry were initiated by him and acquired without a specialized course in this area. He had the combination of intelligence, interest, motivation, and availability of basic scientific information.

Thomas A. Edison (1847–1931). Thomas Edison (Dyer and Martin, 1929) is considered one of the great inventors of the nineteenth and twentieth centuries because of his inventions of the phonograph (1877), the incandescent electric lamp (1879), the motion-picture camera (1891), the magnetic ore separator (1908), and many other mechanical devices.

Edison was raised in an average American midwestern family of his time, his father having been engaged in small business enterprises. His mother, who educated Thomas later, was a former schoolteacher. Throughout his career, he attended public school for only three months. During this time, at the age of 7, he was always at the foot of his class. Furthermore, his teacher reported to the local school inspector in Port Huron, Michigan, that the boy was "addled" and should be kept out of school. His mother became incensed at this recommendation, withdrew the boy from school, and taught him at home, never again admitting him to school.

By the age of 12 he had covered such books as Gibbon's *Decline and Fall of the Roman Empire* and Hume's *History of England*. He was, however, unable to master mathematics. At the age of 15 he became editor of his own paper, called "The Weekly Herald."

The history of Edison shows a creative mind in the development of mechanical and electrical devices. Although he did not contribute greatly to theoretical knowledge, he is considered creative in a practical sense. It is of note, however, that his education was acquired on a tutorial basis, and his achievements were accomplished without the stimulus of formal schooling.

PROFILES OF INTELLECTUALLY GIFTED CHILDREN

To understand the special educational needs of a gifted child it is necessary to make an individual study of that child. One of education's difficulties is that educational programs are organized on the basis of averages derived from studies of groups. The application of averages of populations to an individual is sometimes deceptive, since it does not always follow that what is relevant to a group is relevant to a particular individual. There are, for example, marked differences among children all of whom have been classified as intellectually gifted.

The profiles of George and Ignatius are presented in Figure 4–1. A series of examinations given to these boys at the age of 10 when they were in the fifth grade yields the results shown below.

	George	Ignatius
Chronological age	10–4	10–5
Height age	11–9	9–6
Weight age	11–7	9–3
Motor coordination age	12–1	9–4
Mental age	13–11	13–9
Social maturity age	11–5	9–8
Speech development age	13–0	12–0
Language development age	12–7	12–2
Reading age	12–8	12–7
Arithmetic reasoning age	12–1	11–7
Arithmetic computation age	11–5	11–6
Spelling age	11–6	12–0
General information age	11–10	11–6
Mobility	above average	average
Vision	normal	normal
Hearing	normal	normal
Interpersonal relations	above average	average

FIGURE 4–1

Profiles of two intellectually gifted children

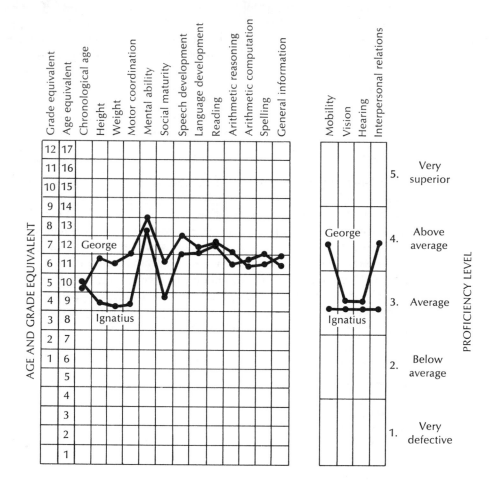

The test results on George and Ignatius and the corresponding profiles in Figure 4–1 show two boys who can be classified as intellectually gifted but whose growth patterns are markedly different. George's IQ on the Stanford-Binet Scale is 135; Ignatius's IQ is 132. Both boys are in the fifth grade. George's age is 10–4, and Ignatius's is 10–5. Physically, George is accelerated, since his height, weight, motor coordination, and mobility are similar to those of 11-year-old boys in the sixth grade. He is likewise accelerated in social maturity, in interpersonal relations, and in school achievement. Actually, with the exception of the accident of birth 10 years and 4 months previous to the examination, George is more like 11- and 12-year-old children. The discrepancies between his physical, social, mental, and achievement levels are really not very great. He is above his chronological age group in all areas of development. He does not have wide discrepancies within himself. Educationally, this child could be accelerated to the sixth or seventh grade, since he is more similar to that group than to the 10-year-olds with whom he is placed under the school's policy of year-by-year promotion.

Ignatius scores about as high as George in mental ability and in educational achievement. But Ignatius has wide discrepancies in growth among his physical, social, mental, and educational abilities. He is not large for his age of 10–5. As a matter of fact, he is more like 9-year-old children in height, weight, and motor coordination. He is also like 9-year-old children in social maturity. His mobility and interpersonal relations are not superior to those of other children in his grade. His only areas of acceleration are his mental ability and his achievement in speech, language, and academic areas. From an educational point of view, this child should not be accelerated to be with older children. The marked unevenness in his physical, social, and mental development presents educational problems different from those presented by George.

These two cases demonstrate why some educators are opposed to acceleration of gifted children while others are in favor of it. Usually those in favor of acceleration are thinking of boys like George, while those opposed to it have in mind boys like Ignatius. That is one reason why easy solutions to the education of this heterogeneous group of the gifted are not readily available.

The cases of George and Ignatius illustrate differences among children of the same age and IQ. There are countless other combinations of abilities. Allen (Figure 4–2), for example, scores higher on intelligence tests than did George or Ignatius. Yet he shows a very different profile. He is an underachieving gifted child who, from his performance, would not be classified as gifted. Below are his test scores in the fifth grade, which are also represented by a profile in Figure 4–2.

Chronological age	10–6
Height age	10–2
Weight age	9–10
Motor coordination age	10–0
Mental age	14–7 (IQ 140)
Social maturity age	10–5
Speech development age	12–2
Language age	13–4

Reading age	10–1
Arithmetic reasoning age	10–3
Arithmetic computation age	9–4
Spelling age	9–4
General information	11–2
Mobility	average for age
Vision	normal
Hearing	normal
Interpersonal relations	below average

The scores on examinations as represented in Figure 4–2 show a boy of high abstract intelligence, accelerated language and speech development, but average physical, social, and educational characteristics for his age. His basic disability is in the area of personality as represented by his below average interpersonal relations. He does not seem to get along well with other children, is not accepted by them, and resents authority and assignments by teachers. He utilizes his intelligence with his peer group by using vocabulary they do not understand and by arguing with them on various issues. He devotes much of his time to being a nonconformist at home and in school. This boy is considered an under-achieving gifted child whose personality problems, anxieties, and attitudes are retarding his performance. His educational program will necessarily be different from the educational programs of George and Ignatius if he is to attain achievement more in harmony with his potentiality.

Characteristics of Intellectually Gifted Children

Gifted children have been the object of interest of numerous investigators. Many of the studies on the characteristics of gifted children, however, are short-term ones and tend to confirm the results of a longitudinal study over a period of a third of a century by Lewis Terman. Since Terman's research is considered the *magnum opus* of all studies of the gifted it is reviewed first.

THE TERMAN STUDIES

Following his revision and publication of the Binet-Simon tests of intelligence in 1916, Lewis A. Terman, a distinguished professor of psychology at Stanford University, became interested in gifted children. He devoted the rest of his life to the study of 1528 gifted children whom he had identified in 1920. He followed this group for 35 years, until his death in 1956. During this period he was instrumental in writing a series of five books entitled *Genetic Studies of Genius* (1925–1959).

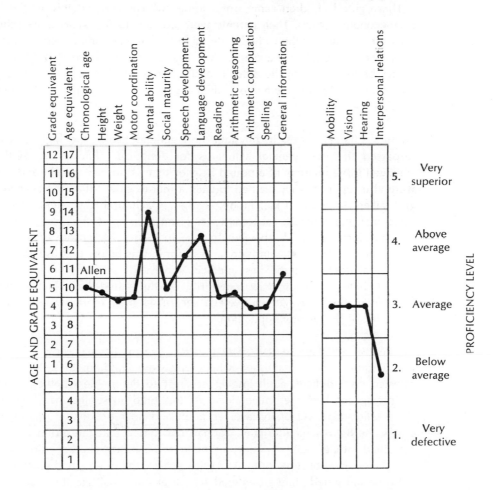

FIGURE 4–2

Profile of an underachieving gifted child

Terman's search for gifted children was conducted in the public schools of California. Teacher nominations and group intelligence tests were used as screening procedures. The final selection of most subjects was based on an IQ of 140 and above on the 1916 Stanford-Binet Individual Intelligence Scale. Terman estimated that this method identified 90 percent of the eligible students. The average IQ for the more than a thousand children selected by the Binet test was 151. The remainder, who were selected on the basis of the Terman Group Test of Mental Abilities, had an average IQ score of 142.6. For the total group of 1528 gifted children, the ratio of boys to girls was 116 to 100. Terman believed that this difference was due to a greater variability in intelligence among males.

These gifted children came from homes which were notably in the higher socioeconomic levels. Their parents averaged four to five years more schooling than the average for the United States, and the median family income was more than twice the California average. There was a low incidence of broken homes. It may be that some of the differences Terman found between the gifted group and the control group were due to their superior homes as much as to their high intelligence.

Physical Characteristics. In physique and general health the high-IQ children surpassed the best general standards for American children. At birth they averaged three quarters of a pound heavier than is normal. Height and strength were also superior. They learned to walk a month earlier than the average child and talked three and a half months earlier. As children they slept significantly more than the controls. Each child was given a complete medical examination, and the doctors' reports showed that the incidence of sensory defects, dental caries, poor posture, malnutrition, and so forth, was below that usually reported by school doctors in the best medical surveys of school populations in the United States. This physical superiority of the gifted has been maintained throughout the years. At the average age of 44 their mortality rate was four-fifths that of the general population.

Intellectual and Educational Characteristics. The intellectual superiority of Terman's subjects was established when they were children. In 1940 they were retested on a difficult adult intelligence test to determine whether superiority of intelligence had been maintained. At this time no subject had regressed to the intelligence level of the average adult and no more than 10 percent were below the 85th percentile rank. Terman concluded that the group as a whole remained intellectually superior, although some bright children did not maintain their degree of superiority. As a rule, he says, the bright child remains bright.

While the gifted children entered school at the usual age (6¼ years), nearly one-half learned to read before the age of 6. Concerning their academic advancement during their school years. Terman and Oden (1947) stated, "It is a conservative estimate that more than half . . . had already mastered the school curriculum to a point two full grades beyond the one in which they were enrolled, and some of them as much as three or four grades beyond" (p. 28). These children tended to be advanced in all areas of schoolwork, showing no more variation among subjects than did unselected children.

The rates of college attendance (90 percent for men and 86 percent for women) and graduation (70 percent for men and 67 percent for women) were eight times those of the general population in California. Although they were graduated a year younger than the average, they participated in extracurricular activities to a greater than average extent. Surprisingly, 8 percent of the men and 2 percent of the women "flunked" out of college (although half of these reentered and graduated).

Interests and Preoccupations. In scholastic areas the gifted children were more interested than the controls in abstract subjects such as literature, debate, and ancient history, and less interested in "practical" subjects such as penmanship and manual training. Gifted and controls were equally interested in games and sports.

The gifted appeared less "sociable" in their interests. They showed a stronger liking for playing with just *one* other person than did the controls. On a scale of sociability of play interest, almost half of the gifted fell in the lowest quartile of control-group scores.

Character Tests and Trait Ratings. A battery of 7 character tests showed gifted children above average on every rating. They were less prone to make over-statements and to cheat. Their book and character preferences were judged more wholesome and mature, and they scored above average on an emotional stability test. On all 7 tests taken together, 86 percent of the gifted boys and 84 percent of the girls scored above the mean for the control groups.

Two facts stood out in the study of character tests and trait ratings for gifted children: (1) Desirable traits tended to be positively correlated with each other, and (2) the upward deviation was not the same in all traits, that is, gifted children were more outstanding in some traits than in others.

Mental Health and General Adjustment. In 1945, more than 20 years after the study began, the subjects were followed up. One of the areas investigated was mental health and adjustment. At this time approximately 80 percent showed "satisfactory adjustment," about 15 percent had "some maladjustment," and 5 percent had "serious maladjustment." This rate is slightly lower than the national expectancy for serious maladjustment. The delinquency rate was far below that of the general population. Alcoholism was found in 1.5 percent of the men and .9 percent of the women. Terman concluded that the superior emotional adjustment seen in childhood was maintained in adulthood.

Marriage, Divorce, Fertility. The marriage rate for the gifted group as adults was about the same as that for the general population (84 percent) and higher than was found for college graduates. The divorce rate to 1955 was somewhat less than that for the general population.

A total of 1525 offspring of the gifted group have been tested. The mean IQ is 132.7. About one-third test above 140 and only 2 percent below 100.

In general, the gifted group tended slightly toward more and happier marriages, fewer divorces, and fewer offspring. However, it is still too soon for these trends to be definite.

Vocational and Occupational Status. The occupational status of the gifted men reported in 1955 showed about eight times as many men in the professions as was true for the general population. About 80 percent of gifted men were in the two highest occupational groups—Group I, the professional, and Group II, semiprofessional and higher business. In the entire population only 14 percent were found in these two groups. The incomes for the gifted group were considerably higher than the national average. The most successful gifted men were compared with the least successful gifted and many striking differences were found. Terman and Oden (1951) state, "Everything considered, there is nothing in which the A [most successful] and C [least successful] groups present a greater contrast than in drive to achieve and in all-round social adjustment" (p. 37). Success for the gifted was associated with well-balanced temperament and freedom from excessive frustration.

The Stanford *Genetic Studies of Genius,* under the direction of Lewis Madison Terman, stand out as one of the monolithic investigations of one kind of exceptional children, thus far unsurpassed by any other study in the field. They will remain as a monument to their brilliant author, who has contributed so much to our knowledge of intelligence.

OTHER RESEARCH ON CHARACTERISTICS OF GIFTED CHILDREN

Racial and Ethnic Differences. Intellectual giftedness is no respecter of color, race, or creed. It is found in every class and culture. The fact that some groups seem to have a higher proportion of gifted individuals than do others may well be the result of the kinds of intelligence tests and other means of identification used. And again, though according to some studies (Barbe, 1956; Terman and Oden, 1947), there are proportionately fewer gifted identified among Negroes than among Caucasians, this finding may be due to limited or subnormal educational and cultural environments. The same thing is probably true of other minority groups. A notable exception is to be observed in the very high rate of giftedness found among Jews. Strodtbeck (1958) suggests a possible relationship between the upward mobility or high achievement of Jewish groups and a belief that man can master and control his environment. The Italian families, in contrast to the Jewish families, were more inclined to feel themselves under the domination of fate or destiny. We may conclude that some racial and ethnic groups do tend to produce disproportionate numbers of gifted children, but quite probably because of cultural and value-system differences rather than because of any inherent differences in intelligence level. More adequate comparisons of race and ethnic differences can be made in the United States only when our pluralistic society has removed race and ethnic prejudices, and when all children have equal economic, health, and educational opportunities.

Peer Acceptance of Gifted Children. The myth that many or most gifted children are social misfits and rejected by their classmates has been thoroughly disproved. Yet it persists because people tend to note and then remember the occasional maladjusted bright person they have known. Terman and Oden (1947) have shown the superior social and emotional traits of the gifted, as discussed earlier. Miller (1956) found that gifted children were significantly more popular than average or retarded pupils. Kerstetter (1952) studied a group of highly gifted children (IQ 160 and above) in special classes and found them, on the whole, socially well-adjusted. She saw no relationship between level of intelligence and poor social adjustment. Gallagher (1958) and Martyn (1957) both found that the gifted rated as high as or higher than the average in popularity. Gallagher concluded that gifted children were better able than average children to predict who would choose them for friends. This social perceptiveness or socioempathy might account for the above average popularity of the gifted group.

Jansen and Gallagher (1966) studied racially integrated, intermediate elementary classes for talented children who were culturally disadvantaged. When they gave the children final choices in seating, working, and playing together, they found that cross-racial social changes were made.

The evidence is clear that the gifted are accepted by their classmates, but several questions are as yet unanswered. The degree of acceptance may vary with the community (many of the studies were done in communities of a high educational level such as Palo Alto, California, and Champaign-Urbana, Illinois). The level of giftedness may also affect popularity, as the suggestion is often made that the very highly gifted (IQ above 165 or 170) may have more social adjustment problems than the less gifted, who numerically constitute the majority of subjects in the studies. The type of program—for example, special class versus enrichment—may have a bearing on popularity with peers. Grade level may prove important, as there are some reasons to believe that elementary children are more warmly disposed toward the gifted than are high school students. Even though these factors and others do influence the social status of the gifted, we may be sure that the gifted are socially accepted by their peers.

Creativity

One common characteristic of gifted children which received increasing attention during the 60's is creativity. Definitions of creativity are many and varied, often quite nebulous. Yamamoto (1965) has compared creativity to the elephant in the story of the three blind men each trying to describe the elephant from his own limited experience:

Something people call an elephant is there—this much is sure. And all of us, blind men, have been touching it, feeling it, figuring it out and describing it to each other. On some facts, we agree among ourselves; on others, we cannot even understand what each is trying to tell the other. But, it is precisely this amorphousness which *is* the elephant—the elephant of creativity. (p. 428)

Yet, in spite of the lack of specific agreement on definitions, theoretical formulations, measuring techniques, and so forth, the focus of interest in the field of the gifted has shown a dramatic swing toward creativity. According to Noffsinger (Frierson, 1969), 64 percent of research on the gifted published in professional journals in 1966 related to their creativity, whereas only 39 percent were oriented in that direction in 1961.

Some sample definitions of creativity are:

behavior involving organization of information into novel combinations. *Yamamoto (1965)*

the ability to produce many unique cognitive associations. *Wallach and Kogan (1965)*

the production of something new, some original idea or invention, or the reconstruction or reintegration of existing products or ideas. *Hildreth (1966)*

Lucito's definition of giftedness given on page 108 also involves the concept of creativity represented by "productive thinking." This is based on the signal work of Guilford (1959; 1967a), who has stimulated much of the subsequent interest in the field of creativity. Guilford has proposed a three-dimensional "structure of intellect" with 120 components. One of the three dimensions (operations) describes five groups of intellectual abilities:

1. Cognition (recognition or discovery)

2. Memory (retention of what is cognized)

3. Divergent-production (reorganizing known facts into new and/or varied relationships)

4. Convergent-production (arriving at more conventional conclusions)

5. Evaluation (reaching decisions as to the correctness or adequacy of what is known).

Of these five abilities, Guilford (1967b) considers divergent production most directly involved in creative thinking. This involves *fluency of thinking* ("the ready flow of ideas"), *flexibility of thinking* ("the readiness to change direction or to modify information"), *originality* ("remote associations," "uncommonness," "cleverness"), and *elaboration* ("the ability to elaborate on ideas, to fill them out with details") (Guilford, 1967a, pp. 138, 154).

Torrance (1966) has applied many of these factors in tests of creativity for children and has conducted extensive research with relevance to educational goals and procedures.

Getzels and Jackson (1960) used tests of creativity to differentiate two groups of high school students: a "high creative" group who were among the top 20 percent on creativity tests but who did not fall in the top 20 percent on intelligence tests (mean IQ 127); and a "high IQ" group who were among the top 20 percent on intelligence tests but who did not fall in the top 20 percent on creativity tests (mean IQ 150). In spite of the advantage of 23 IQ points, the "high IQ" group did not exceed the "high creativity" group on standardized achievement tests, but they were preferred by the teachers. This study has been replicated many times by Torrance (1967) in varying types of schools. He obtained essentially the same results as Getzels and Jackson, except in schools where the children were taught primarily by authority and were given little opportunity to utilize their creative thinking abilities to further their knowledge and skills.

The "high creative" children are not as well rated sociometrically, since they may seem "peculiar." Evidence submitted by Smith (1959) and Lucito (1959) suggests that gifted children in general are more independent and less conforming in behavior than average. It remains to be shown whether this trait is related to degree or type of intelligence.

One result of the studies by Getzels and Jackson and those by Torrance is the realization that there are many children with IQ's below 130 (a common cut-off point for placing children in special classes) who are high in creativity and that these children would be denied the stimulation of the special class if high IQ were used for identification. This, of course, raises a hue and cry against the commonly used intelligence tests, which rely mainly on cognition, memory, and convergent thinking. It probably does not mean, however, "the demise of the IQ concept after a sixty-year reign" as suggested by Frierson (1969). Torrance (1967) has stated:

Our work with tests of creative thinking has caused some people to conclude that I advocate the abolition of intelligence tests and the substitution of creative or divergent thinking tests. The truth is that I have continually said that intelligence tests have long been very useful in guiding and assessing mental growth and intellectual potentiality and that they will continue to be useful. I have tried to show why we need to broaden our concept of "giftedness" from that of the "child with the high IQ" to *include also* the highly creative child and *other types*. (p. 59)

The question of whether creativity is a factor in intelligence or whether the two qualities form a dichotomy has created somewhat of a controversy. The earlier work of Getzels and Jackson (1960) has been interpreted to show that the two are separate qualities, and this has been supported by later research (Torrance, 1959; Clarke, Veldman, and Thorpe, 1965). On the other hand, Marsh (1964) has reanalyzed the Getzels and Jackson data and refutes the earlier interpretation, believing that the IQ is still the best single criterion for indicating creative potential. Cicirelli (1965) found that including creativity scores did not increase the correlation of IQ with achievement.

Martinson (1966) challenges the assumption that creativity is not related to intelligence and notes that our tests of creativity have not been adequately validated and that until they are we should not consider substituting them for our present measures. She also emphasizes Wallach and Kogan's (1965) statement that various creativity scores do not have much interrelationship nor do they indicate a single unified dimension which we might label "creativity." Martinson makes a third point in defense of the IQ by noting that much of the criticism of intelligence tests for not identifying the culturally disadvantaged [Do tests for creativity do better?] arises when such charges are usually backed by data from group tests rather than from individual tests.

A higher than average IQ seems to be necessary for high creativity, but above some undetermined minimum level there is little or no correlation between creativity and intelligence. This is corroborated by Gowan (1967), who states that "whereas intelligence and creativity are highly correlated below about 120 IQ, above that figure they are nearly independent variables" (p. 9). Torrance (1962) also believes that a minimum IQ of 115 to 120 is probably necessary for the emergence of a high degree of creativity. He found, for instance, that among children with IQ's between 132 and 186 there was a negligible correlation (.03) between IQ and creativity. Martinson and Seagoe (1967), on the other hand, found a higher correlation between IQ and judges' ratings of creative products than they found between Guilford tests of divergent thinking and the judges' ratings. They also found that high IQ groups with a mean IQ of 142.7 produced more creative products than did low IQ groups with a mean IQ of 107.5. The Stanford-Binet IQ's, however, were not significantly related to the Guilford tests of divergent thinking.

Regarding the Getzels and Jackson study referred to previously, it should be pointed out that all of the children in the study, both the highly creative group with an average IQ of 127 and the high IQ group with an average IQ of 150, might be considered gifted solely on the basis of an intelligence test. There was also a large group of students not used in the study who were high in both IQ and creativity. Thus, we have many high IQ children who are high in creativity but some who are not.

Damm (1970) found that children who were high on both intelligence and creativity tests were superior in self-actualization. Among the intercorrelations, the highest (.33) was between intelligence (California Test of Mental Maturity) and creativity (Remote Associates Test).

Special Groups of Gifted Children

It has been repeatedly emphasized that gifted children are not a homogeneous group and that one or two patterns of education will not be suitable to all of them. There is a minimum of three types of deviating gifted children who will require special attention over and above the provisions which are being made for gifted children in general. These are (1) the underachieving gifted child, (2) the highly gifted child, and (3) the gifted child with a handicap.

THE UNDERACHIEVING GIFTED CHILD

Some children with high intellectual ability do not achieve. Some are actually failures in school. This fact indicates that it takes more than intelligence to succeed in school as well as in life.

Studies of underachieving gifted children have been made by various investigators. In summarizing the studies on underachieving gifted children, Gowan (1957) speculates that the gifted underachiever is "a kind of intellectual delinquent who withdraws from goals, activities, and active social participation generally. As a child his initial attempts at creative accomplishment may not have been seen by others as 'worthwhile' but only as 'queer' or 'different' " (p. 101). Gowan believes that this blocking of rewards for deviant achievement has blunted the child's work drives and stifled his creativity.

Gallagher (1960), after surveying the literature concerning underachievers, presents a combination of events which leads to underachievement among children of superior intelligence.

1. The underachieving child grows up in, or belongs to, a cultural group which does not value education, independence, or individual achievement.

2. He has poor parental relationships, in which the parents, especially the father, either show limited interest in academic matters or try to put undue pressure on their children to succeed.

3. The child, unable to obtain satisfaction from parental contacts, seeks out his peer group for satisfying human relationships. Since he searches for others of the same interests as himself, he will often find himself allied with other rebellious and angry children.

4. These children will be faced by teachers and other school officials who ask them to meet standards of behavior which are not possible for them, and who treat these children, in many ways, as their parents do. The children thus place the teacher and the school in the same authority category as parents and reject them and their program.

5. The school, in its attempt to deal with these nonconforming and angry children, is likely to take more strict and repressive measures which will turn the children even more emphatically against the school. (pp. 42–43)

In a later publication Gallagher (1964) states:

It appears that low-producing gifted children need to be separated into two major categories. The first consists of youngsters who come from good cultural environments . . . where the difficulties center in the personality of the student and in his often unhappy family relationships. . . . The second large group of underachievers would be those coming from lower-class backgrounds where the cultural environment is generally unfavorable. (p. 74)

In summarizing the literature on underachieving gifted children Gold (1965) states:

Concerted efforts to relieve underachievement have generally failed of their purpose when delayed of inception till the senior high school. A continuous program of guidance, diagnosis, and identification needs its beginning apparently in the primary grades. (p. 411)

HIGHLY GIFTED CHILDREN

Children with IQ's of 170 and above are, of course, extremely rare. DeHaan and Havighurst (1957) state that there are about one in a thousand who have IQ's of 160 and above. Hollingworth (1942) estimated that one in a million have IQ's above 180.

Since most of the studies on the gifted have considered children with IQ's of 130 to 160, there is a question as to whether having an IQ above 170 creates *qualitative* rather than just *quantitative* differences. Because so few children are found with these extreme IQ's, not a sufficient number have been studied for us to understand them. Hollingworth studied 12 children whose IQ's were 180 and above. The early physical development of this group was not unusual. Walking and teething were at average ages. The big difference showed up in the verbal area. They talked somewhat earlier than usual and in reading they showed extreme precocity, learning to read on the average at 3 years of age (only one as late as 4.5 years). On the whole these children were very accelerated in school but presented difficult educational problems. When these problems were identified early and adequately handled through sound educational guidance and fostering of development, the children became well adjusted to school and to society. The cases of clearest adjustment came when the exceptional child attended classes with others approximately of his kind. Hollingworth felt that the problems in personality development and social adjustment were an outgrowth of the deviation between the child's intellectual development and his relative immaturity in other areas.

Terman and Oden (1947) compared 81 children with IQ's of 170 and above with the rest of the gifted children in the Stanford studies. Like Hollingworth's findings, this study noted achievement in reading at the age of 3, 4, or 5 and marked acceleration in elementary school. Although many of these subjects received high grades in college, 25 percent received only fair or poor grades. Furthermore, those with the highest IQ's did not receive the highest ratings in social adjustment. They were poor mixers and tended to participate in solitary activities. Two-thirds of the women wih IQ's of 170 and above were office workers or housewives.

It is rather apparent from the few studies available that the child with an extremely high IQ may have a more difficult time making personal and social adjustments than one with an IQ between 130 and 150 unless he is given special attention by his parents and teachers. A variety of reasons may be postulated for this difficulty, including the effects of ignorant or thoughtless adults, rejection by peers who may think him peculiar, and divergence from the rest of society in his value system. But the difficulties in adjustment can most easily be explained by internal discrepancies in growth. The child's intellectual abilities are growing nearly twice as fast as is usual, and it is too much to expect physical and emotional processes to keep pace with such rapid development. With this irregular development, the child is going to be out of place in any group of average children. If he is placed according to his intellectual level, he will be out of line physically, socially, and/or emotionally. If he is placed with his age peers, he will be out of line intellectually. Furthermore, the greatest deviation occurs at a time when he is least able to understand and handle it, that is, during the early school years. At 5 a child with an IQ of 160 has a deviation of 3 years between his 8-year mental ability and that of his age peers. A 5-year-old child finds it physically and emotionally difficult to compete with 8-year-olds, yet a child with third-grade abilities would be equally out of place living and working with 5-year-olds. At the age of about 20 the young person begins to catch up with himself, since he has reached physical and social maturity and is probably associating with others more nearly like himself.

The educational procedures used with this type of child are undoubtedly of supreme importance. It will be recalled that Hollingworth found the best adjustment among children who had been included in experimental groups for gifted children. Many of our outstanding men of history have not had to face the problem of adjusting to average children in school because they were tutored at home. Some of Hollingworth's subjects were also tutored. There are other cases of successful individuals who received tutoring during their earlier years either in conjunction with formalized schooling or without it until they were ready for high school or the university. DeHaan and Havighurst (1957) have recommended giving the extremely gifted child two groups to deal with—one group not more than a year or two older with whom he can play and associate outside of school and another group closer to his mental age for intellectual pursuits. It may be that for the extremely gifted child tutoring is essential unless there is available a class of high-level gifted children with whom he can have enough in common to stimulate his social, emotional, and educational development. Another possibility is half-day placement in school for physical education, art, and some aspects of school life, and tutoring at home for the rest of the day in academic pursuits.

THE GIFTED CHILD WITH A HANDICAP

The fact that gifted children as a group are superior in physique and health does not mean that all gifted children are healthy, have perfect eyesight and hearing, and are good athletes. The purpose of this section is to point out that there are intellectually gifted among the handicapped.

Helen Keller was both deaf and blind, and had it not been for her superior intelligence and excellent tutelage, she could not have succeeded in scholarly endeavors. Franklin D. Roosevelt was crippled with poliomyelitis. The great physicist Steinmetz was orthopedically handicapped. Beethoven composed music even after he became deaf.

Schools for the physically handicapped and institutions for the emotionally disturbed and for delinquents have within them children who test high on intelligence tests adapted to their handicaps. In general, high intelligence becomes a great asset to a child with a handicap. The education of children with various handicaps will be discussed in later chapters.

Educating Gifted Children

Although interest in making special provision for gifted children has always existed in some quarters, national interest was created after the Soviet Union launched Sputnik. The prevalent idea at that time was the acceleration of Federally sponsored educational programs for the gifted, primarily to use the gifted as a commodity for national defense. Federal aid to education has always been resisted because of fear of Federal control. But, since national defense is a Federal responsibility, the government rationalized the appropriation of funds for the training of scientists under the *National Defense Education Act of 1958.* Since that time, educators and others have pointed out that in a democracy the gifted children are not to be used as a commodity or resource for the state, and that the education of the gifted is necessary for the development of the child for his own dignity and self-development. It is to the latter aim that programs for gifted children should be organized.

Special provisions which are made to adapt the school program to the abilities of gifted children include: (1) accelerating, enriching, or grouping children, (2) devising a curriculum suitable to children with high abilities, and (3) utilizing appropriate instructional procedures.

These three aspects might be called the *where,* the *what,* and the *how* of education.

1. *Where* does the child go to school? What is his *environment?* What administrative adaptations are made?
2. *What* does the child learn? What is the subject matter or *content* of his study?
3. *How* is the child taught? What are the techniques and *processes* used?

Three organizational procedures have been commonly used in providing the environment in which gifted children are taught. These are: (1) acceleration, (2) enrichment, and (3) special schools and classes.

ACCELERATION

Acceleration of gifted pupils has been practiced in various forms for many years. It refers to (1) admitting gifted children to kindergarten or first grade according to mental age rather than chronological age, (2) skipping grades, (3) telescoping grades, (4) early admission to secondary schools or colleges, and (5) other methods such as passing courses in high school and college by examination. All of these administrative procedures are designed to cut down the time a person must remain in school.

Early School Admission. Admission to kindergarten or first grade is a matter of law in most states. The age is generally set at 5 years for kindergarten and 6 years for first grade, with a few months leeway for each. In some states the child's sixth birthday must come by December 1 if he is to be eligible for enrollment in the first grade in the preceding September. A child born December 2 would thus have to wait until the following September before he could be admitted; he would be 6 years and 9 months old when he entered Grade 1.

Research indicates that early admission to kindergarten or first grade for children who are advanced intellectually has not been detrimental as was frequently believed. Hobson (1948, 1956) reported a follow-up of pupils admitted to kindergarten on the basis of mental age. He found that the younger children (the brightest) made the best records in school through the eighth grade and after. They were superior in academic achievement to their older classmates and were also superior in honors received in extracurricular activities and in their success in being admitted to college.

Reynolds (1962) edited a series of studies dealing with early admission and concluded that there is consistent indication that no detrimental effects result from early admission. The children are as well or better adjusted in higher grades as those not admitted earlier. Early admission has the advantage of saving a year or more of time for a gifted child in his school career.

Worcester (1956) also summarized a series of studies of children who were admitted early to kindergarten. He stated that although these children averaged 8 months younger than the others, there was no difference in physical development, and they did as well or better than their older classmates in academic achievement, in social and emotional adjustment, and in acceptance by their peers. Birch (1954) found that gifted children admitted to first grade before the age of 6 were superior later as rated by teachers and administrators.

Skipping Grades. This form of acceleration refers to completely eliminating one grade or one semester in school. Contrary to current belief, and as evidenced by the Terman study and others already cited, children who have skipped grades have shown social, educational, and vocational adjustment superior or comparable to that of equally intelligent nonaccelerates.

Telescoping Grades. Since skipping a grade sometimes leaves a gap in a child's experiences, some school systems have established programs which enable a child to cover the same material as is offered in the regular curriculum but in a shorter period. The ungraded primary program is a good example. In this program children may progress through the first three grades as rapidly as they are able. Some may finish in two years, some take four, and a few even finish three grades in one year. Occasionally seventh and eighth grades are combined in order to accelerate a group of capable students at that level.

Another type of telescoping is sometimes done on an individual basis in high school. By carrying extra courses each term, certain students go through high school in three years instead of four.

Early College Admission. By early admission to first grade, skipping grades, or telescoping grade levels, some children are ready to enter college at an earlier age. In summarizing the studies on this topic Pressey (1949) pointed out that since 1888, when President Eliot of Harvard called for early admission to college, statistics have shown that those who enter college at a younger age (presumably the gifted) are generally superior to the others both in studies and in conduct. "The evidence was practically unanimous that younger entrants were most likely to graduate, had the best academic records, won the most honors, and presented the fewest disciplinary difficulties. The evidence is also that the younger entrants are highest in ability" (p. 7). Pressey also remarked that "Academic programs appear to be paced for the average student, with the consequence that their superiors can readily and often desirably move faster. However, educational convention puts a premium on the educational lock step. Greater flexibility of programs and better guidance should then save time for both students and instructors, with even less handicap for the abler younger persons" (p. 91).

Terman and Oden (1947) divided their group of gifted children into accelerates (those graduating from high school before the age of 16 years, 6 months) and nonaccelerates (those graduating after age 16 years, 6 months). The accelerates were graduated on the average at age 15.9, while the nonaccelerates had a mean age of 17.4 at the time of graduation. These groups were evaluated twenty-five years after the first testing to determine the possible effects of acceleration. Terman concluded: (1) There was little difference between the groups in intelligence; (2) the accelerates did better in college and graduate work; (3) ratings of occupational success favored the accelerates; and (4) the criticism of acceleration as causing social maladjustment is "greatly exaggerated," since there was no difference in this factor between the two groups.

The Fund for the Advancement of Education (1957) provided 1000 scholarships for high school students to attend college. The recipients were below the age of 16.5 years, and the majority had not completed high school. They were selected for the scholarships on the basis of tests of intelligence and achievement and ratings on social and emotional maturity. They were then compared with a group who were 2 years older on admission, had completed high school, and scored equally with the "scholars" on various measures of scholastic aptitude. The findings of this program indicated that (1) the colleges and parents considered the program of early admission successful; (2) the "scholars" had greater difficulty than the comparison group in adjusting initially, but the problems were resolved; (3) the scholastic record of the younger group was better than that of the older group, and (4) a larger proportion of the "scholars" went to graduate school.

Evaluation of Acceleration. The major objection to acceleration of students, whether by early admission, skipping, or telescoping, has been a fear that acceleration displaces the child from his social and emotional peers and thus affects his subsequent social adjustment. This concern has persisted in spite of the evidence that no serious detriment to social and emotional adjustment results from acceleration. The studies submitting such evidence, however, have dealt primarily with acceleration of one or two years. There is little information on the effects of acceleration of four or five years.

Research studies frequently draw conclusions and inferences for a group as a whole. In the case of gifted children, however, no conclusions can apply to all. In a school situation decisions on acceleration have to be made for each individual separately. Deciding on the procedure for the adaptation of instruction for a gifted child should not depend upon the fact of his giftedness alone. It must take into account (1) his deviation from the class in which he is placed and (2) the intraindividual differences.

The growth pattern of George shown in Figure 4–1 depicts a boy who is physically, socially, mentally, and educationally accelerated above his chronological age and grade placement. This boy could probably be accelerated one to two years without untoward effects. The profile shows that he is physically and socially more like 11- and 12-year-old children than like the 10-year-old group in which he is placed. He also is able to achieve adequately at the seventh-grade level. Placing him in the sixth or seventh grade would not be detrimental to his development.

But Ignatius, who is of the same age and IQ as George, shows a different growth pattern. Physically and socially he is more like 10-year-old children, even though in academic achievement he also rates at the sixth- and seventh-grade level. Advancing Ignatius to the sixth or seventh grade would displace him physically and socially, even though his academic achievement is high. Retaining him in the regular grades with children who achieve at a lower level academically is also a displacement. In other words, neither acceleration nor retention in the regular grades is necessarily the answer for Ignatius. Some other solution must be found, perhaps in keeping the child with his age group but providing him with other activities such as interest clubs with children of his intellectual ability and academic achievement or special classes for children who show this kind of discrepancy.

From the arguments for and against acceleration it would appear that those in favor of acceleration are thinking primarily of the Georges (Figure 4–1) while those against it focus primarily on the Ignatiuses. Therefore we cannot say that acceleration is either good or bad, for in some cases it is beneficial and in others it is detrimental. The research in the field is not clear-cut, since the studies have combined subjects such as the Georges, the Ignatiuses, and all the other gifted children regardless of their specific characteristics.

ENRICHMENT

If gifted children are not to be accelerated, how can the schools offer them a challenging program with other children of their own age? To some the answer is enrichment of the curriculum for the gifted child. The term "enrichment" has been applied to an adaptation of the regular program to provide educational experiences over and above those in the regular program. Gallagher (1959) has defined enrichment as "the type of activity devoted to the further development of the particular intellectual skills and talents of the gifted child" (p. 21). He includes in these skills the ability to (1) associate and interrelate concepts, (2) evaluate facts and arguments critically, (3) create new ideas and originate new lines of thought, (4) reason through complex problems, and (5) understand other situations, other times, and other people.

Administratively, such enrichment has been tried through various procedures which include:

1. Encouraging teachers in the regular grades to challenge the gifted child with additional readings, extra assignments, and an opportunity to participate in other than class activities.
2. Grouping children in a class, so that the few gifted children are in a group by themselves, and challenging their interests and abilities with problems requiring independent research and thought, rather than memory processes.
3. Offering additional learnings such as the study of a foreign language or typewriting in the elementary school.
4. Employing a special teacher for the gifted in a school system. His duties would be (a) to identify the gifted children who need additional stimulation and instruction, (b) to assist the regular teacher to secure additional materials of instruction and suggest additional assignments and experiences, (c) to counsel with the gifted child regarding his extracurricular activities and supplementary school assignments, and (d) to hold seminars or special classes for a part of the day in special areas of interest for the gifted children in the school.
5. Encouraging teachers to hold high standards of achievement for the gifted child, and to help him develop habits of independent work, initiative, and creativity.

Although enrichment of a program may be a factor in acceleration, and certainly is a major reason for special schools and classes, the term as commonly used has applied primarily to enrichment of the curriculum for the gifted child in the regular grades. Enrichment has been a very popular byword in schools since many feel that the gifted child should remain in a heterogeneous class. This practice will (1) give the child better opportunities for developing leadership, (2) allow him to remain with children of his own age, which is especially valuable for a child who is uneven in development, (3) make every teacher a teacher of the gifted, thus elevating the quality of instruction for all children, and (4) minimize the financial requirements since enrichment in the regular elementary grades does not necessarily add to the expense of running a school.

The program of enrichment in the elementary grades is easier to state than to execute. Teachers generally do not have the time or in some cases the knowledge and skills to provide all the enriched experiences a gifted child needs. With thirty to forty children in a class, the teacher must utilize his time in group instruction for the majority of children. Enrichment as an administrative procedure for the gifted has been preferred by many administrators but it is felt by some, "in the usual instance, to be a bulwark behind which scarcely anything desirable has in fact, transpired" (Ward, 1962, p. 53).

Kough (1960) has listed the requirements for enrichment in the regular classroom. He states that unless these are met, enrichment becomes an illusion.

1. Has each classroom teacher identified and listed the students who are gifted? If teachers are unable to do this, a well-planned classroom enrichment program is not operating. If only some of the teachers have done it, the gifted child program is not reaching all of the gifted youngsters in the school.
2. Can each classroom teacher describe the specific curriculum modification being made for each bright youngster? Again, if each teacher cannot do this, there is not a complete enrichment program.
3. Does some person have supervisory responsibility for the entire program? Such a person may help classroom teachers in the identification process and provide motivation, ideas, and materials as the program progresses. (p. 47)

It should be noted, however, that many school systems which claim an enrichment program are not complying with the requirements listed by Kough. There are many obstacles to enrichment in the regular classrooms that must be overcome before enrichment becomes a reality. These are the (1) wide ability range within each class, (2) the teacher's limitation in content areas, and (3) the teacher's lack of special methods.

SPECIAL SCHOOLS AND CLASSES

To adapt and enrich the curriculum for gifted children in the regular school, various forms of grouping have been used. These include (1) grouping the children within a regular class in the elementary school, (2) organizing special sections in the subject matters (e.g., English, science, mathematics, and social studies) in the upper elementary school and in the secondary school, (3) offering advanced courses for superior students in secondary schools, and (4) offering honors courses for superior students in college.

The groupings mentioned above are rather generally accepted; more controversial is the establishment of special schools for gifted children, or self-contained special classes within the regular schools. Three forms of such organization have been used: (1) modified special classes, (2) special classes, and (3) special schools.

Modified Special Classes. In this first grouping the gifted child remains in the regular grades with his peer group but has special instruction for a part of the day with other gifted children. The Colfax Plan (Pregler, 1954) in Pittsburgh, Pennsylvania, exemplifies the use of a modified special class. In this large school gifted children are identified in the kindergarten and assigned to a first grade with regular children. This is their home room. For half a day, however, they attend a special class with other gifted children, a workshop for special instruction.

Special Classes. The grouping of gifted children into special classes is practiced in a few city school systems. The children are grouped in grades and progress from one grade to another in a curriculum adapted to their interests, curiosity, and ability. An example of such classes is found in the Major Work Classes in Cleveland, Ohio, which have been in operation as a part of the Cleveland public school system since 1921. They admit children with IQ's of 125 and above. The purpose of these classes in the elementary school is to enrich the program of the grade but not to accelerate. Graduation from the elementary school is at the same age the other children graduate. Here the children learn with gifted children but participate with other children in school activities such as safety patrol, physical education, and other general school programs.

Special Schools. There are few special schools for elementary-school-age gifted children. The Hunter College Elementary School is a special school admitting only gifted children, ages 3 to 11, who are grouped by chronological age. In this school children work independently but participate in unit topics and study themes. In addition to special schools there are neighborhoods in which the majority of children in the school are gifted. These constitute a natural homogeneous group of superior children. In some such schools and classes, as in the specially selected class or school, the average IQ is 120 or 125. At the secondary school level, there are a number of schools devoted entirely to the education of superior students. At the college level there are some schools with very high selection standards, admitting only those students of superior aptitudes and superior grades.

Evaluation of Special Groupings. The special class or special school for gifted children at the elementary level is not accepted by many school systems. As a matter of fact there has been considerable resistance to it. Havighurst (1958) has described the divergent attitudes of two superintendents toward the establishment of special classes for the gifted. One, in a large city, seemed to be very pleased with his organization of classes for the gifted. He had no community opposition and quite a bit of community support. The other, in a smaller community of 20,000, stated that the needs of the gifted children were met without a special program by spending as much money per child on all the children as some communities do on special programs for gifted children. This superintendent felt that the community would not support classes for gifted children and that the way to educate these children was to improve the over-all educational program with better teachers, smaller classes, and expanded facilities. Thus, the type of community and the organization of the school has something to do with the choice between educating gifted children in regular grades or in special classes.

Another reason for resistance to the organization of special classes is the lack of clear-cut experimental evidence that the special class program produces better results than acceleration or enrichment in the regular grades. Sumption (1941) evaluated the Major Work Classes in Cleveland with a follow-up questionnaire by means of which he compared three groups, (1) one group with similar IQ's in Cleveland who did not attend the Major Work Classes, (2) one group who attended up to three years, and (3) one group who attended from four to twelve years. In comparing these groups, Sumption found little difference in physical and mental health or in attitudes toward home or family. The Major Work group did exceed the others in participation in leisure-time activities, in reading, in leadership, and in self-expressive abilities.

Barbe (1955) also made a follow-up study of the Cleveland program by means of a questionnaire to those who were graduated between 1938 and 1952. The majority of respondents approved of the Major Work Classes. Only 8 percent disapproved. In this study the factors listed as best liked were the opportunity to express themselves, the enrichment procedures, and freedom from regimentation. Least liked were the attitudes of other students and teachers and the lack of social contact with other pupils. The girls liked the foreign-language program, while the boys listed foreign language as the least liked.

During the years 1957–1961, the legislature of California appropriated funds for the purpose of studying the effects of special education (acceleration, special classes, and enrichment) on the progress of gifted children. Martinson (1961) reports that a total of 929 children in elementary and secondary schools, with IQ's of 130 and above, were selected, and educational programs were designed for them. Control groups, without these special provisions, were also established.

The results showed marked superiority in academic achievement of the children in the special programs. Although both the control and the experimental groups made notable progress in reading and arithmetic in the first grade, the experimental group made higher gains than the control group.

At the secondary level one surprising finding was the ability indicated on the Graduate Record Examination in social studies, humanities, and natural science. A comparison of both the experimental and the control groups with the scores of college graduates showed that these high school seniors scored higher than the college graduates. Again the experimental group was higher than the control group. The California study has indicated that all special provisions—special classes, acceleration, enrichment—produce results with gifted children.

ADAPTATIONS AND RECOMMENDATIONS AT THE SECONDARY LEVEL

In the preceding sections acceleration, enrichment, and special groups have been discussed as organizational methods by which programs for gifted children can be implemented, especially at the elementary school level. The same basic approaches are found in various combinations in programs at the secondary level. It may be helpful to think of these approaches to educating the gifted as attempts to provide more content, either in a homogeneous or in a heterogeneous setting (special grouping, enrichment), or to provide for faster coverage (acceleration in any form).

One of the major differences between programs for the gifted at the elementary and secondary levels results from a difference in the organization of curriculums. The child in elementary school attends a self-contained class, generally with one teacher handling all of the subjects. The secondary school does not have self-contained classes and in general allows a more flexible scheduling of students to classes according to their abilities and interests.

The comprehensive high school has been designed to offer a wide variety of educational experiences. In the larger high schools different sections of mathematics, science, and English can be adapted to the abilities and interests of the children. Sections in the various subjects can be made up of slow, average, or bright students. In addition, not all enrollees in the high school need take the same sequences of courses.

Many other adaptations have been initiated. Some of them are listed below:

1. Increase in counseling and guidance activities. This program was recently given added impetus by the provisions of the National Defense Education Act.
2. Offering extracurricular activities—school publications, science clubs, hobby clubs, student government, and so forth.

3. Organization of advanced classes in science, mathematics, English, and social studies with emphasis on ideas, concepts, and relationships rather than memory. This is sometimes called an "honors program"; it admits only those superior students who have achieved beyond the minimum requirements.

4. Allowing gifted students to take extra courses each semester to accelerate their graduation from high school.

5. Allowing students to enroll in nearby colleges and universities for courses more advanced than the high school can offer.

6. Allowing students to obtain advanced credit by examination or to enroll in correspondence and television programs for credit by examination.

7. Revision of the sequence and contents of courses in science, mathematics, language arts, social studies, and languages. Such revisions are being made by committees sponsored by professional associations and governmental agencies. An example is the Physical Science Study Committee organized in 1956 at the Massachusetts Institute of Technology. Composed of university professors, technical specialists, and high school teachers, it has been engaged in revamping a physics curriculum for secondary schools. Similar committees are at work in other subject areas—mathematics, social science and English.

WHICH PROGRAM SHOULD A GIFTED CHILD BE IN?

It is obvious that there is no *one* plan for the education of all gifted children. Each gifted child is unique unto himself, and as a group, gifted children cannot be organized under a single plan of education. Efforts to properly educate these children by one specific plan, such as acceleration, special classes, or enrichment in the regular grades, are found inadequate in some situations.

A decision on where to place a gifted child, how to organize for his education, and what teaching techniques and materials to use depends largely upon the pattern of development of that particular child and the provisions for all children in the school system. It is therefore necessary that a gifted child be evaluated in terms of his abilities, disabilities, interests, habits, home environment, and community values. The educational program for the child can be better determined on the basis of this evaluation than by setting up an educational program and fitting all gifted children into it.

Some of the adaptations and adjustments which should be taken into consideration are the following:

1. When a child's patterns of growth in physical, social, mental, and educational areas are all accelerated beyond the chronological age, acceleration in grade placement can be considered.

2. When the physical, social, and emotional areas are equal to the chronological age, but the educational achievement is advanced, a special class can be considered.

3. When the school system is too small (not providing sufficient gifted children of a particular kind for a special class), enrichment, tutoring, or special sections within the class for the gifted children in the regular classroom is necessary.

4. When the class in which a gifted child is placed contains a preponderance of children of superior intelligence, even though it is not designated as a class for the gifted, enrichment of the program is probably more desirable than special classes or acceleration, neither of which may be necessary.

5. When the child is gifted but underachieving, special attention to his social and emotional problems or possible areas of weakness is called for. Intensive counseling and parent education or even remedial instruction may be more important for this child than his placement.

6. When inner discrepancies in growth are quite marked, as we often find in children with extremely high IQ's, a tutorial or individualized method of instruction may be necessary if the child is found to be unable to adjust to other situations.

7. When school systems feel that enrichment in the regular grades is the most feasible plan, a special teacher or coordinator for gifted children is advisable. Many feel that it is unrealistic to expect every teacher to furnish enrichment in the regular grades. Teachers need the help of a specialist or consultant.

8. Since the research cited earlier indicates that acceleration by early school admission, skipping or telescoping grades, or early admission to college is not detrimental to the social and emotional development of most of the gifted children, consideration should be given to these procedures. Establishing a fixed chronological age as an entrance requirement, as is done in most school systems, is not taking into account the mental maturity of gifted children, whose mental level may be beyond 7, 8, or 9 when they are allowed to enter school.

Curriculum Planning for the Gifted

Let us now turn to the "what" of education for the gifted. What subject matter and what skills does our culture believe are essential for its members to acquire? In most schools the basic curriculum has been predetermined by the central administration or even by the state education department. This, of course, applies to the gifted as well as to other children. Special education was defined earlier as that which is over and above regular education. Wherein does the content differ for the gifted?

Some of the ways in which the content can be expanded for the gifted include the following: (1) emphasizing the gross structure and basic principles of subject matter fields rather than emphasizing individual facts; (2) placing emphasis on *how* information is derived instead of on *what* is derived; (3) taking the lead from the child's interests and understanding; (4) expanding the curriculum in breadth and depth; and (5) providing consultation and guidance.

1. *Emphasizing the gross structure and basic ideas of subject matter fields.* With the intensity of the knowledge explosion of the last few decades and the prospects for continued expansion of knowledge, curriculum experts have realized that they must do something more than merely cram more and more information into the traditional format of textbooks and classrooms. Instead of piling fact upon fact like a patchwork quilt, a new approach was needed.

In the mid-1950's experts in the fields of physical science and mathematics, and soon thereafter, those in the social sciences, English, and the humanities began to develop more basic curricula in which individual facts became less important than the structure or the basic principles and theories underlying each content field. Once he has understood these basic principles, the gifted child, with his readiness to absorb new knowledge, can easily grasp the specifics of the field.

The Physical Science Study Committee (1957), for example, selected certain core concepts to be disseminated. These more theoretical bases receive the emphasis while the facts of everyday applications are used as examples. Instead of showing that a stick looks bent when partly immersed in water, the basic principles of optics and refraction can be studied. Instead of emphasizing the mechanics of an automobile engine, the study would center on kinetic energy.

Similar developments have been occurring in other fields—mathematics, biological sciences, social sciences. In summarizing the goals of these curriculum changes Gallagher (1964) states:

There are two major features that all these curriculum developments [produced by various scientific study committees] have in common despite differences in content. One is a desire to present the basic *structure* and order of the content field in as extensive a degree as possible, given the existing knowledge of the field and the mental level of the student who is to receive this information. The second major concept that all of these curriculum projects seem to have in common is the one that *science is a method of investigating phenomena and not a product,* and that the student must be allowed to emulate the scientist. (p. 127)

2. *Placing emphasis on* how *information is derived instead of on* what *information is derived.* The new curricular developments in subject matter fields

have also stressed *method* rather than *product,* as pointed out by Gallagher in the above quotation. In science, mathematics, and social sciences, in particular, an effort is made to help the child think, utilizing the same procedures and processes as the scientist or the scholar by providing those activities and problems in which the child must follow a scientific method to solve the problem. Rather than telling the gifted child facts and figures, he is asked to derive the information himself, to delve for himself, to act like a scientist. He is thereby not only learning facts, but learning how to acquire facts and how to fit facts together to derive more fundamental theories.

Another approach which is applicable to gifted children has been developed by Suchman (1960, 1961) under the general title of *Inquiry Training.* In this type of training Suchman presents elementary school children with short films in physics, economics, and physiology. The short films present problems of cause and effect. The children attempt to solve the problems through questions that can be answered by a "yes" or a "no," or "that's your hunch" (hypothesis). The inquiry training sessions are designed to give the child a plan of operation that will assist him in discovering the causal factor through his own initiative. This procedure is in contrast to a teacher's explanation of cause and effect. The program is designed to make the children more independent, systematic, empirical, and inductive in their solution of problems. Through inquiry training, the child discovers the answers and generalization by data gathering, development of hypotheses, and the testing of them. The problems presented to children are open problems, the answers to which are not found by asking the teacher or looking in a textbook.

Another approach is used by some schools even at the elementary level. They have borrowed the *seminar* style of learning from the graduate school. This is particularly well adapted to a group of gifted children, each of whom can usually contribute something and learn something.

3. *Taking a cue from the child's interests and readiness.* Many times a young child gets interested in and asks questions about a topic that his parents and/or teachers believe he is not ready to understand. They tell him "You're too young to understand," or "You'll learn about that when you get to high school."

Many concepts traditionally reserved for high school mathematics can be taught in simplified form to very young children. Bruner (1960) advocates a spiral curriculum in which "great issues, principles, and values that a society deems worthy of continual concern to its members" should be taught "as early as possible and in a manner consistent with the child's form of thought" (p. 54). The same topics can be redeveloped in later grades, with each new approach expanding the concept within the child's own frame of reference. Thus, mathematics, set theory, logic, probability, and algebra can be instituted in the early grades, then returned to and expanded later.

In high school many gifted students have been frustrated by the rigid sequence of courses. Two young boys of the author's acquaintance were denied permission to take chemistry in their sophomore year when their interest and background information were high. They studied on their own and by the senior year were required to sign up for the required senior chemistry course, much to their own discontent and the eventual annoyance of the teacher. Many frayed nerves would have been avoided if they had either been given more flexibility with course sequences or been allowed to achieve proficiency outside of the classroom.

4. *Expanding the curriculum in both depth and breadth.* Although enrichment has not proven to be an effective approach for the gifted child in the regular class, this is mainly because of logistic and administrative problems. In a special class for the gifted such enrichment provides one of the cardinal differences in content from the regular class. Such expansion of content can be either in depth or in breadth. Enrichment in breadth involves additional reading on the same topic, extra assignments, usually at the same difficulty level, opportunity to participate in other than class activities, and permission to follow other course work, such as a foreign language or typewriting.

Expansion or enrichment in depth involves deeper and often intensive study of some aspect of the curriculum. Gallagher (1964) favors this approach, stating:

For gifted children, the approach should stress a deep and prolonged emphasis on one topic, rather than a superficial bee-flitting approach to many topics. The particular area of study, whether plant life, astronomy, or physics, is probably not terribly important. What *is* important is that the student experience the excitement of inquiry, of striving to solve a difficult problem and, finally, of understanding, in depth, the topic under study. (p. 130)

Enrichment in depth is commonly used in social studies. The gifted student's proclivity for asking "how" and "why" makes him very open to further investigation of a given topic. It allows the gifted student to delve into the historical background of a given event, or the effects of a certain policy on the people or nations involved.

5. *Providing consultation and guidance.* With the broad range of subject matter available and the far-flung interests of gifted children, the teacher would need to be a walking encyclopedia in order to be able to fulfill every need of these children. Therefore, it is often necessary to call an expert into the class or send a child or group of children to an outside expert for further information and guidance. In the elementary school, team teaching is sometimes used so as to give instruction in specific areas by competent teachers. This is an administrative measure affecting the content area.

In academic decisions the gifted child needs guidance which he may or may not recognize. The high school student, for example, wants to take an extra course but may not recognize that he should fulfill certain prerequisites. Another may read widely in unrelated fields and lack the discipline to organize his disparate knowledge. One underachieving gifted boy, for instance, could not be motivated to pursue the requirements of a standard high school course in literature, but when allowed to select a field of reading (science fiction), he pursued a formidable independent reading course and turned in top-notch papers. He would not have had the discipline or direction to accomplish this without the integrating advice he received.

Instructional Procedures

Adaptation of instruction is dependent upon what is to be taught and the characteristics of the individuals. Two general topics will be discussed below: (1) developing creativity and (2) suggestions for instructional practice.

DEVELOPING CREATIVITY

Whether a school provides for its gifted through special schools and classes, through acceleration, or through enrichment in the regular grades, an effort can be made to expand the horizons and extend the abilities of these children. To accomplish this aim workers have taken into consideration Guilford's analysis of the intellectual process discussed on page 128. It should be recalled that Guilford's components of intelligence include five basic operations: (1) cognition, (2) memory, (3) divergent thinking, (4) convergent thinking, and (5) evaluation. The second and third of these abilities are sometimes linked together under the concept of productive thinking. Both divergent production and convergent production have a place in constructive thought, but Guilford has found that divergent thinking produces more creative ideas whereas convergent thinking tends to produce the conventional and more commonly accepted responses.

In another dimension of Guilford's structure of intellect are hypothesized "transformations," in which some item of information becomes something else. "Transformations are changes, revisions, redefinitions, or modifications, by which any product of information in one state goes over into another state" (Guilford, 1967b, p. 64). In this category of behavior are included such activities as seeing unusual relationships, finding hidden figures, finding remote associations, redefining problems, rearranging the letters of a word to make other words. Guilford believes that the use of this type of thinking in conjunction with such qualities as divergent-production typifies the mental activities of the creative individual.

An effective educational program will develop this kind of thinking, utilizing the basic abilities of cognition and memory to provide the raw material and evaluative abilities to measure the end result. But the school must do more than pass on to new generations the facts and ideas it has acquired; it has the responsibility of developing the ability to create new ideas, to see problems in a new light, to realign facts and interrelationships. This should be part of the content for gifted children.

Wilson (1958) has some suggestions for the development of creative thinking in children, some of which follow:

Brainstorming. First the rules are set down: (1) no criticism of any idea presented; (2) the wilder the idea the better; and (3) the greater the number of ideas the better. Then a question is posed, such as: What can we do to make school more interesting?

Stimulating sensitivity to problems. The children are asked to discuss what would happen if everyone in the world became deaf, or if we all had three fingers, or if someone invented a pill as a substitute for all food.

Encouraging ideational fluency. The children are asked to list all the ways a brick can be used, or in how many ways water can be made to work for one.

Encouraging originality. Activities and assignments in class can deliberately seek to produce uncommon or unusual responses. Pupils are asked to look for a different way of doing something.

Encouraging redefinition ability. In this activity the pupil is faced with a problem such as: If you went to a picnic and forgot a frying pan what would you use instead?

It will be noted from the emphasis on creativity that the pendulum has swung from centering educational procedures on developing cognition, memory, and convergent thinking to an emphasis on divergent production and evaluation of ideas. In a strong criticism of education, Silberman (1970) points out that the sterile nature of schools emphasizes conformity to rules and curricula. Instead, he advocates a school that allows initiative and creativity to become predominant in the organization of the school environment. Whether what is good for the gifted is good for everyone is for time to tell. No major evaluation has been made over a sufficient time period to justify drawing definitive conclusions from studies on the educability of creative thinking.

Gifted children have particular mental qualifications for achievement, particularly in the academic subjects of the elementary school. Certain instructional modifications and changes in materials are necessary if a child's program is to be adequate either in a special class, under acceleration, or in the regular grades. The following suggestions for instructional practices are based on qualitative or quantitative differences between gifted and average children:

1. *Characteristic:* Gifted children learn faster than the average child.

Teaching suggestions: Because of their rapid learning, they require less repetition to learn the same material. If a gifted child takes his first-grade reader home some night and finishes it, he should not be required to go over it page by page with the rest of the class but should be allowed to go ahead with supplementary reading, even though the teacher must take precautions to see that he has actually acquired the necessary learning she expects from the basic reader.

Gifted children do need drill on some things, but usually less of it. Not having had to go through endless drill in order to learn things, they are often impatient with excessive drill on mechanical operations such as arithmetic computation facts. They prefer problem-solving exercises to mechanical drill periods. They would usually prefer to figure out why 7 and 8 are 15 than to memorize $7 + 8 = 15$. They tend to learn rationally rather than by sheer memory and sometimes need to be helped to appreciate the efficiency acquired by learning some things automatically, even though that entails the boring task of repetitive memorizing of facts and tables of numbers. Often the drill can be concealed in assignments which have a meaningful appeal. In learning number facts, for instance, some of the drill may take the form of finding out how many ways 10 may be broken up, or playing games which require number combinations.

2. *Characteristic:* The reasoning ability of gifted children is superior to that of other children.

Teaching suggestions: The fact that they see relationships and grasp ideas more readily, wonderful as this is, creates certain pitfalls for the teacher. The child often demands an explanation and a reason which goes into greater detail than the teacher is able to give or is ready to present to the rest of the class. Gifted children would like to be able to reason problems through and understand them, and the teacher must be prepared to help them do so.

The inverse situation is also true at times, when the gifted child must be helped to analyze the steps by which he arrived at a certain result or conclusion. His reasoning ability is sometimes so quick that he derives an answer without going through the routine steps required by the average child. This is particularly the case in some arithmetical problems. The child sometimes needs help in analyzing the thinking process and understanding a routine when he has to apply it later to more complicated situations.

The gifted child's ability to perceive relationships quickly makes it possible for him to complete assignments faster than other children. He may finish in ten minutes what he is allowed thirty minutes to do. Teachers should be on the alert and see that he is not permitted to just sit or get into mischief and distract others.

His reasoning ability creates greater depth of understanding. He is often able to delve deeper into problems, is able to sense more subtle relationships, and comes up with conclusions and generalizations beyond those expected of a child of his age. This trait should not be overlooked but fostered and developed.

3. *Characteristic:* Gifted children usually have a large vocabulary.

Teaching suggestions: Even though the vocabulary used by these children is above the comprehension of the rest of the class, gifted children should be given an opportunity to express themselves, particularly in writing, in reports, and in explanation and discussion in the classroom. One of the goals for their development can be to learn how to say the same thing in simpler terms, to be sensitive to what the rest of the class can understand. As an example, the child might be asked to explain what he has said to a younger child. The gifted child who tends to monopolize the class discussions should be helped to put himself in other people's shoes in order to be more sensitive to those around him.

4. *Characteristic:* The gifted child has a broad fund of information.

Teaching suggestions: Because of his keen memory and ability to relate and retain information, he may be expected to know more than other children. One teacher complained, "This child brings many facts which are not explained in the textbook. I don't know where he gets them." She was not prepared to handle this additional information. Because the child had read and remembered a great deal, he did not stick to the assigned textbook but covered the topic in a much broader way, disconcerting the teacher, who wanted the class to learn a particular lesson in a particular textbook. The teacher should encourage such broader approaches, although it may mean some additional homework for herself.

5. *Characteristic:* The gifted child has an insatiable curiosity.

Teaching suggestions: Because he is fascinated with imaginative activities, is interested in science, wants to know the whys and wherefores of many things, the instructional procedure for this child is, not to try to keep him from delving into new problems, but to utilize this curiosity as a motivating factor in further study.

6. *Characteristic:* The gifted child has a wide range of interests.

Teaching suggestions: Because he often has an intense drive, particularly in intellectual pursuits, it is sometimes difficult to get him to put aside what he has begun in order to follow the class routine. The way to handle this depends on the rigidity of the class organization. Sometimes the routine lesson of the class period is not necessary nor applicable to the more advanced child. If the teacher expects each child to complete identical assignments, whether or not they are of value to all, she may have difficulty with her gifted children. But if individual interest can be utilized to develop the tools and abilities, the gifted child may be able to "kill two birds with one stone." The task of the teacher here is to relate the interests to the developmental area. A particular child who has already mastered a certain technique can be excused from a routine assignment and allowed to take up some other interest. There are times, of course, when routine tasks must be accomplished before more appealing activities are pursued.

7. *Characteristic:* Gifted children are usually socially adjusted and popular with other children.

Teaching suggestions: Although these children are usually not odd or maladjusted (as believed by some in the past) they may be made that way if their creative abilities, deviant behavior, and lack of conformity are dampened. They may develop a self-concept of being eccentric and different and then attempt to isolate themselves from the group. Teachers can assist in fostering a worthwhile self-concept in children who have these bents.

8. *Characteristic:* The gifted child may be critical and dissatisfied with his own achievement.

Teaching suggestions: Auto-criticism is an asset, provided the individual does not become critical of everything he does and ceases to produce because he cannot be satisfied with his own production. Teachers should watch for marked auto-criticism and should help the child to become satisfied with what he can do at each particular stage of development.

9. *Characteristic:* Gifted children are usually observant.

Teaching suggestions: Advantage should be taken of their ability to perceive things to which other children are often oblivious. Since these children tend to grasp more phenomena from a particular experience, they should be encouraged to interrelate them and correlate them with other experiences. Taking advantage of this tendency, teachers may be able to allow them to go beyond the class in some assignments, or the child may be allowed to do a special study assignment on some experience.

10. *Characteristic:* Many gifted children show creative abilities as discussed on pages 127 to 131.

Teaching suggestions: Divergent suggestions should be received with respect, and the child should be helped to evaluate the applicability of his own suggestions to the situation at hand. It sometimes requires considerable flexibility and creativity on the part of the teacher to transform wild suggestion into valid ones, but the teacher should try to find what value or applicability there may be in the divergent suggestion and recognize that the divergent suggestion is the child's own attempt to find a valid suggestion.

Producing creative ideas is an asset that should be cultivated. Torrance (1967) has suggested a number of ways of doing this. These include: (1) encouraging and reinforcing self-initiated learning on the part of pupils, (2) permitting children to learn on their own, without being given assignment, (3) learning through a responsive environment, in which gifted children's curiosity propels them to learn, (4) revising our concepts of readiness such as requiring the child to wait until a certain age to study specific content, (5) assisting them to search for themselves, their self-concepts, and (6) helping them search for and develop their uniqueness. Torrance (1962) has also described and illustrated numerous teaching skills that can be used by teachers to facilitate creative growth.

SUMMARY

1. Gifted children have been defined as those who have superior ability to deal with facts, ideas, and relationships. Talented children and youth have been defined as those who have special aptitudes in specific areas such as music, art, social leadership, mechanics, and so forth. These are not distinct differences since talented children usually are gifted intellectually, and most intellectually gifted children have talent in some area.

2. Identification of gifted children is accomplished by a combination of procedures—teacher's referral, achievement in school, and group and individual intelligence tests.

3. Dissatisfaction with the IQ as the sole measure of giftedness is growing. Newer instruments are being developed to measure creative or productive thinking.

4. The prevalence of gifted children in a school system is contingent upon the criteria used and the socioeconomic status of the community. The prevalence is estimated to be one-half of one percent (in an average community if an IQ of 140 and above is taken as a criterion) to 16 to 20 percent (if an IQ of 115 is the criterion).

5. The studies on gifted children, particularly those of Terman, who defined giftedness as having an IQ above 140, indicated that (a) in physical and health characteristics they were superior to the general population; (b) they were advanced in school subjects two to four years beyond the average; (c) their intellectual maturity was maintained in adulthood; (d) their interests were more in abstract than in practical subjects; (e) their mental health and adjustment were superior to those of other children while in school, and fewer of them developed serious maladjustment or delinquency; and (f) eight times more gifted men entered the professions than was true for the general population.

6. Special attention is directed to special groups of intellectually gifted children such as underachievers, children with very high IQ's, and gifted children with handicaps.

7. Creativity is thought of as divergent-production ability (flexibility, fluency, originality, elaboration) plus the ability to make transformations—to redefine, revise, rearrange facts into new relationships.

8. Creative children, when given an opportunity to uitlize their creativity to gain knowledge, achieve as well in school as noncreative children of higher IQ.

9. Adaptation of a school program to a gifted child can best be accomplished by noting his discrepancies in physical, social, emotional, intellectual, and academic growth.
10. The three organizational procedures which have been used to adapt instruction for the gifted are (a) acceleration, (b) enrichment, and (c) special schools and classes. All of these methods have proved to be of value.
11. Modifications in content include:
    (a) Emphasizing the gross structure and basic ideas of subject matter fields.
    (b) Placing emphasis on *how* information is derived rather than on *what* information is derived.
    (c) Taking a cue from the child's interests and readiness.
    (d) Expanding the curriculum in both depth and breadth.
    (e) Providing consultation and guidance.
12. Modifications in teaching are necessitated by (1) attempts to develop creativity and (2) the unique characteristics of gifted children.

REFERENCES

Barbe, W. B. 1956. A Study of the Family Background of the Gifted. *Journal of Educational Psychology* 47 (May): 302–309.

————. 1955. Evaluation of Special Classes for Gifted Children. *Exceptional Children* 22 (November): 60–62.

Birch, J. W. 1954. Early School Admission for Mentally Advanced Children. *Exceptional Children* 21 (December): 84–87.

Bruner, J. S. 1960. *The Process of Education.* Cambridge, Massachusetts: Harvard University Press.

Cicirelli, V. G. 1965. Form of the Relationship Between Creativity, IQ, and Academic Achievement. *Journal of Educational Psychology* 56 (December): 303–308.

Clarke, C. M.; Veldman, D. D.; and Thorpe, J. S. 1965. Convergent and Divergent Thinking Abilities of Talented Adolescents. *Journal of Educational Psychology* 56 (June) 157–163.

Cox, Catherine M. 1926. *Genetic Studies of Genius: The Early Mental Traits of Three Hundred Geniuses,* Vol. II. Stanford, California: Stanford University Press.

Damm, V. J. 1970. Creativity and Intelligence: Research Implications for Equal Emphasis in High School. *Exceptional Children* 37 (April): 565–569.

DeHaan, R. F., and Havighurst, R. J. 1957. *Educating Gifted Children.* Chicago: University of Chicago Press.

Dyer, F. L., and Martin, T. C. 1929. *Edison: His Life and Inventions,* Vols. I and II. New York: Harper and Brothers.

Education for the Gifted: Fifty-Seventh Yearbook of the National Society for the Study of Education, Part II. 1958. Chicago: University of Chicago Press.

Fliegler, L. A., and Bish, C. E. 1959. Summary of Research on the Academically Talented Student. *Review of Educational Research* 29 (December): 408–450.

Frierson, E. C. 1969. *Education of Exceptional Children: Review of Educational Research* 39 (February): 25–35.

Fund for the Advancement of Education. 1957. *They Went to College Early*. New York: The Fund.

Gallagher, J. J. 1964. *Teaching the Gifted Child*. Boston: Allyn and Bacon.

————. 1960. *Analysis of Research on the Education of Gifted Children*. Springfield, Illinois: Office of the Superintendent of Public Instruction.

————. 1959. *The Gifted Child in the Elementary School*. Washington, D.C.: American Educational Research Association, National Education Association.

————. 1958. Social Status of Children Related to Intelligence, Propinquity, and Social Perception. *Elementary School Journal* 58, (January): 225–231.

Getzels, J. W., and Jackson, P. W. 1960. The Study of Giftedness: A Multidimensional Approach. *The Gifted Student*. Cooperative Research Monograph No. 2, pp. 1–18. Washington, D.C.: U.S. Department of Health, Education, and Welfare.

Gloss, G., and Jones, R. L. 1968. Correlates of School District Provisions for Gifted Children: A Statewide Study. Paper presented at the annual meeting of the Council for Exceptional Children, New York.

Goetsch, Helen B. 1940. *Parental Income and College Opportunities*. Teachers College Contributions to Education, No. 795. New York: Teachers College, Columbia University.

Gold, M. J. 1965. *Education of the Intellectually Gifted*. Columbus, Ohio: Charles E. Merrill.

Gowan, J. C. 1967. What Makes a Gifted Child Creative?—Four Theories. In Gowan, J. C.; Demos, G. D.; and Torrance, E. P. (eds.), *Creativity: Its Educational Implication*. New York: John Wiley.

————. 1957. Dynamics of the Underachievement of Gifted Students. *Exceptional Children* 24: 98–101.

Guilford, J. P. 1967a. Potentiality for Creativity. In Gowan, J. C.; Demos, G. D.; and Torrance, E. P. (eds.), *Creativity: Its Educational Implication*. New York: John Wiley.

————. 1967b. *The Nature of Human Intelligence*. New York: McGraw-Hill.

————. 1959. Three Faces of Intellect. *American Psychologist* 14 (August): 469–479.

Havighurst, R. 1958. In *Education for the Gifted: Fifty-Seventh Yearbook of the National Society for the Study of Education,* Part II. Chicago: University of Chicago Press.

Hildreth, Gertrude H. 1966. *Introduction to the Gifted*. New York: McGraw-Hill.

Hobson, J. R. 1956. Scholastic Standing and Activity Participation of Underage High School Pupils Originally Admitted to Kindergarten on the Basis of Physical and Psychological Examinations. *Newsletter* (September). American Psychological Association, Division of School Psychologists.

————. 1948. Mental Age as a Workable Criterion for School Admission. *Elementary School Journal* 48 (February): 312–321.

Hollingworth, Leta. 1942. *Children Above 180 IQ*. Yonkers-on-Hudson, New York: World.

Jansen, Verna G., and Gallagher, J. J. 1966. The Social Choices of Students in Racially Integrated Classes for the Culturally Disadvantaged Talented. *Exceptional Children* 33 (December): 221–226.

Kerstetter, Leona. 1952. A Sociometric Study of the Classroom Roles of a Group of Highly Gifted Children in Elementary School. *Elementary School Journal* 58 (May): 465–470.

Kirk, Winifred D. 1966. A Tentative Screening Procedure for Selecting Bright and Slow Children in Kindergarten. *Exceptional Children* 33 (December): 235–241.

Kough, J. 1960. Administrative Provisions for the Gifted. In Shertzer, B. (ed.) *Working with Superior Students*. Chicago: Science Research Associates.

Kough, J., and DeHaan, R. F. 1955. *Teacher's Guidance Handbook I: Identifying Children Who Need Help*. Chicago: Science Research Associates.

Lucito, L. 1963. Gifted Children. In Dunn, L. (ed.), *Exceptional Children in the Schools*. New York: Holt, Rinehart, and Winston.

———. 1959. A Comparison of the Independence-Conformity Behavior of Intellectually Bright and Dull Children. Unpublished doctoral dissertation, University of Illinois.

Marsh, R. W. 1964. A Statistical Re-Analysis of Getzels and Jackson's Data. *British Journal of Educational Psychology* 34 (February): 91–93.

Martinson, Ruth A. 1966. Issues in the Identification of the Gifted. *Exceptional Children* 33 (September): 13–16.

———. 1961. *Educational Programs for Gifted Children*. Sacramento: California State Department of Public Instruction.

Martinson, Ruth A., and Seagoe, May V. 1967. *The Abilities of Young Children*. Arlington, Virginia: Council for Exceptional Children.

Martyn, K. A. 1957. The Social Acceptance of Gifted Students. Unpublished doctoral dissertation, Stanford University.

Mill, J. S. 1924. *Autobiography*. New York: Columbia University Press.

Miller, R. V. 1956. Social Status and Socio-emphatic Differences Among Mentally Superior, Mentally Typical, and Mentally Retarded Children. *Exceptional Children* 23 (December): 114–119.

Pegnato, W., and Birch, J. W. 1959. Locating Gifted Children in Junior High School. *Exceptional Children* 26 (March): 303–304.

Physical Science Study Committee, The. 1957. *First Annual Report of the Physical Science Study Committee*. Watertown, Massachusetts.

Pregler, H. 1954. The Colfax Plan. *Exceptional Children* 21 (September): 198–201, 222.

Pressey, S. L. 1960. Concerning the Nature and Nurture of Genius. In French, J. L. (ed.), *Educating the Gifted*. New York: Henry Holt.

———. 1949. *Educational Acceleration: Appraisal and Basic Problems*. Educational Research Monograph, No. 31. Columbus, Ohio: Bureau of Educational Research, Ohio State University.

Reiser, A. 1930. *Albert Einstein*. New York: Albert and Charles Boni.

Reynolds, M. C. 1962. A Framework for Considering Some Issues in Special Education. *Exceptional Children* 29 (March): 367–370.

Silberman, C. E. 1970. *Crisis in the Schools*. New York: Random House.

Smith, D. C. 1959. Inter- and Intrapersonal Adjustment of Adolescents Testing at the Superior and Average Levels of Intelligence. Unpublished doctoral dissertation, Syracuse University.

Suchman, R. 1961. Inquiry Training: Building Skills for Autonomous Discovery. *Merrill-Palmer Quarterly* 7: 147–169.

———. 1960. Inquiry Training in Elementary School. *The Science Teacher* 27: 42–47.

Strodbeck, F. L. 1958. Family Interaction, Values, and Achievement. In McClelland, D. C.

(ed.), *Talent and Society: New Perspectives in the Identification of Talent*. Princeton, New Jersey: Van Nostrand.

Sumption, Merle R. 1941. *Three Hundred Gifted Children*. Yonkers-on-Hudson, New York: World.

Sumption, Merle R., and Luecking, Evelyn M. 1960. *Education of the Gifted*. New York: Ronald Press.

Terman, L. M. (ed.). 1925–1959. *Genetic Studies of Genius*, Vols. I–V. Stanford, California: Stanford University Press.

Terman, L. M., and Oden, Melita. 1951. The Stanford Studies of the Gifted. In Witty, P. (ed.), *The Gifted Child*. Boston: D. C. Heath.

———. (eds). 1947. *The Gifted Child Grows Up: Genetic Studies of Genius*, Vol. IV. Stanford, California: Stanford University Press.

Time magazine, February 17, 1958, pp. 21–25.

Torrance, E. P. 1967. Toward the More Human Education of Gifted Children. In Gowan, J. C.; Demos, G. D.; and Torrance, E. P. (eds.), *Creativity: Its Educational Implication*. New York: John Wiley.

———. 1966. *Torrance Tests of Creative Thinking*. Princeton, New Jersey: Personnel Press.

———. 1962. *Guiding Creative Talent*. Englewood Cliffs, N. J.: Prentice-Hall.

———. 1959. *Explorations in Creative Thinking in the Early School Years VI: Highly Intelligent and Highly Creative Children in a Laboratory School*. Minneapolis: Bureau of Educational Research, University of Minnesota.

Wallach, M. A., and Kogan, N. 1965. *Cognitive Originality Physiognomic Sensitivity, and Defensiveness in Children*. U.S. Office of Education, Cooperative Research Project No. 1316B. Durham, North Carolina: Duke University.

Ward, V. S. 1962. *The Gifted Student: A Manual for Program Development*. Atlanta, Georgia: Southern Regional Education Board.

Weiner, N. 1953. *Ex-Prodigy: My Childhood and Youth*. New York: Simon and Schuster.

Wilson, R. 1958. Creativity. In *Education for the Gifted: Fifty-Seventh Yearbook of the National Society for the Study of Education*, Part II, pp. 108–128. Chicago: University of Chicago Press.

Worcester, D. A. 1956. *The Education of Children of Above-Average Mentality*. Lincoln, Nebraska: University of Nebraska Press.

Yamamoto, K. 1965. Creativity: A Blind Man's Report on the Elephant. *Journal of Counseling Psychology* 12 (Winter): 428–434.

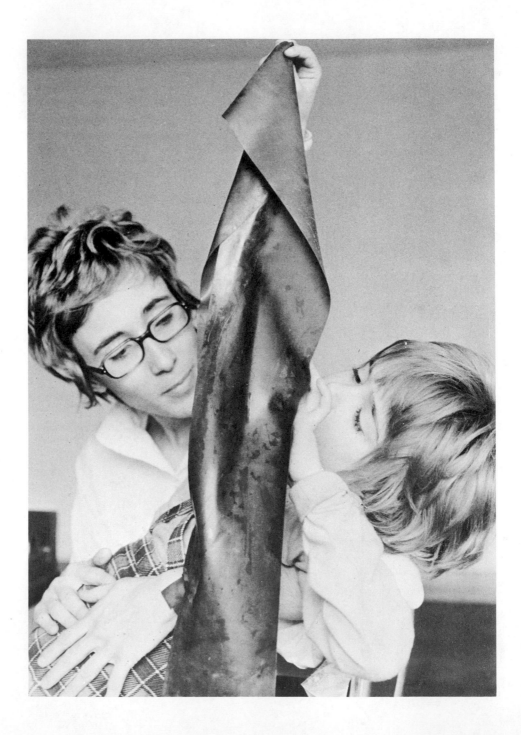

FIVE

CHILDREN

WITH

LOW

INTELLIGENCE

In Chapter 1, Figure 1–1 was presented to show the distribution of intelligence according to the Stanford revision of the Binet Scale. It will be recalled that the lower end of the distribution of intelligence included the slow learner and various degrees of mental retardation. This chapter is devoted to a further study of those children whose learning ability and general adaptation to society are below average.

Children with low intelligence have been of interest to various workers—physicians, psychologists, educators, sociologists, geneticists, and others—and each area has evolved its own classification, concepts, and terminology. As a result, the beginning student becomes quite confused with such different terms as feeble minded, mentally deficient, dementia, amentia, slow learner, mentally handicapped, mentally retarded, idiot, imbecile, moron, oligophrenia, exogenous, endogenous, educable, trainable, totally dependent, custodial, and many other terms referring to children with low intelligence. This chapter will review the different definitions, classifications, causes, and the prevalence of children with low intelligence.

Definitions of Mental Retardation

There have been numerous attempts to define mental retardation. Since the beginning of history, man has had to deal with the problems of children with low intelligence. The problems of identification, definition, classification, and etiology have been extensive in view of the fact that many disciplines work with retarded children and each looks at the child from its own perspective. For that reason, no one definition of "retarded children" has been generally accepted by all.

Although psychologists, psychiatrists, social workers, educators, and others have had a difficult time finding a satisfactory definition for mental retardation, a close analysis of the problem reveals many reasons for the difficulty. Mental retardation is not a disease like tuberculosis or cancer, but a condition. An inclusive definition of mental retardation must describe those manifestations of the condition which pertain to all cases. The difficulty of finding a generally satisfactory definition is obvious when one tries to define a heterogeneous group consisting of different types and degrees of many factors on a continuum. For example, how do we define a "small man"? Are small men all those who are less than 5 feet in height? Suppose some men below 5 feet weigh more than some men above 6 feet. Are they still "small men"? Or do we add a weight criterion and say that all men below 5 feet who weigh less than 120 pounds are considered small men? Similarly, in defining mental retardation we must include many criteria and thus arrive at a multi-dimensional definition. We find ourselves with overlapping medical, social, psychological, economic, physical, and educational factors.

Towards the end of the thirteenth century a legal distinction was made in England between what they called a "born fool," or an idiot, and a "lunatic," the latter being defined as a person who "hath had understanding, but by disease, grief, or other accident, hath lost the use of his reason" (Report of the Mental Deficiency Committee, 1929). Tredgold (1937), one of the early medical authorities, defines mental deficiency as:

A state of incomplete development of such a kind and degree that the individual is incapable of adapting himself to the normal environment of his fellows in such a way as to maintain existence independently of supervision, control, or external support. (p. 407)

It is interesting to note that this definition did not incorporate medical concepts, but used primarily sociological ones. This definition was concerned with the degree of adaptation of the individual to his environment.

Edgar Doll (1941) furnished a more complex definition of mental deficiency. He asserted that a mentally deficient person is: (1) socially incompetent, that is, socially inadequate and occupationally incompetent and unable to manage his own affairs at the adult level; (2) mentally subnormal; (3) retarded intellectually from birth or early age; (4) retarded at maturity; (5) mentally deficient as a result of constitutional origin, through heredity or disease; and (f) essentially incurable.

There have been many other attempts to define mental retardation, all of which are variations of either Tredgold's or Doll's definition. The most recent one (Heber, 1961) has been formulated by the American Association on Mental Deficiency: "Mental retardation refers to subaverage general intellectual functioning which originates during the developmental period and is associated with impairment in adaptive behavior" (p. 499). Subaverage intellectual function in this definition refers to one standard deviation below the general population mean on a standard intelligence test. Impairment in adaptive behavior refers to deficiencies in (1) maturation, (2) learning, and (3) social adjustment.

One can devote a great deal of time in attempting to define mental retardation, but what is really needed is the delineation of the characteristics of children with various degrees of mental retardation. This can be more clearly described after a discussion of attempts to classify these individuals.

Classification

Since mentally retarded children constitute a heterogeneous group, it has become necessary to separate these children into subgroups which have homogeneous characteristics. The following discussion of classification will include subgroupings under (1) the medical-biological classification, (2) the social-psychological classification, and (3) classification for educational purposes.

THE MEDICAL-BIOLOGICAL CLASSIFICATION

From a medical point of view, mental retardation is regarded as a result of some underlying disease process or defective biological condition. It is natural that a medical classification would consider etiological (causal) factors. Heber (1959) lists the medical categories of etiology as diseases due to infection, intoxication, trauma, disorders of metabolism, and so forth. This is a classification of causes, and in general includes about one quarter of the number of the mentally retarded. It is possible that when medical sciences progress further, other diseases will be found which will explain the cause in some of the cases now considered "cause unknown."

SOCIAL-PSYCHOLOGICAL CLASSIFICATION

A functional and descriptive classification was developed by the American Association on Mental Deficiency. This includes the categories mild, moderate, severe, and profound. A description of the developmental characteristics of these four degrees of mentally retarded children is presented in Table 5–1.

EDUCATIONAL CLASSIFICATION

Children with low intelligence are classified educationally into four groups: (1) the slow learner (IQ 80 to 90); (2) the educable mentally retarded (IQ 50–55 to 75–79); (3) the trainable mentally retarded (IQ 30–35 to 50–55); and (4) the totally dependent or profoundly mentally retarded (IQ below 25–30). Since educational programs for the mentally retarded deal with the (1) educable, (2) trainable, and (3) totally dependent, these will be defined further.

The Educable Mentally Retarded Child. An educable mentally retarded child is one who, because of subnormal mental development, is unable to profit sufficiently from the program of the regular elementary school, but who is considered to have potentialities for development in three areas: (1) educability in academic subjects of the school at a minimum level, (2) educability in social adjustment to a point where he can get along independently in the community, and (3) minimal occupational adequacies to such a degree that he can later support himself partially or totally at the adult level.

In most instances the educable retarded child is not known to be retarded during infancy and early childhood. His retardation and growth in mental and social activities can be noted only if observed closely during the preschool years. Most of the time the growth is normal and his retardation is not evident until he shows poor learning ability in school. In most instances there are no obvious pathological conditions that account for his retardation.

The Trainable Mentally Retarded Child. The trainable mentally retarded child is one who is not educable in the sense of academic achievement, ultimate social adjustment independently in the community, or independent occupational adjustment at the adult level. This is what differentiates a trainable mentally retarded child from an educable mentally retarded child. The trainable mentally retarded child, however, has potentialities for learning: (1) self-help skills, (2) social adjustment in the family and in the neighborhood, and (3) economic usefulness in the home, in a residential school, or in a sheltered workshop. In most instances, such children will be known to be retarded during infancy and early childhood. The retardation is generally noted because of known clinical

TABLE 5–1

*Developmental characteristics
of the mentally retarded*

Degrees of mental retardation	Pre-School age 0–5 Maturation and development	School age 6–20 Training and education	Adult 21 and over Social and vocational adequacy
Mild	Can develop social and communication skills; minimal retardation in sensorimotor areas; often not distinguished from normal until later age.	Can learn academic skills up to approximately sixth grade level by late teens. Can be guided toward social conformity. "Educable"	Can usually achieve social and vocational skills adequate to minimum self-support but may need guidance and assistance when under unusual social or economic stress.
Moderate	Can talk or learn to communicate; poor social awareness; fair motor development; profits from training in self-help; can be managed with moderate supervision.	Can profit from training in social and occupational skills; unlikely to progress beyond second grade level in academic subjects; may learn to travel alone in familiar places.	May achieve self-maintenance in unskilled or semi-skilled work under sheltered conditions; needs supervision and guidance when under mild social or economic stress.
Severe	Poor motor development; speech is minimal; generally unable to profit from training in self-help; little or no communication skills.	Can talk or learn to communicate; can be trained in elemental health habits; profits from systematic habit training.	May contribute partially to self-maintenance under complete supervision; can develop self-protection skills to a minimal useful level in controlled environment.
Profound	Gross retardation; minimal capacity for functioning in sensorimotor areas; needs nursing care.	Some motor development present; may respond to minimum or limited training in self-help.	Some motor and speech development; may achieve very limited self-care; needs nursing care.

Source: The Problem of Mental Retardation, U.S. Department of Health, Education, and Welfare, Office of the Secretary, Secretary's Committee on Mental Retardation (Washington, D.C. Government Printing Office, 1969).

or physical stigmata or deviations, and because the children are markedly delayed in talking and walking.

The Totally Dependent or Custodial Mentally Retarded Child. The totally dependent child is one who, because of very severe mental retardation, is unable to be trained in total self-care, socialization, or economic usefulness and who needs continued help in taking care of his personal needs. Such a child requires almost complete care and supervision throughout his life, since he is unable to survive without help.

OTHER CLASSIFICATIONS AND TERMS

With the exception of the medical-biological classification, most disciplines attempt to designate a group primarily by degree of mental subnormality. The National Association for Retarded Children uses a more social adjustment concept for the different degrees, namely—Marginally Dependent (IQ's 50–75); Semi-Dependent (IQ's 25–50) and Dependent (IQ's below 25). The World Health Organization prefers Mild Subnormality (IQ 50–69); Moderate Subnormality (IQ 20–49); and Severe Subnormality (IQ 0–19). The American Psychiatric Association uses Mildly Mentally Deficient (IQ 70–85); Moderately Mentally Deficient (IQ 50–70); and Severely Mentally Deficient (IQ 0–50). With the exception of slight variations in IQ levels, the various terms and levels correspond to the psychosocial and educational classifications.

GROWTH PATTERNS OF CHILDREN WITH LOW INTELLIGENCE

Children with varying degrees of low intelligence present different growth patterns. In Figure 5–1, four children of differing degrees of intelligence are represented. Each child is 10 years old. The chronological age is the only point on the profile which is the same for all four children. Case A is a slow learner; Case B an educable mentally retarded child; Case C, a trainable retarded child; and Case D, a totally dependent retarded child.

It will be noted that the 10-year-old slow-learning child (Case A) is quite a bit like the average 10-year-old in the physical areas of height, weight, and motor coordination. With an IQ of 87 he is a little more than a year retarded mentally below his chronological age, about half a year in social maturity, and between 1 and 2 years on all other characteristics. His reading, for example, is at a third-grade level although he is placed in the fifth grade in school. This child is able to get along in the regular grades even though he is below his grade placement in general educational achievement. In most fifth grades there are a

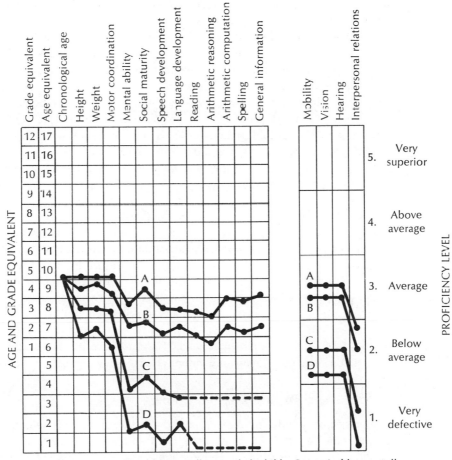

A = slow learner; B = educable mentally retarded child; C = trainable mentally retarded child; D = totally dependent mentally retarded child

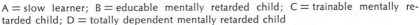

number of children who are doing third-grade work, a few more who are doing fourth-grade work, many who are doing fifth-grade work, some who are doing sixth-grade work, and even a few who are capable of doing seventh- and eighth-grade work. Thus a fifth grade in the regular school has an achievement range of about two years below to two years above that grade. We expect the regular grade to provide instruction adapted to children within this range of ability. For that reason, slow-learning children are not considered mentally retarded and tend to remain in the regular grades rather than being placed in special classes, particularly in the elementary school.

The 10-year-old educable mentally retarded child in Figure 5–1 (Case B) has a Binet IQ of 72. This child is doing beginning second-grade work in school. The discrepancy between his achievement and that of the average child of his age is quite marked and he is unable to cope with the regular school program. Although a child with third-grade reading and arithmetic may be able to struggle through a fifth-grade program, first- or second-grade achievement leaves too large a gap. The educable mentally retarded child therefore requires some special educational provisions in or outside of the regular grades.

The profile of a trainable mentally retarded child (Case C) shows discrepancies in growth much wider than those of the educable child. Here we find an IQ of 40 and a mental level of 4 years. Physical development in terms of height and motor coordination is also considerably retarded, but not as much as mental ability. Speech, language, and general information are also close to the 4-year level. In reading, spelling, and arithmetic the profile is shown with broken lines, indicating that the child has not begun to achieve in these subjects.

Case D with an IQ of 20 shows still greater discrepancies in growth and a wider difference between his development and that of an average child or even an educable or trainable one. This child has not developed to a point where he can do anything for himself. Even as late as 16 or 17 years of age he may not be able to take care of his personal needs. He must be cared for by others and for that reason is called a totally dependent child.

THE DISADVANTAGES OF CLASSIFYING CHILDREN

The preceding sections on definitions and classifications are based on the concept of interindividual differences in which children are compared to each other on a continuum. Classification of children on the basis of intelligence scores, together with current practices for assignment to special programs leaves much to be desired. Class placement according to IQ alone does not consider intraindividual differences which are more relevant to educational needs than are levels of intelligence. Two children classified as educable mentally retarded, both having IQ's in the 70's, may differ widely in their educational needs.

Case E was assigned to a class for the educable mentally retarded. His Chronological Age was 7–6. His Stanford-Binet Mental Age was 5–6, with an IQ of 71. He had not learned to read anything after one year of school, and according to the teacher seemed unable to learn. After enrollment in the special class he was given the Illinois Test of Psycholinguistic Abilities (ITPA). The profile is presented in Figure 5–2.

It will be noted from Figure 5–2 that Case E is retarded in all psycholinguistic abilities. His highest scores on Visual Reception and Visual Sequential Memory are at the 6–6 Psycholinguistic Age (PLA) level. His lowest scores are at the PLA level of 5–0. Since his composite PLA is 5–8, his highest and lowest peaks do not differ more than 10 months from his composite or average PLA. At that age level the difference between the composite PLA and the subtest PLA's should be at least one and a half years before one could consider them possible abilities or disabilities. Since Case E did not have substantial discrepancies in growth he is considered a mentally retarded child with no substantial abilities or disabilities in psycholinguistic development.

Case F was also assigned to the same special class for the educable mentally retarded. His CA was 7–8; his Stanford-Binet MA was 6–0, and his IQ was 76. Like Case E he failed in the first grade, was examined, and placed in a class for the educable mentally retarded. On the ITPA his composite PLA was 5–9. Figure 5–3 shows the profile of his CA, Stanford-Binet MA, Composite PLA, and the profile of the subtests of the ITPA. It will be noted from Figure 5–3 that Case F has marked discrepancies among his abilities and disabilities. His high peaks are at the 8 to 9 year level, actually higher than his chronological age. His lows are at the 3 and 4 year levels. Here we find a discrepancy in growth of approximately 3 years above and below his composite PLA. This can be considered a substantial intraindividual difference. Therefore in spite of the similarity with Case E of IQ, mental age, and classification, Case F should not be considered mentally retarded as should Case E. He should be in a program for children with learning disabilities.

There are currently many children whose IQ's classify them as mentally retarded and who, consequently, are placed in classes for the mentally retarded. Some of these come from minority groups; some are children with learning disabilities.

Jensen (1970) has studied differences between what he calls familial retardation and cultural retardation. His research indicates that some children labeled mentally retarded are not retarded on paired-associate learning and digit repetition. These children tend to come from lower socioeconomic areas. The familial retarded perform poorly on paired-associate learning and digit repetition, even though they have similar IQ's to the culturally deprived.

In many of the larger cities there appears to be a proportionately higher number of minority group children enrolled in special classes for the mentally retarded. These children tend to be assigned to special classes on the basis of low IQ and educational retardation. There have been objections to the use of

FIGURE 5–2

Profile of Case E

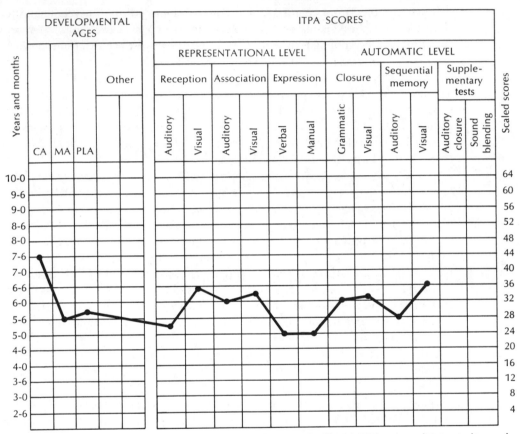

CA 7–6; Stanford-Binet MA 5–6; IQ 71; PLA 5–8. Profile of ITPA scores does not show substantial discrepancies.

tests for minority children which were standardized primarily on Caucasian middle-class children.

Bijou (1968), applying a behavioristic model to mental retardation, rejects the concept that mental retardation is a symptom of "defective intelligence," "clinically inferred brain damage," or "familial factors." He considers mental retardation as a form of limited behavior that has been shaped by the past events in a child's life. These past events are responsible for the delay in

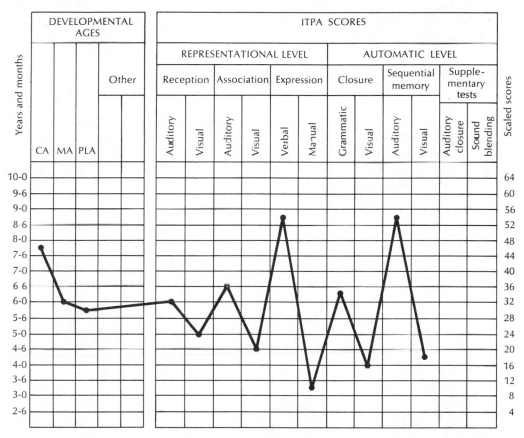

FIGURE 5–3

Profile of Case F

CA 7–8; Stanford-Binet MA 6–0; IQ 76; PLA 5–8. Profile of ITPA scores shows wide discrepancies.

development of adequate ways of interacting with the environment. Furthermore, environment is defined as the biological environment the child carries with him all the time, as well as the social, cultural, and physical conditions that influence the child's life. The retardation in development, according to behavioral theory, is related to the lack of quality and quantity of opportunities for contacts. The more specific factors that contribute to such retardation are (1) abnormal anatomic structure and functioning, (2) insufficient reinforcement (reward) and discrimination history, (3) reinforcement of undesirable behavior, and (4) severe aversive stimulation (punishment). This point of view discards speculation on what goes on in the brain and deals only with observable behavior. It follows from this theory that educators can observe the child as he is and manipulate the environment (stimuli) through reinforcement schedules to shape the behavior and provide a more adequate interaction between the child as a "total functioning biological system and the environment."

It is apparent from the above discussion that classification according to a global criterion like an IQ has not proved satisfactory. There is increasing effort to approach assessment from an intraindividual point of view and to approach treatment behaviorally. An assessment of a child's functioning level, by diagnostic tests, by learning tests, or by functional analysis of behavior, leads to the organization of the environment in a way that will help him make a more adequate adaptation to the surrounding milieu.

Causes of Mental Retardation

The search for causes of mental retardation is motivated by the desire to prevent mental retardation. If the cause can be discovered, it is possible in some instances to introduce measures that would prevent such occurrences. There are many conditions, diseases, and situations that can cause mental retardation. In the following discussion etiological (causal) factors will be discussed under five headings: (1) genetic, (2) prenatal, (3) perinatal, (4) postnatal, and (5) cultural.

GENETIC CAUSES

For many years a number of conditions associated with mental retardation were recorded as "cause unknown." Recent discoveries in biochemistry and genetics have thrown new light on previously unexplained cases. Special techniques have been developed which have made it possible to study tissue cultures and to identify chromosomes. These discoveries in biochemistry and genetics have led to the delineation of a number of genetic causes of mental retardation previously unknown.

Biochemical Disorders. Waisman and Gerritsen (1964) state that there are now nearly ninety diseases that can be traced to inborn errors of metabolism and that these are transmitted genetically by means of a hereditable trait. They assert:

This implies a defect in some gene which controls a certain enzyme system necessary for the normal function of a body tissue. Thus, the intimate relationship between genes and enzymes underlines the significance of biochemistry and genetics in those diseases which are associated with mental deficiency. (p. 308)

Biochemists have identified a number of chemical substances (carbohydrates, lipids, and amino acids) through which a number of abnormal genetic conditions can be traced. Two examples of these are given below:

Phenylketonuria is a well-known inherited disease causing mental retardation. It is caused by an inherited abnormality in amino-acid metabolism. This condition was discovered by Folling in Norway in 1934 and first described in this country by Jervis in 1937. Since then there have been many studies related to this condition. Although phenylketonuria, known as PKU, occurs with a frequency of 4 per 100,000 births (Anderson, 1964) or 1 in 700 mentally retarded, its discovery has led to a search for comparable inborn errors of metabolism that could account for other conditions causing mental retardation.

Phenylketonuric (PKU) children can be diagnosed early by means of urine analysis. In this condition a child is found to have a deficiency in phenylalanine hydroxylase. Waisman and Gerritsen (1964) state that this error of metabolism is transmitted as a recessive trait. If both parents are carriers of this gene there is a chance that 1 out of 4 children may be PKU.

PKU has been of interest because of the efforts to treat the problem. It has been found that if the phenylalanine deficiency is detected at an early age and the child is given a diet low in phenylalanine, the harmful effects on the brain are prevented and the child may not become mentally retarded. It is an illustration of current efforts to prevent mental retardation resulting from a genetic cause by intervening in the course of events—in this case, a phenylalanine-free diet. Birch and Tizard (1967), in reviewing research on PKU treatment, state that the evidence after fifteen years of treatment is still equivocal.

Galactosemia is another example of defective carbohydrate metabolism. It is considered an inherited recessive trait. The child is jaundiced at birth and shows early growth failure, feeding problems, and sometimes early cataracts. This condition, like PKU, can be detected by urine tests, and if detected early can be reversed. Treatment consists of a special diet which excludes galactose by withholding milk and by using a soybean milk substitute. The symptoms decrease or disappear if the galactose-free diet is initiated early in life.

These two conditions are examples of inborn errors of metabolism which can be treated successfully if detected early. Others have been discovered and probably many more will be discovered by biochemists in the near future. Control of genetic deficiencies is currently being explored by many eminent geneticists. Even though the percentage of mental retardation resulting from inborn biochemical abnormalities is quite small, the problem of preventing the resulting mental retardation continues to be most important.

Chromosomal Abnormalities. Developments in the study of tissue culture and identification of chromosomal abnormalities has led to some major discoveries in the genetics of mental retardation. The most common chromosomal abnormality is found in Down's Syndrome, or mongolism. This condition was described by Langdon Down about one hundred years ago. It was originally called Down's Disease, but because of the appearance of slanting eyes it was termed "mongolism." This has been an unfortunate term since there is no resemblance in any respect to the Mongolian race except the epicanthic fold of the eyelids. The name is currently being changed in professional terminology to Down's Syndrome.

This condition can generally be diagnosed at birth. The child born with this syndrome is mentally retarded and at a later age can range in IQ between 20 and 60, with the large majority in the 30 to 50 IQ range. Many studies have been made on children with Down's Syndrome in an attempt to determine its etiology. No definite cause was discovered, biochemical or otherwise, for about 90 years after it was first described. Not until methods had been perfected for the study of human chromosomes was a definite genetic cause determined. Then it was found that in humans there are 46 chromosomes arranged in 23 pairs. In 1959, Lejeune et al. discovered that in children with Down's Syndrome there were 47 chromosomes and that the chromosome pair number 21 was not a pair but a triplet creating a condition known as trisomy.

Other forms of chromosomal abnormalities causing mongolism are translocations in which the child has 46 chromosomes but a part of one is broken and the broken part fused to another chromosome. A third type is called mosaic mongolism. These latter two kinds of chromosomal abnormalities account for only 4 to 5 percent of mongoloid children (Lilienfield, 1969). The incidence of mongolism in the population is 1 to 2 mongoloid births out of 1,000 births.

Other chromosomal aberrations have been found which affect intelligence. Gottesman (1963) states:

The majority of evidence accumulated so far with respect to chromosomal aberrations suggests that practically all parts of chromosomes are capable of affecting measured intelligence and that any upset in the general genetic balance has harmful effects on both physical and mental traits. (p. 284)

PRENATAL CAUSES

In addition to genetic causes of mental retardation there are many conditions that can affect the developing embryo and cause maldevelopment of the nervous system and consequent mental retardation. This problem raises the question of the effects on the intelligence of the offspring caused by the mother's nutritional, psychological, and physical environment. Answers to many of these questions have not been found except in a few specific cases. Examples of some of these will be described briefly.

Rubella. In the early 1940's, it was discovered (Swan et al. 1946) that German Measles (Rubella) contracted by the mother during the first three months of pregnancy may result in congenital defects in the child, including mental retardation. Such defects as cataracts, deafness, heart disease, microcephalis, as well as general mental retardation have been associated with this disease. The earlier reports indicated a high incidence of children with defects following an attack of Rubella by the mother. Later reports, however, as summarized by Fraser (1964) show that only 17 to 24 percent of the children are defective, and that many mothers who contract Rubella during the first trimester of pregnancy do not have defective children. The virus for Rubella has been isolated and a vaccine has been developed. It is anticipated that in the future mental retardation as a result of Rubella will be decreased or eliminated.

The Rh Factor. In 1940, Landsteiner and Wiener (Gates, 1946) reported the study of a condition involving the presence of agglutinin in the blood of rabbits. This was produced experimentally by injecting blood from the rhesus monkey, hence the label Rh. Among humans, the Rh positive factor is found in the blood of 86 percent of individuals. The blood of the remaining 14 percent of human beings does not contain this Rh factor and is said to be Rh negative. Rh positive blood and Rh negative blood are incompatible and, when occurring in the same blood stream, produce agglutinin which causes blood cells to clump together, thus producing immature blood cells due to their failure to mature in the bone marrow.

Yannet and Lieberman (1944) and Snyder et al. (1945) have shown a relationship between the presence of Rh incompatible blood and mental retardation. The writers indicate that when the fetus inherits an Rh factor which is incompatible with that of the mother, the child is apt to be mentally retarded.

PERINATAL CAUSES

Perinatal causes refer to those conditions which may affect the child during or immediately preceding birth. These include primarily birth injuries, asphyxia, and prematurity.

The diagnosis of *brain injury* in children is often a retrospective one. It is inferred later in life when the child is found to be mentally retarded. Histories of the birth process relating to prolonged or difficult labor, forceps delivery, breech presentation, and other mechanical causes may lead a diagnostician to a general diagnosis of "brain injury" without specifying what kind of an injury it is.

A specific form of injury is *asphyxia,* which is caused by lack of oxygen to the brain during the period of birth. Frederick Schreiber (1939) studied this problem extensively and has presented evidence that mental defects in children are sometimes the result of what he terms "cerebral anoxia." According to Schreiber, the brain cannot function without an adequate supply of oxygen. When the oxygen supply to the brain is blocked for more than a few minutes, irreparable damage to the brain cells results. Masland et al. (1958) reviewed the literature concerning the relationship of mental retardation and found that the investigators do not all agree. Although many children with anoxia at birth die in infancy and some are defective later, there are also many who develop normally. He states: "Important changes in the chemistry of the body occur during conditions of asphyxia," but the "newborn infant is capable of tolerating a relatively severe degree of oxygen deprivation." He points out that some of the secondary changes that could occur during asphyxia are more detrimental than the oxygen depletion itself.

Studies on *prematurely born* children have shown a relationship between prematurity and mental retardation. Alm (1953) studied 999 premature boys and compared them statistically with 1,002 boys who were not born prematurely. He found that there were more epileptics, cerebral palsied, and mentally deficient among the prematures. Of those who lived, the height and weight was less for the prematurely born at age 20 and more of them had disorders of some kind. Most studies, although not as extensive as Alm's, show similar results. It should be remembered, however, that such defects apply to only a small proportion of premature births, since the large majority of such births result in normal development of the children.

Wortis (1961) reported that in the Soviet Union the rate of premature births per 100 population in Kiev was 4.7. In New York, at that time, the rate was 9.4 per 100, and in the poorer districts, 16 per 100. It appears that the incidence of prematurity is greater in lower socioeconomic areas than in higher levels. This can be due to lack of adequate medical prenatal treatment, to poor nutrition, or to other factors.

POSTNATAL CAUSES

In addition to genetic, prenatal, and perinatal conditions that can cause mental retardation, there are some conditions and diseases that can result in mental retardation when they occur in infancy and early childhood. These conditions are discussed briefly below.

Encephalitis refers to an inflammation of the central nervous system caused by a particular virus. The term encephalitis refers to a variety of disorders of early childhood, the most familiar of which is *encephalitis lethargica,* which some-times occurs as an epidemic disease and has been fatal to many.

Meningitis has been known as a cause of deafness and blindness, but it has also been recognized as a possible cause of mental retardation.

CULTURAL FACTORS

Cultural factors in the etiology of mental retardation refer to causative factors in the social environment. It should be recalled that reference has been made to environmental factors surrounding the fetus and to the effects of infections of the mother and other conditions. Social environmental factors also play a part after birth.

The relationship of experience to intelligence has been explored by numerous authors. In an exhaustive analysis of the scientific literature, Hunt (1961) con-cludes that adequate early experience is effective in accelerating mental growth. An international symposium on the effects of cultural deprivation on mental retardation (Haywood, 1970) presents considerable information on the posi-tive relationship of early deprivation or intervention to intelligence.

Clarke and Clarke (1965), in a section on the genetic and environmental studies of intelligence, state:

> It may be assumed that heredity plays an essential part in determining the limits of intellectual development, but these limits are considerably wider than was formerly thought. With moderate uniformity of environment, individual differences result largely from genetic variations. The feeble-minded [educable mentally retarded], however, more than any other group in western culture have been reared in most adverse circumstances, followed in many cases by further lengthy periods of residential schools and institutions, with all that this implies. Thus the feeble-minded in such conditions seem likely to be functioning towards the lower end of their spectrum of potentialities, while normals under ordinary conditions of life approximate more closely to their upper limits. (pp. 133–34)

Kirk (1958) has summarized the studies of the effects of environment on mentally retarded children. Of the four groups of studies the first includes case studies of children who had a deprived environment, such as the study by Itard of the Wild Boy of Aveyron. This and other case studies appear somewhat ambiguous and do not show necessarily that a change of environment changed the status of the cases perceptibly. A second approach used by researchers is that of changing the environment by placing children in foster homes. In gen-eral the results show that intellectual development of children is affected in varying degrees by the type of home in which they are placed. A third approach has been the comparison of the intellectual level of children from different en-vironments. These studies do not point to any clear conclusions because many of the variables involved could not be controlled. A fourth approach is the investigation of the effects of environmental enrichment and school programs on the development of retarded children. The studies here are also controversial, with some concluding that altering the rate of development through environmental enrichment or school is possible while others contend that it is impossible.

Skeels and Dye (1939) report a significant study on the effects of earlier environmental intervention. They took 13 children from an orphanage and placed them in a state institution for the mentally retarded. These children were under 3 years of age and had an average IQ of 64, their initial IQ's ranging from 35 to 89. Each was placed in a different ward of the institution with older patients so that they would receive a great deal of individual attention from older girls and attendants. A year and a half later, their IQ's as measured by the Kuhlmann Test of Mental Development had increased on the average 27.5 points.

As a contrast group Skeels and Dye used 12 babies who were retained in the orphanage. These 12 children had an initial average IQ of 87.6 ranging from 50 to 103. After thirty months, this group, who remained in the orphanage under a nonstimulating environment, dropped in IQ on the average 26.2 points.

Skeels has made two follow-up studies of these 25 children. One was made three years after the study and the other twenty-one years later. Skeels (1942) found that after three years the experimental children had retained their accelerated rate of development in foster homes, while the orphanage children retained their decreased intellectual performance.

In the second study, Skeels (1966) followed up the 25 children twenty-one years after the initial testing when they were between 25 and 35 years of age. Every one of the 25 subjects was located and all but one (who had died) were interviewed. Skeels found:

1. The 13 children in the experimental group were self-supporting, and none was a ward of any institution, public or private.
2. In the contrast group of 12 children, 1 died in adolescence following residence in an institution for the mentally retarded, and 4 were wards of institutions.
3. The median grade in school completed by the 13 experimental children was twelfth grade. The median grade for the contrast group was less than third grade. (pp. 54–55)

This study is one of the rare longitudinal studies of children examined at an early age and followed up when the children had become adults. It demonstrates that differential stimulation at the age of 1 or 2 years displaces the rate of mental development upwards or downwards with children who do not reveal any pathology. It also demonstrates that the gains or losses made at an early age are maintained at later ages.

In a series of studies on young mentally retarded children, Kirk (1958; 1965) found similar trends. In one study on institutionalized children, 15 were offered preschool education, while 12 children of similar ages and IQ's were retained in the wards. Both groups were 4½ years of age at the beginning of the experiment and were last examined three years later at ages 7 to 8 years. The results of this experiment are presented in Figure 5–4.

1. The experimental group gained substantially on the Stanford-Binet Scale, on the Kuhlmann Tests of Mental Development, and on the Vineland Scale of Social Maturity.

2. The contrast group dropped on all the follow-up tests.

3. Of the 15 children in the experimental group, 6 were parolled from the institution, either to their own homes or to foster homes, because of increases in IQ and adjustment. Not one of the contrast group was parolled from the institution during that period.

4. Unlike Skeels's children, approximately one-half of the experimental group had a definite medical diagnosis of pathology.

In a similar experiment in the community, 12 children from inadequate homes who attended a special community preschool for mentally retarded were compared with their siblings and twins living in the same home but without the benefits of preschool education. These two groups were also compared to 4 children who had been taken out of inadequate homes, placed in foster homes, and also placed in the preschool.

Kirk concludes:

1. The 4 foster-home children all gained in rate of mental development.

2. Two-thirds of the 12 experimental children who lived in their inadequate homes gained in rate of mental development.

3. Only one-seventh of the twins and sibling controls gained in rate of mental development. The rest either retained their rate of growth or dropped in rate of mental and social growth.

The general conclusions from these data indicate that when intervention is *not* introduced at the preschool level, children from inadequate homes tend to

FIGURE 5–4

*IQ and SQ change scores of institutionalized
retarded children as a function
of preschool experience*

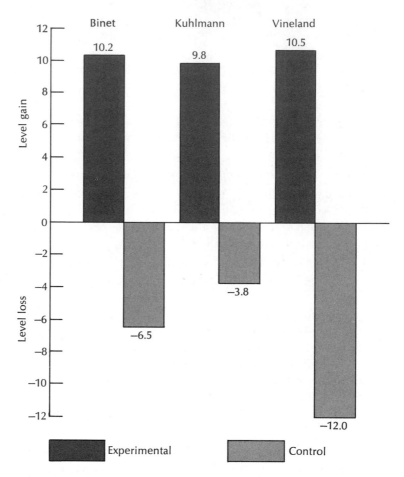

Source: S. A. Kirk, "Diagnostic, Cultural, and Remedial Factors in Mental Retardation." In
Sonia F. Osler and R. E. Cooke, eds., *Biosocial Basis of Mental Retardation* (Baltimore: Johns
Hopkins Press, 1965), p. 137. Reproduced by permission of the publisher.

retain their rate of development or drop in rate of development as they grow
older. When society offers compensatory education in the form of a preschool,
or preschool and change of home, a reversal of this development is accomplished.

Following the Kirk study of 1958 there have been a series of studies on the effects of preschool education on culturally deprived children and on higher grades of the mentally retarded. Only those dealing with children classified as mentally retarded will be reviewed.

Guskin and Spicker (1968) reported on an Indiana study. They applied a specialized curriculum to a group of 28 5-year-old culturally disadvantaged (Caucasian, Appalachian) children ranging in IQ's between 50 and 85. They compared their progress with two other groups, one attending a traditional kindergarten and the other remaining at home. The results of the experiment are presented in Table 5–2. It will be noted from this table that the experimental preschool group of 28 children increased their Stanford-Binet IQ from 75.8 at the kindergarten level to 91.3 after the first grade. The traditional kindergarten group increased their IQ's from 74.1 to 82.9, indicating that traditional kindergarten plus first grade has some effect on IQ but not as great as the specialized curriculum. The home group made no progress while they were at home, but began to increase their IQ after first-grade experience. These results are in harmony with those of Kirk (1958) who found that first-grade experience has some influence on IQ. In other words, schooling is effective whether it is initiated at age 5 or 6.

A similar experiment was conducted by Weikart (1967). The differences between the Indiana project and the Weikart experiment were in race and program. While the Indiana project included white children, the Weikart project involved black children. In the Weikart program the experimental children attended school in the morning, and in the afternoon the teachers instructed the parents at home. The results of the Weikart project are similar to the

TABLE 5–2

Indiana Project Stanford-Binet IQ means
for combined first- and second-year groups

Group	Size	Kindergarten pretest	Kindergarten posttest	First grade follow-up
Experimental preschool	28	75.8	92.4	91.3
Kindergarten contrast	29	74.1	83.2	82.9
At-home contrast	42	74.0	78.6	86.9

Source: Guskin and Spicker, 1968, p. 225. Copyright © 1968, Academic Press.

Indiana project in that the experimental group made substantial gains the first year from 78.4 to 91.1 IQ, while the contrast group made only slight gains. By the second grade, however, there was little difference, with the experimental group having average IQ's of 85.5 and the contrast group 83.9. The most important aspect of the Weikart experiment was the difference between the experimental children and the contrast children in educational achievement (reading, arithmetic, and language skills). At the end of second grade the experimental children were significantly higher on all aspects of educational achievement than the contrast group.

From the experiments of Skeels, Kirk, and others there is strong evidence that early intervention with psychosocially deprived children will accelerate mental, social, and educational development and that lack of intervention will tend to interfere with development. Bloom (1964) states that 50 percent of intellectual development takes place between conception and age 4, about 30 percent between ages 4 and 8, and about 20 percent between ages 8 and 17. If this conclusion is substantiated, prevention of cultural mental retardation (the largest group of mentally retarded) will require the establishment of home training, adequate nursery schools, and kindergarten for all children in low socioeconomic areas. The data presented above lends credence to the concept of environmental experiences providing a cultural etiology in mental retardation.

The question of whether mental retardation is hereditary or environmental can only be answered by, "It is both." The concept of the *norm of reaction* as used in genetics, helps to clarify the controversy. The norm of reaction has been proposed by Dobzhansky (1955) to explain that each child is born with a range of potential ability—his genotypic potential. The point to which he actually develops (his phenotypic behavior) lies somewhere within this range and is determined by his environment. One child may be so constituted genetically that his range is wide while another's is narrow. One may be higher than another but have an area of overlap. For example, a mongoloid child who is known to be genetically defective may have a range of potential between 20 and 40 IQ. A poor environment may result in a child with an IQ of 25. A maximum environment may result in a child with an IQ of 40. Another child without biochemical or chromosomal abnormalities may have a wider range of potential or reaction range from 60 to 100 IQ. In this case, the environment will determine whether the child will remain at the lower end or develop at the upper end of his norm of reaction. The concept of the norm of reaction, then, does not ask the question whether heredity is more important than environment. Rather it asks the question of whether we are providing maximum environments for children—environments which will help them develop to the top of their ranges of potentiality as determined by the genetic endowment of each individual.

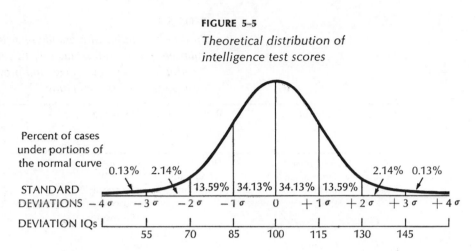

FIGURE 5-5

Theoretical distribution of intelligence test scores

Source: Adapted from *Test Service Bulletin No. 48* (New York: Psychological Corporation, January, 1955). Reproduced by permission of the Corporation.

The Prevalence of Children with Low Intelligence

The numerous surveys of various populations to determine the prevalence of children with low intelligence have shown a wide range of estimates. One reason for the divergence is the fact that different investigators used different criteria for the groups they called mentally retarded.

One method of determining prevalence is to look at the distribution of intelligence on a theoretical distribution curve. It will be noted from Figure 5–5, which presents such a theoretical distribution of intelligence, that 2.14 percent of the population have IQ's between –2 and –3 standard deviation or between 55 and 70 IQ. About one and one-third out of a thousand children (0.13 percent) have IQ's below 55. This constitutes a theoretical prevalence rate. What, then, are the actual or empirical prevalence rates?

Farber (1968) has reported on the studies of prevalence rates by various authors in the United States, England, and European countries and on the methods and criteria used in making studies of prevalence. It is obvious that the prevalence rates depend on the cut-off point used by the investigator. If the investigator uses intelligence tests he would obtain a higher prevalence if he took a cut-off point of 79 IQ than he would if he took a 69 IQ cut-off point. For example, Farber reported that Akkeson in Sweden used a 70 IQ limit and found 17.9 out of 1000 as mentally retarded. Lofthus in Norway used a 75 IQ limit and obtained 38 mentally retarded in 1000.

TABLE 5–3

Prevalence studies of mentally retarded children in the United States, with year, location of study, age range, and prevalence estimate per 1000 population

Year	Location	Report	Age range	Estimate of prevalence (per 1000)
1953	New Jersey	Howard[1]	school age	15.2
1953	Onondaga, N.Y.	Goodman[2]	under 18	35.2
1954	Philadelphia	Ferguson[3]	preschool	32.2
			school age	33.9
			adulthood	19.2
			all ages	23.2
1954	Georgia	Wishik[4]	0–20	37.0
1956	Hawaii	Weiner[5]	Grades K–12	23.6
1956	Delaware	Jastak[6]	all ages (through adult)	
			at 25% cut-off pts.	83.3
			at 9% cut-off pts.	20.3
			at 2% cut-off pts.	3.8
1957	Maine	Levinson[7]	5–20	29.9
1958	Illinois	Farber[8]	6–15	18.8
1957–8	Wyoming	Farber[9]	6–21	50.2
1962	Middle-sized city, California	Mercer[10]	all ages (through adult)	36.1

Source: B. Farber, *Mental Retardation* (Boston: Houghton Mifflin, 1968), p. 58. Reproduced with the permission of the publisher.

[1] John W. Howard, ed., *Found, A Report of the Committee to Study the Education of Handicapped Children* (Trenton, New Jersey: New Jersey Department of Education, 1954.)

[2] Melvin B. Goodman, Ernest M. Gruenberg, Joseph Downing, and Eugene Rogot, "A Prevalence Study of Mental Retardation in a Metropolitan Area," *American Journal of Public Health* 46 (June, 1956), pp. 702–707.

[3] Robert G. Ferguson, "A Study of the Problem of Mental Retardation in a Large Urban Community," *American Journal of Orthopsychiatry,* 27 (1957), pp. 490–501.

[4] Samuel M. Wishik, "Handicapped Children in Georgia, A Study of Prevalence, Needs, and Resources," *American Journal of Public Health* 46 (February, 1956), pp. 195–203.

[5] Samuel A. Kirk and Bluma B. Weiner, "The Onondaga Census—Fact or Artifact," *Exceptional Children,* 25 (January, 1959), pp. 226–228, 230–231.

[6] Joseph F. Jastak, Halsey M. McPhee, and Martin Whiteman, *Mental Retardation, Its Nature and Incidence* (Newark, Delaware: University of Delaware Press, 1963).

[7] Elizabeth J. Levinson, *Retarded Children in Maine, A Survey and Analysis* (Orono, Maine: University of Maine Press, 1962).

[8] Bernard Farber, *Prevalence of Exceptional Children in Illinois in 1958* (Springfield: Illinois Superintendent of Public Instruction, 1959), Circular—Census IA.

[9] *Wyoming Mental Ability Survey, 1957–1958* (Cheyenne: State Department of Education, May 10, 1959).

[10] Computed from data in Jane R. Mercer, Edgar W. Butler, and Harvey F. Dingman, "The Relationship between Social Developmental Performance and Mental Ability," *American Journal of Mental Deficiency* 69 (September, 1964), pp. 195–205.

TABLE 5–4

*Prevalence of low IQ in white children
in relation to socioeconomic status*

Socioeconomic status	Percent of MR below an IQ of 75
High 1	0.5
2	0.8
3	2.1
4	3.1
Low 5	7.8

Source: Adapted from R. Heber, 1970. Courtesy of Charles C. Thomas, Publisher, Springfield, Illinois.

Most surveys, however, use a census method to determine prevalence. Table 5–3 gives selected prevalence studies in the United States that were conducted between 1953 and 1962. It will be noted that, with the exception of the Jastak studies, the prevalence rates per 1000 children range from 15.2 to 50.2. Farber concludes that there is considerable uniformity between the studies in the United States in prevalence rates and that the best generalization that can be made is that 2 to 3 percent of school children are mentally retarded. In general, a smaller percentage are identified at the preschool level, a higher percentage at the middle school-age level, and a drop during the post-school period.

The major variables that affect prevalence in most of the studies relate to (1) socioeconomic level, and (2) degree of retardation.

Heber (1970) reports a study and an estimated prevalence of IQ's below 75. He found the prevalence of white children to be related to socioeconomic status as shown in Table 5–4.

Birch and Dye (1970) found similar data in a study in Aberdeen, Scotland. Although children below 50 IQ had the same prevalence figures for both high and low social class, children between IQ's of 60 to 75 were markedly more prevalent in the lower social classes.

Taking into consideration the surveys made in the British Isles and in various parts of the United States, and also considering the socioeconomic and cultural levels of the community, we can estimate the rates shown in Table 5–5. It will be noted from this table that the prevalence of totally dependent or trainable children does not differ between the low, middle, and high socioeconomic communities. This indicates that pathological conditions, such as mongolism, occur

TABLE 5–5

*Estimated number of children with low IQ's
per 1000 school-age children*

Level of community	Totally dependent	Trainable	Educable
Low	1	4	50
Middle	1	4	25
High	1	4	10

with the same frequency regardless of the cultural level of the family. The differences in frequency of retardation between communities occur primarily among educable retarded. Studies relating to these differences were discussed under cultural factors causing mental retardation.

SUMMARY

1. Children with low intelligence have been classified for educational purposes as (a) slow learners, (b) educable mentally retarded, (c) trainable mentally retarded, and (d) totally dependent. Other similar classifications used by the medical and psychological profession include mildly retarded, moderately retarded, severely retarded, and profoundly retarded.
2. The causes (etiology) of mental retardation include (a) genetic, (b) prenatal, (c) perinatal, (d) postnatal, and (e) cultural factors.
3. The organic and genetic factors in mental retardation are primarily in the domain of the medical and biological sciences. Education is concerned primarily with the cultural and environmental factors, since adequate education and social management can compensate to some extent for deprived environmental situations. How much can be done to improve or compensate for poor heredity or organic pathology remains for future researchers in the biological and social sciences to determine.
4. It is estimated that in an average community the prevalence of mental retardation for each 1000 school-age children is approximately 1 totally dependent, 4 trainable mentally retarded, 25 educable mentally retarded.

REFERENCES

Alm, I. 1953. The Long-Term Prognosis for Prematurely Born Children: A Follow-up Study of 999 Premature Boys Born in Wedlock and of 1,002 Controls. *Acta Paediatrica Supplement* 94.

Anderson, E. V. 1964. Genetics in Mental Retardation. In Stevens, H., and Heber, R. (eds.), *Mental Retardation,* pp. 348–395. Chicago: University of Chicago Press.

Bijou, S. W. 1968. The Mentally Retarded Child. *Psychology Today* 2 (June): 47–51.

Birch, H., and Dye, J. 1970. *Disadvantaged Children: Health, Nutrition, and School Failure.* New York: Harcourt, Brace and World.

Birch, H., and Tizard, J. 1967. The Dietary Treatment of Phenylketonuria: Not Proven? *Developmental Medicine and Child Neurology* 9: 9–12.

Bloom, B. S. 1964. *Stability and Change in Human Characteristics.* New York: John Wiley.

Clarke, A. M., and Clarke, A. D. B. 1965. *Mental Deficiency: The Changing Outlook.* Glencoe, Ill.: Free Press.

Dobzhansky, T. 1955. *Evolution, Genetics, and Man.* New York: John Wiley.

Doll, E. A. 1941. The Essentials of an Inclusive Concept of Mental Deficiency. *American Journal of Mental Deficiency* 46 (October): 214–219.

Farber, B. 1968. *Mental Retardation.* Boston: Houghton-Mifflin.

Fraser, F. C. 1964. Teratogenesis of the Central Nervous System. In Stevens, H., and Heber, R. (eds.), *Mental Retardation,* pp. 395–429. Chicago: University of Chicago Press.

Gates, R. R. 1946. *Human Genetics,* Vol. 1. New York: Macmillan.

Gottesman, I. I. 1963. Genetic Aspects of Intelligent Behavior. In Ellis, N. R. (ed.), *Handbook of Mental Deficiency,* pp. 253–296. New York: McGraw-Hill.

Guskin, S. L., and Spicker, H. H. 1968. Educational Research in Mental Retardation. In Ellis, N. R. (ed.), *International Review of Research in Mental Retardation,* Vol. 3, pp. 217–278. New York: Academic Press.

Haywood, C. (ed.). 1970. *Social-Cultural Aspects of Mental Retardation.* New York: Appleton-Century-Crofts.

Heber, R. 1970. *Epidemiology of Mental Retardation.* Springfield, Illinois: Thomas.

———. 1961. Modification in the Manual on Terminology and Classifications in Mental Retardation. *American Journal of Mental Deficiency* 46 (October): 499–501.

———. 1959. A Manual on Terminology and Classification in Mental Retardation. A Monograph Supplement, *American Journal of Mental Deficiency* (September).

Hunt, J. McV. 1961. *Intelligence and Experience.* New York: Ronald Press.

Jensen, A. A. 1970. A Theory of Primary and Secondary Familial Mental Retardation. In Ellis, N. R. (ed.), *International Review of Research in Mental Retardation,* Vol. 4, pp. 33–100. New York: Academic Press.

Jervis, G. A. 1937. Phenylpyruvic Oligophrenia: Introductory Study of Fifty Cases of Mental Deficiency Associated with Excretion of Phenylpyruvic Acid. *Archives of Neurology and Psychiatry* 38 (November): 944–963.

Kirk, S. A. 1965. Diagnostic, Cultural, and Remedial Factors in Mental Retardation. In Osler, Sonia F., and Cooke, R. E. (eds.), *The Bio-Social Basis of Mental Retardation,* pp. 129–145. Baltimore: Johns Hopkins Press.

———. 1958. *Early Education of the Mentally Retarded.* Urbana, Illinois: University of Illinois Press.

Lejeune, J., Gautier, M., and Turpin, R. 1959. *Études des Chromosomes Somatiques de Neuf Enfants.* C. R. Académie Sci. 248: 1721–22.

Lilienfield, A. M. 1969. *Epidemiology of Mongolism.* Baltimore: Johns Hopkins Press.

Masland, R. L.; Sarason, S. B.; and Gladwin, T. 1958. *Mental Subnormality: Biological, Psychological, and Cultural Factors.* New York: Basic Books.

Report of the Mental Deficiency Committee, 1929. London: His Majesty's Stationery Office.

Schreiber, F. 1939. Mental Deficiency from Paranatal Asphyxia. *Proceedings and Addresses of the Sixty-Third Annual Session of the American Association on Mental Deficiency* 44 (No. 1): 95–106.

Skeels, H. M. 1966. *Adult Status of Children with Contrasting Early Life Experiences.* Monographs of the Society for Research in Child Development 31. Chicago: University of Chicago Press.

———. 1942. A Study of the Effects of Differential Stimulation on Mentally Retarded Children: A Follow-Up Study. *American Journal of Mental Deficiency* 46 (January): 340–350.

Skeels, H. M., and Dye, H. B. 1939. A Study of the Effects of Differential Stimulation on Mentally Retarded Children. *Proceedings and Addresses of the Sixty-Third Annual Session of the American Association on Mental Deficiency* 44 (No. 1): 114–130.

Snyder, L.; Schonfeld, M. D.; and Offerman, Edith M. 1945. The Rh Factor and Feeble-mindedness. *Journal of Heredity* 36: 9–10.

Swan, C.; Fostevin, A. L.; and, Barham-Black, G. H. 1946. Final Observations on Congenital Defects in Infants Following Infectious Diseases During Pregnancy with Special Reference to Rubella. *Medical Journal of Australia* 2 (December): 889–908.

Tredgold, A. F. 1937. *A Textbook of Mental Deficiency,* 6th ed. Baltimore: Willam Worden.

Waisman, H. A., and Gerritsen, T. 1964. Biochemical and Clinical Correlations. In Stevens, H., and Heber, R. (eds.), *Mental Retardation,* pp. 307–348. Chicago: University of Chicago Press.

Weikart, D. P. 1967. Preschool Programs: Preliminary Findings. *Journal of Special Education* 1: 163–181.

Wortis, J. A. 1961. Psychiatric Study Tour of the U.S.S.R. *Journal of Mental Science* 107: 119–155.

Yannet, H., and Lieberman, Rose. 1944. The Rh Factor in the Etiology of Mental Deficiency. *American Journal of Mental Deficiency* 49 (October): 133–137.

SIX

THE

EDUCABLE

MENTALLY

RETARDED

CHILD

The educable mentally retarded child has been defined as one who has potentialities for development in (1) minimum educability in the academic subjects of the school, (2) social adjustment to such a point that he can get along independently in the community, and (3) minimum occupational adequacy to such a degree that he can later support himself partially or totally at the adult level.

Educable mentally retarded children are usually not recognized as mentally retarded at the preschool level. Although they are slightly delayed in talking, language, and sometimes walking, the retardation is not so great as to cause alarm on the part of the parents. Most of these children are not known to be mentally retarded until they enter school and begin to fail in learning the required subject matter. An example of the life of an educable mentally retarded child may be illustrated with the case of Billy.

A Case Study

Billy was the first-born child of a family of mediocre income and education. The father had left school at the age of 15 after completing the sixth grade. The mother was reported to have left school in the ninth grade at the age of 16. The father was employed sporadically at laboring jobs, currently ground maintenance in a small plant. The mother, at the time Billy entered school, was occupied as a housewife with three children. They lived in a small house of two bedrooms in the poorer area of a middle-sized city. The family had been known to social agencies at a time when the father was unemployed and relief was requested.

When Billy was 6 years old he entered school and was placed in the first grade as other children were. On the Stanford-Binet test he obtained an IQ of 68 and a mental age of 4 years, 1 month. Most of the children in the class had mental levels of around 6 and were able to cope with the instruction in reading and other school subjects. But Billy was not ready for first grade. He completed the first year without even beginning to learn to read. Because of this failure, he was retained in the first grade for a second year, when he was 7 years of age.

At the age of 8 Billy still could not read. However, the school had retained him in the first grade once and was reluctant to keep an 8-year-old child with beginning 6-year-olds. Consequently, they placed him in the second grade even though his mental age (5 years, 5 months) was still below that usually required for reading. At the end of the year Billy was still unable to read although he had picked up a few words. He had now attended school for three years without beginning to read. At the age of 9, Billy was retained in the second grade because he could not read. His mental level was now 6 years, 1 month; mentally he was ready to begin reading like normal 6-year-olds. At the end of the second year in second grade he had picked up a little reading and was sent into the third grade, since the school did not wish to retain him in the second grade for a third year. By this time Billy was 10 years old, but he was unable to keep up with 8-year-old children doing third-grade work. Although he began to do some reading and number work and to participate in the oral activities of the class, he felt inferior. At this time he became unpopular with the children because he took advantage of his size, strength, and physical abilities and became a bully. Children did not seek him out as a friend.

The third-grade teacher became frustrated with Billy because of his nonachievement in class. She wondered why he was placed in the third grade when he could barely do first-grade work. She had to devote considerable attention to his problems with other children, and it was necessary to prepare special lessons which could occupy him while she taught the rest of the class.

At this time the school personnel began facing the problem of the educable mentally retarded like Billy and decided to organize special services for them. As finally set up, they organized a class for 14 children, aged from 9 to 14 and with IQ's ranging from 55 to 80. Billy was placed in this class and remained in it as a homeroom until the age of 14 when he entered another special program in a junior high school and remained there until the age of 17. By this time he was achieving academically at the fourth-grade level, and his social adjustment to his classmates was fair. Obtaining a part-time job during the summer as an usher in a theater, he wanted to continue it during the year and so quit school. By the age of 22 Billy had tried seven different part-time or full-time jobs. At this time he was drafted into the army, where he made satisfactory adjustment in the infantry. He was discharged after his period of military service as a private first class.

The example just given is only an illustration of the problems facing an educable mentally retarded child in school and through postadolescence. In the regular classes he was misplaced according to both age and academic achievement yet was unable to profit sufficiently from the regular grades to warrant his retention there.

Billy's social maturity and social adjustment also were retarded. He was not able to get along adequately with children of his own age because their play interests and activities were beyond his. He tended to play with younger children. In spite of such discrepancies it was important for the school to allow him to go through the growing stages, to learn to get along with individuals, learn to respect property rights, learn to respect the rights of others, learn to give and take with other children, so that at the adult level he could participate in the activities of the community, go to work by himself, and do the many things which the average person does for himself. For this reason special programs for the educable mentally retarded have been organized in school systems to adapt instruction to their level of ability.

The Growth Pattern

The profile of an educable mentally retarded child given in Chapter 5, Figure 5–2 (Case E), represents an average educable mentally retarded child. It does not represent a particular individual, since a single person may have many more discrepancies. The profile is the smoothed curve of averages in these characteristics. To more adequately represent the educable mentally retarded child the profile should be a band rather than a line. Using such a band, Figure 6–1 shows the range of development in each area for children usually labeled educable. On each characteristic most of these children will fall somewhere within the shaded area. They range in IQ from 50 or 55 up to 75 or 80. An educable

FIGURE 6–1

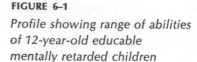

*Profile showing range of abilities
of 12-year-old educable
mentally retarded children*

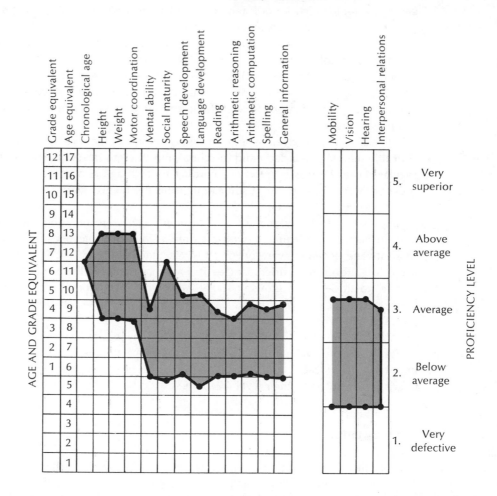

mentally retarded child of 12 will therefore have a mental age between 6 and 9 years, as indicated by the shaded area.

It should be noted that in height, weight, and motor coordination some of the retarded children are higher than average children but the majority of them are average or below. In other words, for physical characteristics there is an overlap between the educable mentally retarded and the average child.

In mental age there is no overlap since all, by definition, are below average. In social maturity there is a wider discrepancy. Some educable mentally retarded children are near average in social maturity, but the large majority are below average. In speech and language development and reading and other academic subjects there is no overlap; the educable mentally retarded child is definitely below the average. In other characteristics the overlap is considerable, for although on the whole there are more defects in ability to see and hear and in mobility among the educable mentally retarded than among the average, many of the former are quite normal in these respects. Similarly there is an overlap in interpersonal relations; some of the educable mentally retarded are near average but the majority are below average.

Characteristics

It is difficult to list characteristics found in all educable mentally retarded children. No single child has all of these characteristics, for some are peculiar to only a certain group. Nevertheless, a teacher or diagnostician should keep the following in mind in identifying or teaching, the educable mentally retarded.

PHYSICAL CHARACTERISTICS

1. In height, weight, and motor coordination most educable mentally retarded children approximate normal children.

2. Because a small number have organic causes for the retardation, these few are likely to be physically inferior to normal children.

3. More handicaps of vision, hearing, and motor coordination are found among the educable mentally retarded. However, a substantial number do not have such defects.

4. Many retarded children come from substandard homes, which are generally inferior in sanitation and attention to health matters.

INTELLECTUAL CHARACTERISTICS

1. The mentally retarded child performs poorly on verbal and nonverbal intelligence tests. His IQ tends to be in the range from 50 or 55 to 75 or 80. This implies a rate of mental development approximately one-half to three-fourths that of an average child.

2. Retarded mental development may include slowness in maturation of specific intellectual functions needed for school work, such as being significantly

low in memory for auditory and visual materials, generalizing ability, language ability, conceptual and perceptual abilities, imagination and creative abilities, and other functions considered basically intellectual. If the child has marked discrepancies in abilities and disabilities as shown in Chapter 5, Figure 5–3 (Case F), general mental retardation should be questioned.

ACADEMIC CHARACTERISTICS

1. The educable mentally retarded child is not ready for reading, writing, spelling, and arithmetic when he enters school at the age of 6 unless he has special abilities. He does not begin to acquire these skills until he is about 8 years old or even, perhaps, until he is 11. This delay in learning is related to mental age, not to chronological age.

2. The rate at which the child progresses in school is comparable to his rate of mental development, that is, about one-half to three-quarters the rate of the average child. He should not be expected to cover a year's material in a year's time, as do average children.

3. At the end of his formal school career his academic achievement will probably have reached second- to sixth-grade level, depending upon his mental maturation and/or special abilities.

PERSONAL AND SOCIAL CHARACTERISTICS

There are no basic social traits which differentiate the educable mentally retarded from the average child. Negative social or interpersonal traits sometimes attributed to the former are usually related to situations in which the children are placed. These social characteristics are by-products of the difference between the expectancies of society and the abilities of the mentally retarded to cope with the requirements.

1. Short attention span or lack of concentration and participation of the mentally retarded child in a regular classroom is often engendered by expecting him to respond like other children to materials he cannot learn or understand in a classroom situation. This characteristic, quite prevalent when retarded children are in the regular grades, tends to disappear when materials and methods are geared to their ability to succeed.

2. Low frustration tolerance has been ascribed to the mentally retarded. It is also related to repeated failure experiences in life and in school since the child is expected to function according to his chronological age. Tolerance for frustration can be increased by a home or school environment which will avoid failure and substitute success experiences.

3. Social values and attitudes generally correspond to those of the home and neighborhood associates and are, in many instances, typical of the culture in which the child is reared.

4. The retarded child's play interests correspond more closely to those of children of his own mental age than to those of similar chronological age.

5. There are more behavior problems and there is slightly more delinquency among the retarded in proportion to their numbers than among children of average intelligence. This may be partially the result of the substandard environment in which a large percentage of these children live. Since behavior problems also stem from the discrepancy between the child's capacity to perform and the requirements of the environment, a finding dramatically evident among retarded children, it is important that the environment of the latter, both home and school, be harmonized with their capacity to perform and to learn. This, of course, is one of the reasons why special education is provided.

OCCUPATIONAL CHARACTERISTICS

1. The educable mentally retarded can learn to do unskilled and semi-skilled work at the adult level.

2. Any failure in unskilled occupational tasks is generally related to personal, social, and interpersonal characteristics rather than an inability to execute the task assigned.

3. Employment records of the educable mentally retarded show that approximately 80 percent eventually adjust to occupations of an unskilled or semi-skilled nature and partially or totally support themselves. The occupational adjustment of the retarded is further discussed later in this chapter.

Purposes and Objectives of Education of the Mentally Retarded

In organizing an educational program for the educable mentally retarded, the first task is to determine its basic goals. Actually, they do not differ from the general objectives for all children. For example, the Educational Policies Commission (1938) has listed four major objectives of education: (1) self-realization, (2) human relationships, (3) economic efficiency, and (4) civic responsibility (p. 47). These apply to the educable mentally retarded as well as to the normal child. The chief differences are the addition of more specific objectives, the limits which the educability of these children imposes on the attainment of the objectives, and the adaptations in instruction needed to attain the more limited objectives.

Kirk and Johnson (1951) have listed the purposes of a program for the educable mentally retarded:

1. They should be educated to get along with their fellow men; i.e., they should develop social competence through numerous social experiences.
2. They should learn to participate in work for the purpose of earning their own living; i.e., they should develop occupational competence through efficient vocational guidance and training as a part of their school experience.
3. They should develop emotional security and independence in the school and in the home through a good mental hygiene program.
4. They should develop habits of health and sanitation through a good program of health education.
5. They should learn the minimum essentials of the tool subjects, even though their academic limits are third to fifth grade.
6. They should learn to occupy themselves in wholesome leisure time activities through an educational program that teaches them to enjoy recreational and leisure time activities.
7. They should learn to become adequate members of a family and a home through an educational program that emphasizes home membership as a function of the curriculum.
8. They should learn to become adequate members of a community through a school program that emphasizes community participation. (p. 118)

Stated in different words and in broader concepts, the program should stress the development of (1) social competence, (2) personal adequacy, and (3) occupational competence. Social competence refers primarily to the ability of the individual to get along with his fellow men, that is, his family, his school and neighborhood mates, and other members of the community. Personal adequacy refers to his ability to live with himself in some sort of equilibrium. Occupational competence refers to his ability to support himself partially or totally in some productive activity.

Educational Overview

Early attempts to educate the mentally retarded following the classical efforts of Itard, Seguin, Montessori, and Decroly (Kirk and Johnson, 1951) dealt primarily with the moderate or severe (trainable) mentally defective. At the turn of the century it became obvious that society could not build institutions fast enough to care for, manage, and educate the mentally retarded in our society. Consequently, many communities delegated to the public schools the responsibility of educating the educable (or higher grade) mentally retarded. Thus, special classes for the mentally retarded began to be organized in school systems around 1900. The special class movement spread rapidly into many school systems, and by 1922 there were enrolled in public special schools and classes 23,252 children. By 1969, 703,800 mentally retarded children were enrolled in school programs.

The development of programs for the educable mentally retarded has not progressed without controversy. Much research has been conducted on the special class programs to answer some questions raised by those administering and operating such classes. Research workers have attempted to answer some questions and to settle some controversies regarding the effectiveness of special classes and the degree of achievement of mentally retarded children in reading, arithmetic, language and speech, art and music, physical education, and adjustment in the community. Prehm and Crosson (1969), Kirk (1964), Guskin and Spicker (1968), and Spicker and Bartel (1968) have summarized current educational research. Some of the general conclusions are discussed below.

ARE SPECIAL CLASSES BENEFICIAL?

A number of studies have attempted to determine whether it is better to place retarded children in special classes or leave them in the regular grades. All of these studies compared children assigned to special classes with children of comparable IQ's remaining in the regular grades. The general results of a large number of such experiments indicate that the benefits of special class placement are equivocal. Specifically:

1. Sociometric studies of mentally retarded children in the regular grades indicate that these children tend to be isolated and rejected by their normal peer groups (Johnson, 1950). Another study by Johnson (1961) of retarded children in special classes indicates that those in special classes are better accepted by their mentally retarded peer groups than are the mentally retarded in the regular grades. Welch (1967) found that an integrated special class was superior to a segregated special class. She studied the self-derogation and academic achievement of mentally retarded elementary school children assigned to (1) a segregated special class, and (2) an integrated special class in which the children spent one-half day in a regular class. She found that the children in the integrated program made higher achievement scores and decreased in self-derogation over an eight-month period, as compared to the children in the segregated class.

2. Although studies are contradictory, the bulk of research evidence supports the thesis that children in special classes are better adjusted, have a better

self-concept and less tension than the mentally retarded children remaining in the regular grades (Kirk, 1964; Guskin and Spicker, 1968).

3. In academic achievement the majority of studies show that the higher levels of the mentally retarded in the regular grades are equal or superior on educational achievement to similar children placed in special classes.

4. There is some, but not conclusive, evidence that lower educable mentally retarded tend to make better educational progress in special classes than in the regular grades, while those at the upper levels (75 to 85 IQ) tend to make better educational progress in the regular grades than in the special class (Goldstein, Moss, Jordan, 1965).

5. Children who are placed in special classes and those placed in regular grades at the age of 6 increase equally in IQ. There is no difference in extent of changes in IQ regardless of placement (Goldstein, Moss, Jordan, 1965).

Along with the rapid expansion of special education classes came a dependence on the IQ and a tendency to label children and place them in classes accordingly. Because the intelligence tests used are usually standardized on white, middle-class Americans, there has been a tendency for minority group children to score lower in IQ because they have not had comparable experiences, rather than because they are inherently less capable. This has resulted in a disproportionate number of minority group children being placed in special classes for the mentally retarded. This disproportionate placement of minority group children in special classes has been severely criticized in many quarters.

One response to this criticism has been the suggestion to abolish all classes for the mentally retarded and return these children to the regular grades. This proposal has been bolstered by the studies which show that, academically, educable mentally retarded children in the regular grades tend to achieve at an equal or higher level in reading, spelling, and arithmetic than do mentally retarded children in the special classes.

Dunn (1968) has presented arguments for abolishing special education for this group of children. He states: "A better education than special class placement is needed for socioculturally deprived children with mild learning problems who have been labeled educable mentally retarded" (p. 5). But he is "not arguing that we do away with our special education programs for the moderately and severely retarded" (p. 61). In an epilogue he states:

The conscience of special educators needs to rub up against morality. In large measure we have been at the mercy of the general education establishment in that we accept problem pupils who have been referred out of the regular grades. In this way, we contribute to the delinquency of the general educators since we remove the pupils that are problems for them and thus reduce their need to deal with individual differences. The *entente* of mutual delusion between general and special education that special class placement will be advantageous to slow learning children of poor parents can no longer be tolerated. We must face the reality—we are asked to take children others cannot teach, and a large percentage of these are from ethnically and/or economically disadvantaged backgrounds. Thus much of special education will continue to be a sham of dreams unless we immerse ourselves into the total environment of our children from inadequate homes and backgrounds and insist on a comprehensive ecological push—with a quality educational program as part of it. This is hardly compatible with our prevalent practice of expediency in which we employ many untrained and less than master teachers to increase the number of special day classes in response to the pressures of waiting lists. Because of these pressures from the school system, we have been guilty of fostering quantity with little regard for quality of special education instruction. Our first responsibility is to have an abiding commitment to the less fortunate children we aim to serve. Our honor, integrity, and honesty should no longer be subverted and rationalized by what we hope and may believe we are doing for these children—hopes and beliefs which have little basis in reality. (p. 20)

In evaluating the placement of children with learning disabilities and/or children coming from different sociocultural environments who appear to have low intellectual potential, consideration must be given to research evidence regarding their placement. Evidence has been given to suggest that the brighter children in a class for the mentally retarded tend to show conformity to the mean performance of the class (Goldstein, Moss, Jordan, 1965). Perhaps this is because the instructional level of the class is significantly below the capacity of the more capable children in the class; perhaps it is because the teacher's expectations are not high enough. Several studies of teacher expectations and children's achievement point to the latter possibility as being very significant.

Representative of such studies is one by Rosenthal and Jacobsen (1966). In this study the Flanagan Test of General Ability was administered to children in grades one through six in a large school system. Twenty percent of these children were selected at random, and the teachers informed that the children would increase in intelligence during the year. At the end of the year all of the children were retested. In grades one and two, the 20 percent whose teachers were told that these children would increase in IQ did make significant gains as compared to the other children. In the third to sixth grades there was no difference between the two groups.

Anderson (1970) attempted to replicate the Rosenthal and Jacobsen study in a community of predominantly Mexican-American and Negro children. She was unable to confirm the Rosenthal and Jacobsen results since the attempt to influence pupils' achievement by modifying teacher expectancy was not successful. On the other hand, the children who were expected to perform at a higher level by the teachers themselves did make higher achievement scores at the end of the year than did the group for whom the teachers held low expectancies. Anderson suggested that "the evidence is sufficient to cast considerable doubt upon the validity of results reported by Rosenthal and Jacobsen" (p. 68).

In another type of experiment Beez (1968) studied the effects of teacher expectancy on 5- and 6-year-old Head Start children. In this experiment Beez asked 60 summer school teachers to tutor 60 children individually, teaching them to recognize words on cards. The teachers were asked to teach as many words as the child could learn in a ten-minute period. One-half of the teachers were told that the child assigned to her was a poor learner, while the other half were told that the child would do well in school. The results were clear cut. The teachers who were told that the child would do poorly covered 5.66 words in the ten-minute period. The teachers who were told that the child would do well, covered 10.43 words. The children labeled as poor learners learned 3.07 words, while those labeled good learners learned 5.90 words.

These studies, although interesting and suggestive, do not give a definitive answer as to whether or not there is a detrimental effect from placing the label of mental retardation on a child who may not be low in general intelligence. Most of these children need an entirely different kind of program, and placing them in a special class for the mentally retarded is not efficacious. It is this author's opinion that the following procedure would be more relevant:

1. Children should be assigned to special classes for the mentally retarded only after a differential psychoeducational assessment indicates that the child shows a general mental retardation requiring a special program geared to his abilities. These classes should be comprised of children who, on the whole, have lower IQ's than children now so assigned.

2. Children with learning disabilities and children from minority ethnic groups whose background of experiences places them at a disadvantage in relation to the general population should remain in the regular grades but be helped by itinerant and resource teachers to adapt to the regular grades and establish adequate learning habits.

3. Regular elementary education, through more individualized instruction and teachers better informed on learning characteristics of educationally retarded children, should adapt to a large proportion of children they are currently referring for special education.

HOW DO RETARDED CHILDREN READ?

Considerable research has been conducted on (1) the level at which mentally retarded children read and (2) what process is most successful in teaching these children to read. The studies on reading reviewed by Kirk (1964) and by Cegelka and Cegelka (1970) yield some interesting conclusions:

1. Mentally retarded children do not read up to their mental-age-reading-grade expectancy, probably because teachers emphasize their social adjustment rather than their academic achievement, and also because the child who is most retarded educationally is referred to the special class.

2. Research on reading methods has not shown the superiority of any one method over others. Some authors found success with the phonic method, some with the experience or other methods. Experiments testing the effectiveness of a particular procedure have been conducted on retarded children who were significantly below their mental-age-grade expectancy. These children made rapid progress during the initial stages of training, then tapered off as they approached their mental-age-grade expectancy.

3. Brain-injured mentally retarded children with perceptual disturbances are able to learn to read as well as non-brain-injured retarded children when emphasis is placed on reading and special methods are used.

WHAT ARE THE ARITHMETIC ACHIEVEMENTS OF RETARDED CHILDREN?

The studies on arithmetic achievement indicate that retarded children achieve in harmony with their mental-age-grade expectancy in arithmetic fundamentals but are below this expectancy in arithmetic reasoning. It appears that, according to present methods of teaching, the retarded child is able to achieve at a higher grade level in the more mechanical computational skills than in arithmetic reasoning. This may be a reflection of the methods of teaching, since it is easier to drill on computational problems than to develop insights into quantitative concepts.

Some of the differences which have been found in the processes of arithmetic suggest that retarded children are inferior to average children of the same mental age in (1) solving arithmetic problems presented verbally, (2) establishing mature habits such as eliminating "counting on fingers," (3) decreasing careless mechanical errors and errors in reading, and (4) understanding the abstract terms of mathematics, space, time, and quantity. As in reading, research workers have not been able to find a significant difference between the arithmetic abilities of brain-injured and non-brain-injured retarded children. (5) In a study of the correlation of mentally retarded children's arithmetic achievement to Piaget tasks and mental age, Winifred Kirk (1968) found that (1) performance on Piaget tasks and mental age correlate equally with arithmetic achievement, and (2) performance on Piaget tasks correlates more closely to arithmetic computation.

As in other areas of achievement, speech and language appear to be highly correlated with mental age. It has been found that speech defects are more prevalent in the mentally retarded than in average children and that the greater the mental defect, the greater the prevalence of speech defects. It has been difficult to show substantial improvement in retarded children's speech as a result of speech therapy.

Like speech, reading, and arithmetic, language development is related to mental age, possibly because language is a factor in intelligence tests of the verbal type. Some studies have shown, however, that language development is also related to opportunities for language usage, and that some socially deprived children have improved in language development temporarily when they received special training.

Since language development is crucial to the intellectual development of mentally retarded children, experimenters have been investigating the effects of specific training in language understanding and language usage with the mentally retarded.

Smith (1962) gave 33 forty-five-minute language lessons over a three-month period to 16 mentally retarded children in a special class. He compared their progress with 16 mentally retarded children in a special class who did not receive such training. On the ITPA the experimental group gained 7 months on the test while the control group remained the same. Thirteen to fourteen months later Mueller and Smith (1964) retested the two groups and found that the experimental group gained 4.4 months while the control group nearly caught up with a gain of 8 months. Although the experimental group was still higher than the control group, the discrepancy was not statistically significant. It was concluded that a three-month training period was not sufficient to make a lasting difference in the psycholinguistic abilities of these children.

Blessing (1964) conducted a similar experiment with mentally retarded children. He gave 45 one-hour language tutoring sessions, three days a week, over a fourteen-week period. He tested the children four months after the cessation of training. He found that the training group made significant gains over the control group in vocal encoding, total word count, and mean sentence length. On the total ITPA, which includes memory factors, the difference between the groups was not significant.

It appears from the foregoing studies that short-term language lessons produce a temporary acceleration, but no lasting differences are evident. What is needed is long-term language training to determine if language facility can be permanently improved in mentally retarded children. Stearns (1966) presents some evidence in the Indiana project with kindergarten children. He found that when the total language development program was conducted throughout each day the experimental children showed significantly higher ability than the children attending a regular kindergarten without such a program.

DO RETARDED CHILDREN HAVE ARTISTIC OR MUSICAL ABILITIES?

Since industrial education and art and music education are standard parts of the curriculum for the mentally retarded, this phase of their education has been evaluated by some researchers.

The consensus of most workers is that art and music competence, like achievement in other areas, is related to mental age. The mentally retarded are slower to learn and remain longer at each stage. It is rare to find a mentally retarded child who has exceptional ability in art or music, although there is wide variation among the mentally retarded as a group and considerable overlap with normal children in ability.

Occasionally, however, we find someone who is classified and who functions as a mentally retarded child, but who has a special ability. Kiyoshi Yamashita is such a case. Kiyoshi was rescued from a broken home and placed in a home for retarded children in Japan. His IQ was recorded as 68. Noticing that Kiyoshi had some graphic skills, an instructor in the school encouraged this ability and stimulated Kiyoshi to produce paper collages of high quality. His artistic abilities broadened into the use of oils and developed to a point where he became, after parole from the institution, a noted artist. The Japanese press referred to him as the Van Gogh of Japan, a wandering genius.[1] Lindsley (1964), who has reviewed the history of this case, rejects the concept of idiot-savant, and proposes that specific skills in children with other deficits should be sought and developed.

WHAT ARE THE PHYSICAL ABILITIES OF THE RETARDED?

A few studies have been conducted on the motor proficiency and physical education achievements of the retarded. These studies (Francis and Rarick, 1960, Rarick and Widdop, 1970) indicate that in motor proficiency retarded children are inferior to normals. Studies on the effects of physical education programs in improving motor proficiency have shown positive results (Solomon and Pargle, 1967).

[1] The author has personally interviewed several people in Japan who knew Kiyoshi Yamashita well. They reported that his highest IQ rating was 78 and that he reached the third grade in school by the time he was paroled. The Japanese insist that he is mentally retarded but with great artistic abilities.

In some cases, however, retarded children have achieved above the average in sports like baseball and boxing. Again, there is a great deal of overlapping in ability with normal children, some mentally retarded being far above some average and gifted children in these areas; but most of them are below normal children in motor proficiency.

Adjustment in the Community

The ultimate purpose of educating mentally retarded children is to help them adjust to the community at the adult level as social participants and wage earners.

During earlier days many of the educable mentally retarded were committed to institutions. It was believed that they could obtain training there and later be paroled to the community as rehabilitated individuals. But the institutions were not being built fast enough to accommodate all the educable mentally retarded as well as those who were more severely retarded. The organization of special classes in the public schools, beginning in about 1900, was aimed at educating the retarded in the community where they would later live and work. Most institutions do not now admit the educable retarded unless the situation is complicated by other serious problems such as dependency or delinquency. Overcrowded conditions permit them to admit only emergency cases. The problem of the educable mentally retarded has therefore become a problem for the schools and the community.

To determine how well the educable mentally retarded adjust socially and occupationally at the adult level, numerous follow-up studies have been conducted.

One of the first of these was made by Channing (1932). She followed up 1000 special class graduates in ten large cities in the United States, approximately five years after they had left school, and found that a large proportion of them were employed and earned wages not far below those of their normal peers. Specifically, 20 percent of the boys and 34 percent of the girls were out of work half the time as compared to 8 percent of unselected boys and 11 percent of unselected girls of comparable age. Channing pointed out that the subnormal can obtain employment but that their employment records are less satisfactory than those for an unselected group.

Kennedy (1948) compared 356 individuals who had been diagnosed as mentally subnormal when they were in school with 129 adults of normal IQ, matched for age, sex, and socioeconomic status. Since the study was conducted during a period of high employment, better work records were found among the retarded than those shown by Channing in the late 1920's. Kennedy found that

(1) there were no differences in marriage rate among the two groups, (2) the retarded had a higher divorce rate, and (3) there was a tendency for the retarded to have an unsatisfactory work record, but little difference in wages earned. The conclusion was that there were many more similarities between the educable retarded and the normals than there were differences. Some of the adjustment differences noted indicated that the retarded participated less in recreational activities (theater, sports, dancing) and read less. Their jobs were primarily of the unskilled type, while many of the normal adults had office jobs requiring some academic education.

The most extensive long-term follow-up study was conducted by Baller in 1935 and followed up by Charles in 1953. Originally Baller (1936) selected 206 individuals who had previously been classified as mentally deficient and enrolled in special classes in Lincoln, Nebraska. He compared their social and economic status with that of a group of others of the same age who as children had been considered normal. He found many more infractions of the law and considerable job instability. Charles found 75 percent of this group fifteen years after they had been studied by Baller. At the time of Baller's study, the United States was in a depression and there was much unemployment. When Charles made his study, unemployment was at a minimum. His findings were as follows:

1. 80 percent of the sample found were married.

2. 21 percent of the married group had been divorced. These marriage and divorce rates were lower than the national averages.

3. About 80 percent of the married subjects had children; the average number of children per family was 2.03. The national average at that time was 2.62.

4. Their children were, on the whole, making satisfactory progress in school. The average IQ of the 73 children tested was 95 and IQ's ranged from 50 to 138.

5. 83 percent of the group located were self-supporting, some living in shacks and some in expensive new homes.

6. Laboring occupations for the males and housekeeping for the females constituted the majority of occupations. A few had managerial positions.

7. 24 of the subjects were retested with the Wechsler-Bellevue Intelligence Scale. The average verbal IQ was 72, the performance IQ was 88, and the total scale was 81. These scores were considerably higher than the original Binet ratings.

8. 60 percent of the men had violated the law. Most of the offenses, however, were traffic or civil violations of some kind. None was serious.

Baller, Charles, and Miller (1967) made a second follow-up study thirty years after the original Baller study in 1936. They compared the adjustment of the ex-special-class students with two other groups of children, one of slow learners and one of normal children. They found that: (1) 65 percent of the mentally retarded group returned or remained in their original communities as compared to 40 percent of the other two groups; (2) a third of the mentally retarded sample was decreased, but the mortality rate of the other groups was low; (3) unemployment and public assistance were somewhat higher among the retarded; and, (4) vocationally successful children in the group of mentally retarded had acquired their skill early.

Organization of Programs

Educable mentally retarded children are educated under many different programs in the regular grades, in special classes, and in residential schools. There is a current trend to retain the children in the community rather than enroll them in public or private residential schools, except in those cases where there are other problems such as delinquency, dependency, or emotional instability.

The most common administrative structure is the organization of special classes within neighborhood elementary or secondary schools. As indicated earlier the number of these special classes in public schools increased substantially following World War II. In addition, the IQ cut-off point for assignment to special classes has gradually increased over the years. In the 1920's when a cut-off point was used it was usually an IQ of 69. Since then it has gradually increased until 80 IQ is now common. This has substantially increased the number of children in classes for the mentally retarded, including many children mislabeled mentally retarded (minority group children and children with learning disabilities) who often score in the 70's and 80's on intelligence tests. This has stimulated the criticism of special classes for the mentally retarded discussed on pages 199–202. Common methods of organizing educational programs are discussed below under (1) preschool programs, (2) primary elementary programs, (3) intermediate elementary programs, (4) secondary programs, and (5) postschool programs.

PRESCHOOL PROGRAMS (BELOW AGE SIX)

There are few special preschool or kindergarten programs that include self-contained special classes for the educable mentally retarded. One reason for this is that these children are not usually identified as mentally retarded at an early age unless the retardation is associated with lack of speech or some physical manifestation such as cerebral palsy. Not until they enter the regular school and fail to learn are they examined and found to be mentally retarded.

Customarily, retarded children are admitted to kindergartens (when such exist in the community) with regular children. If at the end of the year the teacher and the psychological examiners feel that a particular child will fail in the first grade, the child is retained in the kindergarten for another year. A more efficient procedure, both for the child and for the community, would be to identify the children in kindergarten early in the year and provide them with special instruction in language, in perception, and in adaptation to school materials and activities. By using resource or itinerant teachers who are trained in clinical education this procedure may compensate for the experiential deficits in the child who comes from a psychosocially deprived environment; and/or it may serve to activate deficient functions in the child with psycholinguistic disabilities. For the child with a low rate of general intellectual development, the program could design experiences leading to later school activities.

THE PRIMARY-ELEMENTARY PROGRAM (AGES SIX TO NINE)

Most mentally retarded children enter the first grade at the age of six and fail to learn what is required in the first grade. There are three alternate plans that can be used with these children to provide them with special education.

1. The school may leave them in the regular grades but provide instruction by an itinerant or resource teacher.
2. The school may enroll them in a special class, but allow them to attend the regular grades part of the day.
3. The school may organize a self-contained special class for them for the whole day.

The type of placement depends upon the degree of retardation of the children, their abilities and disabilities, the composition of the rest of the class, and the flexibility of the regular grade teacher.

THE INTERMEDIATE-ELEMENTARY PROGRAM (AGES NINE TO THIRTEEN)

The most frequently organized self-contained special class for the mentally retarded has been for children of ages 9 to 13. In most school systems the child attends the regular grades (without special help from a resource teacher) until he has failed for several years. He is then referred for examination, tested, and a decision is made regarding the most beneficial placement or program.

At this age level special education programs may be organized in any of the several ways described for the primary children. Regardless of the type of placement, the goal of the school is to help the child: (1) learn the tool subjects of reading, writing, and arithmetic, (2) adjust to and learn about his physical environment (the community, the state, the nation), (3) learn about his social environment (people, customs, and institutions), and (4) learn about himself and his drives, desires, and aspirations.

Skills in the tool subjects are developed during periods of systematic instruction and during periods of application of the skills to life situations. Work units or experience units have been used extensively with the mentally retarded. These have been found most useful in teaching the children about their physical, social, and personal environment.

THE SECONDARY SCHOOL PROGRAM

In the past, the educable mentally retarded child who attended the intermediate elementary class remained in that class until he left school at the end of the compulsory school age. Recently, however, school systems have organized special classes at both the junior and senior high school levels. Children are admitted to the junior high school special program at ages 13 and 14, and to the senior high school class at age 15 or 16. Special programs in senior high school have tended to increase the school's holding power for these children until the age of 18 or 19.

A special program in the high school usually involves the assignment of the children to one special teacher for a part of the day. In this extended homeroom the pupils continue with instruction in the tool subjects but they go to some classes with other high school pupils—for example, beginning classes in home economics, industrial education, physical education, art, and music.

The curriculum for educable mentally retarded children in the secondary school emphasizes:

1. Experiences to extend their efficiency in the tool subjects of reading, arithmetic, spelling, and writing. Since this is terminal academic education for the educable retarded child, he should learn to utilize these tool subjects in everyday activities.

2. Development of "home building" skills. During this terminal education the pupils should learn to become participating members of a family and to be responsible for family activities. Home economics for the girls and household mechanics for the boys are important aspects of the secondary school curriculum.

3. Occupational education including such attitudes and skills as manners, appearance, methods of getting along with the "boss" or fellow workers, following directions, expressing vocational goals and skills, general job training, and acquiring vocational information. Occupational education should not be confused with vocational education or specific trade training. These children do not necessarily go into the skilled trades and consequently are not placed in vocational schools for that purpose.

4. Getting along in society, holding a job, and participating in community life. This requires adequate social relationships and is an important goal of the secondary school curriculum. The educable mentally retarded youth should have experiences which develop good interpersonal relations with others in the community.

5. Understanding of physical and mental health. This includes good personal hygiene, attractive appearance, following of health rules, using leisure time well, establishing adequate values, acquiring a sense of achievement, accepting one's own limitations, good personal conduct, establishment of security, and pride in accomplishment.

POSTSCHOOL PROGRAM

In the past, most educable mentally retarded youth could obtain unskilled jobs and partially or totally support themselves. This situation continues to some extent. However, because of the increasing complexity of our society, it is becoming more necessary to give additional training and assistance in the placement of the mentally retarded in jobs suitable to their abilities and educational level.

Job training, placement, and follow-up after the school years have been facilitated by Public Law 113, passed by the United States Congress in 1943. Prior to that time the Civilian Vocational Rehabilitation Program was confined to the physically handicapped. Under the new law the vocational rehabilitation program is also allowed to train, place, and follow up educable mentally retarded youth.

This law provides a link between school training and the vocational rehabilitation divisions which exist in all states. The school can provide the general education, and the vocational rehabilitation counselor can carry on from there. Some schools are now incorporating supervised part-time job placement with the terminal school program whenever vocational rehabilitation and the school can cooperate. These new programs are more necessary now than ever before because it is more difficult for the mentally retarded to adjust socially and vocationally in present-day society. In the first place, society is becoming more urban and more complex. In the second place, automation is decreasing the number of unskilled jobs. Our culture now places a premium on intelligence, management ability, technical progress, and machine operation. The mentally retarded will require more help in the future to adjust to a society that emphasizes service positions, professional competence, and technical skill.

Instruction in Special Education

In Chapter 1 special education was defined as the part of education which is extra or in addition to that ordinarily offered to the average children in a school. A legitimate question would be: What additional practices and procedures are used in a special class for the mentally retarded?

Besides the formulation of specific objectives and the organization of special programs, there are certain adaptations of instructional materials and procedures, which we shall examine.

ASSESSMENT

The mentally retarded child must have a special diagnosis including medical, social, psychological, and educational evaluations before he is assigned to a special class. A reassessment should be made at periodic intervals thereafter. His level of development in various areas should be evaluated as was done for each of the children represented in the developmental profiles. This kind of assessment, together with the medical and social history, will give the teacher an indication of the child's assets and liabilities, an insight into his abilities and achievements as shown by his developmental pattern, and facts about his physical and social status before she begins instruction. It will give her a good beginning on the ongoing evaluation she must make. Modifications of educational and instructional practices are to a large extent dependent upon the adequate assessment of the child. This is one feature which differentiates the education of the retarded child from that of the average, since the normal child does not usually need such a comprehensive and thorough evaluation.

This assessment will indicate whether the child is failing in school because of general mental retardation, or whether his lack of learning ability is due to a learning disability or the result of cultural factors that made him appear mentally retarded. Theoretically, these children should be culled out of the program at the outset, but practically, because of the current lag in establishing programs for such children, many are still found in classes for the mentally retarded.

SPECIAL MATERIALS

Educable mentally retarded children need special materials. The physical size of the classroom, the desks, and the furnishings are not different from those of a regular grade, but the instructional materials must be different. For example, the reading books used in regular classes are geared to the development of an average child. Whereas it may take seventeen repetitions of a word before the average child can learn it in a primer or preprimer, the retarded child may need twenty-five or thirty repetitions before he will learn it. This means that the primer or first reader goes a little too fast for efficient instruction of the retarded child, and the teacher must find supplementary material, fill in with additional instructional materials, and use specialized instructional procedures in a variety of situations if the child is to learn efficiently. It is necessary to improvise, adapt, and adjust books and materials to the rate of learning of these children. Likewise, the content of reading material must often be adapted to the chronological ages of these children. A 10-year-old mentally retarded child, although intellectually functioning at a 6-year-old level, is not interested in the physical activities and experiential content of most primers and first readers. This incongruity has been widely recognized and more and more appropriate books are becoming available with mature content and easy reading level.

SPECIAL REMEDIATION

Most mentally retarded children develop fairly evenly but substantially below the normal in most areas. Others show marked deviations among their abilities, performing consistently in most areas but showing lowered ability in others. For example, 12-year-old Bobby may function in the 8- to 10-year range in all areas with only small deviations. On the other hand, 12-year-old Tony may function at the 9-year level in language, speech, arithmetic, etc. but have difficulty learning to read. He has a specific learning disability in reading beyond his general developmental retardation. He may have psycholinguistic disabilities within his range of developmental retardation, similar to a child who is of relatively normal intelligence but with wide discrepancies in abilities as discussed in Chapter 5, Figure 5–3. Similar cases have been reported by Kirk (1940).

Educable mentally retarded children who have specific disabilities over and above their general retardation may need remedial help in communication, or in understanding arithmetic concepts, or in relating abstract ideas, or in rote memory. It is, therefore, necessary for the teacher to find these special problems, to secure more detailed diagnoses, and to introduce remedial procedures.

Throughout the last century there have been attempts to discover specific disabilities and to find appropriate clinical teaching procedures which will remedy them. Strauss and Lehtinen (1947) developed special clinical teaching procedures for certain kinds of brain-damaged children. Hegge, Kirk, and Kirk (1936) developed the *Remedial Reading Drills* for educable mentally retarded children with reading disabilities. Decroly, Montessori, and others all attempted to develop special clinical methods. Recent advances in differential diagnosis and special clinical procedures are discussed in Chapter 2.

APPLYING LEARNING PRINCIPLES

The primary characteristics of mentally retarded children is that they do not learn as readily as others of the same chronological age. They lack a high level of generalization and are usually unable to learn material incidentally, without instruction, as the average child learns it. Much of the knowledge and skills acquired by the average child is learned without specific instruction by the teacher. But for the retarded child instruction needs to be systematically presented without too much reliance on incidental learning. Learning should be programmed in sequence and presented in such a way that the child will learn at a rate compatible with his development. Systematic instruction in every area requires time, planning, and insight, the essentials in a special education program for the educable mentally retarded child.

Many sound learning principles have been applied in behavior modification techniques, including the use of programmed learning. Denny (1966) has discussed some of these principles as related to programmed learning with the retarded. None of these principles by themselves will transform the learning process. However, each has a part to play, and in combination these principles tend to maximize learning.

To implement systematic instruction it is necessary to apply sound principles and techniques that will facilitate learning. Some of the principles which facilitate learning and make teaching more profitable are:

1. *Never let the child fail*. Organize materials and use methods which lead the child to the right answer. Provide clues where necessary. Narrow the choices he has in responding. Lead him to the right answer by rewording the question or simplifying the problem. Never leave him in a failure, but carry him along until he finds success.

2. *Provide feedback* so that he knows when he has responded correctly. Learning is facilitated when the child has knowledge of whether his response is correct or not. If his response is incorrect, let him know it, but let it be only a way station in finding the correct response. Lessons should be so arranged that the child obtains an immediate feedback on the correctness of his

answer. This is one of the principles used in any good programmed learning procedure. If a child is learning to write the word *dog*, for example, he covers the model, writes the word, then compares his response with the model, thus getting feedback on his effort.

3. *Reinforce correct responses.* Reinforcement should be immediate and clear. It can be either tangible, as in providing tokens, candy, etc., or it can be in the form of social approval and the satisfaction of winning a game.

4. *Find the optimum level at which the child should work.* If the material is too easy, the child is not challenged to apply his best effort; if too difficult, he faces failure and frustration.

5. *Proceed in a systematic, step-by-step fashion* so that the more basic necessary knowledge and habits precede more difficult material.

6. *Use minimal change* from one step to the next to facilitate learning.

7. *Provide for positive transfer of knowledge from one situation to another.* This is facilitated by helping the child generalize from one situation to another. By presenting the same concept in various settings and in various relationships, the child can transfer the common elements in each. Itard, for example, when training the Wild Boy of Aveyron, noted that the boy learned to select a particular knife from a group of objects in response to the written word *knife,* but that when a knife of a different shape was substituted he could not respond. The child had not generalized the concept of *knife;* he had failed to transfer the understanding of the label to knives in general.

8. *Provide sufficient repetition of experiences to develop over-learning.* Many teachers have said, "Johnny learns a word one day but forgets it the next day." In such cases, Johnny probably had not had enough repetition of the word in varying situations to insure over-learning, that is, learning to the point where he will not forget it readily. Mentally retarded children seem to require more repetitions of an experience or an association in order to retain it.

9. *Space the repetitions of material over time* rather than massing the experiences in a short duration. When a new concept is presented, come back to it again and again, often in new settings, not as drill but as transfer to a new situation.

10. *Consistently associate a given stimulus or cue with one and only one response in the early stages of learning.* Do not tell the child, "This letter sometimes says *a* and sometimes says *ah.*" Teach him one sound at a time until it is overlearned and then teach the other sound as a different con-

figuration in a new setting. If the child has to vacillate between two responses he will become confused.

11. *Motivate the child toward greater effort by:* (a) reinforcement and the satisfaction of succeeding, (b) variation in the presentation of material, (c) enthusiasm on the part of the teacher, and (d) optimal length of sessions.

12. *Limit the number of concepts presented in any one period.* Do not confuse the child by trying to have him learn too many things at one time. Introduce new material only after older material has become familiar.

13. *Arrange materials with proper cues for attention.* Arrange materials in such a way to direct the pupil's attention so that he will learn to attend to the cues in the situation that will facilitate his learning, and to learn to disregard those factors in the learning situation that are irrelevant.

14. *Provide success experiences.* Educable mentally retarded children who have failed in the regular grades and then been placed in a special class may have developed low frustration tolerance, negative attitudes toward school work, and possibly some compensatory behavior problems which make them socially unpopular. The best way to cope with these problems is to organize a *day-to-day* program presenting the child with short-range as well as long-range tasks in which he succeeds. The self-concept and the self-evaluation of the child are dependent upon how well he succeeds in the assignments given to him. Thus a special class teacher must be very careful to see not only that the child does not fail but also that he experiences positive success and knows that he has succeeded. Although this principle is applicable to all children it is particularly necessary with children who are retarded. They face enough failures in school and in life without having to repeat them over and over again in a classroom situation.

Kolstoe (1970) also deals with the manner in which learning tasks are presented. He states:

1. The tasks should be uncomplicated. The new tasks should contain the fewest possible elements, and most of the elements should be familiar, so he has very few unknowns to learn.

2. The tasks should be brief. This assures that he will attend to the most important aspects of the tasks and not get lost in a sequence of interrelated events.

3. The tasks should be sequentially presented so the learner proceeds in a sequence of small steps, each one built upon previously learned tasks.

4. Each learning task should be the kind in which success is possible. One of the major problems to be overcome is that of failure proneness. This major deterrent to learning can be effectively reduced through success experiences.

5. Overlearning must be built into the lessons. Drills in game form seem to lessen the disinterest inherent in unimaginative drill.

6. Learning tasks should be applied to objects, problems, and situations in the learner's life environment. Unless the tasks are relevant, the learner has great difficulty in seeing their possible importance. (pp. 22–23)

SUMMARY

1. The educable mentally retarded child has been defined as one who is unable to profit sufficiently from the program of the regular school, but who has potentialities for development in: (1) minimum educability in the academic subjects of the school, (2) social adjustment in the home and community, and (3) minimum occupational adequacy to become partially or totally self-supporting.
2. Physical, intellectual, academic, social and personal, and occupational characteristics have been described.
3. Educational provisions are made in regular classes with the help from itinerant and resource teachers, in integrated special classes (part-time in a special class and part-time in the regular grade), in self-contained special classes, and in residential schools.
4. Classification of children as mentally retarded on the basis of an IQ has increased enrollment in special classes and included children from minority groups and children with learning disabilities. The proportion of these children who are not retarded according to other criteria are best served in the regular grades with the help of itinerant or resource teachers.
5. The educability and potential development of educable mentally retarded children in academic, social, and occupational areas have been reviewed.
6. Special principles of learning and teaching are applied to the education of educable mentally retarded children.

REFERENCES

Anderson, Peggy J. 1970. Teacher Expectations on Pupil Self-Conceptions. Unpublished doctoral dissertation. Irvine, California: University of California.

Baller, W. R. 1936. A Study of the Present Social Status of a Group of Adults Who When They Were in Elementary Schools Were Classified as Mentally Deficient. *Genetic Psychology Monographs* 18: 165–244.

Baller, W. R.; Charles, O. C.; and Miller, E. 1967. *Mid-Life Attainment of the Mentally Retarded: A Longitudinal Study.* Lincoln, Nebraska: University of Nebraska Press.

Beez, W. V. 1968. Influence of Biased Psychological Reports on Teacher Behavior and Pupil Performance. Unpublished doctoral dissertation, Indiana University.

Blessing, K. R. 1964. An Investigation of a Psycholinguistic Deficit in Mentally Retarded Children: Detection, Remediation and Related Variables. Unpublished doctoral dissertation, University of Wisconsin.

Cegelka, Patricia A., and Cegelka, W. 1970. A Review of Research: Reading and the Educable Mentally Handicapped. *Exceptional Children* 37 (November): 187–200.

Channing, Alice. 1932. *Employment of Mentally Deficient Boys and Girls.* Department of Labor, Bureau Publication No. 210. Washington, D.C.: Government Printing Office.

Charles, D. C. 1953. Ability and Accomplishment of Persons Earlier Judged Mentally Deficient. *Genetic Psychology Monographs* 47: 3–71.

Denny, M. R. 1966. A Theoretical Analysis and Its Application to Training the Mentally Retarded. In Ellis, N. R. (ed.), *International Review of Research in Mental Retardation.* Vol. 2, pp. 1–27. New York: Academic Press.

Dunn, L. M. 1968. Special Education for the Mentally Retarded: Is Much of It Justified? *Journal of Exceptional Children* 35 (September): 5–24.

Educational Policies Commission. 1938. *The Purposes of Education in American Democracy.* Washington, D.C.: National Education Association.

Francis, R. J., and Rarick, L. 1960. *Motor Characteristics of the Mentally Retarded.* Cooperative Research Monograph No. 1. Washington, D.C.: U.S. Department of Health, Education, and Welfare.

Goldstein, H.; Moss, J.; and Jordan, Laura J. 1965. *The Efficacy of Special Class Training on the Development of Mentally Retarded Children.* Cooperative Research Project No. 619. Washington, D.C.: U.S. Office of Education.

Guskin, S. L., and Spicker, H. H. 1968. Educational Research in Mental Retardation. In Ellis, N. R. (ed.), *International Review of Research in Mental Retardation,* Vol. 3, pp. 217–278. New York: Academic Press.

Hegge, T. G.; Kirk, S. A.; and Kirk, Winifred D. 1936. *Remedial Reading Drills.* Ann Arbor: George Wahr.

Johnson, G. O. 1961. *A Comparative Study of the Personal and Social Adjustment of Mentally Handicapped Children Placed in Special Classes with Mentally Handicapped Children Who Remain in Regular Classes.* Syracuse, New York: Syracuse University Press.

———. 1950. A Study of the Social Position of Mentally Handicapped Children in the Regular Grades. *American Journal of Mental Deficiency* 55 (July): 60–89.

Kennedy, Ruby Jo. 1948. *The Social Adjustment of Morons in a Connecticut City.* Hartford, Connecticut: Mansfield-Southbury Training Schools Social Service Department.

Kirk, S. A. 1964. Research in Education of the Mentally Retarded. In Stevens, H., and Heber, R. (eds.), *Mental Retardation: A Review of Research,* pp. 57–99. Chicago: University of Chicago Press.

———. 1940. *Teaching Reading to Slow Learning Children.* Boston: Houghton-Mifflin.

Kirk, S. A., and Johnson, O. 1951. *Educating the Retarded Child.* Boston: Houghton-Mifflin.

Kirk, Winifred D. 1968. Correlation Between Arithmetic Achievement and Performance on Piaget Tasks. *The Slow Learning Child* 15 (November): 89–101.

Kolstoe, O. P. 1970. *Teaching Educable Mentally Retarded Children.* New York: Holt, Rinehart, and Winston.

Lindsley, O. R. 1964. Can Deficiency Produce Specific Superiority: The Challenge of the Idiot-Savant. *Exceptional Children* 31 (December): 225–232.

Mueller, M. W., and Smith, J. O. 1964. The Stability of Language Age Modification. *American Journal of Mental Deficiency* 68 (January): 537–539.

Prehm, H. J., and Crosson, J. E. 1969. The Mentally Retarded. *Education of Exceptional Children* 39 (February): 5–24.

Rarick, L., and Widdop, J. H. 1970. The Physical Fitness and Motor Performance of Educable Mentally Retarded Children. *Exceptional Children* 36 (March): 509–520.

Rosenthal, R., and Jacobsen, L. 1966. Teachers Expectancies: Determiners of Pupils I.Q. Gains. *Psychological Reports* 19: 113–118.

Smith, J. O. 1962. *Effects of a Group Language Development Program Upon the Psycholinguistic Abilities of Educable Mental Retardates.* Nashville, Tennessee: Peabody College Special Education Monograph Series No. 1.

Soloman, A., and Pargle, R. 1967. Demonstrating Physical Fitness Impairment in E.M.R. *Exceptional Children* 34 (November): 163–168.

Spicker, H. H., and Bartel, Nettie R. 1968. The Mentally Retarded. In Johnson, G. O., and Blank, Harriet D. (eds.), *Exceptional Children Research Review*, pp. 38–109. Arlington, Virginia: Council for Exceptional Children.

Stearns, K. E. 1966. Experimental Group Language Development for Psychosocially Deprived Preschool Children. Unpublished doctoral dissertation, Indiana University.

Strauss, A. A., and Lehtinen, Laura. 1947. *Psychopathology and Education of the Brain-Injured Child.* New York: Grune and Stratton.

Welch, Elizabeth A. 1967. The Effects of Segregated and Partially Integrated School Programs on Self-Concept and Academic Achievement of Educable Mentally Retarded Children. *Exceptional Children* 34 (October): 93–100.

SEVEN

THE

TRAINABLE

MENTALLY

RETARDED

CHILD

The trainable mentally retarded child has been defined as one who, because of subnormal intelligence, is not capable of learning in classes for the educable mentally retarded but who does have potentialities for learning (1) self-care, (2) adjustment to the home or neighborhood, and (3) economic usefulness in the home, a sheltered workshop, or an institution.

Other terms have been used to denote the *trainable child*. The terms "imbecile," "semi-dependent," "severely retarded," "middle-grade defective," and "child with an IQ between about 25 and 50" are somewhat synonymous with "trainable." The term "trainable" appears to be most widely preferred. The World Health Organization (1954) discussed the problem of terminology at length and concluded, "These children are often called 'ineducable' although the term 'trainable' has been suggested as an alternative, and this term is preferred by the Committee" (pp. 23–24).

Kirk (1957) surveyed the programs provided in the states which had established programs by 1956. In a composite statement for school use, he summarized the characteristics incorporated in most definitions. According to this formulation, which is widely accepted today, a trainable child is one who is (1) of school age; (2) developing at the rate of one-third to one-half that of the normal child (IQ's on individual examinations roughly between 30 and 50); (3) of retarded mental development to such an extent that he is ineligible for classes for the educable mentally retarded but will, however, not be custodial, totally dependent, or require nursing care throughout his life; (4) capable of learning self-care tasks (such as dressing, eating, toileting) and capable of learning to protect himself from common dangers in the home, school, or neighborhood; (5) capable of learning social adjustment in the home or neighborhood and learning to share, respect property rights, and cooperate in a family unit and with the neighbors; and (6) capable of learning economic usefulness in the home and neighborhood by assisting in chores around the house or in doing routine tasks in a sheltered environment under supervision, even though he will require some care, supervision, and economic support throughout his life.

The Prevalence of Trainable Mentally Retarded Children

A study of Illinois communities indicated that there are approximately 1.5 trainable children per 1000 school-age children living at home (Office of the Superintendent of Public Instruction, 1954). The institutions had received from these same communities less than one child per 1000. This meant that there were more children of the trainable type in a community than in institutions, but that both combined would be between 2 and 3 per 1000 school-age children.

A similar study was made in Michigan in three communities (State Department of Public Instruction, 1955). Here there appeared to be an average of 1.7 trainable children per 1000 school-age children in the community and 1.6 from those communities in institutions. Thus here there were between 3 and 4 children per 1000 school population.

Another study by Bienenstock and Coxe (1956) in New York, found that there were 1.1 trainable children per 1000 in the community and 1.7 trainable and totally dependent in institutions.

The results of these studies indicate that there are approximately two to four children of the trainable type in a population of 1000 school-age children, and that 1 to 2 out of 1000 are in a community and eligible for classes for trainable children. In terms of the organization of classes this means that there usually has to be a population of about 7000 school-age children, or a total population of 25,000 to 30,000 individuals in a community, before one class for the trainable is feasible. Such a community usually has between seven and twelve children eligible for such a class. The other trainable children would be in institutions.

The figures on prevalence of trainable children in a school-age population appear to be consistent with prevalence figures in England. Birch et al (1970) reported a study made in Aberdeen, Scotland, for children with IQ's below 50.

His prevalence rate was 3.7 per 1000 school-age children. He compared this figure with other studies and found a surprising consistency in prevalence rates with previous studies in the British Isles and in the United States. Table 7–1 is a reproduction of Birch's comparison of prevalence figures. Birch et al found no difference in prevalence rates between high and low socioeconomic levels for children with IQ's below 50, but found a marked relationship between socioeconomic levels and the frequency of educable mentally retarded between 60 and 75 IQ. The prevalence rate for educable mentally retarded was 11.1 per 1000 school-age children for the highest social class, and 43.3 per 1000 for the lowest social class.

Provisions for Trainable Children

INSTITUTIONAL PROVISIONS

The first institution for the mentally retarded in the United States was organized in Massachusetts in 1848. Since that date institutions have been built in most of the states, some states having as many as seven.

TABLE 7–1

Comparison of the prevalence rates of IQ under 50 in age groups where all subjects are likely to be known

Study location and year	Age of children	Total rate per 1000 of IQ < 50
England and Wales (Lewis, 1929)		
1925–1927 urban	7–14	3.71
Middlesex (Goodman & Tizard, 1962)		
1960	7–14	3.45
1960	10–14	3.61
Salford (Susser & Kushlick, 1961)		
1961	15–19	3.64
Wessex (Kushlick, 1964)		
1964 county boroughs	15–19	3.54
1964 counties	15–19	3.84
Baltimore, Md., U.S.A. (Lemkau et al, 1943)		
1936	10–14	3.3
Aberdeen, Scotland		
1962	8–10	3.7

Source: Birch et al, 1970, p. 34. Copyright © 1970 Williams and Wilkins.

The original purpose of most of the institutions was to train the mentally retarded and return them to the community. Some states did not originally admit totally dependent children but accepted only children who were trainable and educable. Few of these institutions, however, could actually refuse admission to emergency cases of totally dependent children. As time went on, all of them began to accept children of all grades of defect, and those remaining in the institution for life were of the lowest abilities.

Thus the admissions to most of the public institutions consisted of children with all grades of mental defect. Originally, and for many years, the admissions to institutions included a larger proportion of educable than of trainable children, and more trainable than totally dependent.

Goldstein (1959) tabulated the first admissions of individuals into institutions from 1900 to 1952. He found that from 1922 to 1939 the institutions admitted approximately 45 percent morons (educable), about 30 percent imbeciles (trainable), and approximately 17 percent idiots (totally dependent). By 1952 the picture had changed. The moron group had dropped to approximately 35 percent while the imbecile group had increased to 37 percent and the idiot admissions to over 20 percent.

Farber (1968) found that by 1963 the moron (educable) group of first admissions had dropped to 23.5 percent as compared to the 45 percent earlier. The percentage of first admissions who were in the imbecile (trainable) group remained the same, while those classified as idiots (totally dependent) rose to 25.2 percent. These figures indicate that the residential institutions are gradually becoming less like training institutions, as they were originally intended, and more like hospitals or life-care institutions.

As communities incorporate more retarded children into their schools the rate of commitment to institutions tends to decrease. Henderson (1957) has shown this tendency among educable mentally retarded in Illinois institutions. He also found that the educable child who is sent to an institution from a community is usually dependent or delinquent. The reason for removal from a community, therefore, is not only mental retardation but also an inadequate home or a tendency toward delinquency. If the child were not retarded, he would probably have been sent either to a home for dependent children or to an institution for delinquent children.

During the depression of the 1930's and during World War II, with its shortages of materials and manpower, few institutions were built or expanded. As population increased (and consequently the numbers of mentally retarded), those institutions in existence were unable to house the number applying for admission. Waiting lists became longer and longer, and the institutions which were built or expanded were far from sufficient to accommodate the new requests and also take care of the backlog of children requiring admission. This situation, together with other factors, caused parents to organize and to request provisions for their retarded children in the community.

COMMUNITY PROVISIONS

It appears, from the large waiting lists, that our society is not willing to build sufficient institutions to take care of all of the trainable children in the community. Furthermore, many parents do not want to send their retarded children to institutions but would rather support them at home. This is a personal problem which in each case must be settled on its own merits.

Many parents who had accepted the responsibility for keeping their children at home instead of having them committed to an Institution felt the need for some kind of group activity and for some kind of organized training program. At first they met together to set up their own classes for the children, hiring their own teachers (often not adequately qualified), procuring their own supplies, and organizing classes in homes, in basements, in churches, or wherever they could find space. At the same time, they tried to make the public aware of their needs and sought the support of social agencies and state legislatures and local school boards. Some communities became cognizant of the problem and accepted the responsibility for helping to support these classes. Some communities incorporated them into the school system, thereby making it possible to improve the standards for teachers, housing, and programs. Better criteria were established for the admission of children which made possible a more homogeneous grouping.

There remains a controversy, however, as to whether training these children fits into the functions of a school or whether it is impossible for a school to offer the children experiences which will be profitable to their growth and development and which cannot be provided adequately by the family or other agencies.

The parents have argued that they, as taxpayers, have helped to pay for the public schools and that their children should not be deprived of the benefits just because they have become less fortunate. They have pointed out that the statutes in many states provide that all children are entitled to an education and that school districts are required by law to supply schools for all children, not just a certain segment of the children. These statutes were drawn up before the advent of the concept of the IQ or the concept that schools can provide for many kinds of children. For that reason it is practically mandatory for schools to admit the mentally retarded and provide adequate training for them just as they provide adequate, though different, training for other children. Some states have provisions for the exclusion of children who disrupt the classroom, who are behavior problems, or who are a danger to themselves and others, but it is recognized that most of the trainable children do not fall into these categories. Thus the schools have found it difficult to exclude them on a legal basis.

On the other hand, some educators and many parents of normal children maintain that public schools should not organize classes for trainable children because this changes the concept of the role of a school. They feel that it is the function of a school to teach academic subjects and that schools should be limited to those who are educable and who can profit at a reasonable level from such a program in order to become socially and economically independent at the adult level. If a child cannot be educated to become relatively independent at the adult level, they believe, the problem is outside the scope of an educational institution.

The controversies of the 1950's, the activities of the National Association for Retarded Children, and Federal involvement in programs for the mentally retarded resulted in major community developments in the form of research and service for trainable mentally retarded children.

Public School Classes. Whereas most school systems previously excluded trainable mentally retarded children, currently, most school systems provide training for these children. Most state departments of education subsidize local school systems for the purpose of providing school programs for the trainable child of school age. Classes are organized for the trainable mentally retarded child in elementary schools or in separate buildings.

Private Community Preschools. Because trainable mentally retarded children are identified at an early age, preschool programs have been organized in many communities. These preschools have been organized by parents' associations and supported financially by community funds, foundations, parents' groups, and tuition.

Sheltered Workshops. Since the majority of trainable children, upon completion of their public school program, are unable to be regularly employed, sheltered workshops have been organized in the larger communities. These workshops enroll adolescent and adult mentally retarded individuals, train them to do routine tasks, contract with industry for piece work on simple assemblies, and also develop and make saleable products. In well-established workshops the mentally retarded come to work or are transported to work on a full-day basis, and are paid wages for their labor. Thus, trainable adults become partially self-supporting. Besides the remuneration that is received from contracts and the sale of products, the sheltered workshops are also supported financially by parents' organizations, foundations, community funds, and donations. In some of the larger cities the community center for this level of mental retardation includes a diagnostic center, a preschool, a sheltered workshop, and a recreation center.

Diagnostic Evaluation Clinics. The Children's Bureau of the Department of Health, Education, and Welfare has organized and supported, partially or totally, diagnostic clinics in communities primarily serving preschool mentally retarded children. These free clinics receive referrals from parents and community agencies. Their main responsibility is to evaluate the child medically, socially, and psychologically and to recommend placement and treatment.

Comprehensive Community Facilities. In 1963 President John F. Kennedy requested and received from Congress history-making legislation on behalf of the mentally retarded. Public Law 88–164 provided Federal grants to states for assistance in construction of specially designed public and other nonprofit facilities for the diagnosis, treatment, education, training, or custodial care of the mentally retarded, including sheltered workshops. Under this law all states have been granted Federal funds to establish comprehensive community facilities to include day-care services, residential care, and diagnostic and evaluation services. These centers attempt to fill in the gaps in services needed and also to reduce the need for large state residential schools.

In addition to the community facilities for the mentally retarded, Public Law 88–164 provided funds for the following: (1) the construction of comprehensive research centers at universities for biological, medical, social, and behavioral research; (2) the construction of university-affiliated facilities to provide the physical and clinical accommodations for training technical personnel (physicians, nurses, psychologists, speech therapists, and educators) required to care for the mentally retarded; (3) funds for training of educational personnel for handicapped children; and (4) financial support for community mental health services.

In 1970, the Federal Congress amended Public Law 88–164, changing the name from Mental Retardation Facilities and Mental Health Centers Construction Act of 1963 to Developmental Disabilities Services and Facilities Construction Act of 1970 (P-L. 91–517). This act does not continue the construction of research centers, but broadens the scope to include other disabilities such as epilepsy and cerebral palsy.

The Organization of Community Classes

Remarkable progress in the quality and organization of classes for the trainable has been made in a decade of trial and error. Beginning with a spontaneous, haphazard program in which parents operated classes on a shoestring in whatever location they could buy, beg, or borrow, classes for the trainable have acquired professional status and financial support. There is considerable variation in the organization and procedure, depending on the location and in large part on the composition of the classes. As criteria for admission became more clearly delineated and as the objectives were better understood, the program became more meaningful.

ADMISSION REQUIREMENTS

The admission requirements for school classes for trainable children have been formulated in many states. The following represent those most generally in effect.

1. The age of admission for trainable retarded children in the public school classes is generally the same as for other children. In most instances this age is 6.

2. The objective criterion which appears to be the most valid for admission is the IQ based on individual psychometric tests administered by a psychologist trained and experienced in the diagnosis of mental retardation. The usual IQ range for these classes is between 30 or 35 and 50 or 55 and the IQ's are derived from such tests as the Stanford-Binet Intelligence Scale, the Minnesota Preschool Scale, the Merrill-Palmer Scale, The Illinois Test of Psycholinguistic Abilities, and the Kuhlmann Tests of Mental Development.

3. Most children admitted into the classes are required to have a medical examination to determine their physical ability to participate in the program.

4. Not all children with IQ's between 35 and 50 are admitted. Other criteria include ability to get along in the class and a minimum ability to take care of their needs, such as toileting, partial dressing, and so forth. Schools tend to exclude children who are a danger to themselves or others and those whose behavior is likely to disrupt the classroom program.

5. Children admitted to these classes must have some minimum communication ability in the form of either speech or gestures. Most trainable children above the age of 6 with IQ's over 30 have these abilities.

6. The general procedure for admission is to have a committee composed of a psychologist, a social worker, teachers, and other school personnel accept or reject the children.

SIZE OF CLASS

The size of class for trainable children varies from about six to fifteen. At first, when the children have not been accustomed to being away from their mothers, the classes should be small; they can gradually be increased in size as the children learn the routines. A homogeneous class of children of approximately the same age and abilities can be larger than a heterogeneous class of children. Another factor determining the size of the class is the age and school experience of the children. Young inexperienced children require more attention from the teacher; hence their class should be small. Older children who have had school experience can be grouped in a larger class, since they will not require as much personal care by the teacher.

TRANSPORTATION

Because of the geographic distribution of trainable children in a community and their inability to go to school unattended, it is necessary to provide transportation for all trainable children. This is a major item which adds to the expense of operating classes for them.

QUALIFICATIONS OF TEACHERS

Teachers of trainable children have been recruited generally from among teachers who have been prepared to teach educable mentally retarded children. There are no special certificates for teachers of trainable children. In addition to the general qualifications for a teacher of the mentally retarded, teachers of trainable children require the following knowledge and experience:

1. Teachers of the trainable mentally retarded should obtain instruction in behavior modification theory and practice. This is particularly necessary in teaching self-help skills.
2. Teachers of the trainable retarded should have instruction in the characteristics of Down's Syndrome (mongoloid) and brain-damaged children. About one-third of the children in the classes are Down's Syndrome children. A large proportion of the other two-thirds have some brain pathology.
3. Skills in arts and crafts, music, industrial arts, recreational games, and homemaking are valuable tools in classes for trainable retarded. Methods of teaching reading, arithmetic, or other school subjects are necessary for the elementary teacher and for the teacher of the educable mentally handicapped, but not necessary for the teacher of trainable children.
4. Courses in child development commonly given to nursery school and kindergarten teachers are of value to teachers of the trainable retarded.
5. A study of the goals, objectives, and activities included in a curriculum for the severely retarded is necessary.
6. Special attention to parent problems is necessary for all teachers of trainable retarded children. Methods of interviewing and counseling parents are important.

7. Teachers who do not expect immediate results or who are not frustrated because children do not learn are often successful as teachers of the severely retarded. One who can appreciate small gains instead of no gains tends to be successful.

8. Practice teaching or experience under supervision with the trainable retarded is essential. Such experience is the only way one can determine whether a teacher has insight into the limitations and abilities of the children, is able to relate to them, and is able to create programs and activities suitable to the growth and development of the children.

The Curriculum and Course of Study

THE GOALS OF THE CURRICULUM

In defining an educational program for any group of children, it is necessary to define the general objectives of the curriculum and then to give the specific elements required in a course of study. The general objectives of the curriculum for a trainable child are inherent in the definition, namely, (1) the objective of developing self-care or self-help, (2) the objective of developing social adjustment in the home and neighborhood, and (3) the objective of developing economic usefulness in the home or in a sheltered environment. These constitute the broad goals of the educational program for trainable mentally retarded children.

Self-Help. The major characteristic which differentiates the trainable mentally retarded from the dependent mentally retarded is self-care. If a child can learn to dress and undress himself, eat properly, to take care of himself in the bathroom, and to follow sleep routines, he is not dependent on someone else for his personal needs. In a restricted sense he becomes independent as far as taking care of himself is concerned. Although such independence is common among normal children after 3 or 4 years of age, it is necessary to educate the trainable child in the elements of self-care. Behavior shaping techniques are especially effective in teaching self-help skills.

Social Adjustment in the Home and Neighborhood. It is not expected that the trainable child will become independent in the community—that is, learn to go around the community by himself or be in charge of his affairs outside of the home. He is, however, expected to get along in the home and in his immediate neighborhood. This particular learning achievement includes language development, sharing with others, waiting his turn, obeying, following directions, sensing the feelings of others, and other aspects of interpersonal relationships, especially those concerned with daily associations. Social adjustment is not a subject which is taught like chemistry or physics. It is an intangible type of development which comes about through recreation and play, singing, dramatics, and working and living with others.

Economic Usefulness. The term "economic usefulness" is applied to the trainable child to differentiate this ability from occupational or vocational activities which are within the capacity of educable children. It is expected that the trainable child will be of some use in the home, the school, or a sheltered environment in either community or institution. In the home, economic usefulness means helping with housework and yard work. These activities can be developed in the classroom through many of the programs which require care of the room, cooking, washing, and wiping dishes, arts and crafts, woodwork, and the ability to complete simple tasks under minimum supervision. This kind of objective is more attainable with older trainable children in school than with younger ones.

THE ELEMENTS OF THE CURRICULUM

The mental ages in classes for trainable children range between about 3 and 7 years. At this mental level the academic program prescribed for educable or for normal children is not warranted. It would be well here to discuss some limitations of and possibilities for these children.

Modified Reading. In general, trainable children do not learn to read from even first-grade books. Their ability is limited to reading and recognizing their names, isolated words and phrases, common words used for their protection, such as "danger," "stop," "men," "women," and other signs which they encounter in a community. Some trainable children with special abilities can learn to read. Most who learn to read, however, are probably educable mentally retarded children.

Arithmetic. Trainable children are not taught formal arithmetic as it is taught in the primary grades. They can learn some quantitative concepts, however, such as more and less, big and little, and the vocabulary of quantitative thinking. They are also taught to count up to 10 and to recognize differences between groupings. The older children can learn to write numbers from 1 to 10 and some of them can learn time concepts, telling time by the clock and possibly understanding the calendar. Some can recognize and remember telephone numbers, their own ages, and some simple money concepts.

Arts and Crafts. Activities in this area include coloring, drawing, painting, simple woodwork, pasting and cutting, and making simple craft objects. Such activities may help in developing motor control, appreciation of color and form, and the ability to complete a task.

Dramatization. Classes for trainable children use considerable dramatization such as acting out a story or a song, playing make-believe, shadow playing, and using gestures with songs, stories, and rhymes.

Physical Hygiene. The routine of a classroom includes drinking juice or milk, discussion about the kinds of food eaten at different meals, the care of the teeth, cleanliness, safety, and posture. These health habits usually need to be fostered both in the school and at home.

Language. This program includes the development of speech and the understanding of verbal concepts. It also includes listening skills, listening to stories, roll calls, discussing pictures, and other activities familiar to the children in the classroom.

Mental Development. Mental activity can be stimulated through experiences. The teacher attempts to keep in mind the development of imagination, concept building, problem solving, and the ability to discriminate and to remember visual and auditory patterns.

Practical Arts. Under this heading are included cooking, sewing, dishwashing, cleaning, gardening, setting the table, chores around the classroom, preparing foods, and learning to help with home activities. This program is best limited to older trainable children.

Motor Development. Motor development is best stimulated through games, recreational activities, various manipulative skills, playing, outdoor recreation, and similar activities.

Self-Help. Self-help includes grooming, toileting, dressing, undressing, eating, brushing teeth, washing, and care of clothes and other personal belongings.

Socialization. It is important for the children to learn certain skills which will assist their socialization, such as greeting people with "Hello," shaking hands with visitors, learning to be quiet while someone else is talking, having acceptable table manners, getting along with classmates in school, helping others who need help, and other activities of an interpersonal nature.

Social Studies. The important area of study here is the home and the way it participates in the community. This includes learning about holidays, transportation, church, knowing the months and days of the week, and so forth.

Music. Music is a medium through which trainable children can learn many things. Singing, rhythm bands, musical games, and other activities help release energy and also serve as a form of expression and a socializing influence.

Is Training Effective?

The results of a training program for trainable mentally retarded children should be evaluated in relation to the goals stated earlier: independence in self care, social adjustment in the home and neighborhood, and economic usefulness at the adult level in home, sheltered workshop, or institution. To make such an evaluation, one would have to set up a series of programs within the public schools and follow them up for twenty-five or thirty years. There has not yet been time for this kind of follow-up and only studies covering shorter periods are available. These do help to answer some questions.

ARE CHILDREN FROM TRAINABLE CLASSES EVENTUALLY INSTITUTIONALIZED?

Studies on this question indicate that many of the children in trainable classes later become institutionalized. Lorenz (1953) followed up a group of children eighteen years after their admission into a public school special class for trainable children. She found that 47 percent of the 66 children studied were institutionalized upon leaving the special class. Boys had a higher percentage of institutionalization than girls. Those institutionalized usually came from the average or below average socioeconomic levels. Tisdall (1960) followed up a group of 126 trainable children five years after their enrollment in a special class. He found that during this period 12 percent had already been institutionalized. In another study Saenger (1957) found that 26 percent were institutionalized. These studies were made before sheltered workshops in communities were common and before comprehensive community facilities were established and functioning. Since these centers are just being established (1968–1970) their impact on eventual institutionalization of the trainable child will not be known until about 1975–1980.

DOES A CLASS FOR THE TRAINABLE ASSIST THE PARENTS?

Many people feel that the organization of a class for trainable children has been justified because of its great value to parents. First, it relieves the mother of the constant care of the child. Second, it gives the parents a chance to become more objective by having an opportunity to see what the child can learn outside of the home. And third, it helps the parents to become more realistic concerning the developmental limitations of the child. Reynolds and Kiland (1953) found that after the children were in the classes for some time the parents reduced their expectations for the children's learning of the academic subjects. Similarly, in the Illinois Study (Office of the Superintendent of Public Instruction, 1954), the parents tended to become more realistic about their children's abilities and limitations. They began to realize that although the children improved in self-care skills they would not become self-supporting.

DO THE CHILDREN BECOME ECONOMICALLY USEFUL?

One of the alleged purposes of a class is to help the children become economically useful. Both the Lorenz and the Tisdall studies found that about one-third of the children who were beyond school age and remained at home were considered economically useful in the home or in a sheltered workshop.

Saenger found that about one-quarter of the group residing in the community earned some pay. Saenger's group, however, was intellectually at the borderline level between trainable and educable. Lorenz found that 2 of the 66 children were employed for remuneration outside of the home, while Tisdall found only one of his sample working in the community. These children had IQ's in the 50's and were borderline trainable-educable. The figures confirm the prediction that trainable children are not able to hold a job in the community or to be occupationally adequate but can be of some nonremunerative help in a limited environment.

The figures on economic usefulness of trainable children do not give us the true picture. Their degree of usefulness will depend on proper selection of such children for the special classes, an adequate training program, and facilities in the home and community for their adjustment. A community, for instance, which does not provide a sheltered workshop or recreational facilities in effect requests the parents to either keep these children at home or send them to an institution. Unless proper facilities and programs are available it is impossible to evaluate accurately the economic usefulness of trainable children.

DO CLASSES FOR TRAINABLE CHILDREN FULFILL EXPECTATIONS?

There have been numerous studies evaluating the results of programs. Invariably the children improve from year to year, but whether the improvement stemmed from the programs or from maturation was not known. Two studies each used two groups of children, one of which was placed in a training program while the other (the control group) remained at home or in an institutional environment. Hottel (1958) compared twenty-one matched pairs of children. He found that although both the experimental and the control (home) groups improved in mental and social age and other measures, the experimental group did not improve more than the control group. Cain and Levine (1961) compared four groups: (1) an institution school group, (2) an institution nonschool group, (3) a community public school group, and (4) a community nonschool group. They found no difference in gain scores in social competence between the school and home groups, but there was a difference in gain scores between the two institution and two community groups in favor of the community children.

SUMMARY

1. Trainable mentally retarded children are those children whose limits of educability have been defined as (a) competence in self-care skills, (b) adjustment in the home and neighborhood, and (c) economic usefulness in the home or sheltered environment.
2. It is estimated that there are approximately 3 to 4 trainable children residing at home or in institutions per 1000 school-age children.
3. Provisions for trainable mentally retarded are made in (a) residential schools, (b) public school classes for school-age children, (c) private or public preschools, (d) sheltered workshops, and (e) comprehensive community centers which include diagnosis, day care and residential care for all the children not served by other agencies.
4. Comprehensive community programs have not been in existence long enough for research to determine their efficacy.

REFERENCES

Bienenstock, T., and Coxe, W. W. 1956. *Census of Severely Retarded Children in New York State.* Albany, New York: Interdepartmental Health Resources Board.

Birch, H. G.; Richardson, S. A.; Baird, Sir Dugald; Horobin G.; and Illsley, R. 1970. *Mental Subnormality in the Community.* Baltimore: Williams and Wilkins.

Cain, L. F., and Levine, S. 1961. *A Study of the Effects of Community and Institutional School Classes for Trainable Mentally Retarded Children.* U.S. Office of Education, Cooperative Research Project No. SAE 8257. San Francisco: San Francisco State College.

Farber, B. 1968. *Mental Retardation.* Boston: Houghton Mifflin.

Goldstein, H. 1959. Population Trends in U.S. Public Institutions for the Mentally Deficient. *American Journal of Mental Deficiency* 63 (January): 599–604.

Henderson, R. 1957. Factors in Commitment of Educable Mentally Handicapped Children to Illinois State Schools. Unpublished doctoral dissertation, University of Illinois.

Hottel, J. V. 1958. *An Evaluation of Tennessee's Day Class Program for Severely Mentally Retarded Children.* Nashville, Tennessee: George Peabody College for Teachers.

Kirk, S. A. 1957. *Public School Provisions for Severely Retarded Children*. Albany, New York: New York State Interdepartmental Health Resource Board.

Lorenz, Marcella H. 1953. Follow-Up Studies of the Severely Retarded. In Reynolds, M. C.; Kiland, J. R.; and Ellis, R. E. (eds.), *A Study of Public School Children with Severe Mental Retardation*. Research Project No. 6. St. Paul, Minnesota: Statistical Division, State Department of Education.

Office of the Superintendent of Public Instruction. 1954. *Report on Study Projects for Trainable Mentally Handicapped Children*. Springfield, Illinois: The Office.

Reynolds, M. C.; Kiland, J. R.; and Ellis, R. E. (eds.). 1953. *A Study of Public School Children with Severe Mental Retardation*. Research Project No. 6. St. Paul, Minnesota: Statistical Division, State Department of Education.

Saenger, G. 1957. *The Adjustment of Severely Retarded Adults in the Community*. Albany, New York: New York State Interdepartmental Health Resources Board.

State Department of Public Instruction. 1955. *Interim Report: The Michigan Demonstration Research Project for the Severely Mentally Retarded*. Lansing, Michigan: The Department.

Tisdall, W. 1960. A Follow-Up Study of Trainable Mentally Handicapped Children in Illinois. *American Journal of Mental Deficiency* 65 (July): 11–16.

World Health Organization. 1954. *The Mentally Subnormal Child*. Technical Report, Series No. 75. Geneva: Palais des Nations.

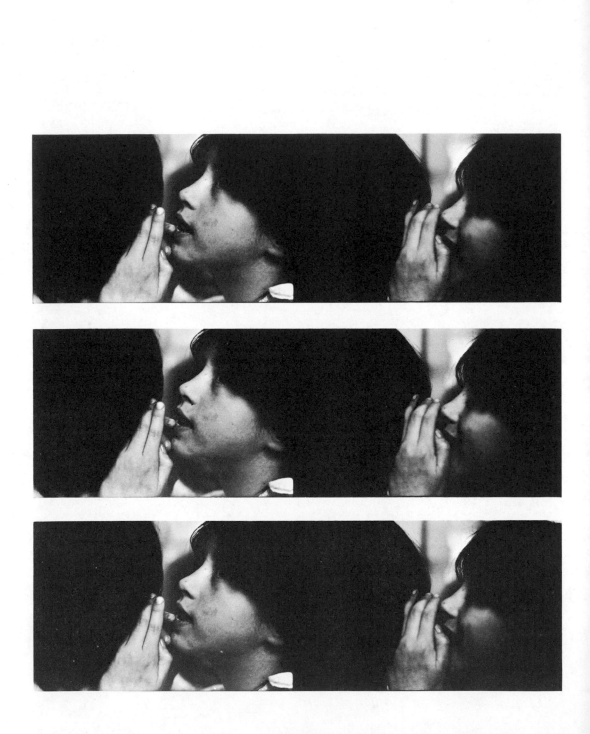

EIGHT

CHILDREN

WITH

AUDITORY

HANDICAPS

Individuals with auditory handicaps may have difficulty hearing in one or both ears or may not hear at all. Professionals and laymen alike have used various terms: "hard-of-hearing," "deaf," "deaf-mute," "deafened," "partially deaf," and "partially hearing." Most of these terms came into use as a means of differentiating some of the auditorily handicapped children from others. "Deafened," for instance, usually refers to someone who once had hearing and developed language and speech, and later became deaf. Such an individual's reactions in the field of learning and communication are quite different from those of a person who was born deaf and never learned to speak or communicate verbally.

Streng et al (1958) give the following definitions:

The child who is born with little or no hearing, or who has suffered the loss early in infancy before speech and language patterns are acquired is said to be deaf. One who is born with normal hearing and reaches the age where he can produce and comprehend speech but subsequently loses his hearing is described as deafened. The hard of hearing are those with reduced hearing acuity either since birth or acquired at any time during life. (p. 9)

Classification

Because of the confusion in terminology and because training programs differ according to the type of problem, the Committee on Nomenclature of the Conference of Executives of American Schools for the Deaf (1938) has made the following classification:

1. *The deaf:* Those in whom the sense of hearing is nonfunctional for the ordinary purposes of life. This general group is made up of two distinct classes based entirely on the time the loss of hearing occurred. These include:
   a. *The congenitally deaf*—those who were born deaf.
   b. *The adventitiously deaf*—those who were born with normal hearing but in whom the sense of hearing became nonfunctional later through illness or accident.
2. *The hard of hearing:* Those in whom the sense of hearing, although defective, is functional with or without a hearing aid. (p. 2)

Hearing loss is generally measured by an audiometer using standards agreed upon internationally, such as the current ISO standard (International Standard Organization) (Davis and Krantz, 1964). The classifications of hearing loss of slight, mild, marked, severe, and extreme are described in Table 8–1 (on pp. 244–245) in terms of ISO standards, the effects of hearing loss on the understanding of language and speech, and corresponding educational needs and programs.

Both of the classification systems just given relate to the degree of hearing loss. Loss of hearing may also be classified according to the time of onset. This is particularly important from an educational point of view because if an individual has already acquired speech before the loss of hearing, the whole communication and educational process is different from that used with persons who have never known speech and language. Therefore the term "deafened" is used in referring to the former. It will be noted that the definition quoted earlier from the Conference of Executives of American Schools for the Deaf included a distinction between *congenitally deaf* and *adventitiously deaf*. This is also an effort to classify according to the time of onset of deafness.

There are many variables to be considered in describing the deaf and hard of hearing. Because of this multidimensional nature of the problem any classification is incomplete unless it takes into account all variables, such as (1) degree of hearing loss, (2) age at onset, and (3) type of hearing loss.

Case Illustrations

Many hearing-impaired children have found social adjustment difficult because they could not interact socially as hearing children do. In school, likewise, progress is likely to be uneven if they hear only part of the material presented. Thus a hearing loss may interfere with social adjustment and educational progress especially in the areas of speech and language. The amount of difficulty will vary with the degree of hearing loss and also with other factors, such as intelligence, emotional adjustment, and neurological integrity. Figure 8–1 illustrates the different effects of varying degrees of hearing loss.

CASE A

Figure 8–1 presents three development profiles. The upper one, labeled A, represents a child with a marginal loss of hearing of 45 (ISO) decibels. It will be noticed from the upper profile that the hard-of-hearing child is 10 years of age and is physically (in terms of height, weight, and motor coordination) average. In mental ability and in social maturity there appears to be no difference between him and the average. In speech development the child is slightly retarded in that he has some difficulty in articulation and requires speech correction. His language development and reading are only slightly retarded while his achievement in arithmetic, spelling, and general information is approximately average. The only difference between this child and an average child is a slight difficulty in speech development, language development, and reading.

Fortunately, this hard-of-hearing child has been fitted with a hearing aid, and has received speech correction. The only special education he has needed is some help in the use of his hearing aid, in speech correction, and in speech-reading. Otherwise, he is so much like the average child that he has functioned adequately in the regular grades. An itinerant speech correctionist has given him speech correction, auditory training, and speechreading lessons once a week for the last year.

CASE B

The next profile on the chart (B) presents the developmental patterns of a child with a severe hearing loss. This child was born with normal hearing but at the age of 4 suffered a serious hearing loss in both ears. He is classified as educationally deaf. Although he is approximately normal in intelligence, social maturity, and physical ability, his speech has deteriorated noticeably. On the audiometric test he had a 75 decibel loss. Fortunately, however, he had learned to talk quite normally before his loss of hearing and had developed considerable language ability, so that now he still can learn through the auditory channel with the help of hearing aids. His retardation in language results from not having developed normally in this area since the age of 4. At present his language is below the 7-year (second-grade) level and his reading and other academic abilities are also around the second-grade level. The hearing loss has interfered considerably with his educational progress, but with the use of hearing aids, speech correction, and other specialized techniques in a classroom for the deaf, he is progressing, though at an understandably slower rate than Case A.

FIGURE 8–1

Profiles of three children of differing degrees of hearing loss

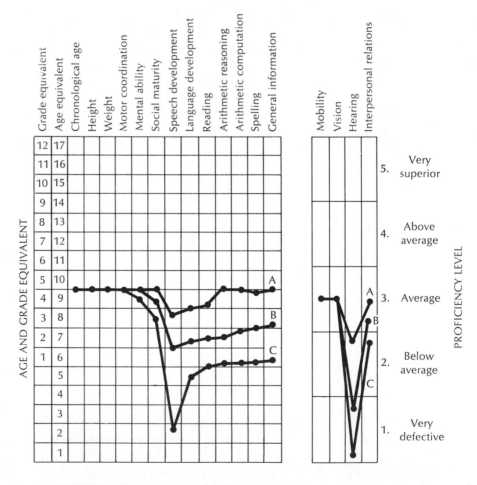

A = hard-of-hearing child; B = deafened child; C = deaf child

CASE C

The third profile is of a child with an extreme hearing loss which existed at birth. This child has never heard sounds. A hearing aid might alert his attention to environmental sounds, but will not help sufficiently in the development of speech and language. Because of the severity of his hearing loss it is necessary to place him in a class for the deaf.

In speech development, this child is still quite defective. He does not talk as well as a child of 2½ years, even though he has had some instruction. His language development is at about the 5-year level. In reading and other academic subjects he is at the beginning first-grade level even though he is now 10 years of age. We would consider him about four years retarded educationally.

Although these three profiles all represent auditorily handicapped children, they differ considerably. They show the progress such children make, depending upon the age at onset of deafness, the intelligence, the degree of hearing loss, and the amount of intensive instruction which has been received during the growing stages.

Prevalence of Hearing Loss

The prevalence of defective hearing is difficult to estimate although many surveys have been made. The rate of occurrence appears to be partly dependent on the method of testing, the criteria used by the investigator, the community, and other factors. For example, Farber (1959) found that in the literature estimates ranged from 1.5 percent to 5 percent of the school population. Yet in Farber's own study the teachers in Illinois reported only .48 percent of the school population as having hearing losses. This figure includes children already placed in classes for the hard of hearing and probably represents the prevalence of moderate and severe hearing losses, losses large enough that teachers are able to recognize them. Mild hearing losses are not readily detected by teachers. Curry (1950) found that teachers refer only 7.4 percent of children with known hearing losses, and Warwick (1928) reports that teachers referred only 14 out of a group of 63 children with impaired hearing.

According to Silverman (1957) a rough estimate of the prevalence of hearing loss is that 5 percent of school children have a hearing impairment, and that 1 or 2 out of 10 in this group or about 5 in 1000 will require special educational attention.

The Illinois Commission on Children (1968) after reviewing studies on prevalence estimated that 1 to 3 percent of school children have a hearing impairment severe enough to warrant medical or special educational attention. They estimated that 1 in 1000 are deaf.

TABLE 8–1

*Relationship of degree of impairment
to educational needs[1]*

Average of the speech frequencies in better ear	Effect of hearing loss on the understanding of language and speech	Educational needs and programs
SLIGHT 27 to 40 dB (ISO)	May have difficulty hearing faint or distant speech. May experience some difficulty with the language arts subjects.	Child should be reported to school principal. May benefit from a hearing aid as loss approaches 40 dB (ISO). May need attention to vocabulary development. Needs favorable seating and lighting. May need lipreading instructions. May need speech therapy.
MILD 41 to 55 dB (ISO)	Understands conversational speech at a distance of 3–5 feet (face to face). May miss as much as 50% of class discussions if voices are faint or not in line of vision. May exhibit limited vocabulary and speech anomalies.	Child should be referred to special education for educational follow-up. Individual hearing aid by evaluation and training in its use. Favorable seating and possible special class placement, especially for primary children. Attention to vocabulary and reading. Lipreading instruction. Speech conservation and correction, if indicated.
MARKED 56 to 70 dB (ISO)	Conversation must be loud to be understood. Will have increased difficulty in group discussions. Is likely to have defective speech. Is likely to be deficient in language usage and comprehension. Will have limited vocabulary.	Child should be referred to special education for educational follow-up. Resource teacher or special class. Special help in language skills: vocabulary development, usage, reading, writing, grammar, etc. Individual hearing aid by evaluation and auditory training. Lipreading instruction. Speech conservation and correction. Attention to auditory and visual situations at all times.

[1] Medically irreversible conditions and those requiring prolonged medical care.

SEVERE 71 to 90 dB (ISO)	May hear loud voices about one foot from the ear. May be able to identify environmental sounds. May be able to discriminate vowels but not all consonants. Speech and language defective and likely to deteriorate.	Child should be referred to special education for educational follow-up. Full-time special program for deaf children, with emphasis on all language skills, concept development, lipreading and speech. Program needs specialized supervision and comprehensive supporting services. Individual hearing aid by evaluation. Auditory training with individual and group aids. Part-time in regular classes only as profitable.
EXTREME 91 dB or more (ISO)	May hear some loud sounds but is aware of vibrations more than tonal pattern. Relies on vision rather than hearing as primary avenue for communication. Speech and language defective and likely to deteriorate.	Child should be referred to special education for educational follow-up. Full-time in special program for deaf children, with emphasis on all language skills, concept development, lipreading and speech. Program needs specialized supervision and comprehensive supporting services. Continuous appraisal of needs in regard to oral and manual communication. Auditory training with group and individual aids. Part-time in regular classes only for carefully selected children.

Source: Adapted from a compiled study in Illinois Commission on Children, 1968, p. 19. Reproduced with the permission of the Commission.

Methods of Measuring Hearing Loss

The identification of hearing loss is a technical problem. Whereas severe or extreme loss is rather easily recognized, children with slight or mild hearing loss are hard to identify. Teachers may feel that the child just does not pay attention or is mentally handicapped or stubborn.

It is important for a classroom teacher to be aware of some of the symptoms which may be misinterpreted, such as those displayed by (1) the child who ignores, confuses, or does not comply with directions; (2) the child who daydreams a great deal; (3) the child who is educationally retarded; (4) the child with a slight speech defect; (5) the child who is "lazy"; (6) the child who seems dull; and (7) the child who is always asking "what?"

TESTING

Informal tests are used by teachers and psychological examiners to obtain a crude measure of hearing ability. These informal tests include conversation at 20 feet, whisper tests, and watch-tick tests. The most accurate method of testing, however, is with an electric pure-tone audiometer, which produces pure tones of known intensity and frequency.

These two dimensions—frequency and intensity—are necessary for evaluating a hearing loss. *Frequency* refers to the number of vibrations (or cycles) per second of a given sound wave: the greater the frequency, the higher the pitch. An individual may have difficulty hearing sounds of certain frequencies whereas those of other frequencies are quite audible to him. For the understanding of speech the most important frequencies range between 500 and 2000 vibrations per second. *Intensity,* on the other hand, refers to the relative loudness of a sound.

To determine an individual's level of hearing it is necessary to know what intensity of sound is needed to cross his threshold of hearing at each of the frequency levels. The pure-tone audiometer presents the individual with sounds of known intensity and frequency and asks him to respond when he hears the tone. The degree of hearing loss is recorded on an audiogram from −10 to 120 decibels. The hearing in each ear is plotted separately. A hearing level of 30 decibels indicates a slight hearing loss; a 91-decibel level indicates extreme deafness.

Routine audiometric procedures cannot be used with infants and young children, but clinical testing of young children can be accomplished by electrodermal and other procedures in audiology clinics, including EEG audiometry and operant conditioning audiometry. These techniques are often used for other hard-to-test individuals such as the severely mentally retarded and psychotic (Bricker et al., 1968). Often hearing loss in a young child is detected by informal means such as observing his behavior and ability to react to sounds in his environment or by the more structured but informal methods described by DiCarlo (1964). Does the child respond to music? to noise? or to voices?

Causes of Hearing Defects

Deafness is a symptom of a defect in the hearing mechanism. Much of the diagnosis is made by inference, and often the exact nature and origin of the defect are unknown. In roughly one-third of the cases the cause cannot be determined with certainty. Some hearing defects are predetermined by the genetic structure of the individual and may be present at birth or develop later in life. Some are acquired through disease, trauma, or other insults to the organism.·

CAUSES OCCURRING BEFORE BIRTH

Prenatal infections and toxic conditions of the mother may create auditory defects in the child. The viruses of mumps and influenza, for example, especially during the early months of pregnancy may cause degeneration of important nerve cells that results in deafness. German measles (rubella) afflicting the mother during the first three months of pregnancy often has quite serious effects. The National Communicable Disease Center (Hicks, 1970) reported that the rubella epidemic of 1964–65 caused deafness in over 8,000 children. The Johns Hopkins Study (Hardy, 1968) reported on 199 children who were diagnosed as having been subjected to the rubella virus. The distribution of defects was found to be 20 percent visual, 35 percent cardiac, and 50 percent auditory.

Some diseases specific to the functioning of the auditory mechanism may occur at any stage in life, including the period *in utero*. In *otosclerosis,* for example, spongy bone is formed in the middle and inner ear, occasionally at birth but usually not until later in life.

Some *malformations* are present at birth, such as abnormalities of the external auditory canal which prevent sound from being carried into the mechanism of the ear. The eardrum or some of the structures of the middle ear may be deformed or absent, and development of the neural mechanism of the inner ear may be arrested.

TRAUMATIC AND OTHER CONDITIONS AT BIRTH

During delivery certain *traumatic experiences,* such as pelvic pressure, use of forceps, and intracranial hemorrhage, may cause damage to the nervous system resulting in auditory and other defects. Fortunately such problems are becoming increasingly rare.

Another untoward condition at the time of birth is prolonged *lack of oxygen* available to the infant as in prolonged labor, heavy sedation, or blockage of the infant's respiratory passages. This may produce rapid degeneration in some of the more delicate neural mechanisms of the ear as well as those of other sensory organs or of the central nervous system itself.

Of fairly recent discovery is the effect of *blood incompatibility* between the mother and infant. The best-known incompatibility is that of the Rh factor, but current research has indicated similar effects from other types of blood incompatibility.

CAUSES OCCURRING AFTER BIRTH

Postnatal diseases and *accidents* account for a large percentage of hearing losses. If they occur early in life, before the acquisition of speech and language, the educational implications are the same as if the child had been born deaf.

Childhood diseases take their toll in hearing defects but their frequency and severity have been lessened by advances in immunization and antibiotics. At one time such infectious diseases as scarlet fever, mumps, diphtheria, whooping cough, measles, typhoid fever, pneumonia, and influenza accounted for a great deal of deafness. Meningitis is still reported as a frequent cause of hearing defects, but this too is becoming more amenable to control. *Otitis media,* which is common to many upper respiratory diseases, may cause loss of hearing through infection in the middle ear. Davis and Fowler (1960) state, "Pus in the middle ear is a more frequent cause of hearing loss than any other except perhaps senility." The presence of *infected adenoids, tonsils,* and *sinuses* favors the production of infection in the middle ear and is therefore an indirect cause of hearing loss.

If acute infections of the middle ear are not properly treated, *chronic otitis media* may follow. If this is extended or recurs frequently, adhesions may form and destroy the eardrum or the bony structure of the middle ear. If the infection extends into the mastoid process of the temporal bone, a *mastoidectomy* may be necessitated. A "simple" mastoidectomy removes only the diseased portion of the mastoid bone; in a "radical" mastoidectomy it is also necessary to remove the bony canal wall plus whatever is left of the eardrum and other diseased parts. The "simple" mastoidectomy does not cause an appreciable hearing loss. The "radical" operation usually leaves a hearing level of 35 to 50 decibels because the middle ear is destroyed either by the operation or by the previous infection (Walsh, 1960; Goodhill, 1957).

Otosclerosis has been mentioned as a hereditary disease which may affect hearing at any stage of life. Similarly, there may be a *degeneration of the auditory nerve* which seems to be hereditary and may affect the individual at any age. Although little is known about this condition, it is stated that ". . . if *both* parents have true hereditary deafness . . . their children will almost certainly be born deaf or soon become deaf" (Davis and Fowler, 1960, p. 110). Even if the parents themselves have normal hearing, but there is a history of such deafness on both sides, the children may have defective hearing.

Concussions on certain parts of the head may cause temporary or permanent loss of hearing. Subjection to prolonged *high-frequency sounds,* as in certain industrial conditions or military experiences, may likewise have a traumatic effect on the nervous mechanism of the ear. It is not yet known what serious effects may result from the present style of high-frequency popular music. Other forms of insult to the auditory nerve may come from *intracranial tumors,* from *cerebral hemorrhage,* or from the *toxic effect of certain drugs.*

It has been found that certain *ototoxic antibiotics,* such as streptomycin, neomycin and others, produce side effects of hearing loss (McGee, 1968).

Old age creates a deterioration in hearing known as *presbycusis* and is possibly the most common of all causes of hearing loss.

Psychological and emotional factors also play a role in some forms of hearing loss. Auditory defects of psychogenic origin include hysterical deafness, in which an individual finds it easier to resolve a deep unconscious emotional conflict by elimination of hearing than by other forms of adjustment. Often military experiences are such a shock to the sensibilities that functional deafness ensues.

Davis and Fowler (1960) report data from Hoff General Hospital (United States Army) showing that, of the last 500 cases admitted for auditory rehabilitation toward the end of World War II, 15 percent had psychogenic factors as all or part of the cause of loss of hearing. In many cases there is some loss or a temporary loss which is exaggerated or prolonged for psychological reasons.

Psychogenic deafness must not be confused with malingering, in which the individual pretends to be unable to hear. Usually the malingerer can be detected by special tests.

Extensive current statistics are not available giving number and proportions of the various causes and classifications of hearing defects. In a national study of the psychological effects of deafness Myklebust (1960) found 39.1 percent exogenous (acquired), 22.6 percent endogenous (hereditary), and 38.3 percent of unknown origin.

In a more recent review of studies, Kloepfer, Laquaite, and McLaurin (1970) found that 46 to 60 percent of all cases of severe hearing loss are genetically determined. Table 8–2 is a breakdown of causes illustrating the lack of definite diagnosis in many cases (in 30.4 percent of the cases, the cause was unknown). It will also be noted that where hereditary factors are concerned there was a definite diagnosis in only 5.4 percent of the cases if the criterion used is that of both parents being deaf; but there is a suspected diagnosis of hereditary causes in 26.4 percent of the cases when the looser criterion of "any family member" is used. This exceeds all other causes.

TABLE 8–2

Major etiologies of hearing loss

Etiology	Definite diagnosis	Suspected diagnosis
Heredity	5.4[1]	26.0[2]
RH factor	3.1	3.7
Prematurity	11.9	17.4
Meningitis	8.1	8.7
Rubella	8.8	9.5
Other	32.3	——
Unknown	30.4	——

Source: M. Vernon, Current Etiological Factors in Deafness, *American Annals of the Deaf* 113 (March, 1968). Reproduced with the permission of the author.

Note: Recent medical research indicates that the actual prevalence of rubella in epidemic years is at least four times the rate reported in this table. The latest genetic data indicates approximately 50 percent of childhood deafness is genetic. This information is drawn from E. D. Mindel and M. Vernon, *They Grow in Silence,* Silver Spring, Maryland: National Association of the Deaf, 1971.

[1] Both parents
[2] Any family member

Types of Hearing Defects

Because of the complicated structure and functioning of the ear, defects in hearing may occur in many different forms. Basically these defects are of two main types: (1) conductive losses and (2) sensory-neural or perceptive losses.

A *conductive hearing loss* is one which reduces the intensity of sound reaching the inner ear, where the auditory nerve begins. To reach the *inner ear,* sound waves in the air must pass through the external canal of the *outer ear* to the eardrum, where the vibrations are picked up by a series of bonelike structures in the *middle ear* and passed on to the *inner ear.* This sequence of vibrations may be blocked anywhere along the line. Wax or malformations may block the external canal; the eardrum may be broken or unable to vibrate; the movement of the bones in the middle ear may be obstructed. Any condition hindering the sequence of vibrations or preventing them from reaching the auditory nerve may cause a conduction loss.

This type of defect seldom causes a hearing loss of more than 60 to 70 decibels, since there will still be available the vibrations carried by the bone to the

FIGURE 8–2

*Audiogram of child with a
conductive hearing loss*

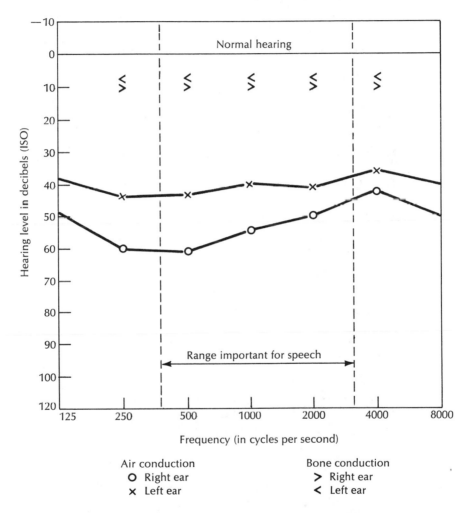

Air conduction
O Right ear
x Left ear

Bone conduction
> Right ear
< Left ear

inner ear. The audiometer has a bone-conduction receiver as well as an air-conduction receiver and can therefore measure the ability of the individual to pick up sound through bone conduction.

Figure 8–2 shows the audiogram of a child with a conductive hearing loss. On the audiometer he heard air-borne sounds at the 40 to 50 decibel level at all frequencies. When using a bone-conduction receiver, however, he responded

FIGURE 8–3

*Audiogram of child with a sensory-neural
or perceptive hearing loss*

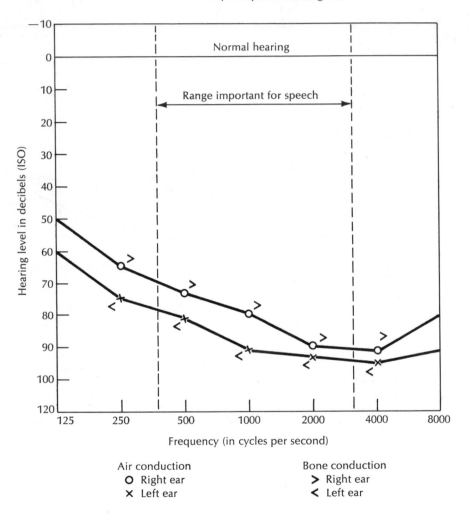

Air conduction
O Right ear
X Left ear

Bone conduction
> Right ear
< Left ear

normally; his difficulty was due to a defect or obstruction in the outer or middle ear rather than to a defect in the sensory nerve of the inner ear. As might be expected, the audiogram of this type of hearing loss is fairly even at all frequencies.

A *sensory-neural or perceptive hearing loss* is caused by defects of the inner ear or of the auditory nerve transmitting the impulse to the brain. Sensory-neural hearing loss may be complete or partial, and it may affect some frequencies (especially the high ones) more than others. Thus in Figure 8–3 the audiogram shows profound loss at the high frequencies and severe loss at the frequencies below 1000 cycles. High-frequency loss is often associated with sensory-neural deafness. The bone-conduction receiver in this case gave no better reception since the defect was in the nerve, not in the mechanism which carried the vibrations to the nerve.

The proper diagnosis of a hearing defect is a very important and very technical matter. The treatment, the educational program, and even the selection of a hearing aid are dependent upon it. It is obvious, for example, that a suitable bone-conduction hearing aid would not help the child whose audiogram is presented in Figure 8–3 whereas it probably would help the child represented in Figure 8–2.

SUMMARY

1. Children with hearing losses are affected in their development in various ways, chiefly in language and speech.
2. Two groupings are made for educational purposes: (a) *Hard-of-hearing* children are classified as children with slight losses, mild losses, and marked losses; they are educated through the auditory channel. (b) *Deaf* children are classified as those with severe losses and those with extreme losses; they are educated primarily through sense modalities other than the ear.
3. The development of speech and language is dependent upon (a) degree of hearing loss, (b) age at onset of loss, and (c) intelligence.
4. The kinds of hearing loss found in children are conductive loss, and sensory-neural loss.
5. The estimates of prevalence of hearing loss among school children range from 2 to 5 percent.

REFERENCES

Bricker, Diane B.; Bricker, W. A.; and Larsen, L. A. 1968. *Operant Audiometry Manual for Difficult-to-Test Children*. Nashville, Tennessee: IMIRID, George Peabody College for Teachers.

Committee on Nomenclature, Conference of Executives of American Schools for the Deaf. 1938. *American Annals of the Deaf* 83.

Curry, E. T. 1950. The Efficiency of Teacher Referral in a School Hearing Testing Program. *Journal of Speech and Hearing Disorders* 15 (September): 211–214.

Davis, H., and Fowler, E. P. 1960. Hearing and Deafness. In Davis, H., and Silverman, S. R. (eds.), *Hearing and Deafness*, 2nd ed. New York: Holt, Rinehart, and Winston.

Davis, H. and Krantz, F. W. 1964. The International Standard Reference Zero for Pure-

Tone Audiometers and Its Relation to the Evaluation of Impairment of Hearing. *Journal of Speech and Hearing Research* 7 (March): 7–16.

Di Carlo, L. M. 1964. *The Deaf.* Englewood Cliffs, New Jersey: Prentice-Hall.

Farber, Bernard. 1959. *The Prevalence of Exceptional Children in Illinois.* Circular Census 14. Springfield, Illinois: Office of the Superintendent of Public Instruction.

Goodhill, V. 1957. Pathology, Diagnosis, and Therapy. In Travis, L. E. (ed.), *Handbook of Speech Pathology.* New York: Appleton-Century-Crofts.

Hardy, Janet B. 1968. The Whole Child: A Plea for a Global Approach to the Child with Auditory Problems. *Education of the Deaf: The Challenge and the Charge.* Washington, D.C.: Government Printing Office.

Hicks, D. E. 1970. Comparison Profiles of Rubella and Non-Rubella Deaf Children. *American Annals of the Deaf* 115 (March): 65–74.

Illinois Commission on Children. 1968. *A Comprehensive Plan for Hearing Impaired Children in Illinois.* Springfield, Illinois: The Commission.

Kloepfer, H. W.; Laquaite, Jeanette; and McLaurin, J. W. 1970. Genetic Aspects of Congenital Hearing Loss. *American Annals of the Deaf* 115 (January): 17–22.

McGee, T. M. 1968. Ototoxic Antibiotics. *Volta Review* 70 (December): 667–671.

Myklebust, H. R. 1960. *The Psychology of Deafness.* New York: Grune and Stratton.

Silverman, R. 1957. Education of the Deaf. In Travis, L. E. (ed.), *Handbook of Speech Pathology.* New York: Appleton-Century-Crofts.

Streng, Alice; Fitch, W. J.; Hedgecock, L. D.; Phillips, J. W.; and Carrell, J. A. 1958. *Hearing Therapy for Children,* 2nd ed. New York: Grune and Stratton.

Walsh, T. E. 1960. The Surgical Treatment of Hearing Loss. In Davis, H., and Silverman, S. R., *Hearing and Deafness,* 2nd ed. New York: Holt, Rinehart, and Winston.

Warwick, H. 1928. Hearing Tests in Public Schools of Fort Worth. *Volta Review* 30 (November): 641–643.

NINE

EDUCATING

DEAF

AND

HARD-OF-HEARING

CHILDREN

The educational provisions and techniques for teaching deaf children are significantly different from those utilized with hard-of-hearing children. Because hard-of-hearing children have the ability to acquire speech and language through hearing, the problem in teaching them is mainly one of making it possible for them to learn through the methods and techniques used with hearing children. With hearing aids, some individual help in speech, speechreading, auditory training, and a few special arrangements, most of these children can acquire an education in classes with hearing children.

The deaf child faces quite a different problem. Because he never hears speech, he does not normally acquire language or the subtleties of meaning which are more readily acquired through the sense of hearing. The important factor to remember in educating deaf children is that their major deficiency is not so much lack of hearing as inability to develop speech and language through the sense of hearing. Their education, therefore, is probably the most technical area in the whole field of special education. It requires more specialized training on the part of the teacher than any other form of special education.

This chapter will first discuss the less technical problem of providing special educational adaptations for hard-of-hearing children and then describe the procedures in educating deaf children.

Educational Provisions for the Hard of Hearing

In fulfilling its responsibilities to hard-of-hearing children, the school has to (1) identify those needing help, (2) see that they are adequately diagnosed and given whatever medical treatment is necessary, and (3) provide an appropriate educational program.

IDENTIFICATION

The first problem the school faces is that of locating the children needing help. Often a child with a hearing loss of 40 or 50 decibels is not detected by parents or teachers since he hears conversational speech and probably learned to talk at an average age. Sometimes deviant behavior is not recognized as related to hearing loss but is attributed to other factors (such as low intelligence, emotional problems, lack of interest) which may or may not be pertinent. A systematic attempt to find the auditorily handicapped would include a screening test for all children and an individual test for those who fail to pass the screening test.

Screening procedures in schools involve either individual or group testing of children in kindergarten to third grade, and periodic examinations in the higher grades. Generally, a sweep-check audiometric test devised for rapid screening of hearing impairments is administered by the school nurse or an audiologist or hearing specialist. Those suspected of having a hearing loss receive a more complete audiometric test. These screening procedures are referred to as "identification audiometry" and are utilized in schools to select the 2 to 5 percent of children who should be referred to otologists and audiologists for more exact diagnosis. Many children who indicate a hearing loss on the screening test are found not to have a loss when given the more thorough pure-tone test (threshold testing). Inattention, poor understanding, and other factors sometimes make a child respond poorly to group or individual sweep-check testing.

Children suspected of having a hearing loss are referred to an otologist, who determines the exact nature of the disability and if possible administers medical treatment. For example, he may find wax in the ears, infected adenoids or tonsils, or some other abnormality which can be corrected.

The steps in identification diagnosis and services may be summarized as follows:

1. Preliminary screening of children.

2. Threshold testing, and if hearing handicap is found, referral for otological examination.

3. Otological examinations and medical treatment if indicated.

4. Audiological examination to include special tests and hearing-aid evaluation.

5. Psychoeducational evaluation and special educational services.

PROGRAMMING

As was suggested earlier, the educational program is not the same for all cases of hearing handicap. The child with a severe or extreme hearing loss needs specialized techniques and materials, which will be discussed in the next section. At present we are dealing with the philosophy and methods of teaching hard-of-hearing children who, despite their handicap, can make some use of auditory stimuli.

For many years hard-of-hearing children were taught in special classes. These classes had some advantages in that the class number was kept small, there was an increased use of visual aids, and auditory training and speechreading could be an integral part of the program. Since the recent improvements in hearing aids, however, it has been found that most of these children gain more from being with normal children. They are usually able to keep up with the work if given a little assistance in the areas of special need.

Hard-of-hearing children (as shown in Fig. 8–1) are not very different from their classmates. They are not seriously retarded academically except possibly in speech, language, and reading. Special classes have been provided for those with marked variation or with variations in many areas, but when a discrepancy occurs in only one or two remediable areas, it is advisable to keep the child in the regular grades and allow him to leave the class for short periods for specific tutoring in his regions of difficulty. For this reason, school systems are eliminating special classes for the hard of hearing.

More widely recommended is enrollment in the regular grades and provision of itinerant or special support services to help the children individually or in small groups. This instruction would consist of (1) training in the use of hearing aids, (2) auditory training, (3) speechreading, (4) speech correction, and (5) assisting the classroom teacher.

Generally an audiologist determines the type of hearing aid to be used by the child, and instructs both parents and the child in the use and care of the aid.

Instruction in the Use of Hearing Aids. With young children considerable care should be used in introducing the hearing aid. At the outset a child should not wear a hearing aid all day. The best procedure is to start using a hearing aid only in the tutoring session and under the supervision of an audiologist. It should be used for short periods of time under instruction and the periods gradually increased, so that the child will learn to use the hearing aid profitably.

Auditory Training. Training the child to listen to sound clues which are available to him and to discriminate between different sounds is called auditory training. Before the advent of hearing aids, auditory training involved speaking into the ear or using tubes to amplify the sound. Now that the transistor type of hearing aid is available, these are extensively used in auditory training.

Modern electronics has vastly improved hearing aids. Specific frequencies can be emphasized, tone quality has been improved to make reproduction more natural and speech more intelligible, adjustments can be made by the wearer, and packaging has become more convenient. With the application of transistors to hearing aids, the size has been diminished until now the necessary mechanisms can even be put in an eyeglass frame.

The major aim of auditory training is to help the child at as early an age as possible to learn to discriminate between sounds. This kind of instruction is given to the hard-of-hearing child by an itinerant hearing specialist in school in accordance with the needs of the child. Of great importance for this type of training is home instruction, particularly during the preschool period. Parents can aid a great deal in auditory training, and one of the goals of the hearing specialist is to so instruct the parents and obtain their cooperation.

Speechreading (Lip Reading). Although we use the auditory sense to understand the spoken word, most of us can hear and understand another person better if we are looking directly at his face. Certain facial expressions and movements add meaning to what he says. That is why television, which uses both auditory and visual aids, is more effective than a radio. If you turn on your television so that the picture shows clearly, but tune down the voice to the point where it is only partially audible from where you are sitting, you will experience what cues a hard-of-hearing person uses. In this situation you will begin to rely on the facial and lip movements of the speaker to supplement the faint voice you hear. If you turn off the visual picture but leave the faint voice on, you will understand less of what the speaker is saying.

Speechreading lessons are given to hard-of-hearing children to sharpen their understanding of what is said to them. By directing their attention to certain cues in lip and facial movements they can learn to fill in from visual clues the sounds they do not hear and the words which are indistinct. Many words look much alike to the speechreader—words such as "cup" and "up." These cannot be discriminated visually. But words like "fish" and "ball" are rather easy to differentiate. It is also fortunate that the vowels, which are harder to tell apart visually, are easier to discriminate auditorily since they belong to the lower-frequency ranges. Some of the consonants, like *s,* are harder to hear because they belong to the high-frequency ranges in speech, where a deficit in sensory-neural or perceptive deafness is more common (O'Neill and Oyer, 1961).

By giving a hard-of-hearing child some help outside of the regular classroom in auditory training, speechreading, and the use of a hearing aid, the itinerant teacher is helping him understand more effectively the speakers who surround him—the teacher, the children in class, and his parents.

In general, three methods of teaching speechreading have been used. The first emphasizes the analysis of details in a word. This is a phonetic approach to speechreading. Instruction is programmed with a series of exercises in phonics, in which the child learns to distinguish phonetic elements by seeing them and repeating them to himself. In one such system, the Jena method, the child memorizes vowel series, then combines vowels with consonants and later uses words and sentences (Bunger, 1952).

A second method, the whole method of teaching speechreading, does not use a phonetic or syllable approach but emphasizes thought units as a whole (Stowell, 1928). The child is told stories even though he understands only parts of them. Nitchie (1950) first advocated a phonic method but later developed a whole method of speechreading instruction. Her methods of teaching involved the synthesis of what was read.

A third method, described by Bruhn (1947), is based on the German Mueller-Walle Method. In her lessons with children she presents the most visible sounds first and the less visible sounds at a later time. The lessons begin with syllables and move on to sentences.

Speech Correction. Many children who are hard of hearing have not heard certain sounds accurately and so have developed speech with sound substitutions and other articulatory defects. In addition, because they sometimes do not hear background noises, they fail to adjust the loudness of their voices to surrounding noises. Some speak too loudly because they cannot hear their own voices, owing to a perceptive loss; others do not speak loudly enough because, having a conductive loss, they can hear their own voices through bone conduction much better than they hear others.

The usual procedure for speech training is first to find out what errors a child makes in speech. Errors can be tabulated in a more formal way by using an articulation test. A child is asked to label or name pictures or objects, and the teacher notes whether the child adds or omits sounds and whether his distortions or substitutions occur in the initial, medial, or final positions. In addition, the teacher will note the voice quality and any abnormalities in speaking.

Following the detection of specific errors, corrective measures can be initiated. In school it is best for the child to remain in the regular grades for his educational program, while the special teachers help him with his speaking and hearing problems in an individual situation or in a small group. Most effective results are obtained when such training is integrated with the work of the regular class and when the parents will cooperate with the program at home.

Educational Provisions for the Deaf

The major emphasis in education of the deaf is the development of language and communication, since this is the vehicle through which the child receives information and expresses himself verbally. All English-speaking educators of the deaf agree that the deaf child must learn the English language and must learn to read and write this language. However, people concerned with education of the deaf have held sharply differing views on the modes of communication to be emphasized in teaching language to deaf children. The two differing modes of communication are oralism and manualism.

The oral method develops communication through speech and speechreading. It is sometimes called the "oral-aural" approach because of its great emphasis upon the use of residual hearing. The manual method includes (1) the language of signs, a language system consisting of formalized movements of the hands or arms to express thoughts, and (2) fingerspelling using the manual alphabet, in which there is a fixed position of the five fingers for each letter of the alphabet (See Figure 9-1). This is a kind of spelling in the air. In communicating manually, deaf persons generally use the two modes together, fingerspelling some words and expressing others through the language of signs.

THE DEVELOPMENT OF EDUCATIONAL PROGRAMS FOR THE DEAF

According to Wallin (1924) the pioneers in the education of the deaf were Juan Pablo Bonet and Jacob Rodrigues Pereire, Spaniards of the seventeenth century. Bonet originated the manual alphabet for the deaf, published in Madrid in 1620. This was a major innovation in the field since it gave the deaf a means of communication with those who knew the manual alphabet. Pereire extended Bonet's alphabet and added to it the manual sign language.

But Pereire also expanded a more far-reaching technique known as *lip reading* or the oral method of teaching the deaf by having them acquire meaning from the movements of other people's lips and facial muscles and form their own words from what they had seen. According to Wallin, Pereire held to the theory that touch is the primitive sense and that all special senses are modifications of

FIGURE 9–1

The American Manual Alphabet
(As seen by the finger speller)

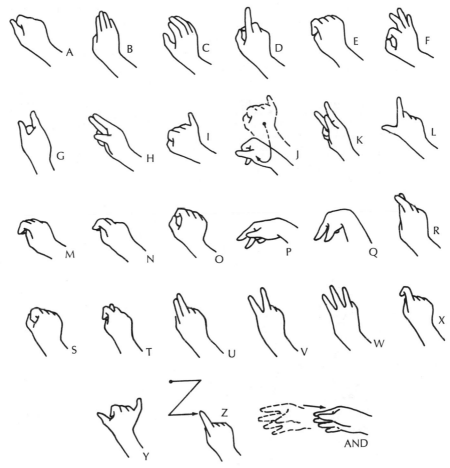

Source: L. J. Fant, Jr., *Say It with Hands* (Washington, D.C.: Gallaudet College Centennial Fund Commission, 1964), p. 1. Reproduced by permission of the author.

touch. Through the tactual sense, he tried to produce voices in deaf children. Thus, through visual apprehension of the movements of the visible speech organs and through the vibrations which could be felt by the deaf child, Pereire introduced the oral method.

Because of Pereire's contribution he was awarded a pension by Louis XV, and the oral method received the official commendation of a committee of the Parisian Academy of Science. Wallin (1924) asserts,

There has perhaps been no achievement in the whole realm of remedial pedagogy or, educational rehabilitation quite equal to the feat of teaching a deaf child who may never have heard a spoken word and who is even unable to hear his own voice, to speak and apprehend speech. It is much more difficult to reach the deaf than the blind, for the deaf are deprived of the greatest stimulus to mental growth, namely, spoken lanaguage. (p. 8)

According to Silverman (1960), it was the Abbé Charles Michel de l'Épée in France and Samuel Heinicke in Germany who advanced the cause of deaf education on the Continent in the eighteenth century. De l'Épée founded the first public school for the deaf in 1755 in Paris, where he taught by the manual method. De l'Épée's contemporary, Samuel Heinicke, founded the first public school for the deaf in Germany, using the oral method. Thus the two methods of teaching the deaf received impetus at about the same time—de l'Épée favoring signs and manualism, Heinicke advocating speech and speechreading.

The first school for the deaf in the British Isles was opened in Edinburgh in 1760 by Thomas Braidwood, who became well known for his oral methods of teaching deaf children. His reputation spread to the United States and stimulated Thomas Hopkins Gallaudet, a divinity student in Hartford, Connecticut, to go to Scotland to study the oral method. Gallaudet was disappointed with what he obtained there. Braidwood was supposedly getting good results from his use of the oral method with deaf children but he was secretive about his methods. Gallaudet therefore crossed the channel to France and studied the manual approach of de l'Épée under Sicard, de l'Épée's successor. After his return to the United States, Gallaudet in 1817 opened at Hartford, Connecticut, the first school for the deaf in this country. Education there was, of course, by the manual method. Gallaudet was also responsible for bringing to Hartford, Laurent Clerc, who himself was deaf. At the Hartford school, then called the American Asylum for the Education and Instruction of the Deaf and Dumb, Clerc became the first deaf teacher of the deaf in the United States.

Although the Hartford school was supported privately, it soon won public support and became the forerunner of state-supported schools throughout the United States, most of which combine oral and manual methods. Private residential schools like the Clarke School for the Deaf in Northampton, Massachusetts, the Lexington School for the Deaf in New York, and the Central Institute for the Deaf in St. Louis, Missouri, were organized and continue to function as advocates of the oral method. The federally sponsored College for the Deaf in Washington, D.C., where the work was carried on by Gallaudet's son, Edward Minor Gallaudet, bears the name of Gallaudet.

In this country Alexander Graham Bell also opened up new channels for teaching speech to the deaf. His method of "Visible Speech" helped the child understand the placement of his speech organs in producing speech. His invention of the telephone led to the development and use of hearing aids and to greater emphasis on the use of amplification of sound in teaching speech to children with severely defective hearing. These inventions advanced oral methods of teaching the deaf and made it possible for many children to understand speech and language who previously could not have done so. Bell was also responsible for founding the Volta Bureau of information on deafness.

The oral method has had many advocates in the United States, although advancement of this technique came somewhat later than teaching by the manual method. The first public day school utilizing the oral method was established in Boston in 1869. Horace Mann, who had studied the education of the deaf in Germany, was influential in this undertaking.

CURRENT COMMUNICATION APPROACHES

Some deaf adults use speech and speechreading almost exclusively in face-to-face communication situations. Some rely solely upon a manual mode of communication. However, the vast majority of deaf and deafened adults utilize various combinations of oral and manual modes, depending upon their proficiency and the nature of the situation.

Controversies on communication center primarily on which approaches are to be used in educating deaf children and in developing their language. Since the time of de L'Épée's emphasis on the manual method and Heinicke's advocacy of the oral method the controversy has continued, but with decreasing enthusiasm for strictly oral or strictly manual procedures. Currently, three basic approaches are in use, (1) the oral approach, (2) the combined approach, and (3) the simultaneous approach.

1. *The Oral Approach* refers to the method of instruction which uses speech, speechreading, use of residual hearing, reading, and writing. School programs which adhere to this approach do not use or encourage the use of the language of signs or fingerspelling on the assumption that manual communication will inhibit the child's learning of language and oral skills and impede his adjustment to the hearing world.

2. *The Combined Approach,* often referred to as the Rochester Method since its establishment at the Rochester, New York, school in 1878, is an approach which combines the oral approach with simultaneous use of fingerspelling. The teacher using this approach spells every word near her face as she says it. Figure 9–1 gives the fingerspelling alphabet.

3. *The Simultaneous Approach* refers to the simultaneous use of oral communication, fingerspelling, and the language of signs (some words are fingerspelled, others are given by signs). A discrepancy may occur in using the simultaneous method since the order of words and the syntax of the language of signs do not conform to those of English. In most cases it is impossible to form different words to show plurals, verb tenses, etc. However, attempts are currently underway to modify the syntax of the language of signs so that it corresponds more closely to English syntax.

It will be noted from the above that the oral, fingerspelling, and manual sign approaches are not completely exclusive. The first method is pure oralism whereas the other methods are additions to the oral method.

For many years controversy has raged between the so-called oralists and manualists without much concrete research to settle the disputes. Recently some research studies have been conducted on the problem.

Markovin (1960) summarized the research on neo-oralism conducted in the Soviet Union. He reports that they initiated simultaneous fingerspelling and speech at an early age (ages 2 and 3) and claim that by age 6 the children had acquired a vocabulary of several thousand words. By the age of 8, the Russians claim, the children had developed sufficient language (through simultaneous presentation of speech and fingerspelling) to abandon fingerspelling. Quigley (1969) reviewed the Russian literature on the subject and failed to find definite substantiation of the claims of superiority over other methods. At the same time Quigley conducted a five-year experiment on the Rochester Method (speech and fingerspelling) and concluded that: (a) fingerspelling plus good oral techniques improves achievement in meaningful language, (b) learning fingerspelling is not detrimental to the acquisition of oral skills, (c) fingerspelling produces greater benefits with younger rather than with older children, and (d) fingerspelling is a useful tool for instructing deaf children but is not a panacea.

In a review of Tervoort and Verbeck's study (1967), Moores (1970) states:

For generations the majority of educators of the deaf have operated under the assumption that the use of manual communication would inhibit the development of speech and language. Tervoort's position appears to be that systematic controlled use of manual communication would facilitate language development and have no adverse effects on speech. (p. 15)

Stuckless and Birch (1966) compared the language development of a group of deaf children exposed to manual communication (because they were reared by deaf parents) with a group of children not exposed to early manual communication. They found that the group with early manual communication was superior to the control group in reading, written language, and speechreading. They were equal in speech intelligibility and in psychosocial development. Meadow (1968) conducted a similar experiment in a state school for the deaf, by comparing deaf children raised by deaf parents (manual communication) with a group of deaf children from homes with hearing parents. Meadow found the group of deaf children who had been exposed to early manual communication to be superior in self-concept, academic achievement, and written language. Speechreading and speech ability were similar for both groups.

The studies cited tend to favor early manual communication for the development of language. Furthermore, with the restricted samples used there were no detrimental effects on speech and speechreading. Yet those who deal with the deaf see many who rely solely on manual communication, reading, writing, and do not use speech and speechreading.

An example of one who learned fingerspelling and who developed excellent language, but who did not learn speech or speechreading was Howard Hofsteater (1959). Raised by deaf parents he was taught fingerspelling at a young age. He learned to read and thus developed written rather than spoken language including a high degree of abstract conceptualization. This is his description of how he developed reading and language:

As soon as my parents became convinced that I had irretrievably lost my hearing, they were confronted with the question of what next to do with me. . . . Quite normally they argued that if a normal hearing child effortlessly acquires spoken language by hearing it and imitating it, a deaf child should be able to do exactly the same by seeing it used. They saw no psychological—nor physiological—difference between a baby's using its vocal cords, tongue, and lips to imitate spoken language and a baby's using his hands to imitate movements of finger-spelled words. . . .

The idea that whenever they manipulated their fingers in my direction would in some way affect my well-being must have percolated through somehow, for I developed at a rather early age the faculty of *concentrated visual attention*—subject, of course, to my fluctuating desire to listen. (pp. 10–12)

It is obvious from these extracts from Mr. Hofsteater's autobiography that he had developed fluent use of the English language. This conceptual and abstract process was developed by extensive reading throughout his school years and after.

Vernon (1970) compared the later educational achievement, communication skills, and psychological adjustment of 32 children who had received early manual training with that of 32 children who had early oral training. The children who had early manual instruction scored significantly higher on the Stanford

Achievement Test than did the early oral-trained group. There was no difference between the groups in communication skills or psychological adjustment.

Both the oral and the manual methods are in use today. Most authorities agree that there is a place for each or for a combined method. No group insists that all deaf children should be taught only by the manual method. Both residential and day schools advocate the oral method for those children who are capable of learning by it. In many residential schools, for instance, most children are given an opportunity to learn the oral method at first, but if they do not make progress they are then taught by the combined method. In most residential schools a simultaneous approach is used as the instructional technique for a large proportion of the children. In addition, when a group of deaf children congregate, as in a residential school, they naturally learn from each other, and the manual method becomes the common denominator of communication because there are some children who never do learn oral speech. Younger children especially rely on the manual method, since adequate speechreading and speech require many years of training and considerable facility.

DAY AND RESIDENTIAL SCHOOLS

At present there are residential schools, day schools, and special classes for deaf children. Table 9–1 shows that approximately half of all deaf children who are receiving education in this country go to the residential schools, either privately or publicly operated. The state schools are administered by a state authority and offer education and maintenance without charge. The education of children in day schools is of two types: either a segregated school is devoted entirely to deaf children or one or more classes are provided for the deaf in a school housing hearing children. The size of the classes ranges from five to ten children. Most of the residential schools combine oralism and manualism, but as indicated earlier a few schools (such as the Central Institute for the Deaf in St. Louis, Clarke School for the Deaf in Massachusetts, and the Lexington School for the Deaf in New York) use the oral method exclusively.

There has been very little research to evaluate the relative advantages of day schools and residential schools or their effects on the future lives of their pupils. In the 1920's Upshall (1929) compared the development of children in institutions with that of children in day schools and found that the intelligence of those in institutions was somewhat lower than that of day school students. Similarly, in comparing 311 day school pupils with 1,470 residential school pupils he found that the achievement of the former was somewhat higher than that of the latter.

The results of Upshall's study do not determine which method is best. All they indicate is that those who are enrolled in day schools tend to have a higher

TABLE 9–1

Enrollment in schools and classes for the deaf, 1955, 1960, and 1968

Kind of School	1955		1960		1968	
	Schools	*Enrollment*	*Schools*	*Enrollment*	*Schools*	*Enrollment*
Public residential schools	72	14,501	72	15,826	102	18,766
Day schools	10	2,019	10	2,050	39	3,950
Day classes in public schools	200	4,374	254	7,082	883	17,190
Denominational and private residential schools and classes	50	2,027	64	2,440	133	3,614
Schools and classes for the multiple handicapped	11	112+	15	191	23	473
Total	343	23,033	415	27,589	1,180	44,020

Source: American Annals of the Deaf 101 (January, 1956), p. 222; 106 (January, 1961), p. 162; and 110 (January, 1969), p. 301.

nonlanguage intelligence test score and higher educational achievement. A selection factor may be operative here, since in some instances day schools refer those with poor learning ability to residential schools. Upshall also discovered that the day schools had a greater proportion of children with better hearing and more who had become deaf later in life. These children also spend more years in school. When Upshall matched cases in day schools with cases in residential schools for age, intelligence, onset of deafness, and degree of hearing loss, he still found a slight educational superiority for those in day schools, but the difference was not statistically significant.

Quigley and Frisina (1961) conducted a different kind of an experiment, matching 120 residential school children with 120 children living at home (day pupils) but attending the same residential schools. The day pupils were found to be superior in speech and speechreading, but there was no difference in fingerspelling ability or vocabulary. In some of the adjustment evaluations the resident pupils scored slightly higher than the day pupils. This difference was more evident among boys than among girls.

Whether to send a child to a day school or to a residential school for the deaf depends upon many factors. If adequate provisions exist in the community, the child should probably go to the day school. If, on the other hand, there are few deaf children in the community and no provisions for their education, it is usually better for the child to be in a residential institution. Therefore, the question is not whether day schools are more effective than residential schools, or vice versa, but what is most beneficial for a particular child in a particular community.

Factors Influencing Educational Development of Deaf Children

As with all children, there are many environmental influences and factors which produce individual differences in development among deaf children. The more tangible and important factors are (1) intelligence, and related psychological functions, (2) degree of deafness (severe or extreme), (3) age at onset of deafness, and (4) other handicaps.

INTELLIGENCE AND PSYCHOLOGICAL CHARACTERISTICS

The progress of a deaf child in school is partially dependent upon his intelligence, his rate of learning, and his ability to generalize, draw conclusions, and make use of subtle cues. There are some deaf children who are superior in intelligence, many who are average, and some who are mentally retarded. Performance on nonlanguage intelligence tests (where the deaf child's language difficulty is minimized) indicates that the IQ's of deaf children attending school range from 60 to 160.

Pintner et al (1941) surveyed the results of various nonlanguage and performance intelligence tests given to deaf children mostly in residential schools. They state, "Our best estimate at present, therefore, is that the average IQ of the deaf does not quite reach 90." In general, however, children attending oral schools and public day schools tend to be close to 100 IQ while the larger group attending residential schools averages around 90 IQ. This difference is not necessarily attributable to the teaching methods since there is a selection factor in effect. The more intelligent children are less likely to be sent to a residential institution, whereas the ones who find it difficult to function in the day schools are often referred to the residential schools.

Since the time of Pintner et al's study many individual performance tests have been developed and administered to deaf children. In general, on individual performance tests not utilizing language, the deaf tend to show the same distribution of IQ's as hearing children. These tests include the Wechsler Intelligence Scale for Children (WISC), the Goodenough Draw-a-Man Test, the Ontario

School Ability Test, the Progressive Matrices, and the Leiter International Scale.

Brill (1962) studied the relationship between intelligence test scores (WISC and WAIS—the Wechsler Adult Intelligence Scale) and later academic achievement. He found the distribution for 499 deaf children to be similar to a random sample of hearing children with a mean IQ of 102 and a standard deviation of 17. The correlation between Wechsler IQ's and the Stanford Achievement test was .54 for 105 of the children. For those later admitted to college the average IQ's were 115.8. For those given an academic diploma from the school the average IQ was 112, and for those given a vocational diploma the IQ was 101.7. The certificate group had a mean IQ of 90.1. The academic achievement level of each group showed similar differences. The college group had a mean grade of 9.4; the academic group a mean grade of 7.2; the vocational group a mean grade of 4.9; and the certificate group had a mean grade of 3.1.

Birch et al (1963) studied the relationship between the Leiter International Performance Scale and school achievement eleven years later. They found a significant relationship between the early intelligence rating and educational achievement.

Vernon (1968) has reviewed the research on the intelligence of the deaf and hard of hearing for the past fifty years. He states that when psychological testing of the deaf was conducted by individuals experienced with deaf children, the results showed the deaf and hard of hearing nearly equal in intelligence. He also concluded that there was no substantial difference between the hard of hearing, the deaf, the congenitally deaf, and the adventitiously deaf; or in other words, no major relationship existed between degree of hearing loss and IQ or age of onset and IQ.

Myklebust (1960) points out in his study of deafness and mental development that although the deaf seem to be inferior to hearing children on some intellectual tasks, they are equal or superior on other tasks. For example, he found that the deaf are superior to hearing children on memory for designs, tactual memory, and memory for movement. But they were inferior to hearing children on digit span, picture span, and memory for dots.

Olsson and Furth (1966) administered visual memory span tests to a group of adolescents who were deaf and a group who had normal hearing. They found that with nonsense forms there was no difference between the deaf and the hearing group, but with digits the deaf were inferior to hearing subjects.

DEGREES OF DEAFNESS

Children placed in classes and schools for the deaf have either (1) a severe loss of hearing in the speech range (71 to 90 decibel level) or (2) an extreme hearing loss at a level of over 91 decibels.

The severely deaf child has considerable residual hearing and can profit in most instances from a hearing aid. Such a child is sometimes called *educationally deaf*; that is, he is not completely deaf but needs the specialized training of a deaf child. In other words, for instructional purposes he *is* deaf. Without intensive training, hearing aids, special techniques, and individual help, he will not develop language and speech. With such help children with this defect usually do develop language and speech. In some instances and with proper instruction they can be reclassified as hard of hearing and can move into the program for hard-of-hearing children; that is, they can be placed in a regular class with additional tutoring by a special teacher part of the day.

The extremely deaf, however, cannot profit as much from a hearing aid and frequently find it very difficult to acquire speech and language. They make slower progress in language, speech, and school subjects than do the severely deaf children.

AGE AT ONSET OF DEAFNESS

It has been emphasized that the age at which a child becomes deaf has a significant influence on his language and speech development. If a child does not lose his hearing until after he has acquired some speech and language, he at least has some concept of the process of communication and a base on which to build more speech and understanding of language. If he is born deaf or loses his hearing before he has learned to talk, he progresses much more slowly in these areas. Of course, the older the child is when he loses his hearing and the more advanced his speech, the easier his education will be later. To illustrate this point, Figure 9–2 gives the educational profiles of Carl, who was born with normal hearing, and Jim, who was born deaf.

Carl developed normally until the age of 7. He entered school when he was 6, and his intellectual ability was slightly above average. His school achievement was comparable to that of the average child. At the age of 7, however, he contracted meningitis, and when the disease subsided, Carl was unable to hear. Believing that this was a temporary condition, the parents waited for Carl's hearing to return. But it did not return, and he was diagnosed as having a total hearing loss of a sensory-neural type. There was nothing that could be done for him medically.

At the age of 10 Carl was given a series of physical, educational, and mental tests, the results of which are presented in Figure 9–2. It will be noticed that he was average in height and weight, and slightly above average in motor coordination and mental ability. In social maturity he was average. In speech development his progress had been slowed down by his loss of hearing and he was considered to have the speech development of a child less than 9 years old.

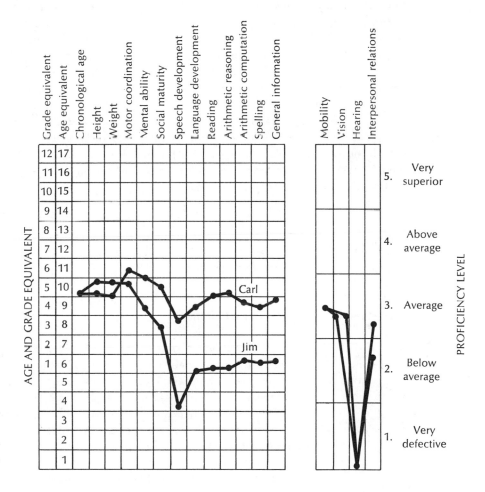

Language development was somewhat better; much of this could be gained from reading, in which, because of a good start in first and second grade, he was able to continue to progress at an average rate. He relied a great deal on reading since this was his best channel for obtaining information. In his other school subjects he was also progressing normally. This profile shows that Carl's major difficulty is in speech and language, which though handicapped by his loss of hearing were sufficiently well established at the time of his illness to permit him to gain ideas through written language.

Jim's profile reveals a much greater retardation. Jim was born deaf; the cause of his disability was unknown. It will be seen from the profile that at the age of 10 Jim was slightly above average in height, weight, and motor coordination and average in intelligence. In social maturity he showed some retardation, but in speech and in language development the retardation was marked. This handicap, of course, took its toll in other school subjects so that when he was 10, Jim was doing only first-grade reading and slightly better in other school subjects. Even this ability was due to the fact that he had been fortunate enough to attend nursery school, where he was taught some speech and speechreading. Had he not had a consistent program for the deaf, he would probably have learned no speech, no oral language skills, and no reading. The discrepancy between his school achievement and his physical, mental, and social abilities had been decreased because of the educational program.

Figure 9–2 demonstrates the effect of the early loss of hearing. Both boys were extremely deaf, with hearing losses of 90 to 100 decibels in each ear due to sensory-neural deafness. But Jim, whose educational retardation was very great, had been born deaf, whereas Carl had acquired his deafness after speech and language had had seven years to develop.

Specialized Curriculum for Deaf Children

In Chapter 8 a deaf child was defined as one whose hearing loss is so great that it interferes with the development of speech and language. Without hearing he does not naturally acquire speech and language; without speech and language he does not acquire knowledge and understanding of other subject matter. Because of the variety of deficits and because of the nature of the techniques necessary to teach the deaf, he needs a small special class and a teacher who understands the problems and is skilled in giving specialized training.

The specialized curriculum of a class for the deaf emphasizes the development of communication through vision and residual hearing and includes: (1) speech development, (2) speechreading and auditory training, (3) language development, (4) reading, and (5) other school subjects.

SPEECH DEVELOPMENT

As the hearing child learns to speak, the observer can recognize a series of stages. At first the child extends his gurgling and swallowing sounds into babbling. He toys with these sounds and experiments with his voice, and as he babbles he hears himself and sometimes repeats the same sound over and over again. Later he may repeat the sounds that someone else says if they are in his repertoire. This is the stage of imitation which at first is only echoing or imitating his own babbling sounds or the sounds his parents make. He may say "ma ma ma" or "da da da" just as repetition of sound, without attaching any meaning to it. As "da da da" is repeated over and over again in the presence of his father, he connects the two and moves into a higher stage in learning to talk: associating meaning with certain sounds. When the mother says "da da" he looks for his father, or when he says "da da" his father comes to him. By these stages the hearing child turns his babbling into meaningful words, and meaningful speech is then well on its way.

But the deaf child cannot hear his own babbling and it soon stops. He does not hear the words of his parents and hence neither imitates them nor attaches meaning to them. In short, he does not learn to speak by ordinary channels. If he is to learn to speak, it must be by other routes which are tedious, less efficient, and extremely slow in developing. But it has been found that a totally deaf child can learn to speak if properly taught by skilled parents and teachers. The intonation and expression may not be those of a hearing child, but he can learn to make himself understood. Vibrations and the sense of touch, visual aids, kinesthetic and proprioceptive cues, and the use of any residual hearing through a hearing aid are all part of the process as he learns to speak. Though often used together, they will be discussed separately.

Speech Training Through Vibration and the Sense of Touch. The tactile sense was used intensively by Kate and Sophia Alcorn (1938, 1942) in teaching deaf-blind children and also in teaching deaf-seeing children. With his eyes closed the child feels speech vibrations by placing his hand on the teacher's cheek, near the mouth, and so begins to discriminate between sounds, words, and sentences. He develops comprehension through touch before he is required to speak, just as a normal child understands through hearing before he speaks. Understanding of ideas precedes expression of ideas.

In all methods of teaching the extremely deaf, the sense of touch is an important factor. Through touch, the child feels the teacher's voice when his hand is in front of her mouth as she articulates consonants such as *b* and *p*. He feels vibrations of some sounds when his hand is on her cheek and other sounds when his hand is on her throat. With his hand on his own cheek, nose, or throat he tries to reproduce the same vibrations and gradually learns to pronounce sounds and words in correct order when he feels the face of the teacher and then his own face. Through these tactile cues the deaf child begins to articulate even though he does not hear. The steps in developing speech from the beginning stages to more complex phases are highly technical and require a teacher who is thoroughly trained. The process is very different from that used in correcting speech in a hearing child.

Speech Training Through the Use of Visual Aids. Although deaf-blind children rely primarily on the tactile sense, the deaf-seeing child is taught to use visual cues in addition to tactile cues. He learns to read other people's speech and by watching the face of the teacher and using a mirror he learns to reproduce what he sees as well as what he feels.

Espeseth (1969) found that intensive treatment could significantly improve the visual sequential memory span abilities of the deaf. He concluded that there exists a relationship between visual memory span and reading achievement; therefore, improvement in this ability should have a positive effect on accelerating the communication skills of the deaf.

Speech Training Through Kinesthetic or Proprioceptive Cues. In addition to vision and touch (both responding to external cues), the child learns to control his speech by sensing the muscular movements within his own mouth, jaw, tongue, lips, larynx, and so forth. Through practice his use of these kinesthetic cues eventually becomes automatic. Initially, however, he must be made conscious of these internal cues. He will eventually learn to control his voice and articulation, not because he hears them, but because he feels them internally.

Speech Training Through Auditory Stimulation. Many deaf children have some residual hearing even though not sufficient to understand or learn speech. Through powerful hearing aids their residual hearing can help them to learn rhythm patterns and discriminate differences, and it is used in teaching speech. This is a supplementary help to the training of speech which must utilize the tactile, visual, and kinesthetic methods. Thus hearing aids are used in classes for the deaf even though extremely deaf children are not able to understand speech by them.

Speech Training and Improvement Through "Visible Speech." Using an electronic instrument called an oscilloscope, it is possible to display on a screen (like a small TV screen) instantaneous wave-like patterns of light corresponding to varying sound vibrations. This has been spoken of as "visible speech." For many years attempts have been made to use such visible displays of speech to develop more adequate speech in deaf children. Potter, Kopp, and Green (1947) published a book describing the possibilities of using visible speech. Later Kopp and Kopp (1963) reported effective results using a cathode ray translator to train speech. Stark (1968) has described the modifications that have been made with the new Bell Telephone Visible Speech Translator. Numerous other studies have been made on the teaching of speech or improving articulation through electronic visual displays of various kinds. An example of one such device is reported by Pronovost (1970) entitled "The Instantaneous Pitch Period Indicator" (IPPI). The IPPI displays the rhythm and intonation patterns of spoken phrases on a five-inch storage oscilloscope screen. The teacher displays his voice on the channel so that the student can match the visual display. Matching occurs immediately. The deaf child is able to monitor his own response, and through this feedback learns to control his rhythm, intensity, and intonation. Pronovost reports rapid learning with this type of visual analyzer.

SPEECHREADING OR LIP READING

The highly technical task of teaching speech to deaf children is only part of the curriculum. Teaching speech is related to teaching language, speechreading, reading, and the content subjects.

Deaf children must rely heavily on their ability to interpret the lip and face movements of other people in order to understand their speech. For this reason speechreading is emphasized from a very young age. As in other areas of education, various methods of teaching deaf children to read speech have developed.

Speechreading requires the ability to interpret speech by seeing a few clues to a word or sentence. Those who are able to speechread well "fill in," or close so to speak, most of the speech they read. For example, one can see the articulatory movements in sounds such as *th, p,* and *f*. But the articulation of sounds such as *k* or *h* or *g* is not visible. Some sounds such as *n* and *t* cannot be visually differentiated. The vowel sounds of *ee* and *ay* are indistinguishable visually. Hence the speechreader must infer the sounds he cannot see from those he can see. Likewise words in a sentence must at times be inferred from the content, since words such as *man* and *bat* are not easily distinguishable by sight.

A combination of various methods is usually used by most teachers of the deaf. When the child is young, the teacher or the parent talks to him in whole sentences. Initially he obtains vague impressions of the idea through the whole or synthetic approach. At first he may not obtain any clues, but as the parent or teacher repeats the same expression over and over again in the same relationship to something which the child is experiencing—an object or an act or a feeling—the child begins to get an idea of what is being said. At a later stage these vague whole impressions are converted into lessons which emphasize details. Exercises are given to aid the child in discriminating between different words and between sounds. For example, two pictures may be presented, one of a ball and another of a boat. The child is taught to "point to the ball" or "point to the boat."

Speechreading for deaf children in special classes for the deaf is used in teaching language, speech, and the regular school subjects. It is not, like arithmetic, taught at certain hours of the day. It permeates the whole class day, whenever the teacher talks to the children. When hearing aids are used it is combined with auditory training. Programmed self-instructional speechreading lessons using movie films have been developed to help deaf children gain this technique.

For many years research workers have been wondering why some deaf children become proficient in speechreading while others do not. Studies on the variables that might account for success or failure in learning to speechread include chronological age, length of speechreading training, intelligence, rate of speech, and concept formation. None of these variables seemed to have a relationship with learning speechreading. Sharp (1970) administered a series of visual closure tests to 18 good and 19 poor speechreaders in two schools for the deaf. She found that good speechreaders were superior to poor speechreaders in visual closure, movement closure, and short-term memory. These results are consistent with other studies with hard-of-hearing adults, which showed that good speechreaders had superior visual synthetic ability (visual closure) over poor speech readers. In a study using speechreading films to teach speechreading, Evans (1965) found that visual recognition was the best predictor of speechreading potential.

LANGUAGE DEVELOPMENT

One of the major by-products of deafness is the deficit which results from the inability to hear language spoken by others. Language is one of the most complex of human skills. It involves many facets, including concept formation. It may be easy to teach a child the concept of a ball through lip reading, and whether the ball is large or small, or gray or white. But how can one develop the idea of "intangibility" or "the" or "of" or "for"? Concrete objects like "comb" and "ball" or action verbs such as "sit" and "jump" can be demonstrated, but the more complex forms of language and particularly the different shades of meaning of the same word are difficult to teach. For example, the word "run" has many meanings: "the boy runs" or "the river is running" or "a road runs in front of the house" or a "run in a stocking."

Reading and language are combined because the deaf child learns language through reading, and reading primarily through language. As a matter of fact, deaf children who develop language of a complex nature usually derive their language facility primarily from reading and experience.

There are two major theoretical approaches to teaching language to deaf children. An approach which has been dominant in the past is based on the hypothesis that all children learn the grammatical forms of language through imitation. They hear or speechread or read words and phrases repeated over and over again, and thus acquire the syntax of the language.

Another approach to the development of language has been proposed by psycholinguists. They point out that grammar (syntax and morphology) is not all developed through imitation. The hearing child is able to generalize rules for words not encountered in his experience. Thus, a child will answer (wugs) to the statement "This is a wug; these are two ————." In a study by Cooper (1965) it was found that deaf children also apply generalized rules to words, but not to the same extent as hearing children. Lennenberg (1965) states that children, deaf or hearing, inherit a predisposition for language in the same way as they inherit a predisposition to stand and to walk. He further states:

Language development, or its substitute, is relatively independent of the infant's babbling, or of his ability to hear. The congenitally deaf who will usually fail to develop an intelligible vocal communication system, who either do not babble or to whom babbling is of no avail (the facts have not been reliably reported), will nevertheless learn the intricacies of language and learn to communicate efficiently through writing. Apparently, even under these reduced circumstances of stimulation the miracle of the development of a feeling for grammar takes place. (p. 589)

Brown and Bellugi (1964) give three processes by which children develop language: (1) by imitation, even though the imitation is an approximation, (2) by expansion in which the parent repeats what the child says ("want milk") in an expanded phrase ("I want some milk"), and (3) by induction in which the child constructs language he has not heard (I sitted, two mans, etc.).

Because of the developmental theories of language advanced by psycholinguists, research teams are currently attempting to develop methods for teaching language to the deaf which implement psycholinguistic theories.

Although language training of deaf children permeates all of their educational activities, numerous, more specific systems of teaching language have been used. These use structured lessons for the purpose of developing English syntax.

The best-known system is the Fitzgerald Key (1954). It is used after children have learned some language forms in a natural way, without crutches or mechanical devices. The teacher introduces this series of symbols and structured sentences with questions: "Who?" "What?" "How many?" and "Where?" in relation to the grammatical structure of their sentences. These four questions are the key words of the method. By a structured procedure the children gradually develop an understanding of grammar. When this becomes automatic in speech and writing they have acquired intelligible language.

Such keys are initially "crutches" which the child uses to follow some sequence or pattern in language. It is necessary for him to develop a vocabulary, to understand and produce different shades of meaning for words in a sentence, and to express relationships. This slow and laborious process cannot be accomplished through speechreading or other activities alone. The greatest aid to the development of language in its higher forms is through the skills of reading and writing.

A common technique is the so-called *natural method* of teaching language. Groht (1958) is one of the advocates of this method, which uses language in natural situations through speechreading and writing, then later presents language principles formally. The method is inductive and is more in harmony with the principles of learning language used by hearing children.

READING

Language development for the deaf child is slow and laborious. Reading achievement is likewise slow and laborious. Surveys of reading achievement show that deaf children are markedly retarded in relation to their chronological and mental ages.

Pugh (1946) studied the reading ability of deaf children in a large number of schools for the deaf by administering the Iowa Silent Reading Test and the Durrell-Sullivan Reading Achievement Test. She found that as a group the deaf are notably retarded at the older ages, less so at the younger ages. That is, they become more and more retarded as the language requirements for understanding increase in complexity. Pugh found a small population of deaf children, however, reading at a high level, exceeding the norms for hearing children of their age.

The Office of Demographic Studies at Gallaudet College annually administers the Stanford Achievement Test to hearing-impaired children. Gentile (1969) reports the results of testing 12,000 hearing-impaired children in residential and day schools throughout the country. Similar to Pugh's results twenty years earlier his survey shows that the hearing-impaired are markedly retarded in reading as compared to their chronological age. Hearing-impaired children in his survey showed that 8-year-old children have a mean reading grade of high first grade, a year and a half retardation. At 12 years of age they were testing at the third grade level, a retardation of 4 years as compared to normal expectancy of achievement. At 16 years of age the mean reading achievement score was at the fourth to fifth grade level, a retardation of 6 to 7 years.

Moores (1967) compared deaf children with hearing children on a "cloze" procedure and concluded that standardized reading tests "give spuriously inflated estimates of the psycholinguistic abilities of the deaf." He arrived at this conclusion by using a "cloze" test to compare 37 adolescent deaf children (16 years, 9 months) whose average reading grade score on reading achievement tests was 4.77, with younger hearing children (9 years, 11 months) whose average reading achievement score was 4.84. The "cloze" test consisted of reading passages from fourth, sixth, and eighth grade reading text books with every fifth word left out. The children were required to fill in the blanks with appropriate words. The younger hearing children with the same reading achievement score were superior to the deaf children who were six years older. Such results have also been found by Odom, Blanton, and Nunnally (1967).

Thompson (1927) conducted an experiment with ten 6½-year-old children. She used a systematic, visual, picture-association technique, teaching the children for an hour a day over a period of one year. Comparing their progress with that of ten similar children taught by the usual methods, she found that for the first year those taught by her method exceeded the control group by two and one-half times, as tested by a picture-word association reading test. She did not follow up these children to determine whether the early gains on picture-word association were maintained. Nor has anyone since then conducted such a longitudinal study. Much research will be necessary before we can know what specific techniques of reading are most effective with deaf children throughout the grades.

OTHER SCHOOL SUBJECTS

In oral schools much class time is devoted to speech development, speechreading, language, and reading. But the curriculum also includes arithmetic, spelling, writing, literature, and the social and physical sciences, just as it does for hearing children.

Many schools utilize the unit plan for these school subjects. The children are given concrete experiences and activities, trips, dramatics, and demonstrations to assist them in understanding. There are no textbooks designed especially for the deaf, since they learn to utilize the books intended for hearing children. The specialized teaching techniques of communication used to teach the content subjects differ from age to age in a developmental sequence for the nursery school, kindergarten, elementary school, and high school.

CAPTIONED FILMS FOR THE DEAF

Before the advent of talking films, the deaf were able to enjoy movies, since they could read the captions. The invention of sound films thereby deprived the deaf of an earlier medium of educational and cultural enrichment. In order to compensate for this loss, Congress appropriated funds in 1958 for *Captioned*

Films for the Deaf. This program was originally designed to improve and enrich the curriculum for the deaf by providing captioned films for use in educational institutions. The original program of Captioned Films provided a loan service, but it has been expanded to include other services: to provide equipment to be used in homes and schools, to contract for the development of educational media, to train personnel in the use of the educational technology, and to establish a national center for the development of educational media and the use of television for educational purposes, and for the development of technology for programmed learning.

EDUCATION AT DIFFERENT DEVELOPMENTAL LEVELS

Early Home Training. Educators of the deaf emphasize early training in the communication skills as soon as a child is known to be deaf. At first the child learns to communicate at home, partly by facial expressions, gestures, and movements. Those who advocate oralism suggest that the parents not gesture with their hands, but rather talk to the child so that he will watch for clues in facial expression instead of watching hand movements.

Thus even the child in the crib obtains clues from his mother through her manner of handling him (tactile and kinesthetic) and through her facial expressions (visual). As the mother says "no," she shakes her head; when she says "yes," she has a different facial expression and nods. The child soon learns to respond to the lip movements and the facial expression or head movement. Through the tactual sense he obtains communication clues by feeling the vibrations of his mother's voice as she sings to him, or by feeling her face and throat as she talks.

Parents are generally instructed to use a whole or natural method of communicating with a deaf child, rather than a special system. They are asked to talk to the child, even though at first, like hearing babies, he does not understand. He will note in time that lip movements, head movements, facial expressions, and vibrations have some communicative meaning. This develops very slowly, but faster if the parent continues to communicate in a natural way without excessive use of signs and gestures.

Parents can get valuable suggestions from teachers of the deaf in school systems or hearing clinics even before the child is enrolled in the school. In addition, a correspondence course has been developed by the John Tracy Clinic (1954) to assist parents with the problems and especially the communication problems of young deaf children.

The Nursery School and Kindergarten. Many schools for the deaf admit children as young as 2½ to 3 years of age. The reason for such early admission is the greater need these children have for opportunities to practice socialization in a group situation and to develop skills in communication. The play activities of the nursery school and kindergarten foster growth in the communication skills through speechreading and in other ways. Although the children cannot hear, rhythm activities use pianos, drums, and other musical instruments, to which they can respond by feeling the vibrations. At a later age speech too will be developed partly through responses to vibration.

In addition, the teacher talks to the children when they are watching her face. They learn, for example, to recognize their names. They learn to jump, or stop, or walk, or dance, in response to the verbal request of the teacher. In this way a beginning is made in language as well as a start in speechreading. At the 5-year level the children begin to respond to words and phrases written on flashcards or on the board. This kind of reading is usually initiated earlier with deaf children than with the hearing child. Whereas the latter relies on hearing and speech for communication, the young deaf child has to rely heavily on vision. Hence the emphasis on beginning reading at an earlier age. Ordinarily, the same vocabulary is used in developing speech, speechreading, and reading.

The major purposes of nursery schools and kindergartens for young deaf children between the ages of 3 and 6 are: (1) to give the child experiences with other children in sharing, playing, and taking turns (a socialization process); (2) to develop language, speech, and speechreading ability; (3) to help the child take advantage of his residual hearing through the use of hearing aids and amplified sounds; (4) to develop in the child elementary number concepts; (5) to develop a readiness for reading words and phrases; and (6) to provide parent education.

The Elementary Years. The elementary school for deaf children is divided generally into a primary level and an upper elementary level. The primary-level instruction for deaf children is much more highly structured than that in the kindergarten. Training in language, speech, reading, and speechreading permeate all activities and all content subjects. If the child does not learn speech and speechreading at this age level, it is unlikely that he will acquire these skills later.

In some residential schools all deaf children are given instruction by the oral method until the age of 9 or 10. If they acquire speech at this level the emphasis on oralism continues. If speech and speechreading have not developed, however, instruction in manual communication by means of signs and fingerspelling is generally given. Language, reading, and the content subjects are pursued through sign language and fingerspelling. In many residential schools deaf teachers of the deaf are employed for instruction in the manual department.

In general, however, the emphasis is on combined forms of communication, fingerspelling and speech, or sign language and speech.

The upper elementary level in schools for the deaf enrolls children of ages 9 or 10 to 16. Since deaf children are generally from two to six years retarded educationally, the instruction is keyed to the content subjects of the fourth through the eighth grades. The large majority of deaf children consequently do not achieve an educational level of eighth grade.

High School and College. Deaf children continue from the elementary school into high school in public school systems and residential institutions. In day schools many of them are assigned to regular classes in the high school rather than to special classes but have an itinerant teacher who helps them understand what they miss from class discussion. With such assistance some of the severely and extremely deaf are able to complete high school.

In 1864 Congress organized Gallaudet College, the only college in the world devoted exclusively to the education of deaf individuals. It has since become an accredited four-year liberal arts college, and has added a graduate school which includes hearing and deaf students. Gallaudet also operates the Kendall School which enrolls elementary and secondary students from the Washington area. In 1965 Congress authorized a Model Secondary School for the Deaf to be supported by Federal funds. An agreement has been made with Gallaudet College to establish and operate a model secondary school which also would serve primarily residents of the District of Columbia.

Not all deaf secondary school graduates attend Gallaudet College. Quigley, Jenne, and Phillips (1968) made a survey of hearing colleges and universities and found 653 deaf individuals who had attended 326 accredited institutions of higher learning in 45 states.

Another development in higher education was the result of the organization of the National Technical Institute for the Deaf in Rochester, New York, which is also supported by the Federal Government. This institution was initiated in 1967 for the purpose of providing opportunities to deaf adolescents and adults for training in technical and vocational pursuits. In addition to this development and because of the expansion of community colleges, a Federally supported project was initiated in 1968–69 to establish three postsecondary programs for deaf students in community colleges. These have been established in three sections of the country at Delagado College, New Orleans, Louisiana; Seattle Community College, Seattle, Washington; and St. Paul Vocational Institute, St. Paul, Minnesota. Career objectives in these community colleges most frequently selected by these students were reported by Craig et al (1970) as including graphic arts, sheet metal, welding and body-repair, food services, machine-tool processing, production arts, prosthetics, and electronics.

Occupational Adjustment

Deaf adults adjust to practically any kind of job which does not have as a prerequisite the ability to hear. The deaf are found in professions, managerial positions, and skilled, semiskilled, and laboring jobs. The most extensive survey was made during the depression of the 1930's by Elise Martens of the United States Office of Education (1936). Of 3,786 employed men who were profoundly deaf, about one-third (1,173) were operatives in mills or factories, 533 were unskilled laborers, 330 were typesetters (a trade frequently taught in schools for the deaf), and all types of other occupations were represented: shoemaker, teacher, painter, forester, farmer, carpenter, cabinetmaker, and so forth. Engineering, medicine, law, real estate and the ministry were listed for from one to seven men. Out of 1,151 profoundly deaf women, 574 were employed as operatives in mills or factories, 120 as hotel or domestic servants, 75 as teachers, and 65 as dressmakers. One was a real-estate agent, one was a trained nurse, and several were managers, librarians, bookkeepers, or cashiers. The others had positions as cook, typist, waitress, housekeeper, clerk, and welfare worker.

In a later study, Lunde and Bigman (1959), in cooperation with the National Association for the Deaf (an association for deaf adults), distributed a questionnaire to deaf individuals throughout the United States. They received 10,101 completed schedules. Of these, 97 percent were from white respondents, 86 percent of whom ranged in age from 20 to 59. Of the total group responding, 7,920, or four-fifths, were employed. The rest were housewives, retired persons, and others.

The occupational distribution of the employed deaf in this study is as follows:

	Employed Deaf	In U.S. (1957) Population
Professional, technical, and similar workers	6.6%	10.6%
Managers, officials, and proprietors	3.2	15.5
Clerical, sales, and similar workers	7.2	20.7
Craftsmen, foremen, and similar workers	35.9	13.4
Operatives and similar workers	35.2	20.1
Others—i.e., service workers, laborers, etc.	11.9	19.7

It is interesting to note from this distribution of occupations that, as compared to the general population, there were fewer deaf in the professional fields, managerial positions, and clerical and sales positions because of the necessity of communication in these jobs. There were greater numbers of deaf serving as skilled and semiskilled workers and machine operators, and in similar jobs.

The industrial stronghold of deaf male respondents was in the printing and publishing industries.

The national surveys have indicated that 85 percent of the deaf workers are successful in their occupations. Observations of others also indicate that deafness as such does not preclude successful employment and independence, especially in occupations that do not require oral communication skills.

During the late 1950's and the 1960's the Vocational Rehabilitation Administration (U.S. Department of Health, Education, and Welfare, 1966) has supported the training of vocational counselors for deaf individuals. These counselors have been assisting the deaf in obtaining vocational training, in placement in appropriate positions, and in follow-up. Case-work standards have been developed to facilitate the work of the counselor.

Like the rest of society the deaf will be affected by the rapid changes in industrial processes, tools, and products. Employers are seeking more highly educated and technically trained workers for modern technology. The development of the National Technical Institute for the Deaf and the new programs for vocational training for the deaf in community colleges will undoubtedly reveal a difference in occupations among the deaf by 1980.

SUMMARY

1. Hard-of-hearing children are generally educated in the regular grades with an itinerant teacher helping them in the specific areas of (a) use of hearing aid, (b) auditory training, (c) speechreading, and (d) speech training. Deaf children are generally educated in a special class or school for the deaf.
2. For educational purposes, *deaf* children are those who were born without hearing or who lost their hearing before they acquired speech and language. Children who lose their hearing after the acquisition of speech and language are classified as *deafened*.
3. Deaf children are educated in public or private residential schools or in day schools and classes which are usually part of public school systems.
4. Three interrelated communication approaches are currently in use in the education of the deaf (a) the oral approach, (b) the combined approach (fingerspelling plus oral), and (c) the simultaneous approach (oral communication, fingerspelling, and the language of signs).
5. On nonverbal intelligence tests, the deaf range from mentally retarded to superior, with the average possibly slightly below 100 IQ.
6. Intelligence, degree of hearing loss, and age at onset of deafness are related to the educational progress of deaf children.
7. The greatest handicap created by the loss of hearing is the difficulty of developing speech and language.
8. The curriculum for deaf children differs from that followed with hearing children and

concentrates on developing (a) speech, (b) speechreading, (c) reading, and (d) language, in addition to the curriculum of the regular school.

9. Because of the handicap in speech and language, deaf children are from two to five years retarded in educational subjects.
10. In adult life the deaf are employed in all types of work not requiring hearing, from professional to unskilled labor, with the majority holding semiskilled and skilled jobs. They are considered satisfactory employees.

REFERENCES

Alcorn, Kate. 1938. Speech Developed Through Vibration. *Volta Review* 40 (November): 633–637.

Alcorn, Sophia K. 1942. Development of Speech by the Tadoma Method. *Proceedings of the Thirty-Second Meeting of the Convention of American Instructors of the Deaf,* pp. 241–243. Washington, D.C.: Government Printing Office.

Birch, J. R.; Stuckless, E. R.; and Birch, J. W. 1963. An Eleven-Year Study of Predicting School Achievement in Young Deaf Children. *American Annals of the Deaf* 108 (May): 236–240.

Brill, R. G. 1962. The Relationship of Wechsler IQ's to Academic Achievement Among Deaf Students. *Exceptional Children 28* (February): 315–321.

Brown, R. W., and Bellugi, Ursela. 1964. Three Processes in the Child's Acquisition of Syntax. *Harvard Educational Review* 34: 133–151.

Bruhn, Martha E. 1947. *The Mueller-Walle Method of Lip Reading for the Hard of Hearing.* Boston: M. H. Leavis.

Bunger, Anna M. 1952. *Speech Reading: Jena Method,* 2nd ed. Danville, Illinois: The Interstate Press.

Cooper, R. L. 1965. The Development of Morphological Habits in Deaf Children. In Rosenstein, J., and Macginitie, W. H. (eds.), *Research Studies on Psycholinguistic Behavior of Deaf Children,* pp. 3–11. Research Monograph Series B, No. B02, Arlington, Virginia: Council for Exceptional Children.

Craig, W.; Craig, Helen; and Barrows, Nona L. 1970. A Progress Report: Post Secondary Opportunities for Deaf Students. *Volta Review* 72 (March): 290–295.

Espeseth, V. K. 1969. An Investigation of Visual-Sequential Memory in Deaf Children. *American Annals of the Deaf* 114 (September): 786–789.

Evans, L. 1965. Psychological Factors Related to Lipreading. *Teacher of the Deaf* 63 (May): 131–136.

Fitzgerald, Edith. 1954. *Straight Language for the Deaf: System of Instruction for Deaf Children,* 2nd ed. Washington, D.C.: The Volta Bureau.

Gentile, A. 1969. *Academic Achievement Test Performance of Hearing Impaired Students.* Washington, D.C.: Office of Demographic Studies, Gallaudet College Bookstore.

Groht, Mildred. 1958. *Natural Language for Deaf Children.* Washington, D.C.: The Volta Bureau.

Hofsteater, H. T. 1959. *An Experiment in Preschool Education: An Autobiographical Case Study.* Bulletin No. 3, Vol. 8. Washington, D.C.: Gallaudet College.

John Tracy Clinic. 1954. *Correspondence Course for Parents of Little Deaf Children.* Los Angeles: John Tracy Clinic.

Kopp, G. A., and Kopp, Harriet G. 1963. *An Investigation to Evaluate the Usefulness of·' the Visible Speech Cathode Ray Translator as a Supplement to the Oral Method of Teaching Speech to Deaf and Severely Deafened Children.* Washington, D.C.: Department of Health, Education, and Welfare, Vocational Rehabilitation Administration.

Lennenberg, E. H. 1965. The Capacity for Language Acquisition. In Fodor, J. P., and Katz, J. J. (eds.), *The Structure of Language,* pp. 579–603. Englewood Cliffs, New Jersey: Prentice-Hall.

Lunde, A., and Bigman, S. 1959. *Occupational Conditions Among the Deaf.* Washington, D.C.: Gallaudet College.

Markovin, B. V. 1960. Experiment in Teaching Deaf Preschool Children in the Soviet Union. *Volta Review* 62 (June): 260–268.

Martens, Elise H. 1936. *The Deaf and Hard of Hearing in the Occupational World,* Bulletin No. 13. Washington, D.C.: Office of Education.

Meadow, Kathryn. 1968. Early Communication in Relation to the Deaf Child's Intellectual, Social, and Communicative Functioning. *American Annals of the Deaf* 113 (January): 29–41.

Moores, D. F. 1970. Review of Analysis of Communicative Structure Patterns in Deaf Children by Tervoort, B., and Verbeck, A. J. *American Annals of the Deaf* 115 (January): 11–15.

———. 1967. Applications of "Cloze" Procedures to the Assessment of Psycholinguistic Abilities of the Deaf. Unpublished doctoral dissertation, University of Illinois.

Myklebust, H. R. 1960. *The Psychology of Deafness.* New York: Grune and Stratton.

Nitchie, Elizabeth H. 1950. *New Lessons in Lip Reading.* Philadelphia: J. B. Lippincott.

Odom, Penelope B.; Blanton, R. L.; and Nunnally, J. C. 1967. Some "Cloze" Technique Studies of Language Capability in the Deaf. *Journal of Speech and Hearing Research* 10 (December): 816–827.

Olsson, J. E., and Furth, H. G. 1966. Visual Memory-Span in the Deaf. *American Journal of Psychology* 79 (September): 480–484.

O'Neill, J. J. and Oyer, H. J. 1961. *Visual Communication for the Hard of Hearing.* Englewood Cliffs, New Jersey: Prentice-Hall.

Pintner, R.; Eisenson, J.; and Stanton, Mildred. 1941. *The Psychology of the Physically Handicapped.* New York: F. S. Crofts.

Potter, R. G.; Kopp, G. A.; and Green, Harriet C. 1947. *Visible Speech.* New York: Van Nostrand.

Pronovost, W. 1970. The Instantaneous Pitch-Period Indicator. *Education of the Hearing Impaired* 1 (Spring): 37–39.

Pugh, Gladys. 1946. Summaries from Appraisal of the Silent Reading Abilities of Accoustically Handicapped Children. *American Annals of the Deaf* 91 (September): 331–349.

Quigley, S. P. 1969. *The Influence of Finger Spelling on the Development of Language,*

Communication, and Educative Achievement in Deaf Children. Urbana, Illinois: Institute for Research on Exceptional Children.

Quigley, S. P.; and Frisina, D. R. 1961. *Institutionalization and Psychoeducational Development of Deaf Children.* Council for Research on Exceptional Children.

Quigley, S. P.; Jenne, W. C.; and Phillips, Sandra B. 1968. *Deaf Students in Colleges and Universities.* Washington, D.C.: Alexander Graham Bell Association for the Deaf.

Sharp, Elizabeth Y. 1970. The Relationship of Visual Closure to Speech Reading Among Deaf Children. Unpublished doctoral dissertation, University of Arizona.

Silverman, S. R. 1960. From Aristotle to Bell. In Davis, H., and Silverman, S. R. (eds.), *Hearing and Deafness,* pp. 375–383. New York: Holt, Rinehart, and Winston.

Stark, C. E. 1968. Preliminary Work with the New Bell Telephone Visible Speech Translator. *American Annals of the Deaf* 113 (March): 205–211.

Stowell, Agnes; Samuelson, Estelle; and Lehman, Ann. 1928. *Lip Reading for the Deafened Child.* New York: Macmillan.

Stuckless, E. R., and Birch, J. W. 1966. The Influence of Early Manual Communication on the Linguistic Development of Deaf Children. *American Annals of the Deaf* 3 (March): 452–460.

Tervoort, B., and Verbeck, A. J. 1967. *Analysis of Communication Structure Patterns in Deaf Children.* Groningen, Netherlands: Z.W.O. Onderzack, N.R.

Thompson, Helen. 1927. *An Experimental Study of the Beginning Reading of Deaf-Mutes.* Teachers College Contributions to Education, No. 254. New York: Teachers College, Columbia University.

Upshall, C. C. 1929. *Day Schools Versus Institutions for the Deaf.* Teachers College Contributions to Education, No. 389. New York: Bureau of Publications, Teachers College, Columbia University.

U.S. Department of Health, Education, and Welfare. 1966. *The Vocational Rehabilitation of Deaf People.* Washington, D.C.: The Department.

Vernon, M. 1970. Early Manual Communication and Deaf Children's Achievement. *American Annals of the Deaf* 115 (September): 527–536.

———. 1968. Fifty Years of Research on the Intelligence of Deaf and Hard of Hearing Children: A Review of Literature and Discussion of Implications. *Journal of Rehabilitation of the Deaf* 1 (January): 1–12.

Wallin, J. E. W. 1924. *The Education of Handicapped Children.* Boston: Houghton Mifflin.

TEN

THE

VISUALLY

HANDICAPPED

CHILD

Educational procedures rely heavily on the sense of vision. Learning colors, watching the hamsters in the cage, observing the expressions on people's faces, using the workbooks and readers, distance perception—all are lost to the child without vision. His horizons must retract to the immediate vicinity where he can touch and hear stimuli. Walk around blindfolded, or even live behind a clouded glass, and some sense of the restricted environment and limited perceptions will be evident.

This chapter and the next will discuss the characteristics of children who are labeled blind or partially blind (legally blind, medically blind, occupationally blind, partially sighted, visually impaired) and the educational adaptations that must be made for children whom we call visually handicapped or visually impaired.

Definitions and Classifications

Human beings are such complex organisms that they can be grouped and regrouped according to many different dimensions. The broad classification of visual impairment can likewise be subdivided along varying dimensions for varying purposes. Visually handicapped children can be classified on the basis of (1) the physical measurements of visual acuity and narrowness of the visual field or (2) the use that is made of the visual sense modality for learning. Each classification evolved for a specific purpose and both are in use in different situations.

EARLIER DEFINITION AND CLASSIFICATION

In 1935 the Social Security Act required a definition of blindness for economic and legal purposes. Federal agencies administering services to the blind required an ophthalmic measurement so that an individual could be declared eligible for state and Federal services such as Federal-state-aid to the blind, income-tax exemptions, receiving talking books from the Library of Congress, and receiving large print, braille, and other materials distributed to the blind and partially sighted by the Federally operated American Printing House for the Blind. The *National Society for the Prevention of Blindness Fact Book* (1966) defined these terms as follows:

> *Blindness* is generally defined in the United States as visual acuity for distance vision of 20/200[1] or less in the better eye, with best correction; or visual acuity of more than 20/200 if the widest diameter of field of vision subtends an angle no greater than 20 degrees.
>
> The *partially seeing* are defined as persons with a visual acuity greater than 20/200 but not greater than 20/70 in the better eye with correction. (p. 10)

From the 1920's through 1940's it was believed that the limited vision of the child should be conserved by as little use as possible and that the child should use his vision only when an object or the print was large. The entire educational approach was designed to avoid straining the eyes. Classes for children who were classified as partially blind were called "sight saving" classes or "sight conserva-

[1] Clinical classifications of visually handicapped children are generally presented in terms of visual acuity or sharpness or clearness of vision. There are many visual tests, but most of them are based on the standards of the Snellen Chart. The form used for young people presents the letter *E* and involves figures of differing sizes and in different positions (ꟺ Ǝ ꟺ). The top figure of the chart is about 3.5 inches square and can be seen by the normal eye at 200 feet. The symbol 20/20 means that the child can distinguish at 20 feet what a normal eye can distinguish at 20 feet. The figure 20/200 means that the child can distinguish at 20 feet what a normal eye can distinguish at 200 feet. The symbol 5/200 means that the child can distinguish at 5 feet what a normal eye can distinguish at 200 feet.

tion" classes. Current opinion, on the other hand, holds that the eyes are very rarely damaged through use, and that the child should learn to use whatever vision he has in as many situations as possible.

CURRENT EDUCATIONAL DEFINITION AND CLASSIFICATION

These medical definitions have for many years influenced educational practice and organization. Gradually, however, educators have become less influenced by the medical classification and have evolved more educationally relevant classifications for instructional purposes.

The former classification of visually handicapped children into two categories (1) the *partially sighted* (with vision of 20/70 to 20/200), and (2) the *legally blind* (20/200 and less) became less tenable in view of the fact that a significantly large proportion of the "legally blind" learned to use their residual vision and could read print.

New practices, then, have resulted in a revision in terminology. The current terminology for educational purposes is:

1. The *visually impaired* which refers to those who can learn to read print;

2. The *blind,* who cannot learn print, but who need instruction in braille.

This change evolved as a result of research findings which demonstrated that there is not a one-to-one correspondence between ophthalmic measurements and educational performance. It has been found, for example, that children with the same degree of a given visual defect on clinical tests may have very different visual abilities in terms of learning. A study by Jones (1961) illustrates quite clearly the difficulties in classification for educational purposes by using clinical acuity tests to determine whether the child should read print or should be taught braille. He studied 14,125 legally blind children registered with the American Printing House for the Blind. This Federal organization has a registry of all legally blind children receiving Printing House service and has the data on each child in terms of the degree of vision and the mode of reading. Table 10–1 presents the data for the 14,125 children in local day and residential schools, giving nine classifications of legal blindness, the percentage of children in each level, and the percent of those reading by each mode.

It should be noted from this table that:

1. Thirty-one percent of children in local and residential schools for the visually handicapped were classified as legally blind with 20/200 vision. Yet 82 percent of them read print, and only 12 percent read braille. Six percent read

TABLE 10–1

*Levels of vision and modes of reading
in local and residential schools*

Vision level	Percent of children in each level	Percent of print readers	Percent of braille readers	Readers of both
20/200, etc.	31	82.0	12	6.0
15/200, etc.	4	68.0	26	6.0
10/200, etc.	9	59.0	32	9.0
5/200, etc.	4	46.0	45	9.0
2/200, etc.	2	31.0	64	5.0
Counts fingers	6	24.0	71	5.0
Hand movement	3	7.0	91	2.0
Light perception	16	.6	99	.2
Totally blind	24	——	100	—

Source: Adapted from Jones, 1961.

both. Of those who could only recognize hand movements at close distance, 7 percent learned print.

2. Of the total group, 24 percent were educationally blind and read braille only. Seventy-six percent of the legally blind had some residual vision, and a large proportion of these read print.

Other data from Jones (not shown in the table) showed a difference in the proportion of print and braille readers between residential schools and local schools. While 92 percent of legally blind enrollees in local schools read print, only 51 percent of the legally blind children in residential schools read print.

Nolan (1965) replicated the Jones study of 1960. After a three-year period Nolan found that from among 2,536 children on the registry of the American Printing House for the Blind, the number of braille readers had decreased by 5 percent, and that those listed as print readers had increased by 5 percent.

In a later study, Nolan (1967) found that the residential-school enrollment in 1966 remained static, but the day-school enrollment increased by 15 percent. He also stated that "there appeared to be a consistent trend in all school systems toward greater use of residual vision."

These studies indicate quite clearly that the designation of legal blindness by means of visual acuity measures does not determine the mode of education the child is capable of using. Whether a child reads print or braille seems to be dependent upon factors other than measured visual acuity. Furthermore, the impact of the Jones and Nolan studies on the use of functional vision by educators of the blind is seen as a significant trend toward (1) greater use of residual vision by legally blind children, and (2) increase in the organization of educational programs for the visually handicapped in local school systems. Educational programs become somewhat the same for all who have limited vision (partially sighted or legally blind with residual vision) regardless of their legal classification for public assistance.

School Assessment of Visual Problems

Total blindness is relatively easy to recognize and is almost always detected in the infant by the time he is a year old, and usually much earlier. Identification of a less severely handicapped youngster is much more difficult. A young child has little or no concept of what others see in contrast to his own view of things; hence, it is difficult for him to report his own visual problems. Thus, it is not unusual for visual defects to remain undetected until the child reaches school age unless specifically evaluated because the child appears awkward, clumsy, careless, or even mentally slow.

The importance of an adequate vision screening program and systematic observations of visual behavior in school cannot be overestimated. Among preschool and school children the following should be observed and noted as possible indications of visual difficulty:

1. Strabismus; nystagmus.
2. How the child uses his eyes: tilting his head, holding objects close to his eyes, rubbing his eyes, squinting, displaying sensitivity to bright lights, and rolling his eyes.
3. Inattention to visual objects or visual tasks such as looking at pictures or reading.
4. Awkwardness in games requiring eye-hand coordination.
5. Avoidance of tasks that require close eye work.
6. Affinity to tasks that require distance vision.
7. Any complaints about inability to see.
8. Lack of normal curiosity in regard to visually appealing objects.

Observation of the child's behavior can give parents and teachers a hint that there may be some visual difficulty. But there are more efficient and accurate methods. Usually, screening tests are given to identify the presence or absence of visual difficulties. The most commonly used screening device is the Snellen Chart which was described in the footnote on page 292. This test, of course, detects only problems of acuity (refractive errors) and the observant parent or teacher should be aware of other problems such as those of fusion, muscle imbalance, conjunctivitis, etc.

If the observations and/or screening tests suggest a defect, tests and examination by an eye specialist make the final determination. A referral for an examination to an optometrist or ophthalmologist can come from a parent or a teacher who suspects some difficulty or from a school nurse as a result of a visual screening test. The eye specialist usually diagnoses the degree and kind of visual handicap and whenever possible pins down the etiology. Correction of the visual handicap through optical aids, eye muscle exercises, or surgery (as in cataracts and squint) is the final stage in treatment. If after correction the child can see normally no special education is offered. If, on the other hand, the child is still visually handicapped and requires special education, the child is referred to a program of special education.

Some Kinds of Disabilities Found Among Visually Handicapped Children

The eye is a complicated organ, any part of which is susceptible to damage. The eyeball itself, the cornea covering the anterior portion of it, or the lens inside may have defects of structure or function. The conjunctiva surrounding the eye may be diseased or injured. The iris, the retina, and the optic nerve (and related areas) may be damaged or diseased so as to affect vision. Until recently the most common location of difficulty affecting vision has been the retina, due mostly to a disease known as retrolental fibroplasia which, fortunately, has had a marked decline (the details of this disease will be discussed later). Structural anomalies of the eyeball account for nearly one-fourth of blindness in children.

Table 10–2 presents data on type and site of eye affliction from a study by Hatfield (1963) who obtained statistics on a sample of 7,757 legally blind children reported by local and residential schools from 36 states. It will be noted from this table that structural anomalies of the eyeball account for 23.4 percent and retrolental fibroplasia for 33 percent of the defects of these legally blind children. The latter figure is probably inflated since the cause of this defect was discovered in 1954 and has been practically eliminated.

Whereas Table 10–2 refers to the site, or location, of visual defects, the diag-

TABLE 10–2

Percentage of blind school children by site and type of eye affection, ages 5 to 20, 1958–59

Site and type of affection	Percent
Eyeball in General	24.8
Structural anomalies	23.4
Multiple anomalies	5.5
Myopia	4.9
Glaucoma (Infantile)	4.6
Albinism	4.2
Coloboma	0.9
Anophthalmos and Microphthalmos	1.2
Aniridia	0.7
Other	1.4
Other general affection to eyeball	1.4
Conjunctiva (Ophthalmia neonatorum)	0.3
Cornea	1.8
Lens	12.1
Cataract	11.5
Dislocated lens	0.6
Uveal Tract	4.8
Retina	40.4
Retrolental fibroplasia	33.0
Retinal and macular degeneration	4.4
Retinoblastoma	1.7
Other	1.3
Optic nerve, optic pathway, and cortical visual centers	9.5
Optic nerve atrophy	8.6
Other	0.9
Other specified affection	3.7
Not reported	2.6
Total, all causes	*Percent* 100.0
	Number 7,757

Source: Adapted from Hatfield, 1963, p. 8. Reproduced with the permission of the author.

nosis of a given eye problem is not usually so stated. Refractive errors, for instance, relate to the lens, phototropia to the uvea, strabismus to the muscles (not included in Table 10–2 since it does not cause legal blindness). Some of the more common visual handicaps are explained below:

REFRACTIVE ERRORS

Refractive errors constitute approximately one-half of all visual defects. In the normal eye (emmetropic) the size, shape, and refractive media are such that the image of an object focuses directly on the retina. In the mature normal eye no muscular effort or accommodation of the lens is necessary to clearly see objects 20 feet or more away. The cornea, the lens, and the fluids at the back of the eyeball make it possible for the image to focus accurately on the light-sensitive membrane known as the retina. When the eye looks at an object closer than 20 feet, the muscles in the eye increase the convex curvature of the lens so that the image of the closer object will still focus on the retina. The increase of the lens curvature through the use of the ciliary muscles is called accommodation.

When the eye is not normal (ametropic), the image does not focus on the retina at 20 feet. In these cases of refractive abnormality the eye is hyperopic, myopic, or astigmatic, or a combination thereof.

Hyperopia, or farsightedness, is a condition in which the eye is too short from front to back, so that the rays of light focus behind the retina, forming a blurred and unclear image on it. To correct this condition a convex lens is placed before the eye to increase the "bending" of the light rays and bring them to a focus within a shorter distance, that is, on the retina rather than behind it. The term "farsightedness" implies only that distant objects can be seen with less strain on the muscles of lens accommodation than can near objects, and does not mean, as is often thought, that the hyperope can see farther or more clearly at a given distance than can the emmetrope.

Myopia, or nearsightedness, is a refractive error opposite in kind to hyperopia. In myopia the eye is too long from front to back or the refractive media bend the light rays too much. In either case the rays of light focus in front of the retina when the eye is at rest and viewing an object 20 or more feet distant. Correction for this type of refractive error is made with a concave lens, which spreads or diverts the rays of light, focusing them farther back in the eye and directly on the retina.

Astigmatism is a refractive error resulting from an irregularity in the curvature of the cornea or lens of the eye. The light rays from any given object or point do not all focus at the same point on the retina. Parts of the image may fall behind the retina, and parts in front, so that vision is blurred. The eye attempts to clarify the image through accommodation, but this affects the entire lens equally, and cannot influence corneal irregularities at all. Most astigmatism is more or less regular and is correctable. Irregular astigmatism is only partially correctable.

DEFECTS OF MUSCLE FUNCTION

Another type of visual defect found in children is abnormality in the external ocular muscles which control the movement of the entire eyeball in its orbit. These muscles are not to be confused with the internal muscles of lens accommodation discussed above.

Strabismus, or crossed eyes, is caused by a lack of coordination of eye muscles; the two eyes do not simultaneously focus on the same object. In most cases one eye turns inward toward the nose, while the other focuses on the object being viewed. When, as in this case, the deviating eye rotates inward, it is called *internal strabismus* or *convergent squint.* When the deviating eye turns outward it is called *external strabismus.* Occasionally, *alternating strabismus* is found, in which either one eye or the other turns in or out. Strabismus can be constant or intermittent.

Heterophoria is a defect in muscular balance of the eyes in which the deviation of the eyes is not apparent, as in strabismus, but latent. In this condition there is (1) a tendency for the eyes to deviate from the normal position for binocular fixation, and (2) a partially counterbalancing tendency toward simultaneous fixation through forced muscular effort. When one eye tends to pull toward the nose, it is called *esophoria,* and when it tends to pull away from the nose it is *exophoria.* When one eye tends to pull upward it is *hyperphoria;* when downward it is *hypophoria.* Heterophoria tends to cause difficulties in visual fusion, that is, in the ability to coordinate or fuse the two images, one from each eye, into a single image.

OTHER ANOMALIES

Many other anomalies, diseases, and pathological conditions affect the functioning of vision and produce visual handicaps in children.

Albinism is a hereditary, congenital condition characterized by relative absence of pigment from the skin, hair, choroid coat, and iris. It is often accompanied by refractive errors, lowered visual acuity, *nystagmus* (quick jerky movement of the eyes, usually lateral, but occasionally in a rotary or vertical direction), and *photophobia* (extreme sensitivity to light).

A *cataract* is a condition of the eye in which the crystalline lens or its capsule becomes opaque, with resultant loss of visual acuity. Cataracts are sometimes removed successfully through surgery by removing the lens or by a "needling" process in which the opacity is broken up and then absorbed. In either case vision is affected. When the entire lens has been removed it is often impossible to achieve normal central acuity by means of external lenses alone, and almost inevitably peripheral vision is distorted. The patient does have very usable vision, however.

Many diseases and conditions other than those already mentioned can attack the eyeball, cornea, lens, vitreous humor, choroid, retina, or optic nerve and cause marked visual deficiencies or total blindness. Common among these diseases are diabetes, syphilis, glaucoma, and keratitis. Retrolental fibroplasia is one of the most important and will be discussed later.

Causes of Blindness

The major causes of blindness have been listed in broad categories as including: infectious diseases, accidents and injuries, poisonings, tumors, general diseases, and prenatal influences (including heredity).

The National Society for the Prevention of Blindness (1966) has for many years attempted to obtain statistics on the prevalence, conditions, and causes of blindness. In one compilation (for the year 1962) it is reported that prenatal conditions (rubella, heredity, etc.) account for 47.7 percent of legally blind children. Retrolental fibroplasia (categorized under "poisonings") accounted for 33.3 percent of legal blindness among school-age children, and infectious diseases together with neoplasms accounted for 7 to 8 percent. Injuries, including accidents, accounted for a little over 2 percent, a substantial drop from earlier figures.

Unfortunately, the decrease in blindness in some categories does not always lower the total frequency of blindness when unforeseen new problems arise. A good example of this is the change in prevalence figures since 1907. At that time ophthalmia neonatorum (caused by gonococci and other micro-organisms) accounted for 30 percent of the blindness among children entering schools for the blind in Great Britain and the United States (*Encyclopaedia Britannica,* 1960). The use of silver nitrate in the eyes of neonates, the improved medical treatment for gonorrhea, and premarital blood tests have resulted in 73 percent fewer cases of blindness due to ophthalmia neonatorum in the school-age group. Similarly, safety measures and the legislative prohibitions against fireworks and guns for children reduced the rate of blindness due to accidents by 47 percent from 1937 to 1955 (Kerby, 1958). This improvement, however, was counteracted by increases in other categories of blindness caused by epidemics of rubella and the man-made defect of retrolental fibroplasia. To illustrate society's struggle for the prevention of blindness, two causes of blindness and their prevention will be described in more detail.

THE DRAMATIC STORY OF RETROLENTAL FIBROPLASIA

Seldom has a disease had a more spectacular history than that of retrolental fibroplasia. It was nonexistent prior to 1938, was not named or diagnosed as a clinical entity until 1942, and had virtually disappeared by 1955, leaving in its wake thousands of blinded children.

Literally, retrolental fibroplasia means "fibrous tissue behind the lens," a misnomer for the detached retina found floating behind the lens in late stages of the disease. This eye disease was so named in 1942 by Dr. T. L. Terry, a Boston ophthalmologist. It was originally noted by Terry that this new and previously unknown type of maldeveloped eye was occurring only in premature babies. Sixty-five percent of the cases of retrolental fibroplasia were diagnosed by 6 months of age, and only very rarely as late as a year.

Beginning in about 1944 the incidence of the disease increased at an alarming rate, reaching its peak in 1952–1953, at which time it accounted for well over half of all the blindness in preschool children. In some hospitals the disease was striking as many as one out of every eight premature babies (Kinsey, 1956).

In 1952, ten long research-filled years after retrolental fibroplasia was first diagnosed, evidence began to accumulate suggesting that the increased concentration of oxygen (possible because of improved incubators) to which premature youngsters were routinely subjected was the culprit. Very quickly it was established that this was the case, and, even more important, that the concentration and duration of oxygen therapy could be significantly reduced without increasing the mortality rate.

In an extensive study of 586 premature infants, Kinsey showed conclusively that the length of time the premature infant was kept in the oxygen-enriched environment was the important factor in the incidence of retrolental fibroplasia. The findings on the cause of retrolental fibroplasia were rapidly circulated and by 1955–1956 the disease was occurring only very rarely, as shown in Figure 10–1.

Now that we have looked briefly at the history of retrolental fibroplasia, let us examine some of the results of its short, but too long, existence. Figure 10–1 presents the so-called rise and fall of the incidence of retrolental fibroplasia from 1940 to 1960. This figure is based on data from 6 states reported in the *National Society for the Prevention of Blindness Fact Book* (1966, p. 88). It will be noted from Figure 10–1 that retrolental fibroplasia reached its peak during the years of 1952–1953. The sharp drop in the graph after 1953 demonstrates the results of the decreased use of oxygen. Retrolental fibroplasia accounted for a large proportion of blind childern born between 1940 and 1952–1953, and since that date the incidence has dropped abruptly due to better control of oxygen.

Meantime, however, the schools and institutions of our country were suddenly confronted with the problem of planning an educational program, providing materials, training teachers, social workers, and counselors, organizing vocational services, legislative programs, and so forth for the thousands of blind children who are now growing up. And this planning had to be done with the realization that by about 1972 these children will have passed through their first twelve educational years, and the need for the programs so hurriedly established will be rapidly disappearing.

FIGURE 10–1

Incidence of blindness due to retrolental fibroplasia in six states, 1940–1960

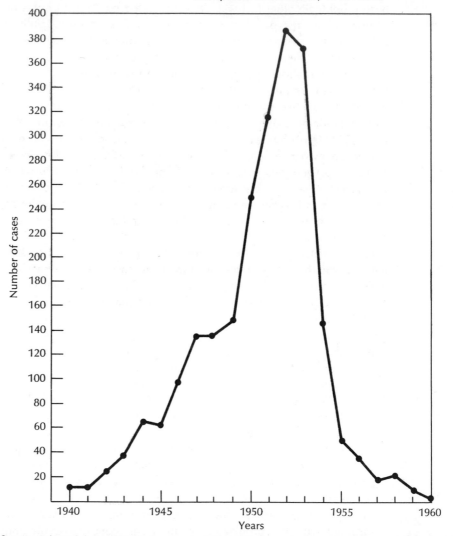

Source: Adapted from *N.S.P.B. Fact Book*, 1966, p. 88. Reproduced with the permission of the Society.

This brief glance at retrolental fibroplasia illustrates one of the problems often introduced by technological or scientific advances. The widespread use of oxygen therapy did indeed save the lives of many premature babies, but at the expense of unnecessarily blinding thousands of children. We knew enough to use oxygen therapy, but not enough to use it judiciously. As we advanced with one foot, we retreated with the other.

As in many areas of ecology, interference by man with the process of nature resulted in an artificially produced disability. The man-made disease of retrolental fibroplasia absorbed the attention of the medical world, and its ultimate prevention or elimination required the expenditure of huge amounts of money, time, and personnel. Now the burden is being felt by families, schools, clinics, and other institutions, and in a few years it will affect the vocational world. Thus, what began as a medical advance to prevent death from prematurity has become a broad educational-psychological-social area of concern. Similarly, today there is considerable speculation on the effects of nuclear bombing and radiation on the incidence of handicapping conditions in children. Will we again witness the spectacle of an advance in one area of physical science producing defects in human development and new social problems? Such a thesis is forcefully presented by the Nobel Prize-winning scientist Linus Pauling (1958). Progress is indeed not made in a straight line.

Silverman (1970) has warned that the control of oxygen in eliminating RLF has in some cases resulted in cerebral palsy. He states "In nurseries which had a marked reduction in retrolental fibroplasia, the incidence of cerebral palsy was high and vice versa." In attempting to control nature there is a fine line between too much and too little.

RUBELLA

Rubella, described earlier in Chapter 5 on mental retardation, commonly produces visual impairments as well as hearing defects, mental retardation, and other disabilities in children. According to Cooper (1969) increases in disabilities and particularly in multiple handicaps occur most frequently in epidemics which recur unpredictably every seven to ten years. The last major epidemic occurred in 1964 and affected an estimated 30,000 infants in the United States. Montgomery (1969) studied a small sample referred to a clinic and reports approximately 30 percent infant mortality. From an analysis of 146 rubella survivors in a clinic he found 49 percent to have visual handicaps. With the advancement in medical research in isolating the rubella virus and in the development of a rubella vaccine, it is anticipated that this condition will be prevented.

Prevalence

The United States Office of Education estimated that approximately 0.1 percent of school children have visual handicaps serious enough even after correction to warrant special educational provisions. Ashcroft (1963) stated that there are 1 in 500 who are partially sighted (visual acuity 20/70 to 20/200), and that there are 1 in 3,000 who are legally blind (20/200 and less).

The total number of blind persons in this country was estimated to be 400,000 in 1962 (*NSPB Fact Book,* 1966) and includes 2,780 under the age of 5, 36,230 between the ages of 5 and 20, and 360,440 over the age of 20. In 1968 the number of children enrolled in public institutions for the blind was 20,266 (American Printing House for the Blind, 1969). At least two-thirds of all blind persons are in the 65-and-older age group. It is anticipated that the number of blind people over 65 will continue to increase as the average life span increases. On the other hand, the incidence of blindness among preschool children has dropped sharply with the prevention of retrolental fibroplasia, which accounted for over half of all blindness in preschoolers during the years 1945–1955.

Characteristics

The various groups of exceptional children, including the blind, have been surveyed extensively with respect to their physical, social, mental, and educational development. Among the visually handicapped, concentration on research has been primarily with the legally blind, and surprisingly little has been done with partially seeing children.

Lowenfeld (1955) has suggested that this paucity of research may be due to the fact that the partially sighted child is "for all practical purposes a seeing child, and his handicap, if it is one, does not affect him in any different way from other children who slightly deviate from the 'normal' " (p. 273).

Blindness affects the development of the child in that the blind child becomes aware of the world through senses other than sight—that is, through the senses of hearing, touch, and smell. Although the tactile sense is primary and is used extensively by young blind children, many objects cannot be perceived through touch either because of physical inaccessibility or because of social restraints. Hills and mountains, space, and the relations of large objects to one another remain a mystery to blind children. Most of these are explained to the child orally and by analogy to what he can hear and feel.

What effect does blindness have on the development of the blind child in the various areas of growth? Does blindness affect his height, weight, mobility, intelligence, and social behavior? These questions and others have been subjects for research and experiment. When we turn to the literature in an attempt to answer them, we are faced with differences of findings and interpretation, for a number of reasons:

1. Many of the studies do not distinguish between causes of blindness. If a youngster has been blinded by an accident there is no reason to believe his intelligence has been affected. However, in a case of blindness resulting from rubella, which often results in mental retardation also, the chance that intelligence will be affected is much larger.

2. Many of the tests used in assessing personality and social adjustment as well as achievement and intelligence have been designed for and standardized upon sighted subjects. Interpretation of scores obtained by blind subjects is at best equivocal.

3. In very recent years there has been some reason to believe that placement of blind children in residential or public schools is selective. This is not always made clear in research which includes both residential and day-school pupils.

4. It is very difficult to know what part of any differences found between blind and sighted subjects is due to the visual deficit and what part to differential treatment accorded to blind children.

PROFILES OF GROWTH PATTERNS

Figure 10–2 shows the developmental profiles of three 12-year-old blind children. William has average intelligence. On the Hayes-Binet Test he obtained an IQ of 95. His school experience, like that of the other two children in the profile, has been in a residential school since the age of 5. Frank is of superior intelligence, having scored 132 IQ on the Hayes-Binet Test. His academic achievement is also superior to that of the other two children. Alice is blind and mentally retarded. Both her blindness and her mental retardation have been attributed to her mother as having contracted German measles (rubella) during the first trimester of pregnancy. All three children were totally blind at birth, and all were enrolled between the ages of 5 and 6 in a residential school for the blind.

These profiles illustrate the differences in development of blind children at different intellectual levels. Other multiple handicaps can produce other kinds of developmental patterns. A deaf-blind child would present a much more retarded picture, although Helen Keller, who was a gifted deaf-blind child, was able to compensate for the multiple handicap by superior instruction, intensive effort, and high intelligence.

HEIGHT, WEIGHT, AND HEALTH

There is no reason to believe that blindness has any effect on the height and weight of individuals. Krause (1955), however, reports that in the early years of retrolental fibroplasia some children were restricted and were not allowed to

FIGURE 10–2

*Profiles of three blind children
of differing intelligence levels*

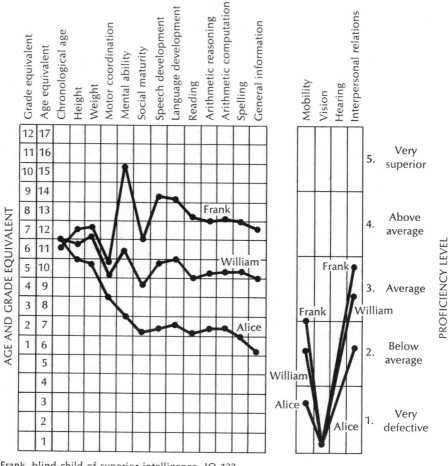

Frank, blind child of superior intelligence, IQ 132
William, blind child of average intelligence, IQ 95
Alice, blind child of retarded mental development, IQ 68

develop independently. He stated that these children's height and weight were less than the average for that age. But since the children had been premature infants, it may have been the prematurity, rather than blindness, which caused both the height-weight difference and the overprotection. Myers (1930) found that according to the judgments of teachers, there was no difference in general health between the children in sight-saving classes and normal, sighted children.

MOTOR COORDINATION

The research by Buell (1950) on motor performance showed quite clearly the inferiority of the blind to the partially sighted and the inferiority of both to normals. Norris, Spaulding, and Brodie (1957) found a high relationship between blind children's opportunities for learning and their mobility or motor performance. It is highly probable that a group of blind children who had had opportunities to climb trees, roller-skate, and wrestle along with their sighted peers from preschool days would not be found seriously deficient in motor coordination. Similarly, it would be expected that a group of sighted children who had been sedentary and had not taken part in such activities would be somewhat deficient motorically.

Two case studies illustrate the dangers of generalizing in this area. Gesell, Ilg, and Bullis (1950) followed the development of a blind child from infancy through the age of 4 and found the sequence of development to be normally progressive in posture, manipulation, locomotion, exploration, language, and social behavior. On the other hand, Wilson and Halverson (1947) observed another blind child and found general developmental retardation which was most pronounced in motor areas.

Cratty et al (1968) has studied aspects of motor response of blind children and finds that (1) laterality is not as well established in the congenitally blind as in the adventitiously blind since the former give evidence of lack of left-right discrimination, and (2) the blind veer with a left-right tilt while walking in the absence of auditory cues. Cratty ascribes this turning-and-veering to perceptual distortions, but finds that training can be effective in overcoming this tendency.

THE INTELLIGENCE OF THE VISUALLY HANDICAPPED

It has been difficult to assess the intelligence of visually handicapped children since most standardized tests of intellectual functioning include visual items. To assess the intelligence of the blind it is necessary to use verbal tests or performance tests using tactile and/or kinesthetic modalities (haptic). Samuel P. Hayes (1950), a pioneer contributor to the field of psychological testing of the blind, used items from the Stanford-Binet Scale (Forms L and M) that did not require vision, naming it the Interim Hayes-Binet. In addition to the Hayes-Binet, the verbal scales of the Wechsler tests are used widely. Dauterman, Shapiro, and Suinn (1967) report a number of performance tests specifically for blind children and adults. These include adaptations of the Minnesota Mechanical Ability Tests and the O'Connor Finger Dexterity Test. The general pattern in the development of tests for the blind is to adapt or invent tests of cognitive functioning that require auditory input and verbal or motor response, or a combination of these stimulus-response channels. For the partially sighted child, intelligence tests such as the Stanford-Binet are sometimes used.

Earlier Myers (1930) utilized two approaches to the question of whether the intelligence of children with defective vision is similar to that of normal children. He asked the teachers to record psychological test data and also to rate the children. On teachers' judgments the children were average or above, while on intelligence test scores they were average or below. Pintner, Eisenson, and Stanton (1941) reviewed the studies which have investigated the relationships between intelligence test scores of partially sighted and of normal children and found contradictory results. They stated that our knowledge on this factor is meager and indicated that intelligence tests devised for normally seeing children may be penalizing partially seeing children.

Livingstone (1958) administered the Stanford-Binet test to sixty 8- and 9-year-old children in classes for the partially seeing and found their average IQ to be 98.6. Enlarging the test print did not help them to score any higher than they did on the regular size. He concluded that although the visually handicapped were below normal on visually presented tests, they performed like normal children on reasoning, language development, and abstract generalization.

In an earlier study very similar to Livingstone's, Pintner (1942) had found a mean Stanford-Binet IQ of 95 for a group of 602 partially seeing children. He, too, could not see that enlarging the test materials made any difference.

Lowenfeld (1955) argues that blindness limits perception and cognition in three ways: (1) in the range and variety of experiences, (2) in the ability to get about, and (3) in the control of the environment and of the self in relation to it. These restrictions would be expected to affect intellectual development.

Assessing the intelligence of the blind has been difficult in that standard instruments designed for and standardized on the sighted are often inappropriate. Hayes (1941) administered the Hayes-Binet to 2,372 blind children in residential schools and found the mean IQ to be slightly below average (98.8). According to this study and others more recent, the percentage of blind children falling in the average range is less than that for seeing children, with fewer in the superior range and notably more in the defective range. No relationship has been found between age at which sight is lost and intelligence or achievement.

A re-evaluation of the intellectual status of blind children is long overdue in view of changing conditions affecting blind children as a result of (1) the accelerated movement to enroll blind children in regular classrooms, (2) the new emphasis on the development of residual vision, and (3) the changing attitudes of parents.

In general, and in spite of the deprivation of experience through limited or no vision, the visually handicapped child shows approximately the same distribution of scores on intellectual tasks as the seeing child, when tests like auditory-vocal or haptic-motor channels of communication are used.

Studies on Differential Cognitive Abilities

Bateman (1963) studied the effects of visual handicaps on the reading and psycholinguistic abilities of 131 children enrolled in classes for the partially sighted in public school classes in Illinois. The subjects in the classes were classified by eye condition, i.e., degree of measureable loss of acuity. Forty percent were classified as very mild or mild (20/70 or more); 40 percent were classified as moderate (20/70 to 20/200); and 20 percent were classified as severe or legally blind (20/200 and less). She found that:

1. The IQ's on the Binet or WISC were normally distributed with an average IQ of 100;
2. On the Illinois Test of Psycholinguistic Abilities (see Chapter 3) these children (a) did not differ from the standardization norms in the auditory-vocal channel subtests, but (b) performed significantly less well on visual reception, motor expression, visual sequential memory, and visual association;
3. Children with mild visual defects (visual acuity more than 20/70) were slightly lower in IQ and also lower on the subtests of the ITPA than those with moderate (20/70 to 20/200) vision;
4. The visual-motor channel deficits were most marked in the severely defective group (those with visual acuity less than 20/200).

Tilman (1967) compared 100 sighted with 100 blind children on the Wechsler Intelligence Scale for Children. An item comparison showed that the blind scored the same as the sighted on arithmetic, information, and vocabulary. The blind were inferior in items of comprehension and similarities.

Tisdall, Blackhurst, and Marks (1967) compared residential and day-school blind children with seeing children on tests of divergent thinking ability and found no significant differences between the blind and seeing children or between residential and day-school blind children.

One study which has investigated the suggestion that retrolental fibroplasia might also be associated with reduced mental capacity was that of Norris, Spaulding, and Brodie (1957). These investigators tested 300 preschool children in the Chicago area whose blindness was due to retrolental fibroplasia. They found no definite evidence that this group of children had a generalized brain defect. The distribution of test scores appeared to the authors to be essentially normal.

EDUCATIONAL ACHIEVEMENT

In the 1930's Myers's (1930) and Peck's (1933) surveys of the educational achievement of partially seeing children indicated that at all grade levels the partially seeing scored as well or rated as well as seeing children of the same chronological age.

A more intensive study of reading levels and reading errors made by children in classes for the partially seeing was conducted by Bateman (1963). Ninety-six partially seeing children, attending public school classes for the partially seeing, grades 2 to 4, were examined on four reading tests, which compose the Monroe Diagnostic Reading Examination. Error types were analyzed to determine whether or not partially seeing children are characterized by any specific kinds of reading errors. Bateman concluded:

1. The reading achievement level of this sample was in general similar to the level of achievement of seeing children.
2. The partially seeing children scored lowest on Gray's Oral Reading Examination (a test which includes a time element) and highest on the silent reading test.
3. The analysis of errors compared with that of a normal sample of 30 seeing children indicated that the partially seeing group made more reversal errors than did the seeing group sample, and either did not differ or made fewer errors in other areas.

Birch et al (1966) surveyed the school achievement of 903 fifth- and sixth-grade partially seeing children to determine their level of educational achievement, and to establish the appropriateness of type size. They found that although these children were of average intelligence, they were overage for grade and 2½ years retarded in academic achievement. They also concluded that no one type size could be considered superior. Nolan and Ashcroft (1959) found the average reading speed of 264 partially seeing children (grades 4 to 12) to be about 100 words per minute, which is less than half the speed of seeing children.

In 1967 Golfish estimated that there were 45,000 braille readers in the United

States. Since the educational achievement of the blind is partially dependent upon their ability to read braille, many studies have been conducted on the levels of achievement attained by blind individuals through this medium of instruction and on the methods of teaching braille.

Nolan (1966) summarized the conclusions from studies on perceptual factors in recognizing braille words. He concluded that children learn braille, not as word wholes, but by the integration of the braille characters. Henderson (1966) trained blind children in grades 3–6 on braille character recognition in 18 daily sessions, and found that the training group reduced their errors in character recognition by 85 percent. The training group also increased their rate of reading by 12 words per minute as compared to blind children not receiving this training.

Lowenfeld, Abel, and Hatlen (1967) studied in considerable detail the programs of teaching braille in the residential and day-school programs throughout the United States. By means of a questionnaire they concentrated on blind students in the fourth and eighth grades. Among other findings their study showed:

1. Braille reading starts in the first grade.
2. Eighty-five percent of the teachers try to teach the children to use both hands in learning braille.
3. Almost all the teachers taught braille writing with reading and used a braille writer.
4. Two-thirds of the teachers emphasized whole word reading. (This is incongruent with the results of Nolan and Henderson, mentioned above.)
5. In comparison with seeing children reading print, the reading comprehension scores on reading tests showed that fourth-grade blind children were equal in braille-reading ability to seeing children, while the eighth graders were superior to seeing, eighth-grade children. This result was explained by the authors as a result of the higher intelligence ratings of the blind eighth graders which averaged 110. Furthermore, the standardized tests administered in braille allow for 2 to 3 times reading time allowed seeing children.

It will be noted that some of the studies indicate that the visually handicapped have relatively normal educational achievement. Even the blind are equal to the seeing child in comprehension of reading when given more time to read the tests. The exception is the study by Birch et al (1966), who found that in their large sample the "partially seeing" children were several years retarded educationally. Since Bateman found that the most educationally retarded in her study were children who had the most minor visual handicaps, is it possible that the Birch sample consisted of children who were referred to classes for the visually handicapped because they were educationally retarded and also had a minor visual handicap?

SOCIAL ADJUSTMENT AND ACCEPTANCE

The study of personality, social adjustment, and attitudes of peers toward the visually handicapped have been probed by several investigators. This kind of research with children always presents some unsurmountable methodological problems. In general, their problems in mobility, the overprotectiveness of parents, and the relationships with peers and sighted individuals have led many to suspect that visually handicapped children have problems in personal adjustment, helplessness, and dependency.

Chevigny and Braverman (1950) and Cutsforth (1951) have expressed the feelings of their associates toward them. Chevigny was told, after losing his sight, that his friends and relatives felt the same about him. He felt, on the other hand, that their attitudes had changed. Cutsforth stated that the emotional problems of the blind are induced in the blind by the attitude of seeing persons. In reviewing the opinions and studies on this problem, Ashcroft (1963) gave three opinions: (1) social and emotional maladjustment are not consequences of a visual handicap, (2) where maladjustment occurs, the behavior is not necessarily related to the visual limitations, and (3) negative attitudes toward the visually handicapped and their own negative self-regard may produce more personality problems than are found among the normally seeing.

If the negative attitudes of others affect the blind, it is necessary to study the attitudes of seeing people toward the visually handicapped. Some such studies have been made.

Sommers (1944) distributed a questionnaire to 72 mothers of blind children. The reactions of the parents fell into five categories: (1) genuine acceptance, (2) denial that either the parents or the child is affected, (3) overprotectiveness and excessive pity, (4) disguised rejection, and (5) overt rejection.

A study of 232 sighted children's perceptions of the abilities of blind children by Bateman (1962) found that when a seeing child has had experience with the blind their estimate of the blind child's ability is higher than when a seeing child has had no experience with blind children.

Jones, Gottfried, and Ownes (1966) studied the social acceptance of 186 high school students to all types of exceptional children by means of a questionnaire. The average and gifted were the most accepted while the mentally retarded were least accepted. The blind were among the groups least accepted.

It is obvious from the selected studies reported above that broad generalizations about the personality of blind children or their social adjustment are not warranted. There appears to be some evidence of negative attitudes toward the blind, especially by those who have not dealt with them. If association with the blind enhances acceptance, it would follow that integrating the blind with the seeing in an educational setting is to be desired.

SPEECH DEVELOPMENT

Brieland (1950) reports the observations commonly made in the literature regarding speech of the blind:

1. The blind show less vocal variety.
2. Lack of modulation is more critical among the blind.
3. The blind tend to talk louder than the sighted.
4. The blind speak at a slower rate.
5. Less effective use of gesture and bodily action is typical of the blind.
6. The blind use less lip movement in articulation of sounds.

While it is true that the blind do not have the visual imitative cues available which are sometimes utilized by seeing children in developing articulation, this is perhaps not a crucial lack. Apparently it is amply compensated for by the greater role that oral and aural communication necessarily plays in the life of the blind.

Miner (1963) surveyed the speech problems of 293 elementary school children from two residential schools. Among this group were 69 emotionally disturbed and mentally retarded children. He found 33.8 percent to have speech deviations; 24 percent articulatory disorders; 3.4 percent had voice problems; and 2.4 had language problems. Rowe (1958) and Brieland (1950) did not find this high percentage of speech problems among comparable groups. It is possible that the Miner sample is not typical of blind children in general since his group included 69 emotionally disturbed and mentally retarded children.

LANGUAGE DEVELOPMENT

Language of children is studied by aural, written, oral, and reading methods. Cutsforth (1951) tested congenitally blind children with a free-association test by giving them a noun and asking them to name its attributes. He found that they responded with words that were unrealistic to them. For example, to "night," some of them said "dark," "black," "blue," "yellow," and only one child out of twenty-six responded "cool." Cutsforth felt that these verbalisms were in terms of learned, associative visual responses rather than of the children's own tactile or hearing experiences. He explained that the underlying purpose

313   *The Visually Handicapped Child*

of verbalism was to obtain social approval. The interest in verbalism, defined as excessive use of words not verified by concrete experience, has attracted the attention of workers with the blind, for this behavior is related to language and to concept development.

Harley (1963) studied the verbalism of 40 children between the ages of 6 and 14 years of age at the Perkins School for the Blind, and related these to CA, IQ, experience and social adjustment. He found that (1) verbalism decreases with age, (2) the higher IQ the less the verbalism, and (3) the more experience with age the less verbalism.

Dokecki (1966) has reviewed the literature on verbalism in the blind and has demonstrated methodological flaws in the procedures. He states that Harley's concept of verbalism differs from that of Cutsforth. Dokecki questioned whether Harley may have been measuring tactile discrimination not really related to verbalism. He questions the view that verbalism is meaningless and leads to loose thinking. Much of our language is nonsensory, and there is no reason to doubt the word-word nature of meaning.

In general, one may conclude that the language of blind children (if we exclude concepts which require vision) is not deficient. Since much of language is acquired auditorily, the blind, unlike the deaf, can develop language usage similar to that of seeing individuals.

MUSIC

It has often been asserted that music is one area in which the blind have exceptional ability and interest. Although music education is emphasized with the blind, and history gives records of some blind individuals who became noted musicians, there is no evidence that the blind in general are superior in musical ability. For a time one of the vocations recommended for the blind was piano tuning, and indeed some have become efficient at this trade. Nevertheless, music, using primarily the auditory sense, is still included in all curriculums for the blind. Various mechanical devices, including typewriters, have been used for typing musical notes, and braille and other notations have been used for reading music. Memorization, of course, plays a large role in the actual performance of blind musicians.

SENSORY PERCEPTION

Research workers have been interested in the question of how other sense functions are affected by visual deficiency. The doctrine of sensory compensation holds that if one sense avenue such as vision is deficient, other senses will be automatically strengthened. It was believed that the blind could hear better and had better memories than sighted individuals. Yet research has not demonstrated this popular opinion. In a study by Seashore and Ling (1918) it was found that there was no difference between blind and seeing subjects in auditory, tactual, or kinesthetic sensitivity.

It is possible that blind people make better use of their abilities in other sense fields. A sighted person may tend to disregard sounds in his environment which have, of necessity, become significant to a blind person. This does not mean that the actual hearing abilities of the two individuals differ.

In a comparison of types of imagery experienced in response to oral words or phrases, Schlaegel (1953) found no differences between blind and sighted subjects. Both experienced visual imagery most frequently, then auditory, kinesthetic, tactual-thermal, and olfactory-gustatory in that order. When the blind were subdivided on the basis of amount of remaining vision, however, visual imagery increased with visual acuity to the extent that the subjects who were the *least* blind had *more* visual imagery than the seeing subjects had.

The ability of a blind child to utilize various types of imagery is an important consideration in his total development and especially in his educational program. Much more work is needed in this field, but at present it is known that differences exist in the extent to which blind persons utilize sensory channels, and that the extent of visual loss and the age at which the loss occurs are important variables.

An interesting development has been the discovery that residual vision in blind children can be developed through training. Barraga (1964), believing that the development of the visual process follows a sequential pattern but that training is necessary to develop maximum efficiency, conducted a significant training experiment. She matched 10 pairs of blind children on the amount of remaining vision, trained one of each pair, leaving the other as a control. She designed 44 sequential lessons and taught the experimental group, 2 children at a time, for 30 days. Testing both groups at the end of the experiment with a reliable visual discrimination test, she found that the experimental group scored significantly higher than the control group. No increase in near acuity measures were noted in either group.

LISTENING

Since the blind child is denied access to visual information, his ability to gain knowledge from what he hears is most important. There is some evidence that listening ability can be improved by training, and the continuing development of procedures for training listening skills is urgently needed.

Talking books for the blind have been used for many years. These talking books are recorded in different speeds up to 190 words per minute. Efforts have been made to study the comprehension of blind children when the speed of talking is increased. Enc and Stolurow (1960) compared the comprehension of blind children under two speeds of presentation of material: fast (194 to 232 words per minute) and slow (128 to 183 words per minute). They found that the blind comprehended more per unit of listening time when the fast rate was presented. Foulke (1967) edited papers from a conference on compressed speech and in summarizing the research concluded that the procedure of presenting educational materials at faster rates appears promising.

The Multiply Handicapped Child

Reference has been made repeatedly to the fact that some visually handicapped children may have other disabilities. Thus, we have deaf-blind, mentally retarded blind, cerebral palsied blind, and other combinations of handicaps.

In a review of the research on multiple disabilities with visual impairments, Wolf and Anderson (1969) discuss the following categories:

The Deaf-Blind Child. The interest in educating deaf-blind children was stimulated by Samuel Gridly Howe who tutored Laura Bridgeman in the middle of the nineteenth century. Helen Keller was later tutored by Anne Sullivan. In 1960 it was estimated that there were 372 deaf-blind children in the United States. In 1970 the U.S. Office of Education estimated that there are 2,461 deaf-blind children in the United States. Because of the low prevalence and wide dispersion, the Federal Government has established regional centers for the care and education of deaf-blind children.

The Blind Speech-Defective Child. In reviewing the studies in this area, Wolf and Anderson (1969) report the prevalence of speech problems among the blind as being between 6 percent and 33 percent.

The Mentally Retarded Blind Child. Such children are found in residential schools for the blind, in local day schools, and in residential schools for the mentally retarded. These children often have more than the two underlying disabilities. In a study of these problems Wolf and Anderson (1969) summarize the results as follows:

Thirty-five percent of the mentally retarded blind children in special classes had two disabilities and sixty-five percent had three or more disabilities. Thirty-one percent had three disabilities, twenty percent had four disabilities, six percent had five disabilities, and five percent had six or more disabilities. (p. 33)

Blind Children with Physical Disabilities. These include children with cerebral palsy, poliomyelitis, epilepsy, and any physical disability found among normal children.

Blind Children with Emotional Problems. As in other groups there exist among the blind a number of children with emotional problems who need special treatment.

It is obvious from the above discussion that a visual handicap can be associated with many other handicaps. As indicated in an earlier section, rubella can result in deafness, blindness, mental retardation, speech defects, and other conditions. Any or all may occur together. The educational program for such children must be adapted to their individual needs. Jones (1966) reported that 73 percent of the 353 local programs studied and 94 percent of 54 residential programs provide services to multiply handicapped children.

SUMMARY

1. Visually handicapped children are classified for educational purposes into (a) the *visually impaired* who can read print, and (b) the *blind* who learn to read braille. The medical, legal, and economic classifications of *partially sighted* (visual acuity of 20/70 to 20/200) and *legally blind* (20/200 and less) have been found not to be educationally relevant classifications.
2. A large proportion of children classified as blind for economic and legal reasons have been found to be (a) capable of using residual vision to learn print instead of braille, and (b) are capable of developing better visual perception through training.
3. There are approximately 400,000 blind persons in the United States. Approximately 20,000 visually handicapped children attend local and residential schools for the visually handicapped. It is estimated that 1 to 2 school children in 1000 require special education because of a visual handicap.
4. Blindness among school children caused by ordinary diseases and injuries has been decreasing due to public health measures. This decrease, however, was temporarily offset by the man-made disease of retrolental fibroplasia. Epidemics of rubella have also offset the decrease but may be on the wane because of the recently discovered vaccine. Rapid increase in population also accounts for increases in prevalence of visual handicaps.
5. Intelligence and educational achievement of visually handicapped children do not deviate substantially from that of the seeing child.
6. Major problems of adjustment relate to the visually handicapped's perception of the attitude of others toward blindness. Approximately one-third of visually handicapped children enrolled in local day and residential schools have multiple handicaps (deaf-blind, blind-mentally retarded, and so forth).
7. There is little differentiation between the educational content for normal children and

that for visually handicapped children except that some blind children rely on reading braille. The major differentiation is in instructional materials and practices.

REFERENCES

American Printing House for the Blind. 1969. *One Hundred and First Report.* Louisville, Kentucky: American Printing House for the Blind.

Ashcroft, S. 1963. Blind and Partially Seeing Children. In Dunn, L. M. (ed.), *Exceptional Children in the Schools,* pp. 413–461. New York: Holt, Rinehart, and Winston.

Barraga, Natalie. 1964. *Increased Visual Behavior in Low Vision Children.* Research Series No. 13, American Foundation for the Blind.

Bateman, Barbara. 1963. *Reading and Psycholinguistic Processes of Partially Seeing Children.* Arlington, Virginia: The Council for Exceptional Children.

———. 1962. Sighted Children's Perceptions of Blind Children's Abilities. *Exceptional Children* 29 (September): 42–46.

Birch, J. W.; Tisdall, W. J.; Peabody, R.; and Sterrett, R. 1966. *School Achievement and Effect of Type Size on Reading in Visually Handicapped Children.* Cooperative Research Project, No. 1766, University of Pittsburgh.

Brieland, D. M. 1950. A Comparative Study of the Speech of Blind and Sighted Children. *Speech Monographs* 17 (March): 99–103.

Buell, C. 1950. Motor Performance of Visually Handicapped Children. *Journal of Exceptional Children* 17 (December): 69–72.

Chevigny, H., and Braverman, S. 1950. *The Adjustment of the Blind.* New Haven, Connecticut: Yale University Press.

Cooper, L. 1969. The Child with Rubella Syndrome. *The New Outlook for the Blind* 63 (December): 290–298.

Cratty, B. J.; Peterson, C.; Harris, Janet; and Shoner, R. 1968. The Development of Perceptual Motor Abilities in Blind Children and Adolescents. *The New Outlook for the Blind* 62 (April): 111–117.

Cutsforth, T. D. 1951. *The Blind in School and Society.* (2nd ed.) New York: American Foundation for the Blind.

Dauterman, W. L.; Shapiro, Bernice; and Suinn, R. M. 1967. Performance Tests of Intelligence for the Blind Reviewed. *International Journal for the Education of the Blind* 17 (October): 8–16.

Dokecki, P. R. 1966. Verbalism and the Blind: A Critical Review of the Concept and the Literature. *Exceptional Children* 32 (April): 525–530.

Enc, M. A., and Stolurow, L. M. 1960. A Comparison of the Effects of the Two Recording Speeds on Learning and Retention. *The New Outlook for the Blind* 54 (February): 39–48.

Encyclopaedia Britannica. 1960. *Education of the Blind.* Britannica Book of the Year 1960. Chicago: Encyclopaedia Britannica.

Foulke, E. (ed.). 1967. *Proceedings of the Louisville Conference on Time Compressed Speech.* Louisville, Kentucky: University of Louisville.

Gesell, A.; Ilg, F. L.; and Bullis, G. E. 1950. *Vision: Its Development in Infant and Child.* New York: Paul B. Hoeher.

Golfish, L. H. 1967. *Braille in the United States: Its Production, Distribution and Use.* New York: American Foundation for the Blind.

Harley, R. K. 1963. *Verbalism Among Blind Children.* New York: American Foundation for the Blind Research Series, No. 10.

Hatfield, Elizabeth M. 1963. Causes of Blindness in School Children. *The Sight-Saving Review* 33 (Fall): 218–233.

Hayes. S. P. 1950. Measuring the Intelligence of the Blind. In Zohl, P. A. (ed.), *Blindness,* pp. 141–173. Princeton, New Jersey: Princeton University Press.

———. 1941. *Contributions to a Psychology of Blindness.* New York: American Foundation for the Blind.

Henderson, Freda. 1966. The Rate of Braille Character Recognition as a Function of the Reading Process. *American Association of Instructors of the Blind. 48th Biennial Conference,* pp. 7–10. Washington, D.C.: The Association.

Jones, J. W. 1961. *Blind Children, Degree of Vision, Mode of Reading,* Bulletin 24. Washington, D.C.: U.S. Office of Education.

Jones, R. L.; Gottfried, N. W.; and Ownes, Angela. 1966. The Social Distance of the Exceptional: A Study at the High School Level. *Exceptional Children* 32 (April): 551–556.

Kerby, Edith C. 1958. Causes of Blindness in Children of School Age. *Sight-Saving Review* 28 (Spring): 10–21.

Kinsey, V. C. 1956. Retrolental Fibroplasia: A Cooperative Study of Retrolental Fibroplasia and Use of Oxygen. *Archives of Ophthalmology* 56 (October): 481–543.

Krause, A. C. 1955. Effect of Retrolental Fibroplasia in Children. *Archives of Ophthalmology* 53 (April): 522–529.

Livingstone, J. S. 1958. Evaluation of Enlarged Test Form Used with the Partially Seeing. *Sight-Saving Review* 28 (Spring): 37–39.

Lowenfeld, B. 1955. Psychological Problems of Children with Impaired Vision. In Cruickshank, W. M. (ed.), *Psychology of Exceptional Children and Youth,* pp. 214–283. Englewood Cliffs, New Jersey: Prentice-Hall.

Lowenfeld, B.; Abel, Georgia; and Hatlen, P. 1967. *Blind Children Learn to Read.* Springfield, Illinois: Charles C. Thomas.

Miner, L. E. 1963. Study of the Incidence of Speech Deviations Among Visually Handicapped Children. *New Outlook for the Blind* 57 (January): 10–14.

Montgomery, J. R. 1969. Congenital Rubella—Baylor Study. Forty-ninth Biennial Conference, pp. 1–7. Association for Education of the Visually Handicapped.

Myers, E. J. 1930. A Survey of Sight-saving Classes in the Public Schools of the United States. In *The Sight-Saving Class Exchange.* New York: National Society for the Prevention of Blindness.

National Society for the Prevention of Blindness. 1966. *N.S.P.B. Fact Book: Estimated Statistics on Blindness and Visual Problems.* New York: The Society.

Nolan, C. Y. 1967. A 1966 Reappraisal of the Relationship Between Visual Acuity and Mode of Reading for Blind Children. *New Outlook for the Blind* 61 (October): 255–261.

———. 1966. Perceptual Factors in Braille Word Recognition. *American Association of Instructors of the Blind, 48th Biennial Conference,* pp. 10–14. Washington, D.C.: The Association.

————. 1965. Blind Children: Degree of Vision, Mode of Reading. *New Outlook for the Blind* 59 (September): 233–238.

Nolan, C. Y., and Ashcroft, S. C. 1959. The Stanford Achievement Arithmetic Computation Tests. *International Journal for the Education of the Blind* 8 (March): 89–92.

Norris, Miriam; Spaulding, Patricia; and Brodie, Fern H. 1957. *Blindness in Children.* Chicago: University of Chicago Press.

Pauling, L. 1958. *No More War!* New York: Dodd, Mead.

Peck, O. S. 1933. *Reading Ability of Sight-Saving Class Pupils in Cleveland, Ohio.* Publication No. 118, National Society for the Prevention of Blindness. Reprinted from the *Sight-Saving Review* 3 (June).

Pintner, R., 1942. Intelligence Testing of Partially Sighted Children. *Journal of Educational Psychology* 33 (April): 265–272.

Pintner, R.; Eisenson, J.; and Stanton, Mildred. 1941. *The Psychology of the Physically Handicapped.* New York: F. S. Crofts.

Rowe, E. D. 1958. *Speech Problems of Blind Children.* New York: American Foundation for the Blind.

Schlaegel, T. F., Jr. 1953. The Dominant Method of Imagery in Blind as Compared to Sighted Adolescents. *Journal of Genetic Psychology* 83: 265–277.

Seashore, C. E., and Ling, T. L. 1918. The Comparative Sensitiveness of Blind and Seeing Persons. *Psychological Monographs* 25: 148–158.

Silverman, W. W. 1970. Prematurity and Retrolental Fibroplasia. *New Outlook for the Blind* 64 (September): 232–236.

Sommers, Vita S. 1944. *The Influence of Parental Attitudes and Social Environment on the Personality Development of the Adolescent Blind.* New York: American Foundation for the Blind.

Tilman, M. H. 1967. The Performance of Blind and Sighted Children on the Wechsler Intelligence Scale for Children. *International Journal for the Education of the Blind* 16 (March and May): Study I, 65–74; Study II, 106–112.

Tisdall, W. J.; Blackhurst, A. A.; and Marks, C. 1967. *Divergent Thinking in Blind Children.* Project No. O.E.–32–27–0350–6003, U.S. Office of Education.

Wilson, J., and Halverson, H. M. 1947. Development of a Young Blind Child. *Journal of Genetic Psychology* 71: 155–175.

Wolf, J. M., and Anderson, R. M. 1969. *The Multiply Handicapped Child.* Springfield, Illinois: Charles C. Thomas.

ELEVEN

EDUCATING

VISUALLY

HANDICAPPED

CHILDREN

As was explained in Chapter 10, educational programs for visually handicapped children were, until recently, organized according to classifications of children designed for medical and legal purposes. Classifying children according to their degree of visual acuity resulted in two different programs for visually handicapped children: one for the blind, and one for the partially seeing. To understand the major changes that have occurred as a result of a shift from a medical/legal classification to an educational classification, this chapter will discuss (1) the history of education of the visually handicapped, (2) the current changes in practice, (3) the general education of the visually handicapped, (4) special education of the visually handicapped, (5) progress through successive educational levels, and (6) the education of the deaf-blind.

History of Education of the Visually Handicapped

The education of the visually handicapped has existed for many centuries, but the education of the visually impaired (partially sighted, or partially blind) is a twentieth-century development.

EDUCATION OF THE PARTIALLY SIGHTED

Special school classes for partially seeing children originated in England in 1908, according to Smith (1938). Although as far back as 1885 medical examiners in England urged specialized education for these children, it was not until 1908 that Dr. James Kerr and Dr. N. Bishop Harmon were able to persuade the educational authorities to establish the first class at Boundary Lane, England. At this time only nearsighted children were admitted to these so-called "myope schools." Soon classes for myopes spread to other schools in England and Scotland.

In the United States the first class for the partially sighted was initiated in Boston in 1913. Miss Helen Smith (1938), the first American teacher of sight-saving classes, has described their beginnings: In 1910 Mr. Allen, Director of the Perkins Institute for the Blind, informed the Massachusetts Commission for the Blind of the work of the myope classes in London. Several years later the School Committee of Boston decided to begin such a class in the Boston schools and selected Miss Smith, from the Perkins Institute, as its teacher. At first named a "semi-blind class," it later was called a "conservation of eye class." This more adequate name was still somewhat awkward, and it was again changed—to "sight-saving class."

Smith reports that it was not easy to convince parents that their children would benefit from special class placement. Many of the parents interviewed declined to permit their children to leave the grades in which they had been placed to enter a special class. After much work, the class was started with six pupils. Once well established, however, it became known to other parents, who voluntarily applied to have their children admitted.

Other cities heard about the myope classes in England, and one was opened in Cleveland, Ohio, in 1913. This class, unlike the Boston class which was segregated, initiated a program in which the children remained in the regular grades but obtained their close eye work in the special class. As will be seen later there has been a recent revival and extension of this cooperative organization with different alternatives for both the blind and the visually impaired in the day school.

EDUCATION OF THE BLIND

The education of the blind, with a longer history than that of the visually impaired, was originally confined to residential schools. According to Farrell (1950), the first school for the blind was organized in Paris in 1785 by Valentin Haüy. In the United States the first residential school for the blind was organized in 1829. It was named "The New England Asylum for the Blind," now known as the Perkins Institute and the Massachusetts School for the Blind. Since that date most states have established residential schools for the blind, under either private or public auspices.

The residential school is a boarding school for blind children which they generally attend for nine months of the year. Here they live, go to school, and even learn vocations. Such schools often admit children as young as 4 or 5 and terminate their attendance at ages 18 to 21. The residential schools for the blind are not as large as residential schools for other kinds of exceptional children such as the deaf or the mentally retarded. School enrollment ranges from 25 in some states to 200–300 in more populated areas.

Historically, it may be pointed out that in the early nineteenth century, when the first schools for the blind were established in this country, the boarding school was considered the most desirable type of educational facility available, as it was so thought in Europe during this period. Even though it provided an opportunity for thorough training, certain disadvantages of an institutional setting became apparent—routine, formality, segregation, lack of family life, and so forth.

At that time, however, there were only two alternatives—either to send the child to an institution or to train him at home. In spite of the disadvantages of institutional living, residential schools offered the benefits of socialization, techniques and facilities, and trained teachers. Even today these advantages must be weighed against the disadvantages and viewed in the light of a particular child's needs and alternative opportunities. The child from a small community which does not have specialized facilities for his education, the child whose home environment is inadequate to cope with his handicap, or the child who has other handicaps may find that the advantages of a residential school outweigh the disadvantages.

In 1871, Dr. Samuel Howe stated:

With a view of lessening all differences between blind and seeing children, I would have the blind attend the common schools in all cases where it is feasible. . . . Depend on it, one of the future reforms in the education of the blind will be to send blind children to the common schools, to be taught with common children in all those branches not absolutely requiring visible illustrations, as spelling, pronunciation, grammar, arithmetic, vocal music and the like. We shall avail ourselves of the special institutions less, and the common schools more. (Irwin, 1955, p. 128)

This prediction by Dr. Howe was not immediately fulfilled, but the proportion of blind children now being educated with the sighted in the public schools is constantly increasing. (See Figure 11–2 on p. 328.)

Since 1900, when the first public school class was organized in Chicago, special classes for blind children have been set up in most of the large cities and in some of the intermediate-sized communities. At the outset, all of the instruction for the blind was conducted in the special class. Gradually, however, blind children in these classes were assigned for part of the day to regular classes.

CURRENT CHANGES IN THE EDUCATION OF THE VISUALLY HANDICAPPED

It became obvious that the categories of partial sightedness and legal blindness did not determine the best mode of education for these children and that the performance on visual acuity tests did not accurately predict what the child could learn through the use of his eyes. In the first place, the medical/legal categories, although useful from an economic and legal point of view, were not useful for educational purposes; in the second place it was difficult to obtain accurate measures of the visual acuity of these children at an early age.

In dealing with exceptional children in general there developed a reaction against determining educational procedures on the basis of numerical test scores. This reaction has been most evident in the field of the visually handicapped. This philosophy in conjunction with educational research during the 1950's and 1960's significantly changed educational practice and programs for the visually handicapped. Major changes that occurred may be summarized as follows:

1. In the 1920's and 1930's, classes for children who were classified as partially seeing or partially blind had been called "sight saving" or "sight conservation" classes. It was believed that the limited vision the child had must be conserved by little use, or used only when an object or print was large. The entire educational approach was designed to avoid straining the eyes. Current opinion, on the other hand, holds that the eyes are very rarely damaged through use, and that the child should learn to use whatever vision he has in as many situations as possible.

2. The common practice was to place children in self-contained classes for the blind, even though some of the children had residual vision, and to educate them as blind children through braille only. Currently, these children are trained to use their eyes wherever possible. Learning print as well as braille has been possible for many of these children.

3. Instead of placing children in self-contained classes for the blind or partially seeing, current practice is to give similar services to these children in the regular classes through itinerant teachers or resource rooms.

4. The tests of visual acuity formerly relied on for classification of visually handicapped children are now being supplemented by another criterion, namely how the child can learn. The concept of intraindividual differences is now the predominating criterion for educational programs.

5. The differentiation of the partially sighted and the legally blind is no longer accepted as the determinant of educational programming. Currently, the educational developments apply to all visually handicapped except that the educationally blind learn braille, while the others learn to read print.

6. Developing more efficient visual perception with children having limited vision is a modern development which is used in addition to optical aids and recent educational technology. Evidence to be discussed later indicates that the central process of visual perception in children with residual vision can be developed by training. Although the peripheral vision does not improve with training, the central processes involved in visual perception become more functional. Here we find an emphasis on the education of the visually handicapped similar to that found in the education of children with learning disabilities (discussed in Chapter 2).

Organizational Patterns and Trends

As was noted in the previous section, the education of visually impaired and blind children has gone through many changes. Two major changes have occurred during the 1950's and 1960's which have had a significant impact on the education of visually handicapped children. These trends and changes include (1) changes in enrollment in day and residential schools and (2) changes in type of services offered.

CHANGES IN ENROLLMENT IN DAY AND RESIDENTIAL SCHOOLS

In a survey of the enrollment of visually handicapped children in local and residential schools (Figure 11–1) Jones and Collins (1966) presented the enrollment (1) by year (1949 to 1964), (2) by number of children, and (3) by percent of enrollment in local and residential schools. (The figures in the graph for 1970 were obtained by this author from the American Printing House for the Blind and were not included in Jones and Collins's study of 1966.)

Figure 11–1 shows a substantial increase in the total number of visually handicapped children enrolled in public and residential schools, increasing from 5,818 in 1949 to 21,223 in 1970.[1] It also shows a year by year decline in the

---

[1] Federal laws providing materials of instruction for the visually handicapped have resulted in the increased registry of such children.

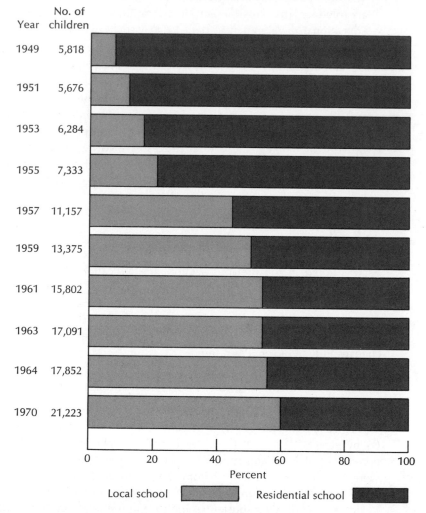

FIGURE 11–1

Number and percent of school children
registered with the American Printing House
for the Blind, by type of school
and year; United States: 1949–70

Year	No. of children
1949	5,818
1951	5,676
1953	6,284
1955	7,333
1957	11,157
1959	13,375
1961	15,802
1963	17,091
1964	17,852
1970	21,223

Percent

Local school   Residential school

Source: Jones and Collins, 1966, p. 2. Data for 1970 obtained from American Printing House for the Blind, January 5, 1970.

percentage of visually handicapped children enrolled in residential schools and a year by year increase in such children in local schools.

Types of visually handicapped enrolled. When children were placed in classes according to their level of visual acuity, the very placement determined whether they would be taught to read print or braille. Currently, among classes for the visually handicapped are found (1) classes that enroll children who learn print and children who learn braille, (2) classes that enroll children who learn only braille, and (3) classes that enroll children who learn only print. The latter class is more common (41 percent) in local school programs than in residential school programs (2 percent).

Residential school enrollment in regular schools. For many years residential schools have sent some visually handicapped children to local public schools. This practice is designed to determine whether the visually handicapped child is ready to profit from regular public school instruction. The number of such children, however, does not exceed 1 to 2 percent of the residential school population. This program is primarily for older children at the secondary school level.

Children eligible for enrollment in classes for visually handicapped. Whereas previously the criterion for admission of a child to a program for the visually handicapped was based on type and degree of visual deficit, the current trend is to rely on other factors as the determinants of eligibility. For the blind, these criteria include (1) the recommendations of the eye specialist, (2) intelligence above an IQ of 50, (3) inability to read large-print texts, and (4) sufficient emotional stability. For the visually impaired, multiple criteria are also used, including: (1) visual acuity of 20/70 or less in the better eye after correction, (2) inability of the child to make satisfactory progress in the regular grades, (3) inability to read regular print, and (4) adequate intelligence and emotional stability. Sixty-three percent of the educators in Jones and Collins's survey based their judgment more on mode of reading than on visual acuity measures, while only 22 percent based their judgment on type or extent of visual loss. Fifteen percent used other criteria. In spite of this trend, most authorities believe the schools are still relying more on visual acuity tests than is appropriate.

Multiply handicapped children enrolled. Another noticeable trend is the increasing acceptance of children with other handicaps in programs for the visually handicapped. According to Jones and Collins 73 percent of the 353 local programs and 94 percent of the residential programs had included children with multiple handicaps in their enrollment. For example, previous programs accepted only children who were average in intelligence or above 70 IQ. In 1963, 85 percent of the residential schools and 54 percent of the local programs accepted visually handicapped children who were educable mentally retarded (IQ's 50 to 70).

Number of children enrolled per teacher. The case load of teachers of the visually handicapped was found by Jones and Collins to be as low as 8 children to one teacher in residential school classes with a median of 15 students per teacher for a teacher-consultant in local school districts.

Broader training of teachers. Yesterday's teachers were trained to educate either visually impaired children or blind children. Currently, teacher training institutions have but one curriculum for teachers of the visually handicapped. Since many programs require the teacher to teach both kinds of children and since there is great overlap in objectives and techniques, teachers are prepared for diverse programs. Furthermore, many children classified for legal purposes as blind are in actuality educated as visually impaired. The increased use of residual vision leaves only about 20 percent who are educationally blind and require braille.

CHANGES IN TYPE OF SERVICES OFFERED

Jones and Collins's extensive survey gathered information from 353 local school programs for the visually handicapped and 54 residential schools in order to determine the educational patterns that were being used at that time. This sample constituted 95 percent of local and residential schools in the U.S. employing a teacher of the visually handicapped. They found that there are many patterns and combinations of patterns of service offered visually handicapped children. Jones and Collins defined the five most important patterns as:

Full-time special class. A specially staffed and equipped room in which blind and/or partially seeing children receive three-fourths or more of their formal instruction.

Cooperative special class. A specially staffed and equipped room in which blind and/or partially seeing children are enrolled or registered with the special teacher, but receive less than three-fourths of their formal instruction there. The remainder of their school day is spent in regular classrooms.

Resource room. A specially staffed and equipped room to which blind and/or partially seeing children who are enrolled or registered in regular classrooms come at scheduled intervals or as the need arises.

Itinerant teacher. An organizational pattern whereby blind and/or partially seeing children spend most of their school day in regular classrooms but receive special instruction individually or in small groups from itinerant teachers who travel among two or more schools devoting more than half of their time to the instruction of such children.

Teacher-consultant. An organizational pattern whereby special teachers serve as itinerant teachers part of the time but spend 50 percent or more of their time in more general duties, such as consulting with regular school personnel and distributing aids. (pp. 6–7)

While special classes for the visually handicapped began as segregated full-time classes, the patterns of organization in school systems have changed dramatically over the three periods reported: (1) prior to 1946, (2) 1946–55, and (3) 1956–63. Figure 11–2 shows the changes in patterns. Whereas resource rooms and itinerant teachers were few in number prior to 1946, after 1956 they were the most common. Furthermore, the full-time special class has shown a marked decline over the three periods studied.

General Education of the Visually Handicapped

As indicated in Figure 11–2 the majority of visually handicapped children in local day schools are assigned to a regular grade according to their age and level of academic achievement. They are given special education through the cooperative plan, resource rooms, itinerant teachers, or by teacher-consultants. It should be evident from this type of service that the aims and objectives of the regular grade become predominant, even though the techniques (by itinerant and resource room teachers) may be special. In other words, the general goals or objectives of education are the same for visually handicapped children as for seeing children, even though the procedures of attaining these goals are achieved by modification of instructional materials and special teaching procedures. The residential schools follow the same curriculum with the exception that the visually handicapped children are not integrated with seeing children. In residential schools the teacher of the visually handicapped teaches the whole curriculum, special and regular.

In her study of 131 visually handicapped children enrolled in Illinois classes for the partially seeing, Bateman (1963) found that 40 percent of the children had visual acuity of 20/40 to 20/70. The question is raised as to why these children were assigned to classes for the visually handicapped. The results of the survey give a partial answer. This group of mildly handicapped tested lower on the Stanford-Binet and were more educationally retarded than the moderate or more severely visually handicapped. It can be assumed that these children were referred to special classes because of slow learning ability and educational retardation rather than for the basic visual handicap. Such children would be more properly placed in programs for children with learning disabilities rather than in classes for the visually handicapped since the special program for the

FIGURE 11–2

*Number and percent of local school
programs which initiated certain
organizational patterns for visually
handicapped children, by type
of pattern; United States: prior
to 1946, 1946–55, and 1956–63*

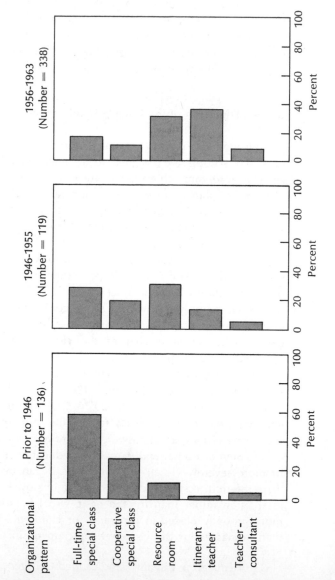

visually handicapped is not designed for the educationally retarded child who might happen to have a mild visual handicap.

As with all atypical children, the visually handicapped child's basic needs and the goals for his education are not different from those of the ordinary child. It is only the means of achieving these goals that are different. The content material and subject matter as well as the attitudes and understandings which are sought are the same as those for seeing children.

Lowenfeld (1952) has proposed the following statement as a more specific goal in the education of blind children:

Education must aim at giving the blind child a knowledge of the realities around him, the confidence to cope with these realities, and the feeling that he is recognized and accepted as an individual in his own right. (p. 96)

Special Education of the Visually Handicapped

Obviously if visually handicapped children were exposed only to the educational experiences and materials used with sighted children (which are approximately 85 percent visual) they would not achieve the goals proposed by Lowenfeld. Thus special methods, materials, and equipment must be employed, utilizing the senses of hearing, touch, smell, residual vision, and even taste. The curriculum for the visually handicapped must include: (1) adaptations of the general curriculum, (2) some additional or specialized content, and (3) specialized materials and equipment.

Most of the adaptations necessary for visually handicapped children stem from an effort to provide comparable experiences which do not involve the use of sight or which utilize the limited vision available. That is, the children must be given tactual experiences and verbal explanations. The visually handicapped child's ability to listen and relate and remember must be developed to its fullest. He must learn efficiency and conservation of time because the techniques he must use to acquire the same information or accomplish the same task are sometimes more cumbersome and time consuming. Therefore the teacher must organize her material better, must be specific in making explanations, and must utilize sound principles of learning.

Teaching, of course, is an art. The ability of the teacher to guide the child in the use of the various adaptations is one of the prime requisites. Lowenfeld (1952) has listed five principles suitable to teaching blind children.

1. *Individualization.* Visually handicapped children, whether in classes for the
   blind or in regular classes, differ from each other as much as or more than

children in a class for the sighted. The degrees of blindness, ages, home backgrounds, differences in intelligence, and the special teaching problems which they present require an individualized program for each child. For that reason the size of a class for the blind is generally six to eight pupils, and each child's program must be fitted to his particular needs.

2. *Concreteness*. The educationally blind child's knowledge is gained primarily through hearing and touch. But if he is to really understand the world about him, it is necessary that he be presented with concrete objects which can be touched and manipulated. Through tactual observation of models of objects he can learn about their shape, size, weight, hardness, surface qualities, pliability, and temperature. Models of objects are enlargements, if the actual objects are too small, or contractions, if they are too large. This type of presentation, of course, is a distortion of the real object, and its differences should be explained to the child. A model of a house, for example, can be used if its dimensions are explained and related to doors, windows, and other parts of a house which he can touch and feel in reality.

3. *Unified instruction*. Visual experience tends to unify knowledge in its totality. A child entering a grocery store will see the relations of shelves and objects in space. A visually handicapped child cannot obtain this unification unless teachers present him with experiences, such as "units of experience" of a farm, post office, or grocery store. It is necessary for the teacher to bring these "wholes" into perspective through actual concrete experience and attempt to unify them through explanation and sequencing.

4. *Additional stimulation*. Left on their own, educationally blind children live a relatively restricted life. To expand their horizons, to develop imagery, and to orient them to a wider environment it is necessary to develop these experiences by systematic stimulation. This requires programming of stimulating experiences from the time the children begin to walk. Mental orientation to their environment can begin by mapping the classroom and having them find their way around it. Later, the orientation is extended to the larger school, and later still to the community through travel instruction.

5. *Self-activity*. For a blind child to learn about his environment it is necessary to initiate self-activity. A blind infant does not reach out for an object, because it does not attract him. He must know of its existence by touch or smell or hearing. Thus his learning is slower. Walking, talking, prehension, feeding, and socialization will be retarded unless training and guidance encourage the development of these behaviors. Maturation must be aided at all stages, and opportunities for doing things himself should be provided and encouraged.

One of the major additions to the curriculum for visually handicapped children is specific training for the utilization of residual vision. As reported in Chapter 10, Barraga (1964) found that visual perception could be improved through training. Since conducting that experiment Barraga (1970) has developed visual training exercises for blind children with remaining vision which are used by teachers of visually handicapped children. In addition, the classroom teacher can use materials and methods in special ways, such as having the child move closer to the chalkboard, or encouraging him to work on materials he does not think he can see clearly. Auditory and tactile aids to visual perception are also used.

THE USE OF BRAILLE

Braille is a system of "touch" reading. Embossed characters use different combinations of six dots arranged in a cell two dots wide and three dots high. The symbols are embossed on heavy manila paper in a left to right order, and the reader usually "reads" with one hand and keeps his place vertically with the other. An advanced reader may use the second hand to orient himself to the next line while he is reading the line above and he may read as much as a third of the line with his left hand. Music, punctuation, and mathematical and scientific notations are based on this same system.

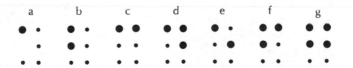

Braille in its original form was developed by Louis Braille, a Frenchman who was himself blind. It was first published in 1829 and further developed five years later. Many other systems have been attempted, including Moon's phonic symbols (modified Roman letters), New York Point (using a cell two dots high and varying in width), American Braille, and British Braille. Each system had its advocates and for many years controversies raged. In an attempt to settle them, a study was undertaken in 1932, which concluded that British Braille was superior to any system being used in this country. One hundred years after Louis Braille first presented his scheme, an agreement was reached on a modified system of British Braille now termed Standard English Braille. Even so, this was not consistently used until about 1950.

Standard English Braille has been developed in several levels of difficulty which differ in the extent to which contractions are used over and above the basic letters and numerals of Grade 1. This is the standard which serves as a common denominator in English-speaking countries.

In 1950 UNESCO adopted a world braille system for all languages, but it has not been highly publicized and there are many details to be worked out. Braille has been adapted in various forms to other languages—Chinese, Esperanto, Spanish, Korean, and many others.

Braille is very bulky. Such works as the Bible or a dictionary require twenty or thirty volumes or more. This presents a storage problem in a school which has an adequate braille library. Fortunately, many braille publications can be borrowed from the American Foundation for the Blind and the Library of Congress.

The eye, of course, is faster than the hand, and as would be expected braille reading is relatively slow, the average speed being about sixty words per minute, or about one-third or one-fourth the rate of sighted readers.

Braille writing is another addition to the curriculum of blind children. It is taught later than braille reading. There are various devices for writing the symbols, easiest and fastest of which is the braille typewriter, or braillewriter machine. This has six keys corresponding to the six dots of the cell. A good braille typist can braille forty to sixty words per minute.

Braille can also be written by hand, using a special slate and stylus. Braille slates, which come in desk and pocket sizes, are boards with a double metal strip, the lower part of which is pitted by cells of six dots each, and the upper punched with corresponding holes. The paper is inserted between the metal strips and the desired dots are embossed by pressing a dull stylus through the appropriate holes. Since this is to be read from the opposite side of the paper, the work must be done in reverse, beginning at the right margin and working toward the left.

Typing, which is seldom included in the elementary curriculum for seeing children, is very important to blind children if they are to communicate with the sighted world, a very small portion of which can read braille. Blind children are taught to use a standard print typewriter as soon as possible, usually in the third or fourth grade. Handwriting is usually very difficult and is no longer emphasized to a great extent, except that an effort is made to teach the writing of one's own signature. The typewriter has all but replaced such devices as wire guide lines, which were needed to help teach handwriting.

COMMAND OF ENVIRONMENT

Teaching command of the environment is of special importance to the blind child in that both his physical and his social independence are involved. The ease with which he can move about, find objects and places, and orient himself to new or strange physical and social situations will be crucial in determining the role he can assume in peer relations, the types of vocations and avocations that will be open to him as an adult, and his own estimation of himself as an individual.

What can be done to aid the blind child in gaining as much command as possible of his environment and himself in it? Certainly from the time he is very young he can be helped to avoid unnecessary fear, both of new experiences and of injury. Sighted children skin their knees, bump their shins, fall from trees, and step in holes. The blind child ought to have the same privileges if he is to experience freedom for the control of himself and his environment.

The blind child must be taught to feel the difference in the weight of his fork when he has successfully cornered a few peas and when it is still empty. A system of marking his clothing and organizing it is essential for both efficiency and good grooming. These are illustrative of ways in which a blind child can be taught to improve his command of the environment.

The use of models, whether of a room, the Empire State Building, or the child's neighborhood, is generally felt to be helpful in showing the relationship of one place or size to another. But this is not to say that models are approved as a substitute for the experience. Rather, they can help give a perceptual or cognitive map of relations and areas too large to be simultaneously included in direct experience.

ORIENTATION AND MOBILITY

The importance of training blind children and adults to get about in their environment cannot be overestimated. It is known that one of the greatest limitations imposed by blindness is on the ability to get about. The situations which force dependence and may cause greatest personality and social problems are very likely to center about mobility. The use of the long cane, the seeing-eye dog, and the sighted guide have been tried with adults. Currently, there has been an effort to introduce mobility training in the curriculum not only for secondary school students but also for young children.

Dr. Richard Hoover (1947) worked with blinded soldiers at Valley Forge Army Hospital and developed a systematic method of travel which employed the use of the long cane. His work has become the basis for instructional programs in orientation and mobility, and is still widely followed. Preparation of specialists in this area is now offered in several colleges. Many public and private schools serving blind children employ such specialists.

While the original techniques were worked out for adults, there is currently an interest in teaching such skills to young blind children with the expectation that they will form habits of independent travel. Lord (1967) identified the sequential skills which young blind children should be expected to perform. A scale was developed to measure the achievement of children with respect to these tasks. The major tasks included skills in using sensory cues, self-help skills, using directions and turns, formal mobility skills, and habitual movement in space. Mobility skills must be stressed in the house as well as at school. Detroit schools began a program (Kirk, 1968) which included instruction and evaluation by both the teacher and the parent. The evaluation related to such skills as posture and walking, use of senses, use of basic knowledge and concepts, indoor mobility and outdoor travel.

Additional support for early instruction resulted from a Los Angeles County project (Lord and Blaha, 1968) in which intensive individual instruction in travel was given to high-school-age youths. After an average of approximately 108 hours of instruction the average student acquired skills in use of the long cane and other skills. In a follow-up study of these youths it was found that many of them have limited travel needs in relation to normal youth of similar age; their parents were protective; their social life was limited; their vocational needs were well ahead of them. They had not grown up with usable travel skills.

Knowles (1969) studied a number of characteristics of the blind in relation to success in vocational rehabilitation. Orientation and mobility led the list of 13 variables which correlate with success.

The whole area of personal mobility and independence has a particular significance in adolescence when the child is ready to break away from family restraints and overprotection. In his peer relations, security and comfort in controlling himself and his environment are most essential to the development of poise and independence and to gaining the respect of others.

PHYSICAL EDUCATION

In relation to orientation and mobility training, physical education, formerly thought dangerous for the visually handicapped, is being stressed as part of the curriculum. In residential schools, classes for physical education are now a routine part of the curriculum. In local day schools the visually handicapped are encouraged to participate in physical education activities with seeing children whenever possible. The classroom teacher and the resource-room or itinerant teacher assists the visually handicapped child to participate in physical education activities. This is accomplished through the verbal directions of the teacher or by assigning a seeing child to give him verbal directions. Generally, physical education is integrated with the program of orientation and mobility.

LISTENING SKILLS

It is very important that visually handicapped children be more proficient than seeing children in listening skills. Much of their education is obtained through listening to talking books, tapes, and verbal intercourse. Special teachers have developed techniques for developing listening skills, and the research on compressed speech and its utilization has helped to decrease the time of auditory comprehension earlier used with talking books. In high school and college blind persons use readers to obtain information and must learn to listen to details.

READING AND WRITING

Large type print has been used with visually impaired children, and braille with blind children. Writing is learned by the visually handicapped through regular writing, typewriters, and braille writers.

ARITHMETIC

Arithmetic is taught in print and in braille. One of the aids that has been used successfully is the Japanese abacus. With this the visually handicapped child can use haptic sense modalities to derive arithmetic concepts.

SOCIAL AND LIVING SKILLS

Part of the job of the blind child's family, teachers, and friends is to help him establish patterns of behavior which are acceptable to others. The seeing child acquires visually much socially useful information which is not accessible to the blind child, who does not, for instance, know who is in a room as he enters or whether his attire is appropriate and neat, or what visual stimuli may have prompted a burst of laughter from his peers. The skills of successfully determining just what is customary in grooming, eating, etiquette, and the social graces, and then finding ways to implement these customs without visual cues are important to the blind child.

SPECIALIZED MATERIALS AND EQUIPMENT

The recommendations that used to be made concerning the adequate lighting and furnishings for classrooms for the visually handicapped are now, fortunately, incorporated into the construction of many regular school rooms.

Lighting is very important for visually impaired children. Illumination must be free from glare and direct sunlight and evenly distributed throughout the room. Artificial illumination must be available for use at different times of the day. Other factors to be considered include the amount and height of window space, adequacy of artificial illumination, and coloring of walls and ceilings.

In addition to physical requisites of the classroom itself, classes for visually handicapped children require special equipment and special materials designed to facilitate instruction and learning. These include the following:

Movable and Adjustable Desks. Movable desks should be adjustable for height, angle, and position. It is preferable to raise the top of a desk for a nearsighted child rather than to have the child lean over in his seat to see visual materials. Different angles are needed for different activities. The desks should be placed at a 30-degree angle to the windows to avoid glare and to preclude facing the window directly. The child should be seated in such a position that the light will fall evenly on his desk. All desks, seats, and tables should be of light neutral color, with a somewhat dull finish.

Chalkboards. Black chalkboards are not recommended for visually handicapped children. Instead a gray or gray-green chalkboard is generally used; it reflects more light and still gives adequate contrast to white chalk. The purpose of this combination, like all materials and equipment in a class for the partially seeing, is to avoid glare and to make seeing as comfortable as possible.

Pencils and Paper. Special care in selecting paper and pencils is desirable. The paper is of cream color, unglazed, and slightly rough. The pencils are of heavy lead (thicker than the ordinary pencil lead) and soft.

Typewriters. Children in resource rooms or classes for the visually impaired can use primary typewriters equipped with larger type than the usual typewriter. The teacher prepares lessons on this typewriter, and the pupils also use it for many purposes.

Dictaphones and Record Players. Since visually impaired children learn a great deal aurally, instead of relying only on reading for information, special classes and resource rooms include dictaphones, phonographs, and tape recorders for presenting lessons and stories and data of many kinds. Teachers may give special assignments, partly in writing and partly on the dictaphone.

Books and Reading Materials. Classes for visually impaired children contain books with large type, usually 18 to 24 points instead of the usual 12 to 14. Other materials such as large maps, enlarged graphs, and special globes with raised relief surfaces are also included in the equipment for a special class. Enlarged phonic charts in classes where phonics is taught are also helpful.

Projection and Magnifying Equipment. Projection equipment which will enlarge charts, maps, and reading material is needed. Care should be taken to adjust this type of equipment so that distortions are avoided and proper contrast results.

Braille materials have already been discussed. It is evident that the use and understanding of these requires a large share of the child's school day.

Audio aids are a basic element in a blind child's quest for knowledge, particularly in the upper elementary grades and beyond. The Talking Book reproducer, other record players, and often a tape recorder may become part of his everyday school life. If he is in the regular grades, the classroom teacher or itinerant teacher may make special explanations or assignments on tape. Textbooks which are not available in braille may be taped or recorded by volunteer workers.

Since braille reading is less than one-third to one-fourth the speed of visual reading, and since the books available in braille are limited, Talking Books have become standard educational media for imparting information to the blind. These long-playing phonograph records of books read by professional readers are heard at the rate of 160–170 words per minute for fiction and about 150 words per minute for texts. The federal government has appropriated funds for their recording and manufacture, and the Library of Congress distributes them free of charge to libraries upon request. Special phonographs are also loaned through libraries. This system makes Talking Books available to blind children and adults in all communities.

In general, the Talking Book has been used for the presentation of fiction rather than for textbooks. Ordinarily, school textbooks are made available through the American Printing House for the Blind, the Library of Congress, or privately.

Talking Books are labeled in braille with a minimum of braille words (to save space), while indicating author, title, and reader. The same information is provided in print for the use of librarians.

Arithmetic aids include an arithmetic board and an adaptation of the abacus. The braillewriter is also used to compute mathematics. Pins and rubber bands are utilized in constructing geometric designs and graphs of various sorts.

Mental arithmetic, of course, is used a great deal in the education of the blind. But higher levels of arithmetic and mathematics require elaborate machines. Calculators can be adapted for use by brailling the dials, or by giving other tactual cues. Similarly, tape measures, rulers, watches, slide rules, compasses, protractors, and so forth have been adapted for use by the blind.

Embossed and relief maps are important in teaching space perception required in understanding geography. Besides braille maps, relief maps, and audible electric maps, jigsaw puzzles and relief globes are also used.

One of the reasons for the importance of maps is not only to supplement the study of geography in general but to help orient the blind to their immediate environment. Mobility around the room or the town requires that the blind person have a mental image of the relation of objects to each other in space. Through sensory cues and the cognitive map he is then able to orient himself, and to move around more freely.

Much engineering research has been conducted to develop aids for the blind. These developments were reported at a conference in Los Angeles in 1970 (The Blind in the Age of Technology: A Public Discussion, 1970).

The Optacon. This device is being developed at Stanford University. It scans print and converts print into 144 tactile pins. These pins, when activated by the print, produce a vibratory image of the letter on the finger of a blind person. The blind daughter of Dr. John Linvil, one of the inventors, is in college and is able to read at 60 to 70 words a minute with the use of the Optacon. When this device is fully developed a blind person will be able to read regular books and notes not available in braille.

Computer Translation of Braille. At the Massachusetts Institute of Technology a computer automaton is being developed which will translate ink print into Grade 2 braille. This procedure is being used extensively at the American Printing House for the Blind.

MIT Braille Emboss. An expansion of the computer braille translator is used with a telewriter. When a teacher of the blind desires a braille output for new materials she can request this by phone from a computer center, and it is returned in braille by means of a teletypewriter.

Mobility Devices. Canes have been used by the blind for many years. Currently, other mobility devices are being developed. One is a laser cane equipped with three beams of light which scan the area in front of the traveler. These three beams are directed in the areas of the head, the waist, and the feet. The traveler receives warnings of obstacles for the feet and the waist by means of vibration and a sound for obstacles at head height.

Compressed Speech. One way of obtaining more rapid information through records and tapes is to increase their speed. This generally produces a distortion. Another system that has been developed is compressed speech, which allows the regular elimination of one-hundredth of a second, or one-fiftieth or one-tenth, without causing distortion of voice. This compressor which is now used at the American Foundation for the Blind can double the word rate while preserving vocal pitch and quality. A blind person can comprehend recorded voices at 275 words per minute which is comparable to reading print.

Artificial Vision. The beginnings of a possible visual prosthesis was encouraged by an experiment in England. The experimenters inserted a prosthetic device in the occipital cortex of a blind nurse. The subject was able to perceive points of light, called phosphenes. This experiment only raises the possibility of developing a prosthesis that can be implanted in the visual cortex which would, in a sense, partially replace the eye.

Progression through Successive Educational Levels

At the preschool level the child is at home or in a regular nursery school. It is at this age that parent involvement with the education of the child is most intimate. It is at this age that the parents need most help. Adequate services to the family through the school or other agencies that are knowledgeable in the education of the visually handicapped can be very helpful.

Visually handicapped children attend regular kindergarten in communities without much difficulty. In the activities of listening to stories, show and tell time, and other oral activities the blind child is not at a disadvantage. In other activities such as painting, playing with three dimensional crafts and other motor activities, minor modifications are made. Teachers allow the blind child to try to participate in as many activities as he can.

Specialized instruction in reading print or braille for the visually handicapped child begins in the first grade. If the local school has a resource room or an itinerant teacher, these personnel will provide the specialized materials and instruction. Materials and aids described above are brought into the class in which the child is enrolled; regular print books, large print books, optical aids, braille, and so forth are furnished each child. The special teacher gives visual training and any other remedial work necessary to fit the child into the regular grades.

In the middle grades (fourth through eighth or ninth grade) supplementary materials are furnished the visually handicapped child. He generally is required to absorb the same information learned by the seeing children. This is accomplished through talking books, recorded audio lessons, and remedial work if the child needs it.

If the child is of average intelligence and has learned to use the aids and materials furnished him earlier, he can enroll in the secondary schools. Readers are furnished the blind child to assist him in "keeping up" with his classmates. Many blind students are found in colleges and universities. With tape recorders, braille writers, and readers many blind individuals graduate from college. Some receive advanced degrees in a variety of fields.

Educating the Deaf-Blind

Whenever the deaf-blind are discussed, the first name to come to mind is that of Helen Keller who has become a symbol of what devoted teaching can do against great odds. This deaf-blind child with a keen mind and a constant companion achieved speech and other ways of communicating and a high level of academic achievement.

The deaf-blind child is defined by the Bureau of Education for the Handicapped (1969) as:

> . . . a child who has both auditory and visual impairments, the combination of which cause such severe communication and other developmental and educational problems that he cannot properly be accommodated in special education programs either for the hearing handicapped child or for the visually handicapped child. (p. 1)

The number of deaf-blind children in the United States is very small. In a survey by the U.S. Office of Education in April, 1970, it was estimated that there were 2,461 deaf-blind children in the United States between birth and 20 years of age. Since these children are scattered throughout the 50 states, it is difficult to arrange for specialized educational facilities in their local communities. Consequently, the education of the deaf-blind has been largely conducted in private residential schools.

During the rubella epidemic of 1963–64 some 20,000 to 30,000 children were born defective. Some of these were deaf-blind and required national attention. In 1968 the Federal Congress authorized the organization of ten regional centers strategically placed throughout the United States to give necessary services to deaf-blind children.

The purpose of the Regional Deaf-Blind Centers is to provide for all deaf-blind children a program designed to utilize modern educational procedures to enable them to develop to their maximum. The regional centers are designed to provide the following services: (1) comprehensive diagnostic and evaluative service; (2) a program of adjustment, orientation, and education; and (3) effective consultative services for parents, teachers, and others who play a direct role in the lives of deaf-blind children in assisting them to understand the problems, adjustments, orientation, and education of these children.

SUMMARY

1. There have been many changes in the educational provisions for visually handicapped children since the days of "sight-saving" classes for the partially seeing and residential schools for the blind.

2. The majority of visually handicapped children are now educated in local day-school classes rather than in residential schools.
3. Enrollments in self-contained classes are being reduced by placing visually handicapped children in regular classes whenever possible and offering the services of resource-rooms and itinerant special teachers.
4. The organizational patterns for the education of the visually handicapped in communities are, in order of frequency: (1) itinerant teacher programs, (2) resource-room programs, (3) full-time special classes, (4) cooperative special classes, and (5) teacher-consultant programs.
5. The curriculum for the visually handicapped is the same as that for the normal child. Only the materials and techniques are different. Special methods of training residual vision have been developed.
6. Children with little or no residual vision acquire knowledge through reading braille, listening to talking books, and utilizing some of the newer technological aids developed to assist in their education.
7. Orientation and mobility training, earlier confined to adults, are now becoming a part of the curriculum for elementary school visually handicapped children.
8. Provisions have been made nationally for the development of Regional Resource Centers for the deaf-blind child.

REFERENCES

Barraga, Natalie. 1970. *Teachers' Guide for "Utilization" of Low Vision.* Mimeographed by author. Austin, Texas: University of Texas.

————. 1964. *Increased Vision Behavior in Low Vision Children.* Research Series No. 13, American Foundation for the Blind.

Bateman, Barbara. 1963. *Reading and Psycholinguistic Processes of Partially Seeing Children.* Arlington, Virginia: The Council for Exceptional Children.

Bureau of Education for the Handicapped, U.S. Office of Education. 1969. *Centers and Services for Deaf-Blind Children.* Washington, D.C.: The Bureau.

Farrell, G. 1950. Blindness in the United States. In Zohl, P. A. (ed.), *Blindness,* pp. 89–108. Princeton, New Jersey: Princeton University Press.

Hoover, R. E. 1947. *Orientation and Travel Techniques.* Proceedings of the American Association of Workers of the Blind.

Irwin, R. B. 1955. *As I Saw It.* New York: American Foundation for the Blind.

Jones, J. W., and Collins, Anne P. 1966. *Educational Programs for Visually Handicapped Children.* Bulletin No. 6, Office of Education. Washington, D.C.: U.S. Government Printing Office.

Kirk, Edithe C. 1968. The Mobility Evaluation Report for Parents. *Exceptional Children* 35 (September): 57–62.

Knowles, L. 1969. Successful and Unsuccessful Rehabilitation of the Legally Blind. *The New Outlook for the Blind* 63 (May): 129–169.

Lord, F. E. 1967. *Preliminary Standardization of Scale of Orientation and Mobility Skills of*

Young Blind Children: Final Report. U.S. Office of Education, Bureau of Research, Project No. 6–2464, Grant No. oEG 4–7–062464–0369. Washington, D.C.: Government Printing Office.

Lord, F. E., and Blaha, L. 1968. *Demonstration of Home and Community Support Needed to Facilitate Mobility Instruction for Blind Youth.* Report R.D. 1784–5, Washington, D.C.: Department of Health, Education, and Welfare, Rehabilitation Services Administration.

Lowenfeld, B. 1952. The Child Who is Blind. *Journal of Exceptional Children* 19 (December): 96–102.

Smith, Helen P. 1938. Pioneer Work in Sight Saving. *The Sight-Saving Class Exchange* 65 (June): 2–14.

The Blind in the Age of Technology: A Public Discussion. 1970. *The New Outlook for the Blind* 64 (September): 201–218.

TWELVE

NEUROLOGIC

ORTHOPEDIC

AND

OTHER

HEALTH

IMPAIRMENTS

Exceptional children considered in this chapter are those who are crippled, deformed, or otherwise physically handicapped (exclusive of the visually and auditorily handicapped) and those who have health problems which interfere with normal functioning in a regular classroom. These children comprise heterogeneous groups with varying disabilities, each a unique problem which limits the effectiveness with which a child can cope with the academic, social, and emotional expectations of the school and community.

The composition of these groups of exceptional children has undergone continuous and rapid change over the years due to the advances made in medical science, the availability of medical services, an increasing consciousness of the health and emotional needs of children, the change in attitude toward handicapping conditions, and the continuing effort on the part of educators to provide educational experiences for the whole spectrum of children. In the past, classes for the physically impaired were comprised primarily of children with mobility problems or problems of manual dexterity. Today, the majority of children found in special classes and other programs for the physically impaired have problems of coordination, perception, and cognition (as well as mobility) resulting from the lack of proper development of, or injury to, the central nervous system. When the main problem was mobility, the role of the educator was to remove the architectural barriers which prohibited or limited the participation of orthopedically impaired children and to create an atmosphere where optimum learning could take place. The children could then be taught in much the same manner as those in a class of nonimpaired children. Today the educator must be prepared not only to modify the classroom environment in terms of space, lighting, furniture, and equipment, but also to identify, evaluate, and remediate learning and adjustment problems peculiar to the neurologically impaired.

Indicative of the change which has taken place in the composition of classes for the physically impaired, three studies published in 1928, 1945, and 1954 respectively, show the changing proportions of postpolio children (mobility problems) and cerebral-palsied children (neurological problems) over this time period. The data are presented in Table 12–1. It will be noticed from Table 12–1 that in 1928 it was reported that about one-third of the class membership were postpolio and that this proportion dropped to about one-fifth in 1945 and remained at that figure in the 1954 report. The proportion of cerebral palsied, however, jumped from about one-seventh (14.5 percent) in 1928 to one-third

TABLE 12–1

Percent of postpolio and cerebral-palsied children in classes for the physically handicapped

Study	Postpolio	Cerebral-palsied
Lisan (1928)	32	14.5
Mackie (1945)	21	17.7
Chicago P.S. (1954)	21.6	33

Sources: (a) Marguerite Lisan, *Care and Education of Crippled Children and Disabled Adults.* Bulletin No. 1. (Madison, Wisconsin: State Department of Public Education, 1928).

(b) Romaine P. Mackie, *Crippled Children in American Education* (New York: Teachers College, Columbia University, 1945).

(c) *The Needs of Physically Handicapped Children* (Chicago: Chicago Board of Education, 1954), p. 14.

(33 percent) in 1954. Unfortunately, more recent data is not available. It is to be expected, however, that the trend would be even more obvious in 1971, due to the continuing use of the Salk vaccine and the reduction in poliomyelitis.

The higher number of cerebral-palsied children in these classes probably reflects, not greater prevalence of this condition, but greater efforts to enroll cerebral-palsied children in schools for the crippled. This campaign was probably a result of the increased interest and promotion on the part of the United Cerebral Palsy Associations and the Easter Seal Society.

Not all children, of course, have the same degree of handicap resulting from the same physical impairment. Some are *mildly involved* and can be adequately educated in the regular classroom. Fortunately, this group includes the majority of these children. Many of the *moderately involved* are also being provided for in the regular classroom, with the remainder placed in special classes and special schools. With the change in attitude concerning the educability of the *severely involved,* and feasibility of programming for them, some are being included in special classes with additional modifications of programs and equipment, although others still thought to be too involved to benefit from group experiences remain in the home, in hospitals, or in public and private residential centers.

For the purposes of the present chapter, those children whose physical needs require some modifications and adaptations of school practice have been classified into three broad categories: (1) neurologically impaired, (2) orthopedically impaired, and (3) children with other health impairments.

The Neurologically Impaired

The neurologically impaired are those children whose handicapping condition is due to lack of complete development or injury to the central nervous system.

The brain is the control center of the body. When something goes wrong with the brain, something happens to the physical, emotional, or mental functions of the organism. The number of things that can happen to the organism are probably as numerous as the nerves and cells of the brain.

Throughout the centuries scientists have been trying to unravel the mysteries of the complex central nervous system. Originally it was believed that the brain functioned as one single organ, like the liver. A little later it was thought that different parts of the brain had separate functions. Only recently scientists have recognized that there is an integrative function of the central nervous system, and also that different parts of the brain have special functions. The theories of both *mass action* (meaning that the brain functions as a whole) and *localization* (meaning that certain functions are located in certain areas of the brain) have been accepted.

As yet scientists have not been able to differentiate and precisely locate the functions of the central nervous system sufficiently to explain all behavior on this basis. What we have at present is partial knowledge of the relation of the central nervous system to behavior and to special disabilities. Figure 12–1 illustrates attempts to localize brain functions. This is a summary representation of various research and hypothetical conclusions. Penfield and Rasmussen (1952), through electrical stimulation of the various parts of the brain in humans during the waking state, were able to produce muscular movements of various parts of the body. In addition, stimulation of the auditory area aroused hearing of tones, and stimulation of the visual areas aroused sensations of color, shape, and other visual representations. When the right temporal lobe was stimulated in one patient there was aroused a memory of being in an office with desks and other people. As a result of these and other studies the brain is being plotted, as shown in Figure 12–1, to indicate the broad areas which appear to be responsible for certain physical and mental functions.

An injury to the brain, or lack of development of the brain, is likely to result in disabilities of various kinds. The major neurological disabilities discussed below are: (1) cerebral palsy, (2) epilepsy, (3) spina bifida, and (4) other brain involvements. The most common type of neurological handicap is cerebral palsy and will be discussed first.

CEREBRAL PALSY

Since "cerebral" means "brain" and "palsy" means "a motor disability," *cerebral palsy* refers to a motor disability caused by a brain dysfunction. There are other kinds of palsy, not caused by brain damage, including spinal palsy, which could be the result of poliomyelitis, or end organ palsy such as that found in muscular dystrophy. An important point to remember is that a brain damage which results in the motor disability called cerebral palsy can also cause language, speech, writing, and other disorders. Furthermore, cerebral disorders can cause psychological disorders without affecting motor ability.

The American Academy of Cerebral Palsy defined cerebral palsy as "any abnormal alteration of movement or motor function arising from defect, injury, or disease of the nervous tissues contained in the cranial cavity" (Fay, 1953). A more inclusive definition has been formulated by the United Cerebral Palsy Research and Educational Foundation (1958):

Cerebral palsy embraces the clinical picture created by injury to the brain, in which one of the components is motor disturbance. Thus, cerebral palsy may be described as a group of conditions, usually originating in childhood, characterized by paralysis, weakness, incoordination or any other aberration of motor function caused by pathology of the motor control center of the brain. In addition to such motor dysfunction, cerebral palsy may include learning difficulties, psychological problems, sensory defects, convulsive and behavioral disorders of organic origin. (p. 1)

Thus, the definition of cerebral palsy includes not only the neuromotor component but also many other mental or psychological disabilities of perception, learning, emotions, and speech. The neuromuscular disorder is primarily the

FIGURE 12–1

Summarizing map of the areas of cortical function

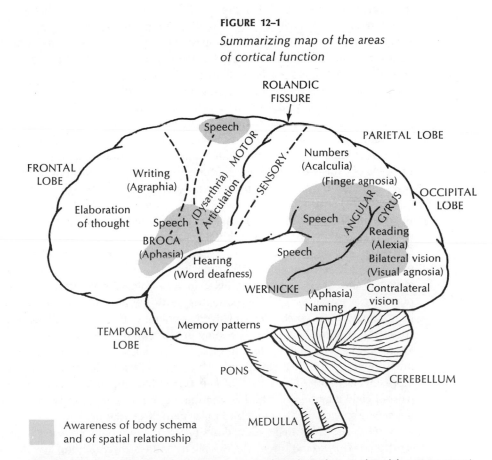

This drawing is based on the conclusions, some hypothetical (e.g., the elaboration zones), others firmly established, in the works of Penfield and Rasmussen (1952) and Penfield and Roberts (1959). The terms agraphia, acalculia, alexia, aphasia, word deafness, visual agnosia, finger agnosia, and dysarthria are terms used by various neurologists to indicate disorders of functions. The localization of these dysfunctions is speculative.

responsibility of the medical profession whereas the associated behavioral disorders become the responsibility of the social, educational, psychological, and speech professions. This is why the problem of cerebral palsy requires a team approach by the members of various professions.

It should also be remembered that damage to the brain need not result in neuromuscular disabilities, and that other behavior disabilities can occur in isolation or in combination. To these general disabilities, including cerebral palsy, Denhoff and Robinault (1960) have applied the term "cerebral palsy and related dysfunctions." They feel that "cerebral palsy" is too narrow a term and that "cerebral dysfunction" is preferable to "brain-injury" or "brain-damage." The present author will use "cerebral dysfunction" as the general term and "cerebral palsy" as referring to cerebral dysfunction when related only to the neuro-muscular disability. It should be pointed out, however, that the majority of cerebral-palsied children have associated handicaps of vision, hearing, and speech, as well as perceptual or behavioral handicaps. In the long run the ultimate treatment or remediation of the associated handicap may be as important as the treatment of the neuromuscular handicap.

Cerebral palsy is not a disease, but a condition characterized by a group of concurrent symptoms. This means that, although it is unlike measles or tuberculosis or cancer, it is a describable syndrome and its description is consistent in some ways. In describing cerebral palsy, a diagnostic team tends to indicate (1) the general condition—cerebral palsy; (2) the parts of the body affected; (3) the degree of involvement, such as mild or severe; and (4) associated disabilities of vision, hearing, intelligence, speech, and learning.

Parts of the body affected by a disability are identified by the terms: (1) monoplegia, (2) hemiplegia, (3) triplegia, (4) paraplegia, (5) quadriplegia, (6) diplegia, and (7) double hemiplegia. In *monoplegia* one limb is affected. In *hemiplegia* one side of the body, that is, both the arm and the leg, is affected. In *triplegia,* three limbs are involved, generally two legs and one arm. In *paraplegia* the involvement occurs only in the legs. In *quadriplegia* all four limbs are somewhat equally affected. In *diplegia* all four limbs are affected with more involvement of the legs. In *double hemiplegia* all four limbs are affected with more involvement of one side of the body than the other. Thus, a cerebral-palsied child may be described as a moderate, right hemiplegic with accompanying severe speech involvement and mild mental retardation.

In 1861, Dr. Little in London described a condition in children as a spastic syndrome. This condition was later called "Little's disease" and has since been variously termed cerebrospastic, infantile cerebral spastic, birth injured, and simply cerebral palsied. Use of the word "cerebral" indicates that the paralysis is the result of a damaged brain, to be differentiated from other kinds of paralysis such as that found in poliomyelitis.

The term "cerebral palsy" was coined by Dr. Winthrop Phelps, orthopedic surgeon and pioneer in work with the cerebral palsied in the United States. Additionally, cerebral palsy is classified as to different forms of neuromuscular involvement. These include: (1) spasticity, (2) athetosis, (3) ataxia, (4) tremor, and (5) rigidity. The first two, the spastic and athetoid groups, comprise about 75 to 80 percent of cerebral-palsied individuals.

Spasticity. Spastics make up the largest group of the cerebral palsied, constituting 40 to 60 percent of the total. Spasticity can occur in one or more limbs with hemiplegia being the most common locus of involvement. The clinical picture is one of hyperactive deep reflexes, hypertonicity, and clonus.

Certain areas of the brain suppress certain impulses, contractions, or stimulations and are therefore called suppressors. When one of these is damaged suppression does not occur, and the muscles remain in a state of spasticity or tension. Normally there is a balance between the suppressors and the antagonistic muscles. In the condition of spasticity the balance is absent and instead of a smooth movement there are jerky, uncontrolled movements with the spasmodic contraction of the muscles. The cerebral cortex (particularly the motor cortex), the pyramidal tracts, and possibly some extrapyramidal tracts which deal with the control of voluntary movements are defective. (The pyramidal tracts are between the sensory and motor regions of the cortex in Figure 12–1, and the extrapyramidal tracts are below the cortical level, deeper in the brain.)

In mild cases the spastic child may extend his arms for balance to control a somewhat awkward gait. In moderate cases he may hold his arms close to his body, bent at the elbow, with the hand bent toward the body, with legs rotated inwardly flexed at the knees, and a "scissoring gait" results. In severe cases the child may have poor control over his body and be unable to sit, stand, or walk without the support of braces, crutches, a walking frame, etc.

Athetosis. Athetoids make up the second largest group in cerebral palsy—about 15 to 20 percent of the total. Athetosis is characterized by uncontrollable, jerky, irregular, twisting movements. The head is frequently drawn back, the neck extended and tense, with the mouth held open, the tongue protruding, and drooling often occurs. Children with athetosis walk in a lurching, writhing, and stumbly manner. Their movements are not rhythmical and do not seem to follow any sequence. Their postural attitude is uncontrolled, and many of them writhe and wriggle in variable fashion.

The athetoid individual is able to put his hand to his mouth, but in so doing he goes through various uncontrollable movements, in the extreme case showing squirming gestures and marked facial grimaces. During sleep, however, the athetoid does not writhe or squirm. These movements occur only in the conscious state. As conscious effort and emotionality increase, the athetotic movements become intensified.

Ataxia. This particular condition, less prevalent than spasticity or athetosis, is due to a lesion in the cerebellum, which normally controls balance and muscle coordination. The ataxic child is unsteady in his movements, walks with a high step, and falls easily. Sometimes the eyes are uncoordinated and nystagmus (jerky movement of the eye) is common. Ordinarily, ataxia is not detected at birth but is apparent when grasping and walking begin. As in spasticity and athetosis, there are varying degrees of ataxia, from mild (barely detectable) to very severe, depending on the extent of damage in the cerebellum.

Tremor and Rigidity. Tremor and rigidity are also, like athetosis, the result of injury to the extrapyramidal system. They occur in a small proportion of cerebral-palsied children. *Tremor* cerebral palsy is sometimes detected at an early age when the whole body shows involuntary vibrating movements of irregular nature. These result from an interference in the normal balance between antagonistic muscle groups. The child is generally consistent and predictable and is able to direct his activities toward a goal more adequately than is the athetoid or spastic. *Rigidity* refers to interference with the postural tone and is the result of resistance of agonist and antagonist muscles. There is more of a diminished motion than abnormal motion. These cases, however, are not very common and can be distinguished from the spastics in that their tremor or rigidity is generally even.

Mixed Types. Although different kinds of cerebral palsy can be identified and classified many cerebral palsy cases are mixed types, with some characteristics of spasticity and athetosis, or spasticity and ataxia, or other combinations. Spasticity has been ascribed to a lesion in the *pyramidal tract,* which is in the motor cortex, while athetosis results from a lesion in the *extrapyramidal* system, located in the forebrain or midbrain. These are not clear-cut areas of deficit, since spasticity may also involve the extrapyramidal system. Although not fully understood, the extrapyramidal system is believed to mediate inhibitory or restraining effects on muscular activity and to control the complex automatic acts like walking and making facial expressions.

THE PREVALENCE OF CEREBRAL PALSY

As with many other kinds of exceptionality, it is difficult to determine very accurately the prevalence of cerebral palsy among children. Many mild cases go undiagnosed and undetected. If the condition is associated with the handicap of mental deficiency, for example, the children tend to be enrolled in institutions for the mentally defective, and are so classified, instead of being classified as cerebral palsied.

Various attempts, however, have been made to estimate the prevalence of cerebral palsy in different populations. Schonell's (1956) study of four county boroughs in England gives the following incidences per 10,000 population.

Birmingham	7.6
Stoke	5.8
Coventry	9.4
Walsall	7.7

Schonell observed that there were a number of cases in institutions which were not included in these surveys and indicated that the overall figure, adding those in institutions, would be an estimated 9 cerebral-palsied individuals per 10,000 population.

Nielsen (1966) quotes a Danish study by Hansen as estimating an incidence of 1 to 2 cerebral palsied per 1000 in Denmark, a much higher figure than that of Schonell of 0.9 per 1,000 population.

Cardwell (1956) has summarized the studies which attempted to determine the incidence and prevalence of cerebral palsy in the population. The studies vary widely, depending on whether they are giving the number in 10,000 population as did Schonell or are estimating the number per 1000 births. Cardwell quotes Wishik as stating that there are between 15 and 30 per 10,000 total population, a much higher figure than that given by Schonell. As with other types of exceptional children, surveys vary in their definitions and criteria; hence the wide variation in estimates of prevalence.

From these studies one can conclude that the Schonell figures are too low, and the Wishik figures too high and that a safe figure would be 1 to 2 per 1000.

The studies of incidence by type vary considerably. Clarke and Clarke (1965) summarize some of the studies done in several countries including the United States. This is reproduced in Table 12–2. It will be noted that the incidence of athetoids ranges from 9.3 to 23.6 percent and the spastics from 45 to 83 percent.

THE CAUSES OF CEREBRAL PALSY

The causes of cerebral palsy appear to be very similar to the causes of some forms of mental deficiency explained in Chapter 5. As Illingworth (1958) has aptly asserted, ". . . the causes of cerebral palsy and of mental deficiency are so interwoven, that with only a few exceptions research into the causes of one cannot and should not be separated from research into the causes of the other"

TABLE 12–2

Incidence of cerebral palsy by type

Study	Athetoid	Spastic	Mixed athetoid and spastic	Other
Asher and Schonell (1950), 349 cases of congenital C.P. in children	10%	83%	5%	1.9%
New Jersey Survey, Hopkins, Bice, and Colton (1951), 1,406 cases	23.6	45.1	3.4	26.9
Hansen (1960), Denmark, 2,621 patients	9.3	78.5	4.6	7.6
Henderson, Eastern Scotland (1961), 240 cases	11.7	77.1	9.6	1.6
Crothers and Paine (1959), 406 cases		64.6	13.1	22

Source: Clarke and Clarke, 1965, p. 237. Reproduced with the permission of the publisher.

Note: In a number of the quoted sources it will be noted that the percentages do not always total 100.

(p. 17). Rather than repeat the etiological factors presented in Chapter 5 we shall briefly summarize the causative (etiological) factors.

Cerebral palsy, like other conditions, may be caused by factors operative before birth (prenatal), during birth (natal or perinatal), or after birth (postnatal), but there appears to be little agreement as to the role played by genetics in the etiology of cerebral palsy.

Prenatal Conditions. In this category are found (1) genetic or inherited conditions and (2) conditions during pregnancy which result in a defect in the child's central nervous system.

Some conditions causing cerebral palsy during the prenatal period include (1) prenatal anoxia from premature separation of the placenta, severe anemia in the mother, a serious heart condition, shock, or threatened abortion, (2) metabolic disturbances of the mother, and (3) the Rh factor.

Perinatal Conditions. One cause which has been firmly established is injury at birth. Difficulties with the cord and placenta can reduce the oxygen supply, causing anoxia. So can other mechanical factors such as breech presentation, holding back of the head, and brain hemorrhage during birth.

Postnatal Conditions. As in other conditions, childhood diseases such as meningitis, encephalitis, influenza, and possibly high fevers in typhoid, diphtheria, and pertussis could cause cerebral palsy, as could head injuries from accidents, certain poisoning causing toxic conditions (lead poisoning, anoxia, carbon monoxide poisoning), or strangulation. According to Illingworth it is estimated that about 10 percent of cerebral palsy is caused by postnatal factors.

In commenting on correlated factors Illingworth (1958) stated:

1. In a small percentage of cases other than kernicterus and heredofamilial degenerative diseases of the nervous system, there is a history of affected near relatives. There is a higher than average incidence of mental deficiency in siblings and near relatives, and a higher than average incidence of other anomalies in affected children.

2. There is a higher than average incidence of males (about 57 percent).

3. There is a higher than average incidence of multiple pregnancies—about 6 percent, as compared to an average of 1.2 percent.

4. There is a higher incidence of previous miscarriages and stillbirths.

5. There is an increased incidence of antepartum hemorrhage in the later part of pregnancy and of toxemia.

6. There is a high incidence of abnormal labor involving conditions which would be likely to cause anoxia rather than mechanical trauma.

7. The condition of affected children in the immediate newborn period is more likely to be poor and to cause concern than that of unaffected babies.

8. Postnatal causes include trauma, encephalitis and meningitis.

9. Anoxia is probably the most important single factor, but other factors are involved. (p. 14)

HANDICAPS ASSOCIATED WITH CEREBRAL PALSY

The cerebral dysfunction resulting in cerebral palsy also may cause a variety of other handicaps, singly or in combinations. As in neuromuscular disabilities, where cerebral palsy can affect one arm (monoplegia), or one leg and one arm (hemiplegia), or both legs and both arms (quadriplegia), a cerebral dysfunction may cause none, one, or a number of significant deviations: intellectual defects, left-handedness, deficiencies in vision, hearing, speech, or visual-motor perceptions.

Mental Retardation. Often poor speech and uncontrolled writhing or spastic movements of cerebral-palsied children give the layman an unwarranted impression of mental retardation. There is actually little direct relation between intelligence and degree of physical impairment in cerebral palsy. An individual with

TABLE 12–3

Distribution of 354 estimated IQ's of cerebral palsy group compared with normal child population

IQ level	Percent of cerebral palsy group	Percent in normal population
130+	.6	3
110–129	3.4	24
90–109	20.1	46
70–89	26.8	24
69 and below	45.2	3
Not assessable	3.9	

Source: Adapted from F. E. Schonell, 1956, p. 66. Reproduced with the permission of the publisher.

severe writhing or uncontrolled spasticity may be intellectually gifted while one with mild, almost unnoticed physical involvements may be severely mentally retarded.

Taylor (1959) summarized many articles and books written on the intelligence of the cerebral-palsied child. Individual intelligence tests such as the Stanford-Binet and the Wechsler Intelligence Scale for Children are sometimes used to obtain a minimal estimate of the cerebral-palsied child's intelligence, but most examiners feel that his performance is unduly handicapped by his motor or speech impairments. With these cautions in mind some of the studies using intelligence tests will be summarized:

Hohman and Freedheim (1958), who obtained IQ's on 1,003 cases referred to a medical clinic, found that 58.8 percent of the cerebral-palsied children had IQ's below 70 as compared to a normal distribution showing only 5 percent in this category. Their distribution of IQ's also shows that 25.1 percent of the palsied group had IQ's of 70 to 90; 13 percent had IQ's between 90 and 110, and only 3.1 percent had IQ's above 110.

Schonell (1956) estimated the IQ's of cerebral-palsied children from a sample of 354 cases and compared them with normal children, as did Hohman and Freedheim. This study, done in England, indicates that 45 percent of the cerebral-palsied children had IQ's below 70. Schonell's distribution of the figures for the group as a whole is shown in Table 12–3.

FIGURE 12–2

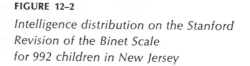

Intelligence distribution on the Stanford
Revision of the Binet Scale
for 992 children in New Jersey

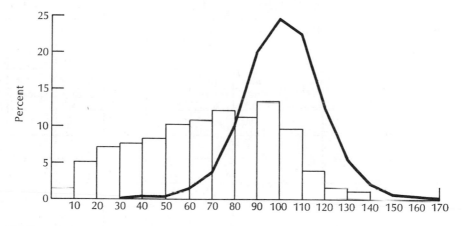

The line graph represents normal distribution (Terman). The bar graph represents total cerebral-palsy cases. Median IQ is 70.4.

Source: T. W. Hopkins, H. V. Bice, and K. C. Colton, 1954, p. 44.

Hopkins, Bice, and Colton (1954) reported the distribution of intelligence on the Stanford Revision of the Binet Scale for 992 children in New Jersey. Figure 12–2 shows the marked difference between the normal distribution and that of the cerebral palsied. This survey indicated that 49 percent of the cerebral-palsied children fell below 70 IQ, 22.5 percent are betwen 70 and 89 IQ, 21.9 percent fell between 90 and 109 IQ, and 6.6 percent above 110 IQ. The median IQ was 70.4. These figures agree quite well with the Schonell figures and are a little more favorable than those presented by Hohman and Freedheim.

Other figures come from Nielsen (1966), who states that in Denmark "between one-third and one-quarter of the cerebral-palsied group are of average to above average intelligence, while the remainder suffer from a mild or severe form of mental retardation" (p. 52).

Myers (1963) tested 24 athetoids, 68 spastics, and 32 normal children ages 4–0 to 9–0 with the Illinois Test of Psycholinguistic Abilities (Experimental Edition). Figure 12–3 gives the comparison profiles. It should be noted from this profile that: (1) both the athetoids and spastics were inferior to the normal groups, (2) the athetoid group was superior to the spastic group in tests at the

FIGURE 12–3

*Comparison profiles of
cerebral-palsied children*

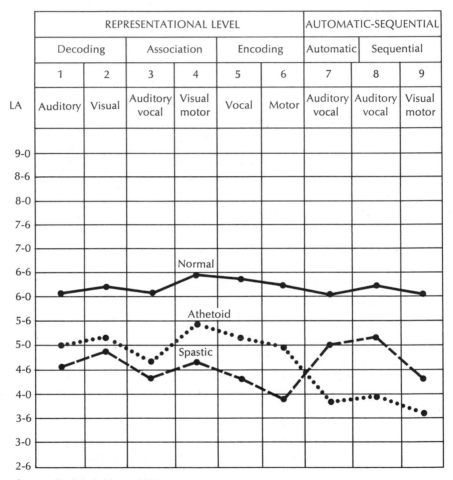

	REPRESENTATIONAL LEVEL						AUTOMATIC-SEQUENTIAL		
	Decoding		Association		Encoding		Automatic	Sequential	
	1	2	3	4	5	6	7	8	9
LA	Auditory	Visual	Auditory vocal	Visual motor	Vocal	Motor	Auditory vocal	Auditory vocal	Visual motor

Source: Patricia I. Myers, 1963.

representational level, and (3) the spastic group was superior to the athetoid group at the automatic sequential level.

Visual Defects. All of the studies on visual deficiencies in cerebral-palsied children have shown that a substantial number of these children have associated visual anomalies. Hopkins, Bice, and Colton (1954) pointed out that in a sample of 1297 cases, 72.4 percent had normal vision while 27.6 percent had defective or questionable vision. Of the children with visual disabilities 42.7 percent were ataxic, 27.3 percent were spastic, and 20.4 percent were athetoid.

According to Denhoff and Robinault (1960), "various authors agree that over 50 percent of the cerebral-palsied children have oculomotor defects and 25 percent or more have subnormal vision" (p. 63).

Hearing Defects. Another problem facing those who diagnose or treat the cerebral palsied is that of whether the cerebral damage has affected hearing as it has vision. Since hearing does not have motor functions comparable to those of the eye muscles, hearing defects should be less frequent. Actually research has found that hearing defects among cerebral-palsied children are not as common as are visual problems.

Hopkins, Bice, and Colton (1954) reported that 13.3 percent of 1,121 cases had hearing defects. Of this group the athetoids comprised 22.6 percent, the spastics only 7.2 percent. In a survey from England, Fish (1955) found that 20 percent of the cerebral-palsied children had hearing losses.

It would appear from these studies that hearing losses among the cerebral palsied, especially among the athetoid group, are greater than among children who are not cerebral palsied, but not as marked as are visual problems.

Speech Defects. Defective speech is the most common type of associated handicap among cerebral-palsied children. In the Hopkins sample of 1,224 children, 88.7 percent of the athetoids and 85.3 percent of the ataxic group were found to have speech defects. Only 52 percent of the spastics were diagnosed as having speech problems.

Denhoff and Robinault (1960) indicate that, because of neuromuscular disorders, speech involvements exist in 70 percent of cerebral-palsied children, being more common in athetoids than in spastics. Among the speech defects are *dysarthria,* an articulation defect caused by poor motor control, *delayed speech* due to mental retardation and the cerebral dysfunction, *voice disorders, stuttering,* and the various forms of *aphasia.* These difficulties are explained in greater detail in Chapter 3, "Speech Handicapped Children."

Perceptual Disorders. One of the psychological disabilities commonly attributed to cerebral dysfunction is perceptual disorder. The term "perception" has been defined differently by different authors and includes auditory, visual, tactile, and other sense modalities. With the cerebral palsied, visual perception has had the greatest attention.

Strauss and Lehtinen (1947) thought of perception as an intermediate step between sensation and the thinking process. It is a sensation with meaning.

Much research has been conducted for the purpose of finding out what kinds of perceptions become distorted in children with cerebral dysfunctions. Cruickshank, Bice, and Wallen (1957) reviewed a part of this extensive literature and conducted experiments in an attempt to differentiate the perceptual problems of the cerebral palsied from those of children without cerebral palsy, and to determine whether spastics and athetoids differ in their response to visual and visual-motor perceptual tasks. They found that in general both of the latter groups showed poorer performance on most of the tasks, and that the spastics performed more poorly than the athetoids on some of them. They concluded that although the study shows impaired perception in spastic and athetoid children the general picture requires much more research.

EPILEPSY

One of the least understood disorders occurring in childhood is epilepsy. Individuals with convulsive disorders have had to struggle in an emotionally charged climate of ignorance and social stigmata. In the past, epilepsy has been regarded as a work of the devil or insanity, and epileptics have been beaten and mistreated on the one hand and treated as prophets and seers on the other. Seizures are symptomatic of functional disturbance of a group of cells in the brain. Four major types of epilepsy have been identified. They are: (1) grand mal, (2) petit mal, (3) Jacksonian, and (4) psychomotor.

Grand Mal. The seizure that is most frequently observed and accompanied by convulsions is *grand mal.* Many epileptics experience a warning of an impending seizure called an *aura.* An aura may be olfactory in that the person is conscious of unusual odors, visual in that he may see different colors or configurations, auditory in that he may hear odd sounds such as bells or clanging, or he may experience an unusual internal feeling. The aura may precede the seizure by only an instant or it may allow the epileptic sufficient time to prepare for the coming seizure. The aura is usually followed by a cry which may be a bird-like sound or a gasp or gurgle to announce the coming of the seizure. The person then stiffens with the muscles becoming rigid. This stiffness is the *tonic stage* which immediately precedes the jerking convulsive state which is the seizure proper and known as the *clonic stage.* The clonic stage is a series of contractions and relaxations of the muscles and usually lasts for 2 to 3 minutes. The contractions become less frequent and severe and the person finally relaxes and goes into a stupor-like sleep. The term *status epilepticus* is applied to a person who has continuing grand mal seizures without regaining consciousness.

Petit mal. The petit mal attack involves a momentary loss of consciousness and is observed as a nod of the head, blinking of the eyes, a vacant stare, or the loss of grasp and dropping of an object. In the petit mal attack there is no aura, cry, or convulsion, and the attack begins and ends suddenly. The entire attack lasts only a few seconds and the child usually has no recollection of what has taken place. Petit mal seizures occur more commonly in younger children and tend to disappear as the child becomes an adult.

Jacksonian. This is a type of focal seizure usually starting with a jerking movement in the foot, hand, or one side of the face and progressing until it involves one side of the body. If it involves the entire body it ends in a *grand mal* attack. Telford and Sawrey (1967) state that "These patients sometimes find that they can prevent the continued spread of the muscular twitchings by rapidly engaging themselves in some task requiring large expenditures of physical energy or extensive intellectual involvement" (p. 353). This seizure pattern is rarely observed in children.

Psychomotor. Psychomotor seizures are also less common in children than grand mal or petit mal and are not characterized by specific behavior. The person acts automatically, in a trance-like attack with bizarre or curious behavior. He may sit motionless and chew or mumble or may become violently active and throw things, scream and run around, or tear off his clothes.

Schools for epileptic children were originally organized because educators felt that a regular teacher could not cope with major convulsions in a classroom and that these children needed attention in a special class or special school. Within the last three decades, however, various anticonvulsant drugs have been successful in greatly controlling seizures without making the child sleepy or sluggish. This advance in medicine has made it possible to retain many epileptic children in the regular grades if they are of average intelligence and have no other disabilities. The necessity for special schools and classes or special education for the epileptic is disappearing.

It should be remembered that convulsions may occur in conjunction with other handicaps. For example, convulsions are associated with cerebral palsy and are frequent among the brain-damaged and severe mental defectives. Special educational provisions for epileptic children who have other handicaps are still necessary.

If a child experiences a grand mal seizure in the classroom with other children present, the teacher should: (1) remain calm, since the other children will reflect the teacher's actions, (2) ease the child to the floor if sufficient warning is given, (3) remove all chairs, desks, tables, etc. from the area to prevent injury to the child, (4) allow the child to rest following the seizure, preferably in the nurse's room, (5) notify the nurse so that the physician and parents may be informed, and (6) use the time that the child is out of the room to explain to the other children that the child has an illness much like other diseases that they have encountered and that with proper medication the child will probably not have a repetition of the illness.

SPINA BIFIDA

Spina bifida is one of the most common birth defects causing disability in infancy and childhood. It is a congenital condition in which the bony elements of the spine have not made a complete closure, leaving an opening in the neural tube. In its slightest form (*Spina bifida occulta*) no neurological symptoms are exhibited and the only evidence of a partial cleft may be a cluster of hair growing from that location. Spina bifida occulta is usually located in the lower back in the lumbar region and does not have the characteristic meningeal sac. If a tumor-like sac is present and no nerve elements protrude into it and if there is no evidence of neurologic disability, the lesion is called a *meningocele*. If nerve elements are contained in the sac or neurologic disability is present, the lesion is called a *myelomeningocele* (Ingraham, 1944).

The myelomeningocele lesion is frequently accompanied by paralysis of the legs and lack of bowel and sphincter control. With physical therapy, bracing, and the use of crutches or walking frame the child can learn to walk and to a great extent take care of his own needs. Incontinence presents the greatest social problem.

The tumor-like sac may occur at any point along the spinal column from the head down, but more frequently occurs in the lumbar-sacral area. Operative closure procedures are performed as early as the first day of life and are becoming increasingly successful as medical research continues to amass additional knowledge of this condition. Spina bifida is frequently accompanied by hydrocephalus which is an increase of cerebrospinal fluid in the cranial cavity causing pressure and enlargement of the size of the head.

Children with spina bifida who do not have hydrocephalus do not deviate significantly in intellectual function from the normal population. They can be educated in regular classes providing modifications are made for those who have orthopedic and urinary involvement. Special classes may be necessary for those children who are not able to adjust to the expectations of the regular class.

OTHER NEUROLOGICAL DYSFUNCTIONS

There are a number of children who have central nervous system deficits which do not necessarily result in cerebral palsy, epilepsy, or spina bifida. These have been labeled "brain injured" or children with minimal cerebral dysfunction. In most cases the neurologist is unable to find definitive neurological signs of damage (hard signs). In most instances brain dysfunction is inferred from behavior (soft signs). It is assumed by many that if the child has a learning disorder and has had ordinary instruction, there must be some cerebral dysfunction present. The explanation of brain dysfunction in such cases is an attempt to establish a cause of the learning disability. Ordinarily, it is not used for developing a remedial program for the child. The reader is referred to Chapter 2, "Specific Learning Disabilities," for a discussion of brain damage and learning disabilities.

The Orthopedically Handicapped

The prevention and treatment of crippling in children has been and is primarily a medical problem. But since children who already are crippled require education, and since many conditions cannot be prevented or cured, it has been necessary to organize special educational programs. According to Solenberger (1918), the first public school for crippled children in the United States was organized in Chicago in 1899 and opened in 1900. Similar classes were opened in New York in 1906, in Detroit and Cleveland in 1910, and in Philadelphia and Baltimore in 1913. The type of program suitable for crippled children is dependent upon the type of children requiring special educational attention. As was pointed out earlier, social and medical changes are reflected in changes in the kind of crippling problem most frequently needing help.

The orthopedically handicapped child is one who has a crippling impairment which interferes with the normal functions of the bones, joints, or muscles to such an extent that special arrangements must be made by the school. Included in the category of the orthopedically handicapped are (1) children who are born with handicaps and (2) children who acquire a crippling condition later in life.

CHILDREN WHO ARE BORN WITH HANDICAPS

Children are sometimes born with defects of nerves, muscles, or bones, the result either of inheritance or of a defect in development during the prenatal period. These defects may include clubbed feet or hands, the absence of an arm or arms, defects in the legs, neck, or hips, and spina bifida.

A small proportion of children are sometimes classified as having miscellaneous orthopedic conditions which in most cases do not incapacitate the child. If the condition is serious enough to require special educational provisions, the child is considered orthopedically handicapped. Such conditions as defective posture (e.g., lordosis, or curvature of the spine), wry neck, and hunched back would fit this classification.

Many orthopedically handicapped children acquire their crippling condition later in life through accidents, infectious disease, a congenital predisposition, or a disease which incapacitates the child later in life. The more common ones are described below:

Poliomyelitis. Poliomyelitis, known as infantile paralysis, accounted for the largest single enrollment of children in schools for the crippled in 1939–1942, prior to the greater influx of cerebral-palsied children. This contagious disease is caused by a virus which in some cases attacks the gray matter of the spinal cord and paralyzes the individual. In some communities epidemics of poliomyelitis have required the expansion or organization of programs for crippled children.

With the discovery and development of vaccines over the past fifteen years starting with the Salk vaccine in 1956, medical science has reduced the incidence of poliomyelitis to where it is not now a serious concern of the educator. Children who are crippled as a result of former epidemics are now in the final elementary grades, in secondary schools, and in higher education.

Hemophilia. Hemophilia, sometimes called "bleeder's disease," is a congenital hereditary defect of blood coagulation. Children with this condition bleed profusely from minor cuts and wounds which would not be considered as serious in a normal child. It is found almost entirely in males with females as the carriers. In order for a female to inherit hemophilia her mother must have been a carrier and her father a "bleeder."

There is currently no cure for hemophilia. It is a lifelong problem with the inability of the blood to clot remaining constant. According to Katz (1970) the incidence of hemophilia in North America is 1 to 2 per 10,000 males. There are no significant differences between races, geographic areas, income levels, or social classes.

The child with hemophilia must guard against cuts and bruises as bleeding may mean another trip to the hospital and more school time is lost. Hemorrhages into the various joints can cause severe pain, limitation of motion, and crippling. These hemorrhages may be spontaneous or caused by a twisting action, fall, tooth extraction, injection, etc.

The average hemophiliac does not have sensory impairment, mental retardation, or other associated disabilities which would serve to limit his academic participation. The reason he may need specialized help in school is because of his rather poor attendance record. Usually the educational problems of the hemophiliac can be met by home teaching or help from a resource or itinerant teacher with the child remaining in the regular classroom.

Arthritis. Juvenile arthritis is a chronic, slowly progressive disease causing pain and swelling in joints of the body. The knees are involved most frequently, then the ankles, wrists, hips, and cervical spine. Juvenile arthritis is frequently referred to as "Still's disease" or rheumatoid arthritis in children. There is at present no accurate data on the incidence of juvenile arthritis. Hill (1965) reports 2 percent of the adult population of the world as having rheumatoid arthritis with the ratio of children to adults as being 10:1. The cause of this disease has not been demonstrated and there is as yet no cure. Medical therapy is administered symptomatically. The prognosis in children is better than in the adult as many children lose the symptoms with development and maturity. Educationally, the child should be kept in the regular classroom as long as possible. In severe cases, placement in a special class or in a home or hospital teaching program may be indicated.

Muscular dystrophy. Muscular dystrophy is a progressive disease of the voluntary muscles such as the arm, thigh, and calf muscles. The internal muscles, such as the diaphragm, are not affected in muscular dystrophy. Muscle fibers are replaced by fatty tissue causing a weakness of the muscles but a continued healthy appearance of the child. The small muscles of the hand are usually the last to be affected. Usually the muscles on both sides of the body are affected equally, leading to a symmetrical weakening and wasting of muscle tissue.

Muscular dystrophy is found throughout the world. Its cause is ascribed to an inherited characteristic coming from either parent. The exact nature of this inheritance is not known at present. Males are affected from five to six times as often as females. Children afflicted with muscular dystrophy rarely live to adulthood.

There is no classification of muscular dystrophy that is universally accepted, but the Public Health Service (1963) lists the following three types:

1. *Childhood muscular dystrophy* which often begins around three years of age. There is sometimes a pseudohypertrophy, or false enlargement, of the muscles due to the accumulation of fatty tissue.

2. *Juvenile muscular dystrophy* which, although it sometimes begins in childhood, is more likely to show up sometime in the teens or twenties. With this type, girls are affected as often as boys. There is a slow wasting of the muscles beginning in the shoulder girdle and affecting the use of the arms, or beginning in the pelvic girdle and affecting the use of the legs. Pseudohypertrophy is not common in this type of the disease.

3. *Facio-scapulo-humeral muscular dystrophy* in which the weakening begins in childhood or in early adult life and in either sex. In this type there is a grad-

ual weakening of the face muscles, the muscles of the shoulder blade, and the muscles of the upper arm. These patients can expect to live to middle ages, and their education should prepare them to earn a living if possible.

The child with muscular dystrophy should be kept as active as his physical condition will permit. Disuse of muscles may lead to more rapid deterioration. Since the child is not affected intellectually and there are no specific learning problems associated with this disorder, he should be retained in the regular classroom as long as he is physically able to adjust to the program. When he becomes so weak that he cannot participate in the regular class he may be assigned to a special education class for the physically handicapped or to the homebound tutoring program.

Other Infectious Diseases. Tuberculosis of the bone and osteomyelitis are examples of other infectious diseases having crippling effects which require special programs. Here, too, much medical progress has been made in remediation.

Other Health Impairments

Children who will be discussed in this section are those with special health problems whose weakened physical condition renders them relatively inactive or requires special consideration on the part of the schools. Children who have cardiac disorders, diabetes, nephrosis, respiratory disorders, and other limiting physical anomalies, and those who are undernourished have been termed "delicate children" or "children with low vitality."

RHEUMATIC FEVER AND CONGENITAL HEART DEFECT

Rheumatic fever is a disease characterized by inflammation in the heart, joints, brain, or all of these. It sometimes follows a streptococcus infection of the throat or scarlet fever. Only about three percent of such infections actually result in rheumatic fever. Most children who develop rheumatic fever get well completely or have so little heart damage that they are able to lead a full and normal life. Some children develop rheumatic heart disease resulting in permanent heart damage with a wide range of severity. Some children are born with an abnormality of the heart or major blood vessel near the heart which results from a failure of the heart to develop normally during the prenatal period.

Most children with heart conditions are able to attend the regular school as long as the teacher is aware of the condition and is able to follow the physician's recommendations in controlling the activity of the child. If the child is confined to the home for certain periods, a home teacher is provided.

DIABETES

Diabetes is a metabolic disturbance wherein the liver is unable to utilize and properly store the body sugar. This condition results when the pancreas is unable to produce a sufficient amount of the hormone insulin.

Diabetes is rather rare in children, with incidence of 1 in about 2,500. The incidence increases with age. In the 60–70 age group the incidence is one in 50. Heredity plays a major role in diabetes with over 80 percent having positive family histories. In adults, it occurs more frequently in women than men. There is no significant sex difference in children.

The diabetic child is treated by controlling his diet and giving him periodic injections of insulin. If the treatment regimen is adhered to the child will be able to lead a normal life. The child with diabetes can normally be educated in the regular grades. In severe cases placement in special classes for the physically handicapped or on a home tutoring program may be indicated.

NEPHROSIS

The word nephrosis simply means condition of the kidney and refers to a disturbance of kidney function especially the renal tubules. This condition is also known as Bright's disease, since Richard Bright differentiated this kidney dysfunction while practicing in London in 1827. It is noninflammatory and results in the escape of large amounts of protein molecules from the blood into the urine. As a result of this loss of protein into the urine, large quantities of water accumulate in the body and a generalized swelling, called *edema,* ensues. Despite the fact that little is known concerning the cause(s) of nephrosis or the membrane leakage, great advances have been made in treatment over the past fifteen years.

Nephrosis is most prevalent in the age period from 18 months to four years. Susceptibility in new cases may go up to 70 years. It occurs about twice as frequently in boys as in girls and has no significant preference as to climate, geography, or race. With onsets and remissions it can be a lifelong problem. The mortality rate of children due to nephrosis is continually lessening and although still a serious disease, the prognosis for the future is optimistic.

RESPIRATORY DISORDERS

Respiratory disorders are debilitating in children and rank very high in disease incidence. Physicians see more patients suffering from respiratory diseases than from any other single group of ailments. More school absence is due to respiratory diseases than all other causes combined. These diseases range from the common cold and influenza to the more chronic forms of cystic fibrosis and asthma. Brief mention here needs to be made of the more chronic disorders affecting children: *cystic fibrosis, asthma,* and *tuberculosis.*

Cystic fibrosis. Cystic fibrosis is an inherited disorder of the pancreas causing a chronic infection and obstructive process in the lungs. Although considerable progress has been made in the treatment of cystic fibrosis, few children survive beyond adolescence. Of those who attend school the majority can be adequately provided for in the regular classroom with limited physical participation. Those who cannot attend school may be placed in the homebound instruction program.

Asthma. Asthma is a disease of the bronchial tubes of the lungs marked by attacks of difficult breathing. These attacks are usually more distressing than dangerous and can be relieved by medical treatment. Most asthmatics are allergic to one or more substances that enter the body from the outside. These substances include certain foods, feathers, fur, powders, pollens, and air pollutants. Ragweed pollen can cause hay fever and asthma at the same time. Asthmatic children may be found in special schools, special classes, homebound and hospital programs, and regular classrooms depending on the degree of severity of the asthma and the physical condition of the child.

Tuberculosis. Children with tuberculosis have been confined to sanatoriums or hospitals during the active stages, and education has been furnished them in these residential centers. With advances in the medical treatment of tuberculosis and the efforts of the National Tuberculosis and Health Association, this disease is gradually coming under control. The number of children with tuberculosis in sanatoriums and special schools is decreasing while those who have contracted the disease can now be treated early and effectively in short periods of time and returned to the regular grades. It is anticipated that the need for special education for tubercular children will diminish further.

Personal and Social Adjustment

In working with the crippled, one of the most difficult tasks is personality adjustment. It is heartwarming to see a child crippled in body but with a friendly, cheerful disposition and a zest for doing the things which he can do. Many of these children have found a good adjustment to their way of life and a means of adapting to what could be great frustration (Cruickshank, 1952).

On the other hand, the group as a whole shows a greater tendency toward a personalized, introspective view of life with concern over the effect of the disability. Closely related to this are the findings of Barker et al (1953), who have surveyed the studies on the adjustment of physically handicapped individuals. Many of the investigations were carried out on adults but some included children. From these studies on crippled children there appears to be some evidence for the following generalizations:

1. Many of the studies found that physically disabled children, more frequently than normal children, exhibit behavior which is commonly termed maladjusted. It should be remembered that even in those studies which found greater maladjustment among the crippled, 35 to 45 percent of the physically handicapped children were just as well adjusted as physically nonhandicapped children. We can conclude that, in addition to crippling, there are other variables operative which could cause maladjustment.

2. The kinds of maladjusted behavior exhibited were not necessarily peculiar to the physically handicapped. Any type of maladjustment found among the physically handicapped was also found among the nonhandicapped. If anything, there is probably more withdrawing behavior than aggressive behavior, a little more timidity, and a little more self-consciousness among the handicapped than among the nonhandicapped.

3. There did not seem to be much evidence of a relationship between the kind of physical handicap and the kind of maladjustment. The same kind of physical handicap results in varying types of maladjustment, and different kinds of physically handicapped individuals can be found with the same maladjustment.

4. The person with a long history of physical handicap has a greater amount of maladjustment than the person with a short history of physical handicap. At the adolescent-adult level, personalities are fairly well formed. A physically disabling condition incurred at that age probably does not change the personality to any great extent.

5. The attitudes of the parents toward their crippled children, whether rejecting or overprotecting, tend to be more extreme than their attitudes toward normal children. They usually overprotect more than reject and are inclined to press for greater accomplishments.

In general the studies have not revealed important factors in adjustment and maladjustment of crippled children. The problems of adjustment faced by the crippled and those faced by the noncrippled differ more in quantity than in quality, for both are barriers to physical accomplishment and both necessitate establishing goals within one's ability to achieve. The greater restriction to their activity and the lowered frustration tolerance of the handicapped, however, make necessary more careful control of the environment and greater help in making the psychological and emotional adjustments necessary.

On the basis of case studies and comparative studies available, one can speculate on some of the factors involved.

MOTIVATION

Like the nonhandicapped, the crippled have certain hopes and aspirations which determine the direction of their drives. Their basic needs are much the same as a normal child's, but their means of satisfying them must be different. They sometimes require help in finding realistic ways to attain certain satisfactions which are within their ability. It is the gap between their ability to perform and their aspirations which creates tension, frustration, unhappiness, and unfortunate compensatory behavior. It might be well to outline a few examples of basic needs which both crippled and noncrippled experience.

Affection and Recognition. To be recognized as a worthwhile individual is one of the most universal desires of mankind. Whatever his age, station, or condition, an individual seeks approval from others. Because society has placed a premium on physical beauty, strength, and ability, it is easy for a crippled child to devaluate himself because he does not have these qualities. He sometimes needs help in realizing that while he lacks these qualities he has others which also are of value. The fact that he is inferior in some ways does not make him inferior as a person. He may need more than the usual assurance, in word or deed, that he is loved for himself as a unique individual.

Self-Realization. The need to overcome obstacles, to do something well, to gain self-esteem is also very strong in our culture. Steering a crippled child's efforts in a direction where he can succeed and giving him a feeling of accomplishment may help him to satisfy this motive of self-realization.

A person's body is something he can never get away from, and quite understandably a child's concept of his *self* is greatly influenced by the concept he has of his body: his *body image.* Thus, if there is shame or disgust or fear in his attitude toward his body, this same attitude is likely to attach itself to his concept of himself as a person. He often needs help and guidance in integrating a physical disability into a healthy self-concept.

Security. There are many kinds of security—physical security, emotional security, social security. A crippling condition may make a child vulnerable in any of these areas. Physically he has many obstacles and threatening situations; emotionally he may be subject to doubts about himself and his abilities; socially he has to compete in limited areas for recognition and approval and is often uncertain as to how others may react to him.

Because of the child's inability to gain a normal feeling of security, and because often he has been overprotected at home, there is a tendency for him to rely on the protectiveness of other people and to prolong his dependency. This reaction is a normal consequence of the striving for a feeling of security. Educational efforts at home and at school should be directed toward substituting more mature and desirable ways of gaining security. Even though one cannot gain physical independence, he can do much to approximate independence, since after all, the feeling of security is a psychological phenomenon rather than purely a physical one.

FRUSTRATION

Although the crippled child has the same needs as other children, his means of satisfying them are more limited. In addition, secondary needs and means of satisfying the more basic motives are developed by the values and aspirations of the culture in which a child finds himself. Whereas the nonhandicapped child experiences many obstacles in his environment which thwart or frustrate the fulfillment of his strivings, the crippled child has two types of obstacles: (1) the usual ones within the environment which are faced by all children, and (2) the crippling condition which poses difficulties over and above those faced by other children. It is sometimes said that crippled children have a low frustration tolerance, but the opposite may actually be the case. When frustration appears, it may not be that the threshold of frustration was low but rather that the frustrating stimuli were very high.

The primitive response to frustration is physical aggression, but children learn from the cradle up that aggression will not be tolerated by others. Thus the child learns to substitute other types of response—some better, some worse—by which to relieve the tension caused by frustration. The problem of frustration will be discussed in greater detail in Chapter 13. It is sufficient here to recognize that frustration is the result of a discrepancy between the goals set by the child or by society and his ability to achieve those goals. When such a discrepancy creates frustration, a crippled child (like anyone else) may respond in one or several of the following ways:

1. He may allow his frustration to make him *aggressive,* if not physically, then verbally.
2. He may *blame other people.*

3. He may *repress his desires* and superficially accept the situation without efforts at other forms of adjustment.

4. He may *withdraw into fantasy.*

5. He may react against the original goal and say it is not worth achieving, degrading others who achieve it (*reaction formation*).

6. He may *regress* into less mature modes of behavior, demanding more help from others.

7. He may *compensate* for his disability by finding an alternate interest which will satisfy the same motives.

COMPENSATION

Compensating for one deficiency by exaggerating abilities in another area often provides much needed satisfaction. Most of us compensate in some direction or other, but we have a wider range of abilities and activities on which to draw. Once these children achieve success, they usually become more objective toward their physical handicaps and are willing to accept them. If they cannot achieve in any area, they do not obtain the satisfaction needed for adjustment.

There has been a tendency to feel that crippled children can compensate for their handicaps by high academic achievement. A number of men who had physical defects did become mental giants, but some parents and schools have pushed children too hard in this area. Not all children can achieve in intellectual pursuits. Perhaps this is not the direction of compensation for them. Some may gain satisfaction from social and personal achievement, others in aesthetics. All that can be said in this respect is that attempts should be made to determine the areas in which these children can really achieve to their own satisfaction.

IMPORTANCE OF THE HOME CONTACTS

In studying crippled children an analysis of the home must be made. It is difficult for a parent to accept a handicapped child, especially at the time the handicap is first discovered. This is a major trauma for parents. Should they institutionalize the child or keep him at home? How will the other children in the family be affected? What goes on in the minds of parents and in their dreams is not known. Teachers sometimes see just the end result, the oversolicitousness or apparent rejection by the parents. An educational program cannot be organized without taking into consideration what has happened to both child and parents during the child's infancy and early childhood. That is the important age for socialization, since the factors of personal security, self-concept, and a feeling of belonging are important in adjustment. If a child has good personal security and stability during the first seven years of life, he can accept many frustrations.

Pupils cannot all be treated alike in school. If the child has been rejected and is insecure, the teacher must compensate for the home and find ways for him to feel accepted and secure. If the child has had too much attention at home and has security but no independence, the teacher must use "scientific neglect," which is neglect according to a plan and not based on feelings and emotions.

THE ROLE OF THE SCHOOL

Can a child develop better adjustment in a school for crippled children or is it better for him to be in classes for normal children when possible? Little evidence for either point of view is forthcoming. The consensus of opinion, however, is that he should be placed with normal children unless other factors contraindicate such placement.

Force (1956), studying the social acceptance and social relationship of physically handicapped children who were educated in classes for normal children, found that the orthopedically handicapped children were chosen fewer times as playmates, friends, and workmates than other children. This finding, although showing lack of popularity of crippled children in regular grades, does not necessarily indicate that they would be better accepted if they were in a special class for crippled children.

Naturally, crippled children in a class for normal children face certain kinds of frustration which do not exist in a special class. They cannot play like other children and with other children in games requiring mobility such as football or baseball. In a special class, games and activities are designed for children with little mobility; hence the problem does not appear. It is likely that the most realistic program for crippled children will be a combination of (1) association with other children with handicaps for the purpose of giving them insight into the problems and achievements of the handicapped and a sense of belongingness to one group, and (2) association with nonhandicapped children so that they will learn about the activities of normal children. When this group becomes too frustrating, they can identify with the handicapped for their own security. When they attain security and some independence, they can then tolerate the problems which arise when they are with nonhandicapped children. Both environments are probably more desirable than either one alone.

Educational Provisions

The reader will surmise from the foregoing discussion that the education of crippled children (excluding those with cerebral palsy) and children with special health problems is not as "special" from the school's point of view as is the education of other types of exceptional children. The provisions which have to be made are for physical, medical, and health reasons, rather than for the promotion of academic accomplishments. This fact is readily understandable when we consider that a child who has been crippled by muscular dystrophy is not necessarily affected in the way he learns to read or write or study history. He may have psychological and emotional hurdles to clear, but the learning process is the same in him as in children who are not crippled. The adjustments necessary are physical and emotional rather than educational. If he is unable to hold his book or to write because of the physical handicap, it becomes necessary to develop devices which will facilitate his holding a book or communicating on paper. In other words, the "special" part of the school becomes an adaptation of the physical surroundings for the facilitation of learning, rather than the devising of special methods of teaching, such as braille for the blind.

SPECIAL ADAPTATIONS AND MODIFICATIONS

Educational programs in special schools and special classes can justify themselves only when the necessary adaptations and modifications cannot be accomplished in the regular grades. Because of the heterogeneity of crippling conditions it is difficult to describe facilities for all of the children. One child may be crippled in one arm, another in both arms, and another in both legs but not in the arms. One is mobile in the classroom, another is mobile on crutches, and still another is confined to a wheel chair. Some of the conditions are of long standing; others may be of short duration. With these differences in physical abilities in mind it becomes obvious that we can consider here only the more general types of modification.

School Housing. Some school buildings with slippery floors, swinging doors, easily overturned equipment, stairways to maneuver, and other features which are taken in stride by the vigorous nonhandicapped child are not suitable for crippled children. If a regular school is to enroll crippled children in either regular or special classes, or if a special school is designed, it will be necessary to make adjustments in the physical plant for them. Ramps, elevators, sturdy equipment, hand rails, wide hallways, and spacious classrooms are designed to encourage the child to be as independent as possible and to promote freedom of movement and physical activity. In addition, lavatories should be readily available and equipped with hand rails and other aids to facilitate independence. In new schools or remodeled older ones doors should be wide enough for wheel chairs, floors should be covered with rubber tile or other non-skid surfaces, and there should be sufficient storage space for wheel chairs and other equipment.

Transportation. The transportation phase of the program for crippled children and those with health problems is expensive. Most of these children will require transportation to and from school, and being scattered in many areas of the city, they will have to be transported for some distance. This means providing facilities for loading some of the children into the bus and arranging their seating for comfort, especially if they have severe handicaps.

Special Equipment. In most of the schools for crippled children special rooms for physical therapy and occupational therapy are equipped with necessary materials used in the treatment of muscle disabilities and in improving motor coordination. Special chairs and cut-out tables which will support a child as he sits or stands are common classroom equipment. Sometimes such equipment has to be made to specifications for a particular child if the physician in charge recommends special supports in his chair or table.

In addition to the modifications necessary in the gross physical environment, the teacher utilizes numerous aids and devices for instructional use. All of these pieces of equipment have special purposes: book racks for children who cannot hold books, ceiling projectors for children in bed in hospitals or at home, electric typewriters with remote control devices for children in bed, cots for special rest periods, and so on. What is actually needed in a particular special class depends upon the children in the class. The child who has to have support as he stands needs a standing table. The child who cannot use his hands to turn pages needs an automatic page turner. The child who can barely use his fingers to type needs an electric typewriter. The child who cannot follow a line or hold a pencil firmly needs a pencil holder or needs guides in writing. Special equipment is usually obtained only when there is a specific requirement for it since it is just an aid and has to be selected on an individual rather than a group basis.

MEDICAL SUPERVISION

Children are assigned to schools and classes for the crippled and for special health supervision on the basis of medical recommendations. The school authorities are responsible for the total program of the child, which includes not only the classroom instruction but also the child's health program. If the physician has recommended the child for a special class he has specifically prescribed that the child is to have rest periods and not become fatigued, or that his diet is to be controlled according to his physical needs, or that a particular postural aid is to be used to correct certain deformities. A teacher organizes her program with health and physical requirements in mind, since it is for health and physical reasons that the child has been placed in that particular class.

Because of the heterogenous nature of the group of children in these special classes, and because of the wide range of adaptations necessary for varying abilities and achievements, much of the work is individualized. This situation, however, should not exclude group instruction for certain activities. For example, many of the children have limited firsthand experiences about their community or about the world. Secondary experiences are therefore necessary, especially through the use of visual aids, and particularly appropriate educational films and television. Carefully planned trips to centers of interest are used in many classes for crippled children.

The attitude of the teacher in these classes toward each child's personality and adjustment is of utmost importance. She must not only understand the physical problems and their requirements but also be an expert in motivating the child who is depressed and withdrawn, handling the tantrums which sometimes follow frustration, and in general promoting the personal and emotional adjustment of these children.

EDUCATIONAL FACILITIES

To provide for the wide range and combinations of intellectual and physical disabilities found among the physically handicapped, different kinds of educational provisions have evolved. While some cerebral-palsied children with adequate intelligence and a mild physical handicap can adjust in the regular grades, a totally dependent mentally retarded child with severe physical disability will require permanent custodial care. The following types of facilities have been organized for the physically handicapped child.

Home Instruction. This type of instruction is provided for children who are physically disabled to the extent that they cannot attend a school, or who live where a school suitable for them is unavailable. Ordinarily children with normal intelligence are offered this service, and in some situations the educable mentally retarded child with severe physical disabilities is offered education by a home instructor.

Hospital Schools. These schools generally enroll physically handicapped children during short-term diagnostic and treatment periods. The children with severe physical handicaps but with normal or near normal intelligence are usually admitted to such schools.

Institutions for the Mentally Retarded. Totally dependent mentally retarded children of all degrees of physical handicaps and trainable mentally retarded children with severe physical handicaps require care and management in an institution if the parents are unable to provide the proper nursing or custodial care at home. No child should be put in this category until he is old enough to be properly diagnosed, which in most instances is not possible before the age of 3 or 4.

Sheltered-Care Facilities. Normal or near normal children with severe physical handicaps who cannot be taken care of at home are provided with sheltered-care (residential) facilities and are offered education in these centers.

Special Schools or Classes. Special schools or special classes in regular schools are the most common type of facility for physically handicapped children. In many cities these are organized as schools for crippled children and include those with cerebral palsy. The schools accommodate the normal and slow-learning child with mild and moderate physical handicaps, and if they have the facilities, as many of them do, they accommodate the severely physically handicapped.

Regular School Classes. The large majority of children with normal intelligence and mild physical handicaps attend regular classes with nonhandicapped children.

Itinerant or Remedial Teacher Program. Whether a physically handicapped child is in a regular grade, or in a special school or class, or in a hospital class, he is offered remediation for special learning disabilities. The most common service is speech habilitation, which can be accomplished in the home or in whatever school the child is attending. Provisions for special remediation for other forms of learning disabilities (such as those in language, reading, writing, or arithmetic) are not as common but should apply to physically handicapped children who have learning disabilities (as defined in Chapter 2) or to children whose learning disability is the result of cerebral dysfunction.

EDUCATIONAL PROGRAMS

Educational procedures for the physically handicapped include (1) the organization of programs for different ages and levels: nursery and kindergarten, elementary school, and secondary school; (2) the adaptation and modification of physical facilities and plant to accommodate children with physical disabilities; (3) provisions for general educational activities offered all children; and (4) special individual and small-group remedial instruction for speech, language, reading, writing, and arithmetic disabilities.

The Beginning Years. As soon as a child is known to be physically handicapped, whether at 6 months or 2 years of age, steps should be taken to guide the parents in understanding and training him. Although most of the diagnoses are made before school age, and the services of physicians, nurses, and social agencies in the community have been mobilized, there should be some coordination with the school in which the child will be enrolled later. At this stage the parents should be helped to understand the disability—how it affects mobility, the natural history of its development, and its possible effects on intellectual development. The parents require guidance in facilitating motor activity of the child at a young age, and in developing babbling, understanding of speech, and other forms of communication. Extra effort is needed on the part of the parents and siblings in developing the child's independence in motor and other activities. Although it is quicker and easier for the parents of a physically handicapped child to do things for him than to teach and encourage him to do things for himself, it is important for the child to function as adequately as possible within the limits of his condition. Wherever possible he should be helped to approximate the abilities of the nonhandicapped child in self-care, play, speech, motor activity, intellectual development, and social and emotional adjustment, even though he cannot attain normal development in all of these areas. At this age level the immediate purpose is to make the child as self-sufficient as possible before he enters school.

Preschool Programs. Nursery schools and kindergartens have been established in hospitals, in clinic schools, and in private and public schools for 3- to 6-year-old children. The general program of the preschool is designed to:

1. Develop motor abilities in the child through special materials, special aids and supports for mobility, and through special methods provided by the physiotherapist, the occupational therapist, the recreational therapist, and the special teacher. In the school situation the teacher is the coordinator of the program even though specific prescriptions are given by the attending pediatrician or orthopedic specialist.
2. Develop language and speech, especially in the cerebral-palsied child, since this is one area where the majority are retarded or defective. This includes the ability to perceive oral language and to express it, to perceive visual stimuli and interpret them, and to express oneself in motor terms. The latter includes both speech and gestures. This phase of the child's development is assisted by a speech correctionist, the parents, and the special teacher.
3. Develop in the child the psychological factors of visual and auditory perception, discrimination, memory, and other factors considered intellectual.

These functions are best developed through the school program which in-cludes language usage, listening, planning, problem solving, dramatization, imagination and creative expression (through art and music media), creative rhythms, visual and auditory memory and discrimination, and perception. At this age level an environment with toys, sand tables, doll corners, and so forth, is provided so that the children will learn to respond to the attractions of the environment both physically and mentally. Through the addition of materials and the verbal and manual suggestions of the special teacher the children are helped to progress from one developmental stage to the next.

4. Develop social and emotional adequacy in the child at home and in the school by providing him with opportunities for acquiring emotional security, belongingness, and independence. The school situation is probably superior to the home in not overprotecting the child and in giving him opportunities to do things himself. The environment of the school which includes other children of the same age gives the child an opportunity to learn to interact with others, to share, and to cooperate. It offers him examples of activities which he can imitate, and at the same time the protection and help which he needs when he really needs it.

The Elementary School Program. The elementary school program for physically handicapped children with slow learning ability or average intelligence is an extension of the preschool program in provisions for special help, physiotherapy, occupational therapy, recreational therapy, and speech correction. These services generally continue as long as the child is able to profit from them.

An elementary class of ten children would probably consist of six cerebral-palsied children, three orthopedically impaired (muscular-dystrophy, spina bifida, bone, joint, or other congenital deformity, hemophilia) and possibly one with some other health problem. The ages of the children range from 6 to 10 or 12, or at the upper elementary age group from 10 or 12 to 15 or 16. Their men-tal levels range from about 5 years to above their chronological ages of 15 or 16. It is difficult to group physically handicapped children for instruction since a wide range of abilities and disabilities is usually represented in one class. Within the class individual adaptation of instruction is made, or at best two or three children can be grouped for instruction.

The curriculum is similar to that used for all children. However, because of physical limitations, sensory defects, some intellectual limitations, and asso-ciated psychological disabilities, many physically handicapped children are re-tarded educationally. Reading progress is hampered by the disabilities men-tioned and by learning disabilities, which are discussed in Chapter 2. Writing is impossible for some and awkward and difficult for many. Larger pencils and paper with widely spaced lines are often provided to facilitate learning to write for those who can achieve in this skill. Schonell includes in the curriculum writing, dramatization, recitation and singing, free activity, nature study, news period, English, literature, art and handwork, history, geography, science, reading, and arithmetic.

The Secondary School and College Programs. Those physically handicapped children who are able to achieve academically may attend secondary schools and colleges. At this level they have acquired some degree of independence and have learned to adjust to their physical handicap. Secondary schools do not change their programs of instruction for these children but attempt to make it possible for them to attend, even in wheel chairs, by providing ramps for them to use.

Some universities, especially since World War II, have made a special effort to provide facilities so that very severely handicapped individuals with superior intelligence can attend college. Notable is the University of Illinois at Urbana, Illinois, where a special division for physically handicapped students has been organized, with living quarters, ramps, special transportation, and special parking areas. The students take courses in many departments of the University. Special recreational facilities are provided for those in wheel chairs. Basketball teams for wheel-chair students (such as the well-known Gizz Kids) compete with other wheel-chair students from other universities.

AUXILIARY EDUCATIONAL PROGRAM

In addition to the educational program generally supplied by the special teacher, a comprehensive program requires the assistance of parent counselors, speech correctionists, recreation and physical education specialists, and a variety of medical specialists. Such a team is necessary to cope with the variety of multiple handicaps found in physically handicapped children.

SUMMARY

1. Children considered in this chapter are those who are crippled, deformed, or are otherwise physically handicapped (exclusive of auditory and visual handicaps), and those who have other health problems which interfere with their normal functioning in a regular classroom.
2. Neurologically impaired children are (a) those who are cerebral palsied (the largest group of physically handicapped children), (b) those with epilepsy, (c) those with spina bifida, and (d) other brain involvements.
3. Orthopedically handicapped are children with (a) poliomyelitis, (b) hemophilia, (c) arthritis, (d) muscular dystrophy, and (e) congenital and traumatic conditions.

4. Other health-impaired children include those with (a) rheumatic fever, (b) diabetes, (c) nephrosis, (d) respiratory disorders, and (e) tuberculosis.
5. Special educational provisions are made for these children in hospital classes, convalescent home classes, sanatoriums, residential schools, and in their own homes as well as in day classes in special buildings, in centers or units in the regular schools, and in single multigrade classes.
6. Educational adaptations are made by changing the physical environment in such a way as to facilitate the educational program.
7. In addition to the adaptation of the physical environment, adaptations are made for different levels of mental ability, special remedial programs for learning disabilities in speech, language, reading, writing, spelling, arithmetic, and other school subjects.
8. Physically handicapped children experience the same needs for recognition, security, and self-esteem as do normal children, and require guidance in adjusting to their handicap and finding compensatory satisfactions.

REFERENCES

Barker, R. G.; Wright, Beatrice A.; Meyerson, L.; and Gonick, Mollie. 1953. *Adjustment to Physical Handicap and Illness: A Survey of the Social Psychology of Physique and Disability,* No. 55, Rev. New York: Social Science Research Council.

Cardwell, Viola E. 1956. *Cerebral Palsy: Advances in Understanding and Care.* New York: Association for the Aid of Crippled Children.

Clarke, Ann M., and Clarke, A. D. B. 1965. *Mental Deficiency,* Rev. ed. New York: The Free Press.

Cruickshank, W. M. 1952. A Study of the Relation of Physical Disability to Social Adjustment. *American Journal of Occupational Therapy* 6 (May-June): 100 109.

Cruickshank, W. M.; Bice, H. V.; and Wallen, N. E. 1957. *Perception and Cerebral Palsy.* Syracuse, New York: Syracuse University Press.

Denhoff, E., and Robinault, Isabel. 1960. *Cerebral Palsy and Related Disorders.* New York: McGraw-Hill.

Fay, T. 1953. Desperately Needed Research in Cerebral Palsy. *Cerebral Palsy Review* 14 (March-April): 4–15 passim.

Fish, L. 1955. Deafness in Cerebral Palsied School Children. *Lancet* 2: 370–371.

Force, D. G., Jr. 1956. Social Status of Physically Handicapped Children. *Journal of Exceptional Children* 23 (December): 104–107, 132.

Hill, R. H. 1965. Arthritis in Children. *Psychotherapy Information Bulletin* (The Canadian Arthritis and Rheumatism Society) 8 (No. 1).

Hohman, L. B., and Freedheim, D. K. 1958. Further Studies on Intelligence Levels in Cerebral Palsied Children. *American Journal of Physical Medicine* 37 (April): 90–97.

Hopkins, T. W.; Bice, H. V.; and Colton, Kathryn C. 1954. *Evaluation and Education of the Cerebral Palsied Child.* Arlington, Virginia: International Council for Exceptional Children.

Illingworth, R. S. (ed.). 1958. *Recent Advances in Cerebral Palsy.* London: J. & A. Churchill.

Ingraham, F. D. 1944. *Spina Bifida and Cranium Bifidum.* Cambridge, Massachusetts: Harvard University Press.

Katz, A. H. 1970. *Hemophilia; A Study in Hope and Reality.* Springfield, Illinois: Charles C. Thomas.

Meyers, Patricia. 1963. A Comparison of Language Disabilities of Young Spastic and Athetoid Children. Unpublished doctoral dissertation, University of Texas.

Nielsen, Helle H. 1966. *A Psychological Study of Cerebral Palsied Children.* Copenhagen: Munksgaard.

Penfield, W., and Rasmussen, T. 1952. *The Cerebral Cortex of Man.* New York: Macmillan.

Penfield, W., and Roberts, L. 1959. *Speech and Brain Mechanisms.* Princeton, New Jersey: Princeton University Press.

Public Health Service, Department of Health, Education, and Welfare. 1963. *Muscular Dystrophy.* Washington, D.C.: The Service.

Schonell, F. E. 1956. *Educating Spastic Children.* Edinburgh: Oliver and Boyd.

Solenberger, Edith R. 1918. *Public School Classes for Crippled Children.* U.S. Department of the Interior Bulletin No. 10. Washington, D.C.: Government Printing Office.

Strauss, A. A., and Lehtinen, Laura. 1947. *Psychopathology and Education of the Brain-Injured Child.* New York: Grune and Stratton.

Taylor, Edith M. 1959. *Psychological Appraisal of Children with Cerebral Defects.* Cambridge, Massachusetts: Harvard University Press.

Telford, C. W., and Sawrey, J. M. 1967. *The Exceptional Individual.* Englewood Cliffs, New Jersey: Prentice-Hall.

United Cerebral Palsy Research and Educational Foundation. 1958. *Program for Calendar Year 1958.* New York: The Foundation.

THIRTEEN

CHILDREN

WITH

BEHAVIOR

DISORDERS

Behavior disorders can be defined in terms of personality dynamics or in terms of the effect of a child's behavior on himself or on other people. For purposes of this chapter a *behavior disorder* will be defined as a *deviation from age-appropriate behavior which significantly interferes with (1) the child's own growth and development and/or (2) the lives of others.*

A child who is extremely withdrawn and does not relate to other people, who does not seem to respond to his environment (even though he is average in intelligence) is one whose behavior is interfering with his own growth process. Such children have been termed "withdrawn," "neurotic," "autistic," or "schizophrenic." A child who behaves in such a way that he has repeated conflict with his siblings, parents, classmates, teachers, and community is interfering with the lives of other people. Parents call him a "bad boy." Teachers call him a "conduct problem." Social workers say he is "socially maladjusted." Psychiatrists and psychologists may say he is "emotionally disturbed." And if he comes in conflict with the law, the judge calls him "delinquent." Behavior disorders in children may be actions which retard social and emotional and sometimes educational growth, or they may be actions which are detrimental to other people.

The major difficulty in delineating behavior deviations is inherent in the use

of certain terms and concepts and appears to be related to (1) the kind of deviation under discussion, (2) the degree of deviation, (3) the situation in which the
deviation occurs, and (4) the individual who concludes that a deviation exists.
A good illustration of the multidimensional nature of behavior deviations is a
boy eating candy. Many will state, "There is nothing wrong or abnormal about
a boy eating candy," and, "Most boys eat candy; hence it is a normal activity."
But a child who ate candy he took from a shelf in a store and did not pay for
would be considered to have been stealing. A child who ate candy in a classroom when the teacher specifically prohibited eating candy in class would be
thought disobedient. A child who ate candy when he was aware that since he
had diabetes eating candy would make him sick might be considered compulsive or masochistic. Furthermore, the mother of the child who took candy from
the store shelf might think his behavior, not deviant, but an innocent response,
since he had been used to helping himself to candy when he saw it. The store-
keeper, on the other hand, would undoubtedly call it stealing, which is a form
of delinquency.

The area of behavior disorders is of interest to many professions: social work,
psychology, psychiatry, sociology, neurology, education, and related disciplines.
Education has traditionally dealt only with the mild behavior disorders, leaving
the more severe disorders to psychiatry; however, the field of mental health has
gradually moved away from a purely medical psychoanalytical approach toward
a behavioral, educational approach (Ullmann and Krasner, 1965; Glasser, 1965;
Hewett, 1968). Education meanwhile, has taken increased responsibility not only
for prevention but also for the treatment of many of the more severe behavior
disorders.

Types of Behavior Disorders

Labels for children, as indicated earlier, are usually of little value for treatment purposes. Although labels are of value in facilitating communication, for
treatment purposes it is necessary to define our categories in more behavioristic
terms. Numerous attempts have been made in various disciplines to classify
behavior disorders in children. To be useful for educational planning, any such
classification should be in terms that delineate behavior manifestations.

One perceptive classification which comes close to this was made by Hewitt
and Jenkins (1945), who analyzed 500 cases of maladjusted children referred to
child guidance clinics. By statistical means they related the patterns of maladjustment to home situations. Three patterns of maladjustment were found, each
being associated with a different home situation. From these relationships
Hewitt and Jenkins defined three types of behavior disorders:

1. *The unsocialized aggressive child* is one who defies all authority, is hostile toward authority figures (policemen, teachers, and so forth), is cruel, malicious, and assaultive, and has inadequate guilt feelings. Children of this type come from broken homes where they received no love or attention in infancy. They have developed no attachments to anyone or any group. In psychoanalytic terms they did not develop a superego or conscience.

2. *The socialized aggressive child* has the same characteristics or behavior problems as the unsocialized aggressive, but he is socialized within his peer group, usually the gang or companions, in misdemeanor and crime. Unlike the unsocialized aggressive child he had some security with the mother or mother figure in infancy, but was later rejected.

3. *The overinhibited child* is shy, timid, withdrawn, seclusive, sensitive, and submissive. He is overdependent and easily depressed. Such children in the study came from overprotective families in the higher socio-economic levels.

In terms of the behavior observed, it will be noted that categories one and two in the above classification are identical. They both display the kind of behavior which is unacceptable to society. The third category represents those children with personality problems who are overinhibited, sensitive and shy. In other words, from an observation of behavior Hewitt and Jenkins's three categories boil down to the traditional dichotomy of (a) social maladjustment (including delinquency) and (b) emotional disturbance.

The differentiation between social maladjustment and emotional disturbance is a difficult one because on the surface the behavior may look the same. It is the dynamics behind the behavior that is different. Children who are socially maladjusted display behavior which may be highly valued within a small subgroup (usually a juvenile gang or peer group) but which is not "within the range of the 'culturally permissible,' either at home, in the school, or in the community" (Mackie, Kvaraceus, and Williams, 1957). The socially maladjusted are able to adapt "on the street" with responses approved by the peer group of which they are a part (i.e., the gang), but come in conflict with parents, teachers, and others outside of their immediate peer group. These children are usually unmanageable in the home, generate problems in the school, are retarded in educational achievement, and are destructive, quarrelsome, and socially immature. They are generally characterized by a lack of anxiety and they display antisocial behavior which interferes with the lives of others. Delinquents are usually a subgroup of the socially maladjusted, "delinquent" being a legal term referring to children who have come in conflict with the law.

Emotionally disturbed children are characterized by inner tensions and anxiety, and they display neurotic and psychotic behavior. The behavior of many emotionally disturbed children also interferes with the lives of others. Where such behavior in the socially maladjusted child is characteristic of peer group behavior, in the emotionally disturbed child it is the result of inner conflicts and the inability to control anxiety. The isolate or withdrawn child would be considered emotionally disturbed because his behavior, although an attempt to avoid anxiety, actually interferes with his own growth and development.

In an attempt to bring their classification more in line with observed behavior, Quay, Morse, and Cutler (1966) have relabeled and redefined these two categories and added a third category which better describes the behavior of one group of children. They made a factor analysis of the ratings of the teachers of 441 children in classes for the emotionally disturbed. The instrument used was the Behavior Rating Check List developed originally by Peterson (1961). The sample consisted of 80 percent boys and 20 percent girls. They found three patterns of behavior clusters as follows:

1. *Conduct disorders,* sometimes referred to as unsocialized aggressive or psychopathic behavior. Included in this dimension is such behavior as defiance, disobedience, impertinence, uncooperativeness, irritability, boisterousness, attention seeking, bullying, temper tantrums, hyperactiveness, restlessness, and negativism. These maladaptive behaviors are similar to those described by Hewitt and Jenkins (1945) under the two categories they labeled as socialized and unsocialized aggressive.

2. *Personality Problem Dimension,* sometimes referred to as neurotic or overinhibited. These children were rated as being hypersensitive, shy, having feelings of inferiority, lacking in self-confidence, self-conscious, easily flustered, fearful, and anxious. Hewitt and Jenkins (1945) referred to their samples as overinhibited. Such children lacked close friendships and were overdependent and easily depressed.

3. *The Inadequate Immature Dimension.* This dimension refers to children who were rated as inattentive, sluggish, lacking interest in school, lazy, preoccupied, day dreamers, drowsy, and reticent. These children resemble categories from other classifications such as autism or a prepsychotic condition. These children appear to be less able to function in the regular classroom than children who are labeled "neurotic" or children with personality problems.

The label *delinquency* is a legal term and reserved for those youngsters whose behavior results in arrest and court action. The youngsters who were elsewhere described as "socialized aggressive" and "unsocialized aggressive" frequently display behavior that brings them in contact with the law and results in their being labeled "delinquent." After surveying the numerous definitions of delinquency Wirt and Briggs (1965) formulated a definition:

The delinquent, then, would be a person whose misbehavior is a relatively serious legal offense, which is inappropriate to his level of development; is not committed as a result of extremely low intelligent intracranial organic pathology, or severe mental or metabolic dysfunction; and is alien to the culture in which he has been reared. (p. 23)

Although this category cuts across all of the others it is very significant in the light of the marked increase in the rate of crime among the young which has increased significantly faster than the rate of population increase. Quay (1965) reports a constant increase in juvenile delinquency, as reported by the Federal Bureau of Investigation from 1953 to 1961. He reports an increase in that period of less than a decade from 300,000 to one million. Rakstis (1970) states that:

According to the Federal Bureau of Investigation juvenile arrests for serious crimes climbed 78 percent between 1960 and 1968, while the juvenile population rose only 25 percent. In 1968 youthful offenders accounted for 61 percent of all auto thefts, 54 percent of larcenies, 55 percent of burglaries, and 33 percent of robberies. (p. 21)

Characteristics of Children with Behavior Disorders

In a study by Morse, Cutler, and Fink (1964) characteristics of 441 children in programs for the emotionally disturbed were listed as follows:

1. The range of ages was from 5 to 15, with a mean for the boys of 9.4 and for the girls 9.8 years.
2. Of the group, 83.2 percent were boys and 16.8 percent were girls.
3. The teachers rated the majority of children as educationally retarded compared to their chronological-age educational-expectancy.
4. The IQ range was 68 to above 132. The majority of children had IQ's over 100.
5. More than half of the sample were classified as neurotic, with "acting out" behavior as the dominant conduct problem. Another large group was classified as "primitive neglected," or immature.

Another listing of characteristics was presented in a study by the California State Department of Education (1961). A group of emotionally handicapped and another group of non-emotionally handicapped children were identified by teachers in 1955–1956. In 1960 a follow-up of the records of these two groups was made. The significant differences between the groups led the authors to conclude that the emotionally handicapped, as compared to the normal group, were (1) seriously below average in school achievement; (2) sent to the vice-principal more often for disciplinary action; (3) more often dropped from school or left school; (4) more often absent from school without excuses; (5) more frequently sent to the health department for illness, need of rest, or discomfort; (6) more often served by school counselors; (7) more often the subject of home calls by child welfare workers and attendance officers; (8) subject to more contacts with police; (9) more likely to be on probation; (10) found more frequently to commit penal and vehicle code violation; (11) more frequently referred to local guidance clinics.

With respect to delinquency, Kvaraceus and Miller (1959) have defined delinquency as "behavior by nonadults which violates specific legal norms or norms of a particular societal institution with sufficient frequency and/or seriousness so as to provide a firm basis for legal action against the behaving individual or group."

Kvaraceus (1958) has listed eighteen characteristics which can be observed in school. He calls this compilation a "Delinquency Proneness Check List."

DELINQUENCY PRONENESS CHECK LIST

	Yes	No	Not Sure
1. Shows marked dislike for school.	....	....	....
2. Resents school routine and restriction.	....	....	....
3. Disinterested in school program.	....	....	....
4. Is failing in a number of subjects.	....	....	....
5. Has repeated one or more grades.	....	....	....
6. Attends special class for retarded pupils.	....	....	....
7. Has attended many different schools.	....	....	....
8. Intends to leave school as soon as the law allows.	....	....	....
9. Has only vague academic or vocational plans.	....	....	....
10. Has limited academic ability.	....	....	....
11. Is a child who seriously or persistently misbehaves.	....	....	....
12. Destroys school materials or property.	....	....	....
13. Is cruel and bullying on the playground.	....	....	....
14. Has temper tantrums in the classroom.	....	....	....
15. Wants to stop schooling at once.	....	....	....
16. Truants from school.	....	....	....
17. Does not participate in organized extracurricular programs.	....	....	....
18. Feels he does not "belong" in the classroom. (p. 17)	....	....	....

Kvaraceus (1971) estimates that 11 percent of children between the ages of 7 and 19 have a juvenile record. Of these there are 5 boys to 1 girl. In addition to these statistics, the delinquency rate in large cities and particularly in slum areas in large cities is high compared to that in rural districts and small towns and in neighborhoods of higher socioeconomic levels.

Factors Contributing to Behavior Disorders

There are two contrasting approaches to the study of behavior disorders. The psychodynamic group see behavior disorders as a result of intrapsychic conflicts that must be treated before the education of the child can take place. The behaviorist psychologists, especially those dealing with operant conditioning, recognize that complex historical events determine behavior, but they feel that modification of behavior is not dependent on the reconstruction of the past or on inferences about the nature of the cognitive or affectional state of the individual. Why a fear exists and how it was started is of little concern to the behaviorist when he is attempting to remove or extinguish the fear. *What* behavior the child exhibits is the concern of the behavior modifier rather than the *why*. Regardless of the differences in philosophy, the main reason for studying factors that produce behavior disorders in children is that of prevention.

There have been many explanations for deviations in behavior. Only a few will be mentioned here: (1) psychological factors, (2) psychosocial factors, and (3) possible organic factors.

PSYCHOLOGICAL FACTORS IN BEHAVIOR DISORDERS

The laboratory research of Pavlov (1928) in Russia led to theories of behavior disorders as resulting from frustration. While conditioning dogs to react to specific stimuli, Pavlov and his colleagues found that the dogs developed what Pavlov called *experimental neurosis* when their discriminative capacity was strained. These experiments have been repeated with other animals and with children with the same results. Subjects, when faced with insoluble problems, have been shown to exhibit behavior deviations and also lose habits they had earlier acquired (Hilgard and Marquis, 1940; and Maier, 1949). These observations suggested the hypothesis that frustrating experiences lead to *aggression, regression,* and/or *resignation.*

Aggression. Dollard, et al (1939) postulated the well-known frustration-aggression hypothesis. They explain that when goal-directed behavior meets interference the individual is frustrated, and this frustration leads to aggression—striking, fighting, abusive language, and anger. In most instances the aggression reduces the tension aroused by the frustration and no permanent personality changes occur. In children, aggression takes the form of hostility and destructiveness. Play therapy is an attempt to allow the child to express his aggressions in a controlled situation.

Regression. Barker, Dembo, and Lewin (1941) demonstrated with young children that frustration can lead to regression, defined as returning to an earlier form of behavior. In their experiment they allowed children to play with toys, then restricted them to one part of the room with only some of the toys. The children could see the toys in the other part of the room but were prevented by a wire screen from obtaining them. According to the authors some of the children showed aggression, but the majority regressed one and one-half years in their play activities. This was interpreted as regression to earlier forms of play caused by frustration. It is possible that dependence on the mother, whining, excessive crying, infantile speech, and nonconstructive play are examples of regressive behavior caused by frustration.

Resignation. Maier (1949) cites resignation as another reaction to frustration. This behavior deviation seems to be a loss of motivation and inability to respond constructively following repeated frustration. It is characterized by a *lack* of overt behavior rather than a positive action such as aggression or regression. It is one way of avoiding further frustration.

The Concept of Discrepancy. Although experimentation with humans under controlled frustrating situations is not always practical, there are, as has been indicated, many analogies from everyday life and human experimentation in which the behavior deviations and problems of children can be explained as responses to frustration. When children or adults are placed in situations which are too difficult for their capabilities or in which they are unable to satisfy their motives and drives, they are frustrated and behavior deviations of aggression, regression, compulsive behavior, fixations, resignations, or other out-of-the-ordinary or abnormal reactions may result. When children are unable to choose between one of two courses of action (the proverbial donkey between two bales of hay), or when the courses of action do not reduce their tensions, they are frustrated and react in an emotional way—by temper tantrums, fighting, sulking, regressing, and other bizarre types of behavior. These situations lead to the statement that *behavior disorders are the outcome of frustration resulting from the discrepancy between the child's capacity to behave and the requirements of the environment.*

The concept of a discrepancy between the child's ability to perform and some of the requirements of the home or the school may be applicable to the situations in experiments with animals and those cited with humans. In some cases where the child is forced to attempt a task which he cannot perform he becomes tense and excited and may get angry at objects or people. Or he resorts to irrational or silly maneuvers. In many situations he escapes the requirement. For example, truancy from school is more prevalent among slow learners and among the educationally retarded than among those who are succeeding in school. Although other factors also operate in truancy, it seems apparent that when the home and school require of the child certain tasks which he cannot perform he tends to run away from the situation or become aggressive and hostile.

Many examples of situations can be given wherein the child becomes frustrated because he is unable to perform as required by parents and teachers. In one instructional period the author noticed that when a teacher was quizzing a child, first with a problem he could answer, then with a little harder one, until the question became so difficult that the child was unable to find a solution, the child diverted his own attention and the attention of the teacher by saying, "You have a pretty dress on today." This response was not a neurosis or a breakdown, but when the situation persists and the child is repeatedly taxed beyond his capacity, he may become more aggressive, or he may regress to more immature behavior. Many parents are overly ambitious for their children's progress in school. They are not satisfied with average or even above-average progress. They want their children to be top students in class even though the children do not have the capacity. Persistence in this attitude develops in the children various forms of deviant behavior. They may rebel against school and do less well than they would have otherwise, or they may withdraw from efforts to succeed.

PSYCHOSOCIAL FACTORS IN BEHAVIOR DISORDERS

Not all behavior disorders arise from frustration in an immediate situation or from the discrepancy between the child's capacity to behave and the requirements of the environment. Other factors include (1) early home experiences and (2) the social and economic aspects of the child's environment.

The psychoanalytic school initiated by Sigmund Freud has attempted to explain behavior deviations by the experiences of children at an early age. According to psychoanalytical theory certain unpleasant early experiences may become repressed in the unconscious but continue to determine behavior and deviations in behavior. Behavior disorders would be explained in these terms.

The influence of early home experience has been studied by numerous investigators. Many factors within the home, especially relations with the mother, father, and siblings, have been associated with behavior deviations. Some studies of this nature will be reviewed here to point up the connection between early home factors and maladjustment.

Child-rearing Factors. Hewitt and Jenkins (1945), discussed earlier, related their patterns of maladjustment to home conditions as an explanation of the behavior of the child. The *overinhibited child* came from restrictive families at the higher socio-economic levels. The *unsocialized aggressive* came from lower class families who had no attachments to or love from parents in early childhood. The *socialized aggressive,* who later had attachments to the gang or peer group, had security from the parents in early childhood but was later rejected.

Later Jenkins (1966) studied 500 cases from the Michigan Child Guidance Institute. He related clusters of behavior to certain types of home environments. The shy, seclusive, inhibited child tended to come from a family where both parents were present, where there was little feeling of rejection, and where the mother was not hostile toward the child. In the neurotic, over-anxious group many of the mothers were considered neurotic. The aggressive delinquent tended to come from neglectful homes and poor neighborhoods.

Many studies have shown that child-rearing methods featuring inconsistent discipline and rejection or hostility on the part of parents are positively correlated with conduct disorders. These same factors are thought to be related to many forms of personality problems. In relation to delinquency, for example, Bandura and Walters (1959) found that certain child-training factors and family interrelationships differentiated a group of aggressive boys who had come into conflict with school authorities or county probation authorities from a group of high school boys not in such conflict. They found that parent attitudes rejecting dependence, encouraging aggressiveness outside the home, and placing fewer demands for obedience, responsibility, and school achievement were significant. There was also less affection shown between father and mother and between parents and the boy.

An investigation which highlights the interplay of sociological factors with those of family life is that done by McCord and McCord (1959). Many aspects of home life and environmental influences were examined. Of significance was the frequency with which delinquency was associated with lax or erratic discipline which was punitive in nature, membership in gangs, and quarrelsome and neglecting home life. Certain constellations of factors seemed to indicate higher relationships than did single factors—for example, a quarrelsome home plus lax discipline, or a neglecting mother who provided a deviant role model and whose discipline was erratic and primitive.

Community Factors. Over and above the influence of family and home, there are other influences from the community at large which help determine the course of a child's social and emotional development. Much of the conflict with the law which arises in lower-class urban areas is complicated by community factors as well as family influences.

The classic studies of Shaw and McKay (1942) indicate that in Chicago, delinquency areas were identifiable. The highest rates were in the inner zone (the business area), the next highest in the bordering slum areas, and the next in the workingman's area. The lowest rates were in the outer zones of the city. It is in the high-delinquency areas that the criminal tradition is handed down from one generation to the next through what is known as "cultural transmission." In studies of other factors, Maccoby, Johnson, and Church (1958) found that in areas of high delinquency the community was heterogeneous in religious beliefs and ethnic background and that there was greater impersonality among the neighbors.

It is now rather widely accepted that we do not have a classless society in this country. Miller (1958), a cultural anthropologist, believes that social class status is now superseding the ethnic differences prevalent during surges of immigration to this country and that we do have a growing and distinct "lower class" with a hard core of some 15 percent of the population and probably twice that many influenced to a lesser degree by the mores of that group. Miller uses the term "lower class" in a descriptive sense rather than as a negative evaluation.

To discriminate *between* important subsegments of our society is not to discriminate *against* them. . . . [Lower-class culture is] a cultural system in its own right, with an integrity of its own, with a characteristic set of practices, focal concerns, and ways of behaving that are meaningfully and systematically related to one another rather than to corresponding features of middle-class culture. (1959, pp. 222–223)

"Lower-class" concerns center on immediate problems. Goods are to be used, money is to be spent, and life is to be lived. The focal concerns of this group, according to Miller, are: trouble, toughness, smartness, excitement, fate, and autonomy. It should be pointed out that these concerns of "getting into trouble," "staying out of trouble," being masculine and strong and able to endure pain and fatigue, outsmarting others, being one's own boss, and so forth, rather than the economic factor of being rich or poor are what differentiate this group. This lower-class subculture can be further subdivided into lesser subcultures, one of which is the delinquent gang.

Many sociologists believe that the social values of lower-class culture are an inversion of middle-class standards and derive from the disadvantageous position in which the members of the lower class find themselves. Cohen (1955) has dwelt at length on a delinquent subculture characterized by elements of nonutility, negativism, and maliciousness, which he postulates is a reaction against middle-class standards by a lower-class group placed in a disadvantageous position because of their social status. He states:

This . . . may require a certain measure of reaction-formation, going beyond indifference to active hostility and contempt for all those who do not share his subculture. . . . The problems of adjustment to which the delinquent subculture is a response are determined, in part, by those very values which respectable society holds most valid. (pp. 136–137)

School Factors. The factors in the home and the community which influence behavior in children are reflected in the school—the community agency which deals with all children. Teachers must understand these influences if they are to handle effectively children whose maladjustments stem largely from these out-of-school factors such as a conflict between the subculture of the home and the middle-class values of the school. Although the social and cultural forces in a society are beyond the control of a school, the school can contribute to the home and the community through the activities of children. It is this role that the school must play to ameliorate or compensate for the detrimental influences of the home and community on the mental health of children.

PHYSIOLOGICAL FACTORS IN BEHAVIOR DISORDERS

Neither psychological factors nor psychosocial factors explain all forms of behavior deviations. Central nervous system dysfunction is considered by many to be another cause. There is probably no question about the role of cerebral dysfunctions in some cases of behavior deviations. In addition to brain dysfunction, many physiological conditions may exist which are not detected and corrected. Physiological factors have sometimes been noted to relate to irritability, lack of school progress, and other conduct disorders.

Strauss and Lehtinen (1947), Cruickshank et al (1961), and others discussed in Chapter 2 ascribe hyperactivity and perceptual-motor problems to brain damage, even though it is difficult in most cases to find definite signs of neurological damage. Morse, Cutler, and Fink (1964) asked the teachers of the 441 children in their study to indicate which children in their classes for the emotionally handicapped had neurological impairments. They found that only 7 percent of the children were so designated and concluded that organicity was not a major cause of emotional disturbance as viewed by the teachers. It is very possible, however, that additional children have undiagnosed neurological dysfunctions or minimal brain disorders. Irritability caused by incipient rheumatic fever or glandular disturbances such as hyperthyroidism may be the basis of hyperactivity and apparent emotional disturbance. Many children displaying such symptoms have had cursory examinations, but such conditions are not always easily detected.

We have heard a great deal about the term "psychosomatic disturbances," meaning the effect of the mind on the body. Because of considerable discussion and literature from psychoanalysis we tend sometimes to forget that there is also a somatopsychological factor, that is, the effect of the body on the mind and the emotions.

The Prevalence of Behavior Disorders in School

The large majority of children with behavior disorders are enrolled in regular classrooms with normal children. A study by Ullmann (1952) found that teachers identified 8 percent of their pupils as maladjusted. Their ratings correlated .86 with the ratings of 22 clinicians. Ullmann also reports that the ratio of boys to girls was 4 to 1. (Interestingly he notes that among adult applicants to psychiatric clinics women outnumber men.) The 8 percent figure, he comments, compares favorably with 7 percent maladjusted reported by Wickman and 12 percent reported by Rogers.

Bower (1960) studying the methods of identification of the emotionally handicapped (personality disorders) in school, found that 87 percent of the clinically known emotionally handicapped children were likewise so rated by their classroom teachers. The teachers rated 10.5 percent of school children as overly aggressive or defiant (conduct disorders) or overly withdrawn and timid (personality disorders).

Rutter and Graham (1970), using data from an Isle of Wight survey, found that 5.7 percent of some 2,200 nine- to eleven-year-old children were considered to have some clinically significant psychiatric disorder. Neurotic (personality) and antisocial (conduct) disorders were the two largest diagnostic groups. Among those with conduct disorders boys outnumbered girls 34 to 9. However, among those with neurotic disorders, girls outnumbered boys 26 to 17.

Wright (1969) found that third- and fourth-grade teachers referred 5.2 percent of their total classroom population as being conduct problems. Among those referred, boys outnumbered girls 74 to 23.

Stennett (1966), using a modified Bower's (1960) screening device, estimated that 22 percent of the fourth, fifth, and sixth grades in a Minnesota school district were moderately or seriously "emotionally handicapped." Teachers reported that 78 percent of the boys and 66 percent of the girls referred had learning problems. In a follow-up study three years later, he found 39 percent of the original group were still identified as emotionally handicapped. A major difference between the improved group and the persistent group occurred in the area of academic functioning. The improved group was functioning almost up to expectancy, while the persistent group was found to be functioning almost a year below expectancy.

From the studies on prevalence that have been reviewed it should be obvious to the reader that a prevalence figure depends on the definition and degree of behavioral disorders an investigator establishes. The U.S. Office of Education

(Chapter 1) gives a conservative estimate of prevalence of emotionally disturbed children as 2 percent of school children.

Educational Strategies

As indicated earlier the treatment of children with behavior disorders was for some time considered a psychiatric medical problem. The small number of such children who were treated by psychiatrists, psychologists, and social workers was infinitesimal as compared to the need. The results of treatment in offices and in residential institutions led many within the psychiatric profession to call upon the schools to assume the major responsibility. As a result there has been a shift of emphasis and responsibility from (1) the medical profession being the responsible agent for treatment, using teachers as ancillary personnel, to (2) the schools becoming the responsible agents for treatment, with the ancillary assistance of psychiatrists, psychologists, social workers, and others as conjunctive personnel.

As the school increased its responsibility for education or treatment of children with behavior disorders it was necessary to take over, modify, or develop strategies for the organization of programs and teaching procedures for the heterogenous group of children variously labeled as behavior disorders, emotionally disturbed, socially maladjusted, or maladapted.

Different strategies have been developed for the educational treatment of children with behavior disorders. The more commonly identifiable strategies, although overlapping in some respects, are (1) psychodynamic, (2) behavior modification, (3) developmental, (4) learning disability, (5) psychoeducational, and (6) ecological. These strategies will be explained briefly. For more details the reader is referred to the original sources.

THE PSYCHODYNAMIC STRATEGY

Proponents of the psychodynamic or medical model place heavy emphasis on psychiatric involvement in terms of diagnosis, treatment, decision making, and evaluation which places the educator in an ancillary role. The model is based on Freud's psychoanalytic theory of personality development and intrapsychic organization. Maladaptive behavior is viewed as symptomatic of intrapsychic conflict involving the id, the ego, and the superego. The focus of treatment is to remove the "underlying cause" for the behavior. It is believed that the removal of a symptom without alleviating the cause will result in the substitution of another symptom, perhaps more maladaptive than the first.

The underlying causes are said to originate biographically in traumatic childhood events and conflicts which are subsequently repressed. Sexual feelings and conflict are considered to be particular sources of difficulty. Treatment focuses on the analysis of the unconscious and the interpretation of symptoms and dreams in an effort to develop insight on the part of the patient. Insight along with a positive transference relationship with the therapist is considered essential for the type of personality reorganization that takes place during psychotherapy.

The major emphasis is on treatment through psychotherapy with educational aspects as secondary. Acceptance of the child and the establishment of a positive interpersonal relationship between the pupil and teacher are considered essential (Berkowitz and Rothman, 1960).

There is little doubt that Freud's theory has had a marked influence on educational practices with so-called disturbed children. Nevertheless, because of the length of treatment, the questionable success of psychotherapy (especially with children), the expense involved, and the lack of trained personnel to implement the model, its widespread use is seldom found outside psychiatric hospitals and psychiatric residential centers.

THE BEHAVIOR MODIFICATION STRATEGY

The proponents of behavior modification view all behavior, maladaptive as well as adaptive, as learned. Unlike the psychodynamic workers who see behavior disorders as symptoms of intrapsychic conflict that must be uncovered, analyzed, and treated, the behaviorist views the manifest behavior as the problem that must be dealt with. While the behaviorists admit that complex historical events determine behavior, they do not believe the reconstruction of the past is necessary to successfully effect a change in behavior. Wolpe, Salter, and Renya (1965) have described the different kinds of therapies that have been used by applying the principles of respondent and operant conditioning. As background, we should note the features of these two types of conditioning: (1) classical or respondent conditioning and (2) operant conditioning.

According to Bijou (1961) *respondents* are those responses which are learned by stimuli that *precede* them. The classical experiments of conditioning fear in a child by pairing a rabbit with a loud noise which the child already fears is an example. By presenting these stimuli together a number of times preceding the response of crying, the child shows a fear reaction when only the rabbit is presented without the loud noise. Another example would be a dog which salivates to a stimulus of a red light, after meat powder and the light are presented together a number of times.

The treatment of fears, phobias, and other emotional reactions is accomplished by extinguishing the response through pairing the rabbit, for example, with a pleasant stimulus such as candy to which the child responds positively (without crying). This is done gradually with the rabbit at a distance at first and without the loud noise.

Operants, on the other hand, function through controlling the stimuli that *follow* the responses. For example, a child sucks his thumb as he watches television. The mother arranges to press a button which will turn off the television when the thumb is in the mouth, and turn on the television when the child is not sucking his thumb. Soon the child learns not to suck his thumb in order to keep the television on. In this situation the operant (thumb sucking) is controlled by the stimulus (television off) that follows. Operant conditioning is based on the principle that behavior is a function of its consequence. The application of a positive stimulus (television on) immediately following a response is called positive reinforcement (reward); the withdrawal of a positive stimulus (television off) constitutes punishment or negative reinforcement.

The principles of operant conditioning have been applied extensively to the control of behavior of children with behavior disorders. This is accomplished by first making a functional analysis of behavior, or specifying what behaviors are to be changed. Just labeling a child or saying he is emotionally disturbed or is a "bad boy" is not helpful. The analysis should specify in behavioral terms what the child is doing that is not acceptable. One common behavior which is of concern to teachers is a boy's failure to work on his lessons because he is constantly getting out of his seat, bothering others, and running around the room with one excuse after another. To shape his behavior in a classroom would require providing step by step lessons he can do in his seat, and then reinforcing acceptable behavior. Ordinarily, teachers pay attention to children when they are out of their seats disrupting others and ignore them when they are working quietly. Such teacher behavior actually reinforces disruptive student behavior. To change this situation the teacher must positively reinforce the child for doing his lessons and staying in his seat. Sometimes social approval of the teacher for appropriate behavior is sufficient. She praises him when he is working at his seat and ignores him when he is out of his seat. If this does not work, tangible rewards (candy or something that he likes) is given to him every time he is working and in his seat. Marks or tokens may be given for the completion of a particular task or other appropriate behavior.

O'Leary and Becker (1967) selected eight children in a third-grade adjustment class for children with behavior disorders. The teacher gave token reinforcements to the children for appropriate behavior; these tokens were exchangeable for candy or trinkets at the end of the day. The investigators reported an abrupt reduction in deviant behavior in the classroom with the introduction of the token system. Hewett (1968) (whose program will be discussed later) has successfully used token reinforcements in special classes for emotionally disturbed children.

The usual procedure in such classes is to establish goals and organize the tasks to be accomplished by the child in small steps so that the child can experience continuous success and obtain positive reinforcement for each step or task as he completes it (arithmetic, reading, spelling, etc). Materials presented to the child are programmed in easy steps. As the child completes a task that he can accomplish successfully in a specified period of time, the teacher checks the work, praises the child (social reinforcement), gives him a mark, a grade, a token, or some other tangible reinforcement like candy. In this way the child is able to work at his assignments for longer and longer periods with increasingly more difficult assignments.

Programmed learning materials and teaching machines utilize operant conditioning techniques. These rely heavily on positive reinforcement through knowledge of results. The children are helped to succeed at each step by prompting and confirmation. The main responsibility of a teacher as a behavior modifier is (1) to delineate specifically the behavior or behaviors that are considered maladaptive, (2) to determine the situations or environmental events that are sustaining or reinforcing this maladaptive behavior, and (3) to restructure the environment of the child to modify, change, or alter the maladaptive behavior.

THE DEVELOPMENTAL STRATEGY

Hewett (1968) is the principal advocate of the developmental strategy for the education of children with behavior disorders. He has established an educational program which is primarily a behavior modification procedure, with a developmental sequence of seven educational goals. These developmental sequences are (1) attention, (2) response, (3) order, (4) exploratory, (5) social, (6) mastery, and (7) achievement. In Hewett's (1967) own words the developmental strategy:

. . . hypothesizes that in order for successful living to occur, the child must pay attention, respond, follow directions, freely and accurately explore the environment, and function appropriately in relation to others. It further hypothesizes that the learning of these behaviors occurs during the normal course of development from infancy to school age, and failure to learn any or all of them may preclude the child's being ready for school. For such a child they constitute the "somethings" he must learn in the process of getting ready for school while he is actually there. (p. 42)

To assist the teacher to move the child up the hierarchy, Hewett (1967) has organized what he considers to be the three essential ingredients for effective teaching: (1) selection of a suitable task; (2) selection of a meaningful reward following accomplishment of that task; (3) maintenance of a degree of structure under the control of the teacher.

Table 13–1 is Hewett's (1967) description of the hierarchy of educational tasks (the sequence of educational goals). At each level of the sequence is (1) the child's problem, (2) the educative task, (3) the reinforcement (reward), and (4) the teacher's structure.

Hewett has implemented his approach in what he calls the "engineered classroom." The engineered classroom is divided into work sections corresponding to levels on the developmental hierarchy. There are three areas in the classroom: (1) the mastery center, (2) the order center, and (3) the exploratory center.

The mastery center is designed for mastery and achievement tasks primarily in academic fields. The order center is designed to train children to follow directions, complete assignments, and control their behavior. The exploratory center is used for science, art, and communication activities.

The role of the teacher is to assign the child to the appropriate center, give him tasks he needs to learn, is ready to learn, and on which he can be successful. The teacher rewards the child by the use of a check-mark system. The child receives two check marks for starting the assigned task or activity, three for completion of the task and up to five for "being a student." One child may receive check marks for writing his name, another for writing an essay. Rewards are individualized for each child depending on what he can do. The teacher gives the marks with an explanation: "You get two marks because you completed four arithmetic problems," or "because you paid attention," etc.

It is at this point that Hewett departs from the strict behavior modification strategy. Being reinforced for being "a student" is quite different from being reinforced for progress toward some specific goal behavior. In Hewett's model the child continues to be reinforced even if he has a bad day and regresses somewhat. The child is not penalized for maladaptive behavior on one level if he can stabilize his behavior on another. For this reason, assignments are quickly changed at the first sign of maladaptive behavior on any assigned task.

Proponents of a strict behavior modification model would contend that removing a child from a demanding task and assigning him to a less demanding task while continuing to reward his behavior, would actually constitute rewarding inappropriate behavior. They suggest that children may misbehave in an attempt to be assigned to more rewarding, less frustrating activity. Hewett (1967) contends that this phenomenon has seldom occurred because teachers anticipate such problems and attempt to control them by limiting the amount of mastery work given the child and by assigning him to alternate centers before his behavior becomes disruptive.

Hewett (1968) compared engineered classrooms with classrooms using the same materials and schedule, but not on a behavior modification check mark

TABLE 13–1

Summary of the developmental sequence of educational goals

Level	Attention	Response	Order	Exploratory	Social	Mastery	Achievement
Child's problem	Inattention due to withdrawal or resistance	Lack of involvement and unwillingness to respond in learning	Inability to follow directions	Incomplete or inaccurate knowledge of environment	Failure to value social approval or disapproval	Deficits in basic adaptive and school skills not in keeping with IQ	Lack of self-motivation for learning
Educational task	Get child to pay attention to teacher and task	Get child to respond to tasks he likes and which offer promise of success	Get child to complete tasks with specific starting points and steps leading to a conclusion	Increase child's efficiency as an explorer and get him involved in multisensory exploration of his environment	Get child to work for teacher and peer group approval and to avoid their disapproval	Remediation of basic skill deficiencies	Development of interest in acquiring knowledge
Learner reward	Provided by tangible rewards (e.g., food, money, tokens)	Provided by gaining social attention	Provided through task completion	Provided by sensory stimulation	Provided by social approval	Provided through task accuracy	Provided through intellectual task success
Teacher structure	Minimal	Still limited	Emphasized	Emphasized	Based on standards of social appropriateness	Based on curriculum assignments	Minimal

Source: Hewett, 1967, p. 461. Reprinted with the permission of the author.

system. Although the results slightly favored the developmental behavior modification classes, Hewett concluded that:

. . . the engineered classroom design appears basically a launching technique for initiating learning with children who often fail to "get off the ground" in school. It does not appear to be essential in its present form for more than one semester with many children. (p. 333)

THE LEARNING DISABILITY STRATEGY

The proponents of this strategy maintain that a specific learning disability creates a discrepancy between the capacity of the individual to behave and the requirements of the school environment, or between the child's ability in one area and what he and others expect because of his ability in other areas. This situation results in frustration, conduct and personality problems, and sometimes in school truancy and delinquency. The child might strike out against the situation by becoming hostile and aggressive, or he might withdraw. As indicated in Chapter 2 the correlates of a specific learning disability are physical, environmental, psychological, or a combination of these.

Research reviewed earlier has indicated that a sizeable portion of the children in schools or classes for the emotionally disturbed are retarded educationally, and that a number of them can be classified as learning disabilities. How much of the emotional problems can be ascribed to the learning disability, or how much of the disability can be ascribed to the emotional problem in an individual case is difficult to determine. Generally, it is a vicious circle in which one affects the other.

The learning disability strategy intervenes directly into the remediation of the specific disability: language, reading, writing, spelling, thinking, perceiving, etc. Effective remediation tends to decrease the conduct and personality problems by assisting the child in decreasing the discrepancy between his capacity to perform and the requirements of society.

The reader is referred to Chapter 2 for a discussion of learning disabilities and the strategies used for diagnosis and remediation of children with learning disabilities. Suffice it to say that classes and programs for children with learning disabilities contain many children with emotional problems and many classes for the emotionally disturbed contain children with learning disabilities. Most programs for emotionally disturbed children, using any of the other strategies discussed, include provisions for remediation of learning disabilities.

THE PSYCHOEDUCATIONAL STRATEGY

The psychoeducational strategy is, in a sense, an eclectic approach. It is concerned with *what* the child does (similar to behavior modification) and *why* he does it (similar to the psychodynamic approach). It is also concerned with the learning disability strategy since many of the emotionally disturbed are retarded educationally. In the psychoeducational strategy psychiatric and educational emphases are equally balanced, and joint planning is accomplished among workers. Morse et al (1964) in their survey of classes for the emotionally handicapped found that about one quarter of the children in the classes and/or their mothers had conjunctive therapy, that is, were receiving psychotherapy as a planned part of their educational program by personnel other than the teachers.

In the psychoeducational strategy the child is viewed as possessing an innate biological potential which in combination with early experiences determines the child's self-concept, aspirations, and the manner in which he copes with reality and tension. When the child enters school he is expected to possess certain social and readiness skills which will allow him to perform in a prescribed manner acceptable to school, home, and society. Failure of the child to meet certain externally imposed demands will result in internal anxiety and frustration which lead directly to maladaptive behavior. If the teacher and/or peers counter with hostile, rejecting responses, anxiety and frustration are increased. This leads eventually to a school crisis. The crisis then provides the child with another example of his inability, further lowering his self-concept, increasing his frustration, and creating a vicious cycle that will affect the child, the teacher, the parents, and his peers.

The goal of intervention is to interrupt this cycle. Some of the factors that should be examined in an attempt to reach this goal would include: (1) the nature of the demands and pressures placed on the child; (2) the ability of the child to meet these demands; (3) peer group relations; (4) pupil-teacher relations; (5) the youngster's motivation for the behavior; and (6) his self-concept. For example, the task in which the child is involved may contain the seeds of acute frustration, or group relations may show evidence of scapegoating or pressure for certain types of behavior. The child who feels inferior in academic pursuits may try to compensate by exhibiting his fighting ability. To ignore these factors may result in improper handling and increased frustration for the child (Morse, 1965).

On the other hand, the child must be taught to maintain his behavior within acceptable limits. Long and Newman (1965) have described four alternatives to behavior that may be used by the teacher. The first is called *preventative planning* and suggests a hygienic environment which will allow the child to bring his behavior under control. The second is called *permitting* and suggests that certain types of behavior should be sanctioned by the teacher at times such as running and shouting on the playground. The third is called *tolerating* and suggests that the teacher should tolerate the behavior because it is temporarily beyond the child's ability to control; but it is explained to the child that improvement is expected. Fourth, the teacher may *interfere* or *interrupt* a behavior sequence for the protection of the child, for the protection of others in the class, or for the protection of ongoing classroom activities.

Those coping skills which the child lacks may also be taught by proper handling and the skillful use of the life-space interview at times of crisis (Redl, 1965). The variety of interventions match the variety of personality patterns and forces operating on children.

Proponents of the psychoeducational approach view acceptance of the child and positive interpersonal adult-child relationships as essential for effective treatment. Acceptance, however, does not mean acceptance of the behavior but rather of the child. Further, this acceptance must correspond to the child's personality in such a way that the teacher's responses help him to learn the necessary conformity.

An advantage of the psychoeducational model over the more historically oriented psychodynamic model is that it can be organized and implemented within the scope of the school's responsibility. The teacher is not left on the side line as an observer. She is considered an integral part of a team with much decision-making responsibility.

THE ECOLOGICAL STRATEGY

Proponents of the ecological strategy believe that a total redefinition of the nature of social pathology is required. Rhodes (1967) states:

In this alternative view of disturbance it is suggested that the nucleus of the problem lies in the content of behavioral prohibitions and sanctions in the culture. Any behavior which departs significantly from this lore upsets those who have carefully patterned their behavior according to cultural specifications. The subsequent agitated exchange between *culture violator* and *culture bearer* creates a disturbance in the environment. It is this reciprocal product which engages attention and leads to subsequent action. (p. 449)

The proponents of the ecological model are critical of those interventions that deal with the child alone, assuming that the behavior disorders are the exclusive property of the child. Psychotherapy and behavior modification assume that the target is the child, and it is the child who must change or adjust to his environment. The ecological model, on the other hand, proposes that human problems result from an agitated transaction between the excitor (the child) and the responder (the environment—family, siblings, teachers, children, etc.). The behavior disorder is a point of misfit between the child and his environment.

Culture-violating behavior becomes upsetting to surrounding individuals when its message is received and recognized under the overlay of sanctions and prohibitions which the responding individuals have acquired from the storehouse of the culture (Rhodes, 1967).

Rhodes further states:

Although it is probably true that the condition of disturbance can be attributed to the excitor as well as the responder, . . . we do know that the condition of emotional disturbance does produce strain in the community of responders, and that this strain is one of the definers of the child as the problem. (p. 451)

Hobbs (1969) and his colleagues have implemented the ecological strategy with programs for emotionally disturbed children which he calls Re-Ed (a project for the reeducation of emotionally disturbed children). As indicated earlier the ecological approach rejects reliance on psychotherapy and assumes that "the child is an inseparable part of a small social system, of an ecological unit made up of the child, his family, his school, his neighborhood and community."

Two residential schools were organized to house approximately forty children each, ages 6 to 12. The plan was to reeducate these children for a short period of time (4 to 6 months) and, at the same time, through a liaison teacher, to modify the attitudes of the home, the school, and the community. The entire program was oriented to reestablishing the child as quickly as possible in his own home, school, and community. The general program of reeducation follows a number of principles. These principles are explained by Hobbs as follows:

1. *Life is to be lived now.* This was accomplished by occupying children every hour of the day in purposeful activities, and in activities in which they could succeed.

2. *Time is an ally.* Some children improve with the passage of time. But a child should not remain in a residential setting for long periods since this length of time may estrange him from his family. Six months in the residential center was the stated goal of Re-Ed.

3. *Trust is essential.* Trust, according to Hobbs, is not learned in college courses, but some of those working with emotionally disturbed children "know, without knowing they know, the way to inspire trust in children" (p. 302).

4. *Competence makes a difference.* The arrangement of the environment and learning tasks must be so structured that the child is able to obtain confidence and self-respect from his successes.

5. *Symptoms can and should be controlled.* The treatment of symptoms instead of attempting to use the medical model of treating causes is emphasized.

6. *Cognitive control can be taught.* This is accomplished by immediate experience, by the moment to moment know-how, and by day-to-day relationship between the teacher and the child.

7. *Feelings should be nurtured.* Situations are arranged with animals and people to allow the child to show affection or other feelings.

8. *The group is important to the children.* Children in Re-Ed are organized in groups of eight with two counselor-teachers. Discussions of difficulties or sharing experiences develop the kind of human relations to which these children are unaccustomed.

9. *Ceremony and ritual give order, stability, and confidence.* Rituals and ceremonies, like nightly backrub or being a member of a club, or a Christmas pageant, serve a major purpose.

10. *The body is the armature of the self.* This is accomplished through the physical activities of swimming, climbing, clay modeling, etc.

11. *Communities are important.* Activities to give the child a sense of responsibility to the community such as trips to fire departments, etc., are provided by Re-Ed. In addition, a liaison teacher could prepare the family, school, and community for the return of the child to the community.

12. *Finally, a child should know joy.* In Re-Ed the counselor-teacher arranges for each child to recognize joy each day and to anticipate joy the next day.

An evaluation of the Re-Ed program was based on follow-up information from 93 graduates a minimum of 6 months after discharge. The results of evaluation gave a success rate of approximately 80 percent.

Educational Organization

Children with behavior disorders vary widely in their needs for special services, depending on the severity and the types of the behavior disorders. Reynolds (1962) presented in the form of a triangle the variety of services that might be provided for special education, ranging from the regular classroom to hospital treatment centers. This chart is included in Chapter 1, p. 31. Since this chart is particularly applicable to children with behavior disorders it is adapted in Figure 13–1 which shows the following services:

1. *Regular classes.* At the bottom of the chart is the regular classroom which provides for the largest number of children with behavior disorders. These children usually have minor problems and are the responsibility of the regular

FIGURE 13–1

Hierarchy of services for special education
programs for children with behavior disorders

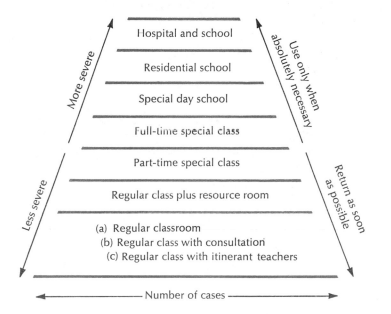

Source: Adapted from M. C. Reynolds, "A Framework for Considering Some Issues in Special Education," *Exceptional Children* 28 (March, 1962).

classroom teacher. Three alternative procedures have been used within the regular classroom depending on the needs of the children:

a. The regular classroom teacher assumes the sole responsibility for minor problems.

b. The regular classroom teacher obtains consultative help from psychologists, social workers, counselors, principals, and others as needed. The major efforts of the consultants are to give the teacher a better understanding of the child and suggestions for treatment. The major treatment responsibility remains with the classroom teacher.

c. The third alternative is to enroll the child in the regular classroom, but provide the child and the regular classroom teacher with special services from itinerant teachers. Such itinerant teachers come into the classroom to assist the child in adjusting to the regular class. The itinerant teacher tutors the child in his academic subjects when needed, and/or assists him in adjustment to the regular class and to his peers. These itinerant teachers include speech clinicians, remedial reading teachers, and child therapists.

2. *Regular class plus resource room.* In this type of organization the child is assigned to the regular class, but for part of the day the child works in a resource room where the resource teacher diagnoses and offers remedial work and assists the regular teacher with appropriate assignments and with consultation. Most larger schools have such facilities.

3. *The part-time special class* enrolls children in a special class but assigns the children to a regular class for part of the day, especially during activities in which the children with behavior disorders can participate and achieve successfully.

4. *The full-time special class* is reserved for children who are unable to participate in the activities of the regular grades even on a part-time basis. The total-day program is in a special class in an elementary or secondary school.

5. *The special day school* is generally a school that enrolls a large number of children with behavior disorders in a separate facility in order to provide special services not available in most public schools. Here the children live at home, but attend the day school.

6. *The residential school* is reserved for those children whose needs are not met in their home community, and who require twenty-four-hour-a-day education, management, and supervision. The Re-Ed program described earlier is such a residential school. There are a number of varying kinds of residential schools throughout the country which enroll children with the more severe types of behavior disorders. Many of these children are removed from the community and home for various reasons, including the effect of the child on other siblings, inability of the parents to manage the child, and in some instances because the children have no home or the home is unsuitable for aid in rehabilitation.

7. *The psychiatric hospital* is planned for the very severe emotionally disturbed children who require medical and psychiatric supervision. Most psychiatric hospitals now have residential schools on the grounds. Children in residence attend a hospital school if at all possible where education is provided in a program designed by the teachers and psychiatric personnel. Some children in hospitals are so severely disordered that they are unable to attend the hospital school and must remain in the wards.

8. *Mental Health Clinics.* The community mental health clinics (not shown in Figure 13–1) also play a role in the treatment of children with behavior disorders. Such a clinic can (1) provide consultative services to regular and special class

teachers, (2) provide itinerant personnel to the school to assist regular and special class teachers, (3) provide a resource room in the clinic where the child can attend on a part-time basis, and (4) provide an all-day class for children with behavior disorders.

9. *Residential schools for delinquents.* Children who are in trouble, especially those whose homes cannot manage them, are placed in detention homes, usually under the supervision of the Juvenile Court. Education is offered these children in small groups or individually while they are awaiting examination and court action. Education in such a situation is often on an individualized basis since the children are generally of a wide age range and a wide range of intellectual abilities. Ordinarily, the children are in a detention home for short periods of a week to six or eight weeks. The educational program is utilized in this setting partly for educational but mostly for therapeutic purposes.

Residential schools have been established for delinquent children or youths who are unable to be at large in society, or whose home is of such a nature that the child cannot live at home and attend a day school. In some of the large cities like New York and Chicago these schools, sometimes known as parental schools, are operated on a twenty-four-hour-a-day basis and are administered by the public school board of education. The schools are for the more severe delinquents who are not profiting from a special class or a day school.

By far the most common type of residential school is the state training school. It accepts court commitments for juveniles and has been variously termed an industrial school, reform school, correctional school, or training school. Usually these residential institutions accept only boys or only girls. Their purpose is to rehabilitate the delinquents under their care and to return them to the community.

Unfortunately, most of our residential institutions for delinquents are custodial and punitive rather than geared to intensive rehabilitation, which requires much more in the way of money and personnel than the public is at present ready to allot. Furthermore, until we have more empirical data on causation and remedial methods, much exploratory work will be necessary.

SUMMARY

1. Children with behavior disorders are those children who deviate from age-appropriate behavior which significantly interferes with (a) the child's own growth and development, and/or (b) the lives of others.
2. Three patterns of behavior disorders have been identified as (a) conduct problems, (b) personality problems, and (c) inadequate immature behavior. A fourth type, delinquency, is of a different dimension since it is a legal term and includes any of the above types.

3. Prevalence of behavior disorders in the school population ranges from 2 percent to 22 percent, depending on the criterion of behavior disorders used by the investigator.
4. Educational strategies include (a) psychodynamic approaches, (b) behavior modification procedures, (c) developmental strategies, (d) learning disability approaches, (e) psychoeducational strategies, and (f) ecological strategies.
5. Educational provisions for behaviorally disordered children include (a) adjustment in the regular grades with or without consultation and itinerant teachers, (b) resource rooms, (c) part or full-time special classes, (d) special day schools, (e) residential schools, and (f) hospitals.

REFERENCES

Bandura, A., and Walters, R. H. 1959. *Adolescent Aggression*. New York: Ronald Press Co.

Barker, R.; Dembo, T.; and Lewin, K. 1941. *Frustration and Regression: An Experiment with Young Children*. Iowa City, Iowa: University of Iowa Press.

Berkowitz, P., and Rothman, E. 1960. *The Disturbed Child*. New York: New York University Press.

Bijou, S. W. 1961. The Behavior of Developmentally Retarded Children as a Function of Loss of Reinforcement to a Peer. *Dissertation Abstracts* 22: 1714.

Bower, E. M. 1960. *Early Identification of Emotionally Handicapped Children in School.* Springfield, Illinois: Charles C. Thomas Publisher.

California State Department of Education. 1961. *The Education of Emotionally Handicapped Children*. Sacramento, California: The Department.

Cohen, A. K. 1955. *Delinquent Boys: The Culture of the Gang*. Glencoe, Illinois: The Free Press.

Cruickshank, W. M.; Bentzen, Frances; Ratzburg, F. H.; and Tannhauser, Mirian T. 1961. *A Teaching Method for Brain Injured and Hyperactive Children*. Syracuse, New York: Syracuse University Press.

Dollard, J.; Doob, L. W.; Miller, N. E.; Mowrer, H. O.; and Sears, R. R. 1939. *Frustration and Aggression*. New Haven, Connecticut: Yale University Press.

Glasser, W. 1965. *Reality Therapy*. New York: Harper and Row.

Hewett, F. M. 1968. *The Emotionally Disturbed Child in the Classroom*. Boston: Allyn and Bacon.

————. 1967. Educational Engineering with Emotionally Disturbed Children. *Exceptional Children* 33 (March): 459–470.

Hewitt, L. E., and Jenkins, R. L. 1945. *Fundamental Patterns of Maladjustment: The Dynamics of their Origin*. Springfield, Illinois: State of Illinois.

Hilgard, E. R., and Marquis, D. G. 1940. *Conditioning and Learning*. New York: Appleton-Century-Crofts.

Hobbs, N. 1969. Helping Disturbed Children: Psychological and Ecological Strategies. In Dupont, H. (ed.), *Educating Emotionally Disturbed Children*, pp. 293–311. New York: Holt, Rinehart, and Winston.

Jenkins, R. 1966. Psychiatric Syndromes in Children and Their Relation to Family Background. *American Journal of Orthopsychiatry* 36 (April): 450–457.

Kvaraceus, William C. 1958. Juvenile Delinquency. *What Research Says to the Teacher,* No. 15. Washington, D.C.: American Educational Research Association of the National Education Association.

———. 1971. *Prevention and Control of Delinquency: The School Counselor's Role.* Boston: Houghton Mifflin.

Kvaraceus, W. C., and Miller, W. B. 1959. *Delinquent Behavior: Culture and the Individual.* Washington, D.C.: National Education Association.

Long, N. J., and Newman, Ruth G. 1965. Managing Surface Behavior of Children in School. In Long, N. J.; Morse, W. C.; and Newman, Ruth G. (eds.), *Conflict in the Classroom,* pp. 352–363. Belmont, California: Wadsworth.

Mackie, Romaine P.; Kvaraceus, W. C.; and Williams, H. 1957. *Teachers of Children Who Are Socially and Emotionally Maladjusted.* U.S. Office of Education. Washington, D.C.: Government Printing Office.

Maccoby, Eleanor E.; Johnson, J. P.; and Church, R. M. 1958. Community Integration and the Social Control of Juvenile Delinquency. *Journal of Social Issues* 3: 38–51.

Maier, N. R. F. 1949. *Frustration: The Study of Behavior Without a Goal.* New York: McGraw-Hill.

McCord, W., and McCord, Joan. 1959. *Origins of Crime: A New Evaluation of the Cambridge-Somerville Youth Study.* New York: Columbia University Press.

Miller, W. B. 1959. Implications of Urban Lower-Class Culture for Social Work. *Social Service Review* 33 (September): 222–223.

———. 1958. Lower-Class Culture as a Generating Milieu of Gang Delinquency. *Journal of Social Issues* 14: 6–17.

Morse, W. C. 1965. Intervention Techniques for the Classroom Teacher of the Emotionally Disturbed. In Knoblock, P. (ed.), *Educational Programming for Emotionally Disturbed Children: The Decade Ahead,* pp. 29–41. Syracuse, New York: Syracuse University Press.

Morse, W. C.; Cutler, R. L.; and Fink, A. H. 1964. *Public School Classes for the Emotionally Handicapped: A Research Analysis.* Arlington, Virginia: The Council for Exceptional Children.

O'Leary, K. D., and Becker, W. C. 1967. Behavior Modification of an Adjustment Class: A Token Reinforcement Program. *Exceptional Children* 33 (May): 637–644.

Pavlov, I. P. 1928. *Lectures on Conditioned Reflexes.* Translated by Gantt, W. H. New York: International.

Peterson, D. R. 1961. Behavior Problems of Middle Childhood. *Journal of Consulting Psychology* 25 (June): 205–209.

Quay, H. C. (ed.). 1965. *Juvenile Delinquency.* New York: Van Nostrand.

Quay, H. C.; Morse, W.; and Cutler, R. L. 1966. Personality Patterns of Pupils in Special Classes for the Emotionally Disturbed. *Exceptional Children* 32 (January): 297–301.

Rakstis, T. J. 1970. Why Our Kids Steal. *Today's Health* (American Medical Association): 21–23, 68–70.

Redl, F. 1965. The Concept of the Life-Space Interview. In Long, N. J.; Morse, W. C.; and Newman, Ruth G. (eds.), *Conflict in the Classroom,* pp. 363–371. Belmont, California: Wadsworth.

Reynolds, M. C. 1962. A Framework for Considering Some Issues in Special Education. *Exceptional Children* 28 (March): 367–370.

Rhodes, W. C. 1967. The Disturbing Child: A Problem of Ecological Management. *Exceptional Children* 33 (March): 449–455.

Rutter, M., and Graham, P. 1970. Epidemiology of Psychiatric Disorder. In Rutter, M.; Tizard, J.; and Whitmore, K.; *Education, Health and Behaviour.* London: Longman Group Limited. U.S. Distributor, John Wiley and Sons, New York.

Shaw, C. R., and McKay, H. D. 1942. *Juvenile Delinquency and Urban Areas.* Chicago: University of Chicago Press.

Stennett, R. G. 1966. Emotional Handicap in the Elementary Years: Phase or Disease? *American Journal of Orthopsychiatry* 34: 444–449.

Strauss, A. A., and Lehtinen, Laura E. 1947. *Psychopathology and Education of the Brain Injured Child I, Fundamentals and Treatment.* New York: Grune and Stratton.

Ullmann, C. E. 1952. *Identification of Maladjusted School Children.* Public Health Monograph No. 7. Washington, D.C.: Government Printing Office.

Ullmann, L., and Krasner, L. 1965. *Case Studies in Behavior Modification.* New York: Holt, Rinehart, and Winston.

Wirt, R. D., and Briggs, P. F. 1965. The Meaning of Delinquency. In Quay, H. C. (ed.), *Juvenile Delinquency.* New York: Van Nostrand.

Wolpe, J. A.; Salter, A.; and Renya, L. (eds.). 1965. *The Conditioning Therapies.* New York: Holt, Rinehart, and Winston.

Wright, Loyd. 1969. Perceptual and Cognitive Characteristics and Their Relation to Social and Academic Factors in Third Grade Conduct Problem Boys. Unpublished doctoral dissertation, University of Illinois.

FOURTEEN

ADMINISTRATIVE

ORGANIZATIONS

Each of the preceding chapters has dealt with one unique exceptionality, giving minimal attention to administrative requirements of funding, preparing personnel, stimulating research, and providing direct services to children. This last chapter will discuss briefly the administrative agencies that provide services, supervision, and funding for training, research, and service.

Special education in the United States is administered at three levels: (1) the Federal level, (2) the state level, and (3) the local level. Each of these agencies serves a different purpose. Funds for training, research, and exemplary services are provided from Federal sources while direct services to children are organized at the state and local levels.

The Role of the Federal Government

Traditionally, the United States Federal government has not had a direct legal or administrative role in education. Its function has been to promote, stimulate, and improve education by (1) providing funds and resources to aid state educational programs in certain areas; (2) establishing limited educational programs for certain groups, such as the Indian population and military dependents; (3) providing scholarships and fellowships for certain groups of students; (4) establishing advisory, consultative, and research services in education; and (5) disseminating information on education.

The United States Department of Health, Education, and Welfare has a number of constituent agencies which promote and facilitate the care and education of exceptional children. The major agency concerned exclusively with education is the U.S. Office of Education, which was established in 1867. Not until 1930 did the Office organize a Section of Exceptional Children and Youth, whose concern is to promote and facilitate adequate programs for exceptional children within the respective state and local school systems. Work with handicapped and gifted children in the Office of Education remained at the section level with only a few employees administering programs until 1963.

In 1963, President Kennedy signed Public Law 88–164, announcing the creation of a Division of Handicapped Children and Youth within the U.S. Office of Education and with an authorized appropriation for research and the training of personnel for all handicapped children. Later, in 1967, Congress elevated the status of this work by creating within the U.S. Office of Education a Bureau of Education for the Handicapped to administer appropriated funds for research, training, and services to handicapped children.

Figure 14–1 shows the organization and function of the Bureau of Education for the Handicapped, with its Divisions of Research, Educational Services, and Training. It will be noted that each division contains a number of branches, each with a specific responsibility.

In 1970 the Bureau of Education for the Handicapped (BEH) administered or monitored the following programs under a Congressional bill entitled Education of the Handicapped Act, P.L. 91–230. Presented below is a brief description of the activities and the 1970 appropriations for the programs in (1) research, (2) training, and (3) services (U.S. Office of Education, 1970):

RESEARCH

1. *Regional Resource Centers for the Improvements of Education for the Handicapped.* Congress appropriated $1,800,000 to allow the Bureau of Education for the Handicapped to grant funds to universities and state education agencies, or combinations of the two, within particular regions to develop centers for educational diagnosis and remediation of handicapped children.

2. *Research on the Education of Handicapped Children and Related Activities.* An appropriation of $13,060,000 was made by Congress to promote new knowledge and developments with reference to the education of handicapped children. Grants are made for this purpose by BEH to state or local education agencies, to universities, and to other private or public nonprofit organizations.

3. *Physical Education and Recreation for the Handicapped.* $300,000 was appropriated by Congress to assist state and local education agencies, universities, and other private and public nonprofit organizations to conduct research in areas of physical education and recreation for handicapped children.

FIGURE 14–1

*Organization chart, Bureau of Education
for the Handicapped, U.S. Office of Education*

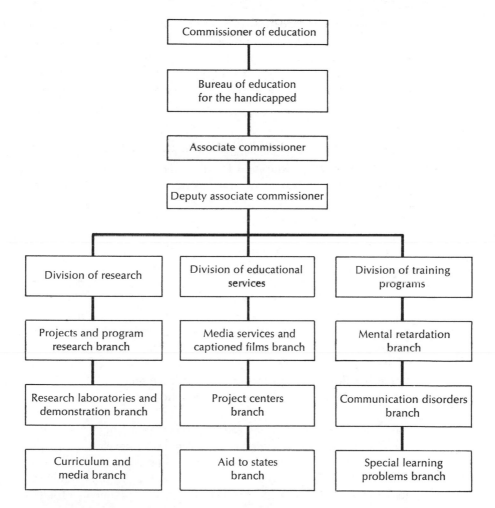

TRAINING

1. *Training Personnel for the Education of the Handicapped.* $29,700,000 was appropriated for the preparation of teachers and other personnel serving in the education of the handicapped. Grants for this purpose are made by the BEH to universities, state departments of education, and to other appropriate nonprofit institutions or agencies.

2. *Training of Physical Education and Recreation Personnel for the Handicapped.* A sum of $300,000 was allotted by the BEH to institutions of higher education to train personnel in physical education and recreation for the handicapped.

3. *Programs for Children with Specific Learning Disabilities.* Although this act was not passed in time for funding, it provides for research, training of personnel, and the establishment and operation of model centers for children with specific learning disabilities. The proposed funds will be granted to universities, state and local education agencies, and other public nonprofit agencies.

SERVICES

1. *Programs for the Handicapped at Preschool, Elementary, and Secondary Levels.* To strengthen educational and related services for handicapped children on the preschool, elementary, and secondary levels, $29,190,000 was allocated to State Departments of Education. Each state's allotment is directly proportionate to the population of the state.

2. *Programs for the Handicapped in State-Supported Schools.* Congress appropriated to State Departments of Education $37,483,000 for the purpose of strengthening educational programs for children in schools operated or supported by the state, such as residential schools for the deaf, blind, mentally retarded, etc.

3. *Supplementary Educational Centers and Services.* Under Title III of the Elementary and Secondary Education Act, as amended, funds have been made available through state departments of education to provide grants for supplementary, innovative, or exemplary projects for the educational improvement of the handicapped. Fifteen percent of the cumulative Title III funds for state agencies, or $17,458,950, constituted the allotment for handicapped children in 1970.

4. *Early Education for Handicapped Children.* An allocation of $3,000,000 was made to public and private nonprofit agencies to develop model preschool and early education programs for handicapped children.

5. *Vocational Education Programs for the Handicapped.* Congress appropriated $30,749,745 to provide, through the State Departments of Education, vocational education and services to handicapped children.

6. *Media Services and Captioned Film Loan Program.* $4,750,000 has been allocated for the purpose of:

a. advancing the education of the handicapped through films and other media, including a captioned film loan service for cultural and educational enrichment for the deaf. This is administered by state or local public agencies and school organizations or groups which serve the handicapped, their parents, and employers or potential employers of the handicapped;

b. contracting for research in the use of educational and training films and other educational media for the handicapped and for their production and distribution;

c. contracting for the training of persons in the use of educational media for the handicapped;

d. establishing and operating a national center on educational media through an institution of higher education.

7. *Centers for the Deaf-Blind.* Congress appropriated $2,000,000 to state education agencies, universities, medical centers and public or nonprofit agencies for the development of centers and services for deaf-blind children.

8. *Information and Recruitment Grants.* To improve recruitment of educational personnel and dissemination of information on educational opportunities for the handicapped, $475,000 has been allocated.

INFORMATION

As pointed out earlier, the collection and dissemination of information has been one of the chief functions of the U.S. Office of Education for over one hundred years. Recently this function has been greatly accelerated due to increased Federal support and the use of new technology. The reader who desires more information on any phase of public education will find it at the Bureau of Education for the Handicapped, U.S. Office of Education in Washington, D.C.

Educational Research Information Center (ERIC) is one of the most useful services for students. Central ERIC has a dozen external clearinghouses, each of which is concerned with a specific subject matter area such as Educational Administration, Reading, Disadvantaged, Exceptional Children, etc. The clearinghouse, which relates to exceptional children—both handicapped and gifted—is located in the offices of the Council for Exceptional Children, in Washington, D.C. ERIC acquires abstracts, indexes, and stores, retrieves and disseminates nationally the most significant and timely educational research and research related documents. *Exceptional Children Abstracts* is the official publication of the ERIC clearinghouse for exceptional children. Copies of the original research publications may be obtained at a nominal cost either in microfilm or hard copy from the Documents Reproduction Service, a service of a subcontractor.

The Role of State Agencies

Previous chapters have described the educational needs and school programs for each group of exceptional children. These are the children who are served by the organized programs in the several states. Not all states, of course, have special legislation which provides services for all these groups. The role of the state is very important in providing enabling legislation and supplementary financial aid. The leadership which emanates from the state school office is important in developing quality programs at the local level.

LEGISLATION

All states have specific legislation for the support of programs for handicapped children. The scope of the services provided by the laws as well as the financial support to districts vary considerably. Legislation is likely to prescribe services for the major handicaps as viewed historically—the educable retarded, the deaf, the blind, and the crippled. In the case of states which have small populations, the legislation relating to the deaf and to the blind child is likely to refer to services at a residential school rather than at a day school.

Twenty-two states have legislation relating to services for the multihandicapped. Specific learning disabilities, a very new program in special education, was covered within the legislation of at least 12 states in 1970. The gifted child is no doubt given special attention in many schools without the pressure of specific legislation. However, 17 states have defined the gifted child in legislation and specified some type of program.

The general functions of state programs for exceptional children are summarized below:

1. *Legislative Acts.* The state legislature designates that a district may (or must) provide programs for exceptional children, and also designates which groups of children are to be served. The services may be *mandatory* and the districts are required to meet the standards as specified, or the state laws may be *permissive* and districts allowed to have programs with all available benefits.

2. *Financial support of districts.* In order to encourage the development of programs, the state usually offers a subsidy or financial assistance to the districts, since the cost of educating handicapped children is higher than for normal children. This extra allowance of state funds (over and above what the state provides for normal children) is always considered as a supplement to the local funds which the district spends for the education of normal children. These excess costs may be granted on a per-capita basis or per-teacher-station (classroom) basis. In some states the subsidy is sufficient to pay all excess costs, while in other states the funds only reimburse the districts for a portion of the excess

costs. By way of an illustration of the principle of state reimbursement to a district, let us assume that the district now expends $375 for each child in the elementary school. This amount is considered the district's obligation toward all children at this level. If the district has a class for the educable mentally retarded which costs an average of $600 per child, the excess cost is $225. Sometimes a ceiling is fixed on the amount of excess which the state grants. It is common however, for districts not to receive full reimbursement for the extra costs due to insufficient state appropriations.

3. *State Standards.* States, by legislative action, set standards for their programs since they are responsible for the quality of educational services. These standards include regulations relating to eligibility for admission to the services, size of class, length of minimum school day, standards for teacher preparation, and enumeration of expenditures which are permitted to be included in the state subsidy.

4. *Teacher Certification.* Usually teachers of exceptional children are required to have preparation beyond that of teachers in regular grades. This preparation is often as much as an academic year of course work and student teaching. The preparation includes courses in the nature of exceptional children, including pathology when appropriate, curriculum and methods, and laboratory practice. A certificate or credential is usually awarded at the completion of this professional preparation. In recent years the Federal grants, previously referred to, have assisted in increasing the supply of well-qualified teachers.

5. *Supervision.* The state provides supervisors or consultants to assist districts in initiating programs and in the improvement of services. In some of the larger states with well-developed programs two or three consultants may be available in such areas as the educable and trainable retarded.

The school district is the prevailing geographical unit for the organization of educational services. The public school services for exceptional children are structured within the administrative framework of these local units. In recent years there have been some variations (which will be discussed later), of this historic American pattern.

The Role of Local Administration

The operating program, as it serves the children, comes from the initiative and, in part, from the financial resources of the local district or comparable unit. Accordingly, during the past half-century most of the practices described in the previous chapters have been developed by local districts. The major instructional plans used by districts to deliver the services to children may be again summarized as follows:

Special schools, including residential schools
Special classes (self-contained classes)
Resource rooms and resource teachers
Itinerant special teachers

REGIONAL AND COUNTY ORGANIZATIONS

The local district is a satisfactory unit for the administration of special education when the school population is sufficient to justify a particular service. Since the incidence of trainable children (as presented in Chapter 1) is 4 per 1,000, a district would be expected to have at least 2,000 children to organize a class of 8 children. Districts with limited population are unable to justify an independent program since a strong program requires numbers. For example, if a district had four or five classes for deaf children, it could have a better chance to group children with similar abilities. The teachers could share problems and experiences and perhaps a part-time supervisor or principal would be justified.

In order to extend offerings and to provide stronger programs, there has been a trend toward increasing the size of the geographic area. This is being accomplished by encouraging districts to join together and form cooperatives, by establishing intermediate districts, and by organizing regional service areas (Lord and Isenberg, 1964).

Michigan, for example, has organized the counties into intermediate units for special education purposes. The term *intermediate* refers to a unit of administration which is between the state on the one hand and the local district on the other, i.e., the counties. In the intermediate unit all special education services, except those programs which the larger districts within the county provide for themselves, are supplied by the county school office. The county really takes on the functions of a district in the usual sense. The intermediate district (county) can provide special education programs for children who reside in several different districts in the county. The Michigan intermediate districts have developed rapidly; this is, in part, due to the financial support which is derived from a special county tax levy which is authorized by the law.

Illinois encourages districts to develop joint agreements or cooperatives which provide an effective range of special programs—far beyond the capacity of a single district. In fact, the cooperative may employ a director, a school psychologist, or other auxiliary personnel.

There are many other types of cooperative programs such as multicounty units, special education districts, etc. However, all such plans are designed to provide a population base sufficient to justify one or more of the special programs which were described in the previous chapters. Currently, there is an interest in organizing regional units for a variety of educational services including special education. A region extends beyond district lines and includes a geographic area which is more of a natural service territory. The state of Wisconsin, for example, has established nineteen subunits which are called Cooperative Educational Service Agencies. The administrator of each agency assists the schools in his territory in extending and improving services to teachers and to children. Common services include library resources, computer services, audio-visual programs, etc. Programs for exceptional children are very common regional services.

The Texas Educational Agency has designated twenty educational service centers within the state. These centers will assist in planning and identifying promising educational developments. Again, the services which relate to exceptional children may become an interest of the center. These concepts of regional services are promising administrative devices to enable smaller districts to care for the few exceptional children within their boundaries.

Recently the United States Office of Education has established regional services for deaf-blind children. Each of these regions may include several states. The low incidence of such children requires this regional approach.

The description of these administrative plans may lead one to believe that all exceptional children are now able to receive appropriate help. This is far from the truth. It was pointed out in the introductory chapter that, on the average, approximately 10 percent of the nation's children have special needs and that only approximately 40 percent of the nearly seven million children are receiving special services. There is much yet to be done in this field. Would you like to help?

SUMMARY

1. Special educational services are administered at the (a) federal, (b) state, and (c) local levels.
2. The Federal government provides financial assistance for (a) the training of professional personnel, (b) research, and (c) services.
3. State education agencies are responsible for (a) implementing state and federal legislation in behalf of exceptional children, (b) providing local communities with financial support for excess cost, and (c) establishing state standards, teacher certification, and (d) providing supervision for local programs.

REFERENCES

Lord, F. E., and Isenberg, R. M. (eds.). 1964. *Cooperative Programs in Special Education.* Arlington, Virginia: Council for Exceptional Children.

U.S. Office of Education, Department of Health, Education, and Welfare. 1970. *Federal Programs Administered or Monitored by the Bureau of Education for the Handicapped.* Washington, D.C.: The Department.

APPENDIX A

A GUIDE TO AGENCIES

AND ORGANIZATIONS

CONCERNED WITH

EXCEPTIONAL CHILDREN

The CEC Information Center acts as a referral center for information requests from professional and nonprofessional personnel in the areas of special education and child health. In providing this service the Center has found that a great need exists for a current annotated directory of public and private organizations in this field. Therefore this annotated listing of agencies whose services relate to exceptional children has been compiled from responses to questionnaires distributed by CEC.

Each organization is described in terms of its purpose, membership requirements, publications, sponsorship of conferences, and affiliation with local chapters. Although this listing is not to be considered complete, it is hoped that it will serve as a useful resource in helping educators and parents obtain needed information and service.

ALEXANDER GRAHAM BELL ASSOCIATION FOR THE DEAF, INC.
1537 35TH ST., NW, WASHINGTON, D.C., 20007

The Association works to promote the teaching of speech and lipreading and the use of residual hearing to the deaf. Membership is open to interested persons for $12 a year. The official journal of the Association is *The Volta Review* (9 issues yearly, $12.50). Numerous books and pamphlets (some free) are published, as well as a newsletter, "Speaking Out." Biennial meetings are held in even-numbered years, regional meetings in odd-numbered years.

Source: Exceptional Children 3 (April 1969). Published with permission of the Council for Exceptional Children.

AMERICAN ACADEMY FOR CEREBRAL PALSY
UNIVERSITY HOSPITAL SCHOOL, IOWA CITY, IOWA 52240

The Academy strives to foster and stimulate professional education, research, and interest in cerebral palsy and related disorders and to correlate all aspects of this endeavor for the welfare of those with the handicap. Publications are the *Journal of Developmental Medicine* and *Child Neurology*. An annual meeting is held in November or December.

AMERICAN ACADEMY OF PEDIATRICS
1891 HINMAN AVE., EVANSTON, ILL. 60201

A national organization of specialty board certified pediatricians in the United States, Canada, and Latin America, the American Academy of Pediatrics fosters and stimulates interest in pediatrics and correlates all aspects of the work for the welfare of children which come within the scope of pediatrics. Membership is limited to specialty board certified pediatricians and other certified physicians (affiliate members). State chapters have been established in all 50 states and in practically all countries in Latin America. Canadian members belong to proximal state chapters in the US. The Academy sponsors an annual national meeting, an annual regional meeting, postgraduate courses, and regional conferences. Publications are the monthly journal, *Pediatrics,* and a bimonthly newsletter.

AMERICAN ACADEMY OF PRIVATE PRACTICE IN SPEECH PATHOLOGY AND AUDIOLOGY
P.O. BOX 53217, STATE CAPITAL STATION, OKLAHOMA CITY, OKLA. 73105

The Academy's purpose is to foster the highest ideals and principles of private practice in speech pathology and audiology within the American Speech and Hearing Association. Membership is limited to those who hold membership in and certification of clinical competence by the American Speech and Hearing Association, have earned the doctoral degree in speech pathology or audiology, have 5 years of experience in the field, and are actively engaged in private practice. Membership dues are $25 annually. Conventions are held biannually. The periodical publication is *Bulletin of American Academy of Private Practices in Speech Pathology and Audiology.*

AMERICAN ASSOCIATION FOR HEALTH, PHYSICAL EDUCATION, AND RECREATION
1201 16TH ST., NW, WASHINGTON, D.C. 20036

A national organization to support, encourage, and provide guidance for personnel who are developing and conducting school and community programs in health education, physical education, and recreation, AAHPER includes professional, student, and associate members. Periodical publications are the *Journal of Health, Physical Education, and Recreation* (which includes a monthly column, "Programs for the Handicapped"), the *Research Quarterly,* and "Challenge" (bi-monthly newsletter dealing with physical education and recreation for the mentally retarded). Other publications are also issued. AAHPER includes six district associations and state associations. National, district, and state association conventions are held annually in addition to numerous national, district, and local conferences dealing with specific topics. One unit of AAHPER is Programs for the Handicapped which is designed to provide leadership preparation, research, interpretation and development of programs, and distribution of materials for all areas of adapted physical education, corrective therapy, recreation for the ill and handicapped, therapeutic recreation, and health and safety problems of the handicapped.

AMERICAN ASSOCIATION OF PSYCHIATRIC CLINICS FOR CHILDREN
250 W. 57TH ST., RM. 1032, FISH BLDG., NEW YORK, N.Y. 10019

The purposes of this Association are to provide for the coordination of the activities of psychiatric clinics serving children in the U.S., its territories, and Canada; to help maintain the highest possible standards of clinic practice; to provide opportunities for the exchange of ideas, and for mutual help in the study and solution of clinic problems; to promote the training of clinic personnel; to cooperate with appropriate groups or organizations doing professional placement work in the clinic field; to cooperate with appropriate organizations throughout the world whose purposes may coincide with those of the Association; and to carry on such activities as may advance the field of child psychiatry. Membership is limited to clinics and other organizations offering psychiatric services to children and meeting specific membership requirements. Annual meetings are conducted in March and November. A Membership Directory is published annually.

AMERICAN ASSOCIATION OF WORKERS FOR THE BLIND, INC.
1151 K ST., NW, SUITE 637, WASHINGTON, D.C. 20005

The American Association of Workers for the Blind works to render all possible assistance to the promotion of all phases of work for and in the interest of the blind and to the prevention of blindness throughout the Americas. Membership ($15 regular, $5 student) is open to persons interested in the welfare of the blind or in the prevention of blindness. State and local chapters exist throughout the country. Periodical publications are *Blindness* (annually), *The New Outlook for the Blind* (monthly, $6), annual convention proceedings, pertinent papers, and the newsletter "News and Views." In addition, professional handbooks are published. Meetings include biennial conventions, biennial regional conventions, annual state chapter conventions, and other institutes and workshops.

AMERICAN ASSOCIATION ON MENTAL DEFICIENCY
5201 CONNECTICUT AVE., NW, WASHINGTON, D.C. 20015

The organization works to promote human progress and the general welfare of mentally subnormal and deficient persons by furthering the creation and dissemination of knowledge of mental deficiency, by facilitating cooperation among professional persons engaged in work in the field of mental deficiency and allied fields, and by encouraging the highest standards of treatment of the mentally deficient. There are several membership classifications for both experienced professionals and other interested persons. Dues range from $8 to $25 according to membership classification. Periodical publications are the *American Journal of Mental Deficiency* and *Mental Retardation* (both bimonthly). In addition, books and monographs are published. An annual national convention and 10 annual regional conventions are held.

AMERICAN CORRECTIVE THERAPY ASSOCIATION, INC.
811 ST. MARGARET'S RD., CHILLICOTHE, OHIO 45601

The work of the Association is directed toward applying the principles, tools, techniques, and psychology of medically oriented physical education to assist the physician in treating handicapped individuals. Active membership ($25 annually) is for those with a physical education degree and clinical training. Professional and associate memberships are $10 annually. Twelve regional chapters have been established. *The American Corrective Therapy Journal* is published six times annually. A national conference is held annually in addition to clinical and business meetings of regional chapters.

AMERICAN FOUNDATION FOR THE BLIND
15 W. 16TH ST., NEW YORK, N.Y. 10011

The American Foundation for the Blind is a private, nonprofit agency which serves as a clearinghouse on all pertinent information about blindness and promotes the development of educational, rehabilitation, and social welfare services for the blind and deaf blind children and adults. Services include publications in print, large type, recorded, and braille forms (limited), manufacture and sale of special aids and appliances for use by blind people, and recording and manufacture of talking books. Additional services are field consultation, research, personnel referral service, legislative consultation and action, public education, operation of a special library, fostering of improved programs, service information and referral, and processing and distribution of identification cards for one-fare travel concession for blind persons. Several periodical publications are issued including "AFB Newsletter" (quarterly, free), *New Outlook for the Blind* (monthly, $6, ink, braille, recorded), and "Talking Book Topics" (six times a year, free to blind persons). Numerous professional and public information books and pamphlets are published (some free). Institutes and conferences are held.

AMERICAN HEART ASSOCIATION, INC.
44 E. 23RD ST., NEW YORK, N.Y. 10010

Through programs of research, public and professional education, and community services, the American Heart Association, Inc., works to reduce premature death and disability caused by cardiovascular diseases. Membership is open to interested persons. Dues range from $2 to $5 annually. Periodical publications are *American Heart* (quarterly), "Heart Research Newsletter" (quarterly), *Management Digest* (quarterly), *Circulation Research* (monthly), *Cardiovascular Nursing* (quarterly), *Stroke—A Journal of Cerebral Circulation*, and "The Heart Bulletin" (bimonthly). Affiliated Heart Associations exist throughout the

United States. Annual scientific sessions, an annual meeting, and various local conferences on cardiovascular diseases are held.

THE AMERICAN LEGION, NATIONAL CHILD WELFARE DIVISION
P.O. BOX 1055, INDIANAPOLIS, IND. 46206

The Division is a child welfare program with emphasis on services and assistance to children of veterans. Through legislative efforts, dissemination of information on child welfare problems, direct aid to veterans' children, and cooperation with other national organizations, it seeks to improve conditions for all children. Membership in The American Legion is limited to wartime veterans; dues vary according to local chapters. Five annual regional child welfare conferences are held.

AMERICAN NURSES' ASSOCIATION, INC.
10 COLUMBUS CIRCLE, NEW YORK, N.Y. 10019

The ANA is a national professional organization which works to foster high standards of nursing practice and promote the welfare and professional and educational advancement of nurses for better nursing care. Five divisions are responsible for advancing the standards, knowledge, and skills in specific areas of nursing practice. Membership is open to registered nurses. Dues are $12.50 a year. Publications are the *American Journal of Nursing* (monthly, $5), "ANA in Action" (bimonthly membership publication), division newsletters, and monographs. The Association has 55 state and territorial associations and holds a biennial conference in even-numbered years and regional clinical conferences in odd-numbered years.

AMERICAN OCCUPATIONAL THERAPY ASSOCIATION, INC.
251 PARK AVENUE S., NEW YORK, N.Y. 10010

Designed to promote and improve the practice of occupational therapy, the Association accepts members who have a degree in occupational therapy and who have passed the registration examination of the Association. Dues are $30 annually. *The American Journal of Occupational Therapy* (bimonthly, $7.50) and other periodicals and publications are issued. Conferences are held annually. Affiliations exist with regional or state occupational therapy associations.

AMERICAN OPTOMETRIC ASSOCIATION
7000 CHIPPEWA ST., ST. LOUIS, MO. 63119

As a federation of associations of state, zone, and local optometric societies, the American Optometric Association works to advance, improve, and enhance the vision care of the public and to encourage and assist in the improvement of the art and science of optometry. Membership is for optometrists who have graduated from an accredited school of optometry and passed the licensing examination of the board of optometry in the state of practice. Dues vary according to the local society. Publications of the Association are the *Journal of the American Optometric Association* (monthly, $7.50) and "The AOA News" (monthly). An annual congress and various educational conferences are held.

AMERICAN ORTHOPSYCHIATRIC ASSOCIATION, INC.
1790 BROADWAY, NEW YORK, N.Y. 10019

The Association works to unite and provide a common meeting ground for those engaged in the study and treatment of problems of human behavior and to foster research and spread information concerning scientific work in the field of human behavior, including all forms of abnormal behavior. Membership ($25 for members, $35 for fellows) is limited to those who have worked 3 years in the field, meet the requirements of the professional organization in their discipline, and have obtained the masters degree. Publications include the *American Journal of Orthopsychiatry* (5 issues yearly, $12), the Association newsletter, and individual books. An annual scientific meeting is held.

AMERICAN PHYSICAL THERAPY ASSOCIATION
1740 BROADWAY, NEW YORK, N.Y. 10019

The organization fosters the development and improvement of physical therapy service and education through the coordinated action of physical therapists, allied professional groups, citizens, agencies, and schools to meet the physical therapy needs of people. Several types of professional and nonprofessional membership are available. Local chapters work with the national organization. Publications include the monthly periodical *Physical Therapy* (monthly, $10), a bimonthly listing of available physical therapy positions, monographs and other professional publications, career literature, and visual aids for rental or purchase. The Association holds an annual conference and periodic symposia.

AMERICAN PRINTING HOUSE FOR THE BLIND
1839 FRANKFORT AVE., LOUISVILLE, KY. 40206

Operating under an annual appropriation from the US Congress to promote the education of the blind, the Printing House is a nonprofit publisher of literature for the blind and partially seeing. Braille books, braille music, large type textbooks, talking books, recorded educational tapes, and tangible and educational aids for the blind are produced.

AMERICAN PSYCHIATRIC ASSOCIATION
1700 18TH ST., NW, WASHINGTON, D.C. 20009

Purposes of the Association are to further the study of the nature, treatment, and prevention of mental disorders, to promote mental health and the care of the mentally ill, to advance standards for mental hospitals and facilities, and to make psychiatric knowledge available. Membership is open to physicians with some specialized training and experience in psychiatry; dues range from $15 to $55. The Association includes local societies and district branches. Publications include *The American Journal of Psychiatry* (monthly, $12), "Psychiatric News" (monthly newsletter, $3), *Hospital and Community Psychiatry* (monthly, $8), special books and pamphlets, reference works, and research reports. The Association holds an annual meeting and an annual mental hospital institute in addition to divisional meetings and regional research conferences.

AMERICAN PSYCHOLOGICAL ASSOCIATION
1200 17TH ST., NW, WASHINGTON, D.C. 20036

The purpose of the American Psychological Association is to advance psychology as a science and as a means of promoting human welfare. Membership is open to professionals who have met specific requirements of education and experience dependent upon class of membership (dues range from $30 to $45). Within the Association are 29 divisions and affiliated state associations. Annual conventions are held in the fall. Journal publications are *American Psychologist* (monthly, $10), *Contemporary Psychology* (monthly, $10), *Journal of Abnormal Psychology* (bimonthly, $10), *Journal of Applied Psychology* (bimonthly, $10), *Journal of Comparative and Physiological Psychology* (bimonthly, $30), *Journal of Consulting and Clinical Psychology* (bimonthly, $10), *Journal of Educational Psychology* (bimonthly, $10), *Journal of Experimental Psychology* (monthly, $40), *Journal of Personality and Social Psychology* (monthly, $30), *Psychological Abstracts* (monthly, $40), *Psychological Bulletin* (monthly, $20), *Psychological Review* (bimonthly, $10), *Developmental Psychology* (bimonthly, $10). Also published are the *Employment Bulletin* (monthly, $8), convention proceedings, and position papers.

AMERICAN PUBLIC HEALTH ASSOCIATION, INC.
1740 BROADWAY, NEW YORK, N.Y. 10019

The Association works to protect and promote public and personal health and acts as an accrediting agency for schools of public health. Membership is open to professionals working in public health and to persons interested in public health (dues range from $15 to $25). Periodical publications are the *American Journal of Public Health and The Nation's Health* (monthly, $15), *Health Laboratories Science* (quarterly, $6), and *Medical Care* (bimonthly, $10). Handbooks, guides, monographs, and other publications are also issued. The Association meeting is conducted annually.

AMERICAN REHABILITATION COUNSELING ASSOCIATION OF THE AMERICAN PERSONNEL AND GUIDANCE ASSOCIATION
1607 NEW HAMPSHIRE AVE., NW, WASHINGTON, D.C. 20009

The Association which is one of eight divisions of the American Personnel and Guidance Association works to emphasize the social concept that conservation of human resources merits skillful services in the rehabilitation of the handicapped. Membership is for professionals, associates, and students; dues range from $11 to $22. *Rehabilitation Counseling Bulletin* (quarterly, $5) is published by the American Rehabilitation Counseling Association and various books, periodicals, and films are available through the American Personnel and Guidance Association. ARCA has state and local branches and participates in the APGA Annual Convention.

AMERICAN SCHIZOPHRENIA FOUNDATION
BOX 160, ANN ARBOR, MICH. 48107

By promoting research and public and professional education on schizophrenia, the Foundation works for the betterment of schizophrenic patients and their relations with society. Various categories of membership are available to interested persons. The Foundation sponsors forums, conferences, and committee meetings and publishes *Schizophrenia* (quarterly) and "Schizophrenia: Newsletter of the ASF" (quarterly).

THE AMERICAN SPEECH AND HEARING ASSOCIATION
9030 OLD GEORGETOWN RD., WASHINGTON, D.C. 20014

The Association is a scientific and professional organization which encourages basic scientific study of the processes of individual human speech and hearing, fosters improvement of therapeutic procedures with such disorders, and stimulates the exchange and dissemination of information. Members must hold a masters degree or equivalent; dues are $32 a year. Three journals are published: the *Journal of Speech and Hearing Disorders* (quarterly, $15), the *Journal of Speech and Hearing Research* (quarterly, $15), and *ASHA Journal* (monthly, $15). Monographs and reports are published irregularly. Twenty-eight state associations sponsor institutes and workshops and an annual convention is held.

ASSOCIATION FOR CHILDREN WITH LEARNING DISABILITIES
2200 BROWNSVILLE RD., PITTSBURGH, PA. 15210

The Association is designed to advance the education and general welfare of children and youth of normal or potentially normal intelligence who have learning disabilities of a perceptual, conceptual, or coordinative nature or related problems. Membership, available through the state organization, if established, or through the national organization, is open to parents and professionals. An annual conference is held as well as regional conferences. *Items of Interest* (monthly) and annual conference proceedings are published.

ASSOCIATION FOR EDUCATION OF THE VISUALLY HANDICAPPED
711 14TH ST., NW, WASHINGTON, D.C. 20005

The Association works to provide periodicals and other communicative media to evaluate problems and provide solutions, to disseminate professional information, and to stimulate an effort toward higher standards in personnel programs and facilities. Membership is available to professional workers, parents, and interested adults (dues range from $15 to $25). Publications are the newsletter "Fountainhead" (5 times yearly, $4) and the journal *Outlook*.

THE ASSOCIATION OF REHABILITATION CENTERS, INC.
7979 OLD GEORGETOWN RD., WASHINGTON, D.C. 20014

As a federation of rehabilitation centers the Association helps to improve rehabilitation service to handicapped and disabled persons by providing a focal point for unified effective joint action, cooperation with other professional associations, and mutual consultation, together with the study and exchange of ideas among rehabilitation facilities. Publications include manuals, guides, and workshop proceedings. An annual workshop and several educational seminars are sponsored.

BOY SCOUTS OF AMERICA
US RTS. 1 & 130, NEW BRUNSWICK, N.J. 08903

With its 508 local councils, Boy Scouts of America works to provide scouting programs for all boys, both normal and handicapped. Units for all types of handicapped boys have been established throughout the United States. Scouting affiliation is open to all boys. The national registration fee is $1; unit dues are determined by the boys themselves. Publications include numerous books, films, and pamphlets (some free). A meeting is held annually.

CHILD STUDY ASSOCIATION OF AMERICA
9 E. 89TH ST., NEW YORK, N.Y. 10028

The Association works to stimulate and further the education of adults in all that pertains to the moral, mental, and physical training and education of children. Membership is open to all interested persons and groups; dues are $15. A conference is held annually.

CONFERENCE OF EXECUTIVES OF AMERICAN SCHOOLS FOR THE DEAF
C/O DR. HOWARD M. QUIGLEY, 5034 WISCONSIN AVE., NW, WASHINGTON, D.C. 20016

The Conference works to further the welfare of the deaf by promoting the management and operation of schools for the deaf along the broadest and most efficient lines and establishing and maintaining minimum standards for teachers through certification procedures and approval of teacher training centers. Membership is comprised of executive heads of schools for deaf children in the United States, Canada, and Mexico (dues range from $50 to $100). *American Annals of the Deaf* (5 issues yearly, $6) is published in conjunction with The Convention of American Instructors of the Deaf. The Conference holds an annual meeting and cosponsors the International Conference on Education of the Deaf.

THE CONVENTION OF AMERICAN INSTRUCTORS OF THE DEAF
C/O DR. HOWARD M. QUIGLEY, EXECUTIVE SECRETARY, 5034 WISCONSIN AVE., NW, WASHINGTON, D.C. 20016

Comprised of persons engaged in educating the deaf, the organization provides an opportunity for the interchange of views concerning methods and means of educating the deaf.

Publications are *American Annals of the Deaf* (5 issues yearly, $6), "News Release" (5 issues yearly), and convention proceedings.

THE COUNCIL FOR EXCEPTIONAL CHILDREN
1411 S. JEFFERSON DAVIS HIGHWAY, ARLINGTON, VA. 22202

As a professional organization, CEC works to promote the adequate education of handicapped and gifted children through cooperation with educational and other organizations and individuals and through encouraging good professional relationships with various disciplines. Membership, which is organized with chapters at the local level and federations or branches at the state or provincial level, is open to special educators and other interested persons. Dues range from $15 to $21 depending upon state of residence. CEC contains the following divisions for persons interested in a particular exceptionality or aspect of special education: Association for the Gifted; Council of Administrators of Special Education; Council for Children with Communication Disorders; Division for Children with Learning Disabilities; Division on the Physically Handicapped, Hospitalized, and Homebound; Divison for the Visually Handicapped; Division on Mental Retardation; and Teacher Education Division. Publications include *Exceptional Children* (10 issues yearly, $10), *Education and Training of The Mentally Retarded* (quarterly, $5), *Teaching Exceptional Children* (quarterly, $5), books and pamphlets, research monographs, and annual convention papers. Annual international conventions, regional conferences, and special conferences are conducted.

COUNCIL OF ORGANIZATIONS SERVING THE DEAF
4201 CONNECTICUT AVE., NW, SUITE 210, WASHINGTON, D.C. 20008

The Council, working to promote the best interests of deaf persons, serves as a central clearing house and contact point for information and combined action by national organizations serving deaf persons. Membership is comprised of organizations (dues from $35 to $100) and interested individuals ($5). The Council publishes a periodic newsletter and the proceedings of the annual forum.

COUNCIL ON EDUCATION OF THE DEAF
C/O DR. GEORGE T. PRATT, PRESIDENT, CLARKE SCHOOL FOR THE DEAF,
NORTHAMPTON, MASS. 01060

Comprised of representatives from The Alexander Graham Bell Association for the Deaf, The Conference of Executives of American Schools for the Deaf, and the Convention of American Instructors of the Deaf, the Council provides a forum for those organizations concerned primarily with the education of deaf children, so that problems and concerns might be brought under advisement and solutions sought. One international congress has been held; future congresses are planned.

GIRL SCOUTS OF THE UNITED STATES OF AMERICA
830 3RD AVE., NEW YORK, N.Y. 10002

Working with 400 local Girl Scout Councils, the national organization is designed to inspire girls with the highest ideals of character, conduct, patriotism, and service so that they may become happy and resourceful citizens. Active membership is granted to any girl from age 7 to 17 who has the endorsement of the local council (dues are $1). Publications include *Handicapped Girls* and *Girl Scouting* as well as handbooks, pamphlets, books, and periodicals. The National Council of Girl Scouts meets every 3 years.

GOODWILL INDUSTRIES OF AMERICA, INC.
9200 WISCONSIN AVE., WASHINGTON, D.C. 20014

The corporation is organized to provide rehabilitation services, training, employment, and opportunities for personal growth as an interim step in the rehabilitation process for the handicapped, disabled, and disadvantaged who cannot be readily absorbed in the competitive labor market. Membership is available to rehabilitation facilities and workshops at the dues rate of up to 1 percent of earned income. Informative pamphlets and manuals (some free) are published. The Delegate Assembly is held annually in June and the annual Conference of Executives is held in February. Autonomous Goodwill Industries number 136; there are 43 branch workshops.

HUMAN GROWTH, INC.
307 5TH AVE., NEW YORK, N.Y. 10016

Begun in 1965 by parents and friends of children with growth problems, Human Growth, Inc., works to help the medical profession understand more about the process of human growth and development and all its deviations, such as dwarfism, gigantism, and failure to thrive. Opportunities are provided for families of children with growth disturbances to meet; financially indigent families are assisted in obtaining medical help. Membership is $5; sixteen chapters serve members in certain geographical areas. An annual national meeting is held. "HGI Newsletter" is scheduled to begin as a monthly publication in 1969.

INFORMATION CENTER—RECREATION FOR THE HANDICAPPED
OUTDOOR LABORATORY, LITTLE GRASSY, SOUTHERN ILLINOIS UNIVERSITY,
CARBONDALE, ILL. 62901

The Information Center is primarily concerned with the collection and dissemination of information pertaining to recreation for all handicapped persons. Publications include "ICRH Newsletter" (monthly), *Recreation for the Handicapped: A Bibliography* (yearly), and monographs. The Training Institute for Directors and Staff of Day Camps for the Mentally Retarded is held annually under the sponsorship of ICRH.

THE INTERNATIONAL ASSOCIATION OF PUPIL PERSONNEL WORKERS
5515 SHERIDAN RD., KENOSHA, WISC. 53140

The Association subscribes to the philosophy that education as an experience is not only for the purpose of developing the intellectual capacities of the individual but also the physical, emotional, spiritual, and social being. Any person working in the field of education which deals with special services to children is eligible to join (dues are $10). A quarterly journal is published and an annual convention is held.

INTERNATIONAL LEAGUE OF SOCIETIES FOR THE MENTALLY HANDICAPPED
12, RUE FORESTIERE, BRUSSELS-5, BELGIUM

The purpose of this international organization is to advance the interests of the mentally handicapped without regard to nationality, race, or creed, by bringing about cooperation between organizations representing national endeavor on their behalf. Four types of membership are available to all national organizations working primarily in the interests of the mentally handicapped. Annual dues are adjusted to the size and resources of the member society. Forty-six countries are represented in the League. Publications include working papers and a newsletter. Five International Congresses have been held and the General Assembly meets every 2 years.

INTERNATIONAL SOCIETY FOR REHABILITATION OF THE DISABLED
219 E. 44TH ST., NEW YORK, N.Y. 10017

As a federation of organizations in 59 countries, the Society works to promote the rehabilitation of the disabled throughout the world. Regional conferences, seminars, workshops, and a Triennial World Congress are sponsored. Publications are a newsletter, "Prosthetics International," and International Rehabilitation Review (quarterly).

JOSEPH P. KENNEDY, JR. FOUNDATION
719 13TH ST., NW, SUITE 510, WASHINGTON, D.C. 20005

The Foundation works to support research into the prevention of mental retardation and to promote programs to give retarded persons a better life. Two corporations established by the Foundation are Flame of Hope (a sheltered workshops program) and Special Olympics, Inc. (athletic competition for the retarded). An international awards competition and periodic scientific symposia are sponsored. Leaflets and general informative brochures are published.

LITTLE PEOPLE OF AMERICA, INC.
P.O. BOX 126, OWATONNA, MINN. 55050

The purpose of the organization is to provide fellowship, interchange of ideas, solutions to the unique problems of little people, and moral support. Membership dues schedule is $5 per person, $7.50 per family. Twelve chapters function on the district level. District and national (monthly) newsletters are published. An annual national convention (July) and annual district meetings are held.

MUSCULAR DYSTROPHY ASSOCIATION OF AMERICA, INC.
1790 BROADWAY, NEW YORK, N.Y. 10019

The objectives of the agency are to foster scientific research into the cause and cure of muscular dystrophy and related neuromuscular diseases; to render services to patients; and to carry on a program of education among physicians, members of the paramedical professions, and the general public. Membership is voluntary with no qualifications or dues required. Publications are *Muscular Dystrophy News* (quarterly) and professional literature. Annual chapter conferences (350 local chapters) and periodic medical and scientific conferences are sponsored.

THE NATIONAL ASSOCIATION FOR GIFTED CHILDREN
8080 SPRINGVALLEY DR., CINCINNATI, OHIO   45236

The Association aids schools, parents, and communities in providing for the gifted. Membership is open to interested persons; dues are $20 and up. An annual convention is held in addition to local chapter and regional meetings. Publications are the *Gifted Child Quarterly* (quarterly, $10) occasional newsletters, and special feature publications.

THE NATIONAL ASSOCIATION FOR MENTAL HEALTH, INC.
SUITE 1300, 10 COLUMBUS CIRCLE, NEW YORK, N.Y. 10019

The National Association for Mental Health is a coordinated citizens' voluntary organization working toward the improved care and treatment of the mentally ill and handicapped; for improved methods and services in research, prevention, detection, diagnosis, and treatment of mental illness and handicaps, and for the promotion of mental health. Membership in the National Association is through the local chapters and/or state mental health associations. Dues are set by the local or state associations. Publications include monographs, leaflets, and the periodical *Mental Hygiene* (quarterly, $8). Specialty conferences are sometimes held in addition to the annual meeting in November.

NATIONAL ASSOCIATION FOR MUSIC THERAPY, INC.
BOX 610, LAWRENCE, KANSAS 66055

The Association works for the advancement of research in music therapy by establishing qualifications and standards of training for music therapists and perfecting techniques of music programming which aid medical treatment most effectively. Membership is open to professionals, interested persons, and organizations; dues range from $5 to $50. *Journal of Music Therapy* (quarterly, $5), brochures, and handbooks are published. A conference and regional workshops are held annually.

NATIONAL ASSOCIATION FOR RETARDED CHILDREN
420 LEXINGTON AVE., NEW YORK, N.Y. 10017

Working through more than 1,300 state and local units, the Association helps to advance the welfare of the mentally retarded of all ages. Membership is through the local unit. An annual convention and an annual youth conference are sponsored. "Children Limited" (10 issues yearly, $2.50) is the periodical publication.

NATIONAL ASSOCIATION OF THE DEAF
2025 EYE ST., NW, SUITE 321, WASHINGTON, D.C. 20006

Comprised of deaf persons, relatives of deaf persons, and individuals working in the area of deafness, the Association promotes educational, sociological, and economic development of the deaf. Dues are $10. A youth organization, the Junior National Association of the Deaf, is active in over 50 schools for the deaf. A biennial convention and various programs and seminars are sponsored. Periodical publications are *The Deaf American* (monthly, $4) and "NAD Newsletter," in addition to numerous pamphlets, books, and films.

NATIONAL ASSOCIATION OF HEARING AND SPEECH AGENCIES
919 18TH ST., NW, WASHINGTON, D.C. 20006

The Association works toward solving the problems of hearing, speech, and language handicapped individuals. Approximately 200 local chapters and member agencies assist in the improvement of both the quality and quantity of care for the communicatively handicapped. Membership is open to agencies, professionals, and interested persons; dues are $10 and up. Annual conventions are held in June. Periodical publications are *Hearing And Speech News* (bimonthly, $5) and a newsletter, "Washington Sounds" (monthly, $15).

NATIONAL ASSOCIATION OF SHELTERED WORKSHOPS AND HOMEBOUND PROGRAMS
1522 K ST., NW, WASHINGTON, D.C. 20005

The purpose of the organization is to establish and maintain high standards of service to handicapped people in agency work programs and to demonstrate the significance of these services in the rehabilitation process. Membership is open to agencies and individuals (dues are dependent upon the size of the workshop). The *Monthly Information Exchange Service* provides information on ongoing programs pertaining to workshops. Studies and surveys are also published. The Association has 17 state chapters and holds an annual conference in addition to short-term institutes.

NATIONAL ASSOCIATION OF SOCIAL WORKERS
2 PARK AVE., NEW YORK, N.Y. 10016

The Association is a professional organization which works to promote the quality and effectiveness of social work practice, prevent and control social problems through a program of legislative and social action, and strengthen research and administration in social work. Members must have a masters degree from a school of social work; dues are $25 a year. Publications are *Social Work* (quarterly, $6), *Abstracts for Social Workers* (quarterly, $4 for members, $10 for nonmembers), newsletters, books, and pamphlets. There are 170 local chapters. Numerous national and regional conferences are sponsored.

NATIONAL ASSOCIATION OF STATE DIRECTORS OF SPECIAL EDUCATION
C/O DR. STELLA A. EDWARDS, PRESIDENT, DIVISION OF SPECIAL EDUCATION,
STATE DEPT. OF EDUCATION, FRANKFORT, KY. 40601

The Association renders services for exceptional children and adults through the establishment of active leadership in educational facilities, planning at state and local ' cussion forums, and consideration of current problems and issues. Membership . open to any person employed as director, supervisor, or consultant in special education by a national or state department of education. Persons employed in provinces of Canada are eligible for associate membership. Membership dues are $15. "State Leadership" is published quarterly. The Association holds an annual meeting.

THE NATIONAL ASSOCIATION OF TRAINING SCHOOLS AND JUVENILE AGENCIES
C/O WINDELL W. FEWELL, EXEC. SECRETARY-TREASURER, 5256 N. CENTRAL AVE.,
INDIANAPOLIS, IND. 40220

The Association works to prevent and control juvenile delinquency and crime by better understanding of the causes and needs of socially maladjusted children. Membership is open to individuals and agencies; dues range from $3 to $25. The Association cosponsors the National Institute on Crime and Delinquency and holds an annual conference. Conference proceedings are published.

NATIONAL CATHOLIC EDUCATIONAL ASSOCIATION, SPECIAL EDUCATION DEPT.
4472 LINDELL BLVD., ST. LOUIS, MO. 63108

The NCEA Special Education Department coordinates and promotes all the educational activities of the church which relate in any way to the education, training, and care of handicapped children, youth, and adults. Areas of disabilities organized under the framework of the Department include acoustical, emotional, mental, orthopedic, and visual. Membership is open to individuals or agencies engaged in some area of Catholic special education. Dues are $10 for individuals and $50 for agencies. Publications include "Special Education Newsletter" (3 issues yearly), *N.C.E.A. Convention Proceedings,* and "Directory of Catholic Special Facilities & Programs in the U.S. for Handicapped Children & Adults." The Special Education Department participates in the annual NCEA Convention and arranges individual conferences.

NATIONAL COMMITTEE FOR MULTI-HANDICAPPED CHILDREN √
239 14TH ST., NIAGARA FALLS, N.Y. 14303

The Committee works to inform the general public of the educational, therapeutic, recreational, and social service needs of children who have more than one handicap. Serving as a clearinghouse for information concerning existing programs for the handicapped, the Committee researches the literature in the fields of the blind, deaf, cerebral palsied, and brain injured. Membership is open to interested persons: no dues are required.

NATIONAL COUNCIL FOR THE GIFTED
700 PROSPECT AVE., WEST ORANGE, N.J. 07052

The Council fosters research in the development of practical programs for the education of the gifted to assure American leadership in fields of education, science (basic, political, and social), and business.

NATIONAL COUNCIL ON CRIME AND DELINQUENCY
44 E. 23RD ST., NEW YORK, N.Y. 10010

Working on a community, statewide, and national level, the Council strives to develop effective family and criminal courts to improve probation, parole, and institutional services, and to stimulate community programs for the prevention, treatment, and control of crime and delinquency. Membership is open to interested persons; dues are $10. The Council has local affiliates and 18 state citizen action program councils. Two journals, *Crime and Delinquency* (quarterly, $4.50) and *Journal of Research in Crime and Delinquency* (semiannually, $4.50), and a newsletter, "NCCD News" (5 issues yearly), are published. The Council cosponsors the National Institute on Crime and Delinquency.

THE NATIONAL EASTER SEAL SOCIETY FOR CRIPPLED CHILDREN AND ADULTS √
2023 WEST OGDEN AVE., CHICAGO, ILL. 60612

The Society is a voluntary agency providing direct services for crippled children and adults; education of the public, professional workers, and parents; research into the causes and prevention of handicapping conditions and into methods of care, education, and treatment of the patients involved. Members are the affiliated State Societies. Publications are *Rehabilitation Literature* (monthly, $6), "Easter Seal Bulletin" (quarterly, free), *Employment Bulletin* (quarterly, free to professional persons and placement service registrants), and numerous informational fliers. Research institutes, inservice training institutes, special workshops, and annual conventions are held.

NATIONAL EPILEPSY LEAGUE, INC.
203 N. WABASH AVE., RM. 2200, CHICAGO, ILL. 60601

The League is a voluntary agency which encourages research in epilepsy and provides information about epilepsy, medical resources, and employment to epileptics. The League provides epilepsy medication at low cost and works to increase public knowledge about epilepsy and to widen opportunities for education and employment of epileptics. Publications include the newsletter "Horizon," general information pamphlets, and technical publications.

THE NATIONAL FOUNDATION—MARCH OF DIMES ✓
800 2ND AVE., NEW YORK, N.Y. 10017

The National Foundation exists to lead, direct, and unify the fight against birth defects through support of programs of research, medical care, professional and public education, and community services. Lay and professional volunteers participate in programs through nearly 3,000 local chapters. National, regional, and local meetings and symposia for professional and lay audiences are held. General interest and professional education publications are issued. Films and exhibits are available for loan.

NATIONAL HEALTH COUNCIL, INC.
1740 BROADWAY, NEW YORK, N.Y. 10019

The principal functions of the Council are to help member agencies work together more effectively, to identify and promote the solution of national health problems of concern to the public, and to further improve governmental and voluntary health services for the public. Membership is limited to national organizations concerned with health. Books and pamphlets concerning health are published. The National Health Forum is held annually.

NATIONAL RECREATION AND PARK ASSOCIATION
1700 PENNSYLVANIA AVE., NW, WASHINGTON, D.C. 20006

As a nonprofit service organization, the Association is dedicated to the wise use of free time, conservation of natural and human resources, and beautification of the total American environment. There are several categories of membership including professional and organization membership (dues range from $10 to $50). Several periodical publications, including *Therapeutic Recreation Journal* (quarterly), are issued in addition to books and pamphlets on all phases of parks and recreation. A convention plus eight regional conferences are held annually.

NATIONAL REHABILITATION ASSOCIATION ✓
1522 K ST., NW, WASHINGTON, D.C. 20005

The Association works to advance rehabilitation of physically and mentally handicapped persons through public understanding, disseminating information, fostering research, encouraging an interdisciplinary approach to rehabilitation, and developing professional standards and professional training opportunities. Five professional divisions with membership subject to membership in NRA (dues range from $10 to $20) further meet the needs of members. The *Journal of Rehabilitation* (bimonthly, $5) and the "NRA Newsletter" (bimonthly) are published, as well as a legislative newsletter. Seventy affiliated state and local chapters hold chapter conferences in addition to an annual national and eight regional conferences.

NATIONAL SOCIETY FOR LOW VISION PEOPLE, INC.
2346 CLERMONT, DENVER, COLO. 80207

Through programs of training, education, and research, the Society works to help people with low vision achieve greater independence. Although the Society is not a membership organization, it sponsors various workshops for parents of low vision children.

NATIONAL THERAPEUTIC RECREATION SOCIETY
1700 PENNSYLVANIA AVE., NW, WASHINGTON, D.C. 20006

As a branch of the National Recreation and Park Association, the Society is concerned with the improvement of therapeutic recreation services and the development of the recreation profession. Members include professionals and agencies; dues range from $12 to $35. The Society participates in the annual convention of the National Recreation and Park Association and holds its own district conferences. *Therapeutic Recreation* (quarterly, $4) is the journal publication.

PAN AMERICAN HEALTH ORGANIZATION
PAN AMERICAN SANITARY BUREAU, REGIONAL OFFICE OF THE WORLD HEALTH ORGANIZATION, 525 23RD ST., NW, WASHINGTON, D.C. 20037

The organization is an agency of the United Nations with membership open to all countries of the region. It acts as a coordinating authority on international health work, assists governments in strengthening health services, and furnishes appropriate technical assistance. Other functions are to establish and maintain epidemiological and statistical services; to stimulate advance work to eradicate diseases; to promote the improvement of nutrition, housing sanitation, and other aspects of environmental hygiene; and to promote maternal and child health and welfare. Several periodicals, including *World Health* and "WHO Bulletin," are published, as well as pamphlets, papers, and reports.

THE PRESIDENT'S COMMITTEE ON EMPLOYMENT OF THE HANDICAPPED
US DEPARTMENT OF LABOR, WASHINGTON, D.C. 20210

The President's Committee on Employment of the Handicapped is concerned with promoting full and equal employment of all handicapped persons and encourages the removal of barriers which stand in the way of their employment. Members, appointed for 3-year terms by the chairman, are national leaders who have an interest in greater opportunities for the handicapped. Each state has a Governor's Committee on Employment of the Handicapped, and nearly 1,000 cities have local committees. All are voluntary. Publications include "Performance" (monthly) and booklets, pamphlets, brochures, and posters.

An annual meeting is held in May of each year and ongoing promotional campaigns are conducted throughout the year.

PRESIDENT'S COMMITTEE ON MENTAL RETARDATION ✓
WASHINGTON, D.C. 20201

The Committee works to promote cooperation and coordination among agencies and organizations giving services in mental retardation and allied fields. It promotes awareness of mental retardation needs, surveys mental retardation programs and needs, and advises the President on needed measures. The Committee is comprised of the Secretary of Health, Education, and Welfare, the Secretary of Labor, the Director of the Office of Economic Opportunity, and 21 citizens. Special workshops and forums are sponsored. Publications include "PCMR Message" (bimonthly), an annual report to the President, and special reports.

SOUTHERN REGIONAL EDUCATION BOARD
130 6TH ST., NW, ATLANTA, GA. 30313

Comprised of the 15 southern states, the Board is an interstate compact for cooperation in the expansion and improvement of higher education, with a special interest for the broad range of problems in mental health research and training. Periodicals include *Mental Health Briefs* (quarterly), *Regional Action* (quarterly), *Regional Spotlight* (monthly), *Summary of State Legislation Affecting Higher Education in the South* (spring and fall). Research monographs and reports are also available. The SREB annually supports the following meetings: SREB Board, Commission on Mental Illness and Retardation, Policy Commission for the Institute for Higher Educational Opportunity in the South, Educational Plans and Policies Advisory Committee, and the Legislative Advisory Council. In addition, a variety of special interest and area meetings are held.

UNITED CEREBRAL PALSY ASSOCIATIONS, INC. ✓
66 E. 34TH ST., NEW YORK, N.Y. 10016

As a voluntary health agency, UCP works to: (a) promote research in cerebral palsy, the treatment, education and habilitation of persons with cerebral palsy and to promote professional training programs of all types related to the problem of cerebral palsy; (b) further by professional and public education information concerning all aspects of the problem of cerebral palsy; (c) promote better and more adequate techniques and facilities for the diagnosis and treatment of persons with cerebral palsy; (d) cooperate with governmental and private agencies concerned with the welfare of the handicapped; (e) promote the employment of persons with cerebral palsy; (f) solicit, collect, and otherwise raise funds and other property for above purposes and for supporting facilities for the care, treatment, and study of persons with cerebral palsy; (g) and to establish and work with local and state affiliates (over 300 currently). Conferences, workshops, and seminars are conducted. Publications include *The UCP Crusader* (bimonthly free) and professional literature.

US DEPARTMENT OF HEALTH, EDUCATION, AND WELFARE ✓

The eight major program units of the Department of Health, Education, and Welfare listed here were selected because each administers several programs for the handicapped. For more detailed information about the specific programs of these and other units within HEW, consult the directory, *Financial Assistance Programs for the Handicapped*, US Department of Health, Education, and Welfare, 1968. Available for $1.00 from the Superintendent of Documents, US Government Printing Office, Washington, D.C. 20402.

US OFFICE OF EDUCATION, BUREAU OF ADULT, VOCATIONAL AND LIBRARY
PROGRAMS
7TH AND D ST., SW, RM. 5050, WASHINGTON, D.C. 20202

As one of five bureaus within the Office of Education, the Bureau of Adult, Vocational and Library Programs administers grants to states for vocational and technical education programs, adult education programs, development and construction of public libraries, and acquisition of library resources. Examples of specific programs are the establishment of library services for the physically handicapped and provision of vocational education for the handicapped. Periodic conferences are conducted. Publications include professional literature, curriculum guides, and general information publications.

US OFFICE OF EDUCATION, BUREAU OF EDUCATION FOR THE HANDICAPPED ✓
7TH AND D ST., SW, WASHINGTON, D.C. 20202

As one of five bureaus within the Office of Education, the Bureau of Education for the Handicapped serves as the principal arm of the Office of Education in administering and carrying out programs and projects relating to the education of handicapped children, including training of professional personnel, research and development, and the provision of special education services. Bulletins, pamphlets, reports, and surveys are published. The Bureau sponsors conferences of professional personnel on subjects involving the education of handicapped children.

US PUBLIC HEALTH SERVICE, HEALTH SERVICES AND MENTAL HEALTH ADMINISTRATION,
NATIONAL INSTITUTE OF MENTAL HEALTH
5454 WISCONSIN AVE., CHEVY CHASE, MD. 20015

The agency works for the promotion of mental health, the prevention of mental illnesses, and the treatment and rehabilitation of the mentally ill by conducting or supporting research programs, manpower development and training, demonstrations, and community service. Special mental health problems such as delinquency and child and family mental health are within the work of the Institute. NIMH produces scientific papers, abstract and index publications, and public information publications. Numerous conferences on topics within the wide subject of mental health are conducted.

US PUBLIC HEALTH SERVICE, NATIONAL INSTITUTES OF HEALTH
HEW SOUTH BLDG., RM. 5312, WASHINGTON, D.C. 20201

As one of the three major units of the Public Health Service, NIH works to improve the health of citizens by conducting and supporting basic clinical research, training researchers, and educating health professionals to bring research results to practice. Research activities are conducted by six disease-oriented institutes: National Cancer Institute, National Heart Institute, National Institute of Allergy and Infectious Diseases, National Institute of Arthritis and Metabolic Diseases, National Institute of Dental Research, and National Institute of Neurological Diseases and Blindness, and also through the National Institute of Medical Sciences and the National Institute of Child Health and Human Development. Numerous publications are issued including periodicals, abstract and index publications, technical publications, and public information pamphlets. Meetings and conferences are conducted.

SOCIAL AND REHABILITATION SERVICE, ASSISTANCE PAYMENTS ADMINISTRATION
330 INDEPENDENCE AVE., SW, WASHINGTON, D.C. 20201

Working as a unit within Social and Rehabilitation Service, the Assistance Payments Administration provides leadership in planning, development, and coordination of SRS programs providing for the administrative and money aspects of public assistance programs. Specific programs provide financial aid to needy handicapped persons. Public information publications are available.

SOCIAL AND REHABILITATION SERVICE, CHILDREN'S BUREAU
330 C ST., SW, WASHINGTON, D.C. 20201

The Children's Bureau is a governmental agency established to investigate and report upon all matters pertaining to the welfare of children. It assists in extending and improving maternal and child health and crippled children's and child welfare services through grants to the states and grants for special projects. The journal *Children* (bimonthly, $1.25) is published in addition to materials on child health and handicapped children.

SOCIAL AND REHABILITATION SERVICE, OFFICE OF RESEARCH, DEMONSTRATIONS, AND TRAINING
HEW NORTH BLDG., RM. 3315, WASHINGTON, D.C. 20201

The Office of Research, Demonstrations, and Training is one of several offices within the Office of the Administrator, Social and Rehabilitation Service. The Office is responsible for directing and promoting a research and demonstration program to solve physical, mental, social, cultural, and economic deprivation problems and coordinating and directing all SRS intramural research. Specific programs provide assistance for vocational rehabilitation of the physically and mentally handicapped. Conferences for state and local specialists in staff development are held. "Research and Demonstrations Brief" is published periodically.

SOCIAL AND REHABILITATION SERVICE, REHABILITATION SERVICES ADMINISTRATION
330 INDEPENDENCE AVE., SW, RM. 3139 D, WASHINGTON, D.C. 20201

As part of the Social and Rehabilitation Service, this unit provides leadership in the planning, development, and coordination of SRS programs providing rehabilitation and social services to physically, mentally, culturally disabled, and handicapped persons as provided for in the Vocational Rehabilitation Act, as amended, and the Social Security Act, Titles I, II, X, XIV, and XVI. Publications available include research reports, bibliographies. *Rehabilitation Record* (bimonthly, $1.75), and a wide range of publications for both professionals and the general public.

WESTERN INSTITUTE FOR THE DEAF
215 E. 18TH AVE., VANCOUVER 10, BRITISH COLUMBIA, CANADA

The Institute is a nonprofit service organization dealing with the problems of the hearing handicapped. Services include job placement, audiological assessment hearing tests, provision of hearing aids to the needy, and education of the general public concerning the many problems of the hearing handicapped. A newsletter, "WID News" is published monthly.

WESTERN INTERSTATE COMMISSION FOR HIGHER EDUCATION, SPECIAL EDUCATION
AND REHABILITATION PROGRAM
30TH ST., UNIVERSITY EAST CAMPUS, BOULDER, COLO. 80382

The Special Education and Rehabilitation Program is funded by the United Cerebral Palsy Research and Educational Foundation, Inc., and the Rehabilitation Services Administration. It was established to assist in developing western college and university programs in special education and rehabilitation at the graduate and undergraduate levels and to stimulate coordination of agencies and institutions for the use of all resources available for special education and rehabilitation training. The Program sponsors numerous conferences concerning teacher preparation, patterns of service, and research. Publications include reports and brochures.

APPENDIX B

GLOSSARY OF TECHNICAL TERMS[1]

Adductor A muscle used to draw toward or past the median axis of the body, also to bring together similar parts such as the fingers.

Agglutinin An antibody in the blood serum causing particles to collect into clumps.

Agraphia Impairment in the ability to write.

Albinism Hereditary lack of pigment in the iris, skin, and hair.

Alexia Loss of the ability to read written or printed language.

Amino acids One of a group of acids which are both basic and acid and are obtained from protein by hydrolysis.

Angular gyrus A cerebral convolution that forms the back part of the lower parietal region of the brain.

Aphasia Loss or impairment of the ability to use oral language.

Asphyxia A lack of oxygen or excess of carbon dioxide in the blood causing unconsciousness.

Aspirate To pronounce a vowel or a word with an initial *h* sound.

Asthma A disease marked by recurrent attacks of wheezing coughs, labored breathing (particularly on expiration of air), and a sense of constriction due to spasmodic contraction of the bronchi.

Ataxia A form of cerebral palsy marked by incoordination in voluntary muscular movements.

Athetosis A form of cerebral palsy marked by slow, recurring, weaving movements of arms and legs, and by facial grimaces.

Audiogram Graphic record of hearing acuity at selected intensities throughout the normal range of audibility recorded from a pure tone audiometer.

Audiometer Instrument for testing acuity of hearing.

Auditory association Ability to relate concepts presented orally.

Auditory closure The ability to recognize the whole from the presentation of a partial stimulus.

[1] The author is indebted to La Martha Wallace for most of the work on this glossary.

Auditory reception   The ability to derive meaning from orally presented material.

Auditory sequential memory   The ability to reproduce a sequence of auditory stimuli.

Aura, epileptic   A subjective sensation that precedes and marks the onset of an epileptic attack.

Autism   A childhood disorder rendering the child noncommunicative and withdrawn.

Aversive stimulus   A stimulus which a subject would avoid if possible.

Bilingual   Using or able to use two languages.

Bright's disease   Inflammation of the kidney affecting its vascular system.

Bronchiectosis   A chronic dilation of one of the two main branches of the windpipe or their subdivisions.

Carbohydrate   Any of various neutral compounds as sugars, starches, and cellulose which constitute a major part of human foods.

Cataract   A condition of the eye in which the crystalline lens and/or its capsule become opaque with consequent dimming of vision.

Catastrophic reaction   Response to a shock or a threatening situation with which the individual is unprepared to cope. Behavior is inadequate, vacillating, inconsistent, and generally retarded.

Central nervous system (C.N.S.)   That part of the nervous system to which the sensory impulses are transmitted and from which motor impulses pass out; in vertebrates the brain and spinal cord.

Cephalic   Pertaining to the head.

Cerebral dominance   Assumption that one cerebral hemisphere generally leads the other in control of bodily movements. In most individuals the left side of the brain controls language and is considered the dominant hemisphere.

Cerebral palsy   Any one of a group of conditions affecting control of the motor system due to lesions in various parts of the brain.

Cerebrospinal fluid   The fluid that circulates in certain spaces within the brain and down the central canal of the spinal cord.

Chromosome   One of the minute bodies in the nucleus of a cell which contain the genes or hereditary factors.

Cleft palate   Congenital fissure of the roof of the mouth, often associated with cleft lip (harelip).

Clonic   Pertaining to a spasm (clonus) in which rigidity and relaxation alternate in rapid succession.

Clonus   Involuntary rapid contractions and relaxations of a muscle.

Conductive hearing loss   A condition which reduces the intensity of the sound vibrations reaching the auditory nerve in the inner ear.

Congenital   Present in an individual at birth.

Conservation In Piaget theory the ability to retain a concept of area, mass, length, etc. when superficial changes are made in the appearance of an object or scene.

Cystic fibrosis A hereditary disease due to a generalized dysfunction of the pancreas.

Decibel A relative measure of the intensity of sounds, zero decibel represents normal hearing.

Diabetes mellitus A disorder of carbohydrate metabolism characterized by an excessive amount of glucose (sugar) in the urine and in the blood.

Diplegia Bilateral paralysis affecting like parts on both sides of the body.

Disinhibition Lack of ability to refrain from response to what is perceived, often resulting in hyperactivity and distractibility.

Dysarthria Difficulty in the articulation of words due to involvement of the central nervous system.

Dyscalculia Inability to perform mathematical functions.

Dysgraphia Inability to produce motor movements required for handwriting.

Dyslexia Impairment of the ability to read.

Edema The presence of abnormally large amounts of fluid in the intercellular tissue spaces of the body.

Electroencephalograph An instrument for graphically recording electrical brain waves.

Encephalitis lethargica An infectious inflammation of the brain (sleeping sickness).

Epicanthic fold A congenital formation of the eyelid consisting of a vertical fold of skin on either side of the nose.

Epilepsy The name given to a group of nervous diseases marked primarily by convulsions of varying forms and degrees.

Etiology The study of causes or origins of a disease or condition.

Exaphoria Insufficient action of certain muscles of the eye so that one eye tends to deviate outward but can be controlled by extra muscular effort.

Familial Occurring in members of the same family, as a familial disease.

Figure-ground disturbance The inability to discriminate a figure from its background.

Finger agnosia Inability to recognize the name or identify the individual fingers of one's own hand.

Galactosemia An inherited condition of mental retardation caused by an error in the metabolism of the galactose in milk.

Genetic Inherited.

Glaucoma Increased pressure inside the eyeball caused by accumulation of fluid in the front portion.

Gonorrhea Contagious inflammation of the genital mucous membrane due to infection.

Grammatic closure Ability to make use of the redundancies of oral language in acquiring automatic habits for handling syntax and grammatic inflections.

Grand mal   An epileptic seizure in which the convulsions are severe and widespread with rather prolonged loss of awareness.

Haptic   Pertaining to the sense of touch.

Hemiplegia   Paralysis of one side of the body.

Hemophilia   A hereditary condition characterized by delayed clotting of the blood with consequent difficulty in checking hemorrhage.

Hydrocephalus   A condition of excess cerebrospinal fluid within the ventricular and sub-arachnoid spaces in the brain.

Hyperactivity   Excessive mobility or motor restlessness.

Hypertonicity   Excessive tension in the condition of a muscle not at work.

Hypoactive   Diminished motor function or activity.

Insulin   A protein hormone produced by the pancreas and secreted into the blood where it regulates carbohydrate (sugar) metabolism.

Interindividual   Pertaining to a comparison of one person with another or of one person with a group of individuals.

Intonation   Rise and fall in pitch of the voice in speech.

Intraindividual   Pertaining to a comparison of different characteristics within an individual.

In utera   Period of time in a baby's life from conception until birth.

Jacksonian epilepsy   A form of epilepsy in which the seizure manifests no loss of awareness but a definite course or series of convulsions affecting a limited region.

Jaundice   Yellowish pigmentation of the skin, tissues, and body fluids caused by excessive amounts of pigment in the bile secreted by the liver.

Keratitis   Inflammation of the cornea.

Kinesthesis   The sense whose end organs lie in the muscles, joints, and tendons and are stimulated by bodily movements and tensions.

Larynx   The modified upper part of the windpipe; the organ of the voice.

Laterality   The preferential use of one side of the body, especially in tasks demanding the use of only one hand, one eye, or one foot.

Lipids   Any one of a group of organic substances which are insoluble in water but soluble in alcohol or other fat solvents. Lipids form one of the structural components of living cells.

Malocclusion   Abnormality in the coming together of the teeth.

Mastoidectomy   Surgical removal of the mastoid cells of the temporal bone in the ear.

Maxilla   The irregularly shaped bone forming the upper jaw.

Meningitis   Inflammation of the meninges (the membrane converting the brain and spinal cord) sometimes affecting vision, hearing, and/or intelligence.

Metabolism   The physical and chemical processes in living cells by which energy is provided for vital activities.

Meticulosity   Rigid and undiscriminatory precision, order, and neatness.

Monoplegia   Paralysis of one body part.

Mosaicism   A form of Down's Syndrome (mongolism) in which adjacent cells will be found to contain different numbers of chromosomes.

Muscular dystrophy   One of the more common primary diseases of muscle. It is characterized by weakness and atrophy of the skeletal muscles with increasing disability and deformity as the disease progresses.

Mylomeningocele   A sac containing part of a malformed spinal cord protruding from a hole in the spine.

Myopia   Nearsightedness in which the rays from distant objects are brought to a focus before they reach the retina.

Nephrosis   A noninflammatory, degenerative condition of the kidney.

Neurological   Pertaining to the normal and abnormal function of the nervous system.

Neurophysiological   Pertaining to the physiology of the nervous system.

Obturator   That which closes or stops an opening.

Opthalmia neonatorum   Gonorrheal inflammation of and discharge from the conjunctiva of the eye of the newborn baby under two weeks.

Opthalmologist   A physician who specializes in diagnosis and treatment of defects and diseases of the eye.

Optometrist   A person who examines, measures, and treats certain eye defects by methods requiring no physician's license.

Osteomyelitis   Inflammation of bone which begins with a hematogeneous abscess and, if not checked, may spread through the bone to involve the marrow and other parts.

Otitis media   An inflammation of the middle ear.

Otolaryngoscopic   Referring to an examination of the ear, nose, and throat, A laryngoscope is an examination of the inside of the larynx by means of a laryngoscope.

Otosclerosis   The formation of spongy bone in the capsule bone in the ear.

Ototoxic   Caused by poison or toxin creating damage to the ear.

Pancreas   A large gland behind the stomach; the secretions of which pass into the duodenum and are concerned with digestion. Its internal secretion, insulin, helps to control carbohydrate metabolism.

Paraplegia   Paralysis of the legs and lower part of the body; both motion and sensation being affected.

Perinatal   Occurring at or pertaining to the time of birth.

Perseveration   Continuations of an activity after cessation of the causative stimulus.

Petit mal   Epileptic seizure in which there may be only a momentary dizziness or blackout or some automatic action of which the patient has no knowledge.

Pharynx   That part of the throat that leads from mouth and nose to the larynx.

Phenylketonuria (PKU)   An inherited error of metabolism resulting in a lack of the necessary enzyme for oxydizing pehylalanine which in turn promotes accumulation of phenylpyuric acid and mental retardation.

Phonation The production of speech sounds.

Phoneme A speech sound or closely related variants commonly regarded as being the same sound.

Poliomyelitis An acute viral disease characterized by involvement of the central nervous system, sometimes resulting in paralysis.

Postnatal. After birth.

Prenatal Occurring or existing before birth.

Proprioceptive Pertaining to stimulations from the muscles, tendons, and labyrinth which give information concerning the position and movement of the body and its members.

Prosthesis The replacement of an absent part of the body by an artificial one.

Prosthodontics Making dental substitutes such as crowns, bridges, dentures.

Psycholinguistics The study of the processes whereby the intentions of speakers are transformed into signals and whereby these signals are transformed into interpretations of hearers.

Psychomotor epilepsy A form of epilepsy in which the seizures consist of purposeful but inappropriate acts; a difficult form to diagnose and control.

Psychopathology The study of the causes and nature of mental disease.

Recessive trait A trait, controlled by heredity, that remains latent or subordinate to a dominant characteristic.

Reinforcement A procedure to strengthen (or weaken) a response by the administration of immediate rewards (positive reinforcement) or punishment (negative reinforcement).

Resonance The vibrating quality of a voice sound.

Response The activity of an organism or an organ, or the inhibition of previous activity resulting from stimulation.

Retinoblastoma Malignant intraocular tumor of childhood; occurring usually under the age of five.

Retrolental fibroplasia A disease of the retina in which a mass of scar tissue forms in back of the lens of the eye. Both eyes are usually affected and it occurs chiefly in infants born prematurely who receive excessive oxygen.

Rheumatoid arthritis A systemic disease characterized by inflammation of the joints and a broad spectrum of manifestations often involving destruction of the joints with resultant deformity.

Rubella German measles.

Schema A number of ideas or concepts combined into a coherent plan; a model that displays the essential or important relations between concepts.

Schizophrenia A group of psychotic reactions characterized by fundamental disturbances in reality relationships, by a conceptual world determined excessively by feeling and by marked affective, intellectual, and overt behavioral disturbances.

Sensorimotor Any act whose nature is primarily dependent upon the combined or integrated functioning of sense organs and motor mechanisms.

Sensory-neural hearing loss A defect of the inner ear or the auditory nerve transmitting impulses to the brain.

Sound blending Ability to synthesize the separate parts of a word and produce an integrated whole.

Spasticity Excessive tension of the muscles and heightened resistance to flexion or extension, as in cerebral palsy.

Sphincter A ring-like muscle which closes a natural orifice.

Spina bifida occulta A defect of closure in the posterior bony wall of the spinal conal without associated abnormality of the spinal cord or meninges.

Status epilepticus A condition in which a grand mal seizure is immediately followed by another without regaining consciousness.

Still's Disease Juvenile rheumatoid arthritis.

Stimulus The physical, chemical, biological, and social events which act on the individual.

Strephosymbolia Reversal in perception of left-right order especially in letter or word order, "twisted symbols."

Stuttering A speech impediment in which the even flow of words is interrupted by hesitations, rapid repetition of speech elements, and/or spasms of breathing.

Synergic Acting together or in harmony.

Syntax That part of a grammar system which deals with the arrangement of word forms to show their mutual relations in the sentence.

Synthesis Process of putting data together to form a whole.

Syphilis A contagious venereal disease.

Tachistoscope A machine that exposes visual material for a variable period of time.

Tactile (tactual) Sense of touch.

Tonic Characterized by contraction of a muscle sufficient to keep the muscle taut but not sufficient to cause movement.

Translocation A type of chromosomal aberration found in some cases of Down's Syndrome (mongolism) in which a chromosome has broken and become fused to another chromosome.

Trauma Any experience that inflicts serious damage to the organism. It may refer to psychological as well as to physiological insult.

Triplegia Paralysis of three of the body's limbs.

Trisomy 21 Mongolism caused by having three instead of a pair of chromosome 21.

Tuberculosis An infectious disease characterized by formation of tubercules (small, rounded nodules produced by the bacillus of tuberculosis) in the tissue of the lungs.

Uvula The pendent fleshy lobe in the middle of the posterior border of the soft palate.

Verbal expression Ability to express one's own concepts verbally in a discrete, relevant, and approximately factual manner.

Visual association The organizing process by which one is able to relate concepts presented visually.

Visual closure Ability to identify a visual stimulus from an incomplete visual presentation.

Visual fusion The coordination of the separate images in the two eyes into one image.

Visual reception Ability to gain meaning from visual symbols.

Visual sequential memory Ability to reproduce sequences of visual items from memory.

Whooping cough An infectious disease affecting the respiratory tract and characterized by coughing and a prolonged whooping or crowing respiration.

INDEX

OF

NAMES

Terman, Lewis M., 8, 107, 122–26, 127, 133, 137
Terry, T. L., 301
Tervoort, B., 266
Thompson, Helen, 281
Thorpe, J. S., 130
Tilman, M. H., 309
Tisdall, William, 233, 234, 309
Tizard, J., 173
Torrance, E. P., 129, 130, 154
Travis, Lee Edward, 88
Tredgold, A. F., 162

Ullmann, Charles E., 401
Upshall, C. C., 268, 269

Van Riper, C., 87, 89, 90, 93
Veldman, D. D., 130
Verbeck, A. J., 266
Vernon, M., 267, 271
Von Braun, Wernher, 117–18

Waisman, H. A., 172, 173
Wallach, M. A., 128, 130
Wallen, Norman E., 364
Wallin, J. E. Wallace, 262, 264
Walsh, T. E., 248
Walters, Richard H., 398
Ward, V. S., 140

Warwick, Harold L., 243
Watson, John B., 106
Weaver, C. H., 75
Weikart, D. P., 181
Welch, Elizabeth A., 199
Werner, Hans, 48
West, R., 87, 88, 90
Wickman, 401
Widdop, J. H., 205
Wiener, 175
Wiener, Norbert, 116, 118
Wilson, J., 307
Wilson, Robert C., 150
Wirt, R. D., 393
Wiseman, D. E., 57
Wishik, 357
Wolf, J. M., 23, 316
Wolfe, W. G., 96
Wolpe, J. A., 403
Wood, Nancy E., 91
Worcester, D. A., 136
Wortis, J. A., 176
Wright, Beatrice A., 7
Wright, Loyd, 401
Wundt, 6

Yamamoto, K., 128
Yamashita, Kiyoshi, 205
Yannet, H., 175

INDEX

OF

SUBJECTS

Discipline, erratic, in home, 398
Discrepancy, concept of, 396–97
  in growth, 8, 9, 12, 14, 23, 35, 44, 121, 133, 145, 168, 169
Distortions, sound, 82, 83, 97, 261
Divergent thinking, 108–9, 128–29, 149, 309
Divorce, 125, 207
Double hemiplegia, 354
Down's Syndrome, 174, 229
Dramatization, 232, 384
Drill, excessive, 151
Drug therapy, 365
Drugs, toxic, 249
Durrell-Sullivan Reading Achievement Test, 280
Dysarthria, 363
Dyslexia, 42, 46, 47, 64

Ear, infections of, 248
  structure and functioning of, 250
  See also Auditory defects and Listening
Early admission to school and college, 135–36, 137, 145
Easter Seal Society, 351
Economic usefulness, 221, 230–31, 233, 234
Edema, 371
Edinburgh, first school for deaf in, 264
Educable mentally retarded Children, 161, 164, 166, 169, 177, 186, 191–217, 224
  case study of, 192–93
  characteristics of, 195–97
  in the community, 186, 206–8
  education of, 168, 197–206, 208–12, 330
  growth pattern of, 193–95
Educating Exceptional Children (Kirk, 1st ed.), 62
Education, administrative services in, 421–29
  aims of, 197–98
  of the blind, 310–11, 324–26, 331
  of the crippled, 377–84
  of the deaf, 257, 262–84
  equal opportunity for, 3, 106
  of exceptional children in general, 5–7, 30–34
  of the gifted, 105–7, 134–45
  of the hard of hearing, 257, 258–62
  mass, 106
  of the mentally retarded, 197–206, 208–12, 225, 230–33
  of parents, 145, 181, 259, 260, 382; see also Counseling
  of the partially seeing, 310–12
  and political philosophy, 3, 106
  of the socially and emotionally disturbed, 402–15
  state departments of, 424, 426–27
  of the visually handicapped, 323–44
  See also Schools, Teachers, and Teaching
Education of the Handicapped Act, 422–25
Educational Policies Commission, 197

Educational Research Information Center, 425
Educationally deaf children, 241, 272
Elementary school, deaf children in, 283–84
  mentally retarded children in, 208, 209–10
  speech correction in, 99
  See also Public school
Elementary and Secondary Education Act, 424
Emmetropic eye, 298
Emotional factors, in hearing loss, 241, 249
  in stuttering, 89
Emotionally disturbed children, 30, 33, 41, 91, 208, 317, 389–415
  characteristics, 393–95
  contributing factors, 395–401
  education for, 402–15
  prevalence of, 401–2
  teachers of, 400, 404, 406, 413–15
Employment records of the mentally retarded, 206–7
Encephalitis, 12, 176–77, 359
End organ palsy, 352
Endogenous causes, of deafness, 248–49
  of mental retardation, 161
England, cerebral palsy in, 357, 360, 363
  classes for the partially seeing in, 324
  first school for the deaf in, 264
Enrichment, 127, 139–40, 145, 148
Entrance requirements. See Admission
Environment, adaptation of, for crippled children, 378–79, 383
  classroom, 50, 67, 350
  influence of, on giftedness, 113, 126
  influence of, on speech, 97
  and mental retardation, 162, 171, 177–82, 196, 197
  orientation to, for the blind, 334, 336–37, 341
  protective, 6
  responsive, 154
  See also Community and Home
Epilepsy, 26, 176, 317, 364–66
Equality of educational opportunity, 3, 106, 127
Equipment, special. See Special materials and equipment
Esophoria, 299
Ethnic differences among the gifted, 126–27
Evaluation, of giftedness, 111–12, 144–45
  of mental retardation, 212, 227
  self-, 153, 216
  of special groupings, 142–43
  in thinking process, 128, 149
  of training program for mentally retarded, 233–35
  of visual condition, 295–96
  See also Assessment
Exceptional children, defined, 4–5
  history and philosophy of education, 5–7, 34–36

High-frequency sounds, 249
High school. *See* Secondary school
Hoff General Hospital, 249
Home, importance of attitude in, for crippled, 374–77
inadequate, and removal from community, 224
influence of, in causing maladjustment, 374–75, 397
See also Parents
Home-building skills, 210
Home instruction, of the crippled, 380
of the hard-of-hearing and deaf, 260, 262, 282
Home rooms, special rooms as, 193
Homogeneous grouping, 225
Honors program, 141, 144
Hospital schools and classes, 34, 380, 414
Hunter College Elementary School, 141
Hypernasal speech, 85
Hyperopia, 298
Hyperphoria, 299
Hysterical deafness, 249

Ideational fluency, 150
Identification, of hearing loss, 245, 258–59
of mental retardation, 164
of speech defectives, 77–79
Idiopathic speech, 77
Idiots, 161, 162, 224
Illinois, Commission on Children, 243
deaf children in, 243
mentally retarded children in, 222, 224, 234
University of, 384
Illinois Test of Psycholinguistic Abilities, 52, 54–57, 65–66, 92, 169, 204, 228, 309, 361
Illumination, 399
Imagery, mental, 90, 315, 334
Imbeciles, 161, 162, 221, 224
Imitation period in speech development, 76, 275
Incidental learning, 214
Independence, for the cerebral-palsied, 383, 384
for the crippled, 383, 384
Individual differences, 7–8
Individualized instruction, 68, 145, 202, 333–34, 380
Infantile paralysis. *See* Poliomyelitis
Influenza, 247, 248, 359, 371
Inhibitions, 391, 392, 398
Inner ear, 247, 250–51, 252
Inquiry Training, 147
Instantaneous Pitch Period Indicator, 277
Institutions, for the blind, 325
for the mentally retarded, 177, 178, 198, 206, 222, 223–25, 233, 357, 380–81
See also Residential schools
Integrated plan for teaching the blind and partially seeing, 330–31

Integration of handicapped into society, 6
Intelligence, in the blind, 305, 307–9
in the cerebral-palsied, 359–62
in the deaf, 270–71
low; *see* Mentally retarded children
superior; *see* Gifted children
Intelligence tests, 4, 7, 53, 109, 110, 112–13, 124, 129, 137, 161, 163, 168, 170, 183, 200, 204, 208, 269, 270–71, 360, 361
Intensity of sound, 246, 250
vocal, 82, 86, 97
Interests, of gifted children, 152–53
Interindividual differences, 7–8, 168
Internal strabismus, 299
International Standard Organization, 240
Interpersonal relations, 7, 122, 195, 231, 403; *see also* Personal adjustment
Intracranial tumor, 249
Intraindividual differences, 7–8, 12, 41, 55, 121, 168, 169, 327
Iowa Silent Reading Test, 280
IQ, of blind children, 305, 308
of cerebral-palsied children, 360
of children of the mentally retarded, 207
of deaf children, 270–71
distribution of, 8
of the educable mentally retarded, 168, 192, 193, 200, 207
of the gifted, 8, 108, 109, 113, 114, 120, 123, 129, 130–31, 132, 141
of the trainable mentally retarded, 228
Isle of Wight, behavior deviations, 401
Italians, giftedness among, 126
Itinerant teachers, 30–32, 34, 67, 99, 202, 209, 259, 260, 261, 284, 326, 330, 331, 338, 341, 368, 381, 414

Jacksonian epilepsy, 364, 365
Jena method of lip reading, 261
Jews, giftedness among, 126
John Tracy Clinic, 282
Johns Hopkins Study (rubella), 247
Junior high school, 210
Juvenile Court, 415

Kendall School, 284
Keratitis, 300
Kindergarten, cerebral-palsied in, 382–83
for the deaf, 283
mentally retarded children in, 181, 182, 209, 229
speech correction in, 99
Kinesthetic cues, 275–76, 282
Kinesthetic method of teaching reading, 59–60
Kinesthetic sensitivity in the blind, 315
Kuhlmann Tests of Mental Development, 178, 179, 228

Language development, for the blind, 313–14
for the cerebral-palsied, 382

for the deaf, 53, 265–68, 272, 278–80
for the educable mentally retarded, 204–5
for the trainable mentally retarded, 232
levels of, 54
Laser cane, 342
Law violations by mentally retarded, 207
Learning, disabilities in, 41, 201, 202, 208,
212, 213, 408
incidental, 214
principles of, for mentally retarded, 216–
17
See also Education and Teaching
Learning Disabilities Act of 1969, 43
Left-handedness, 87
Leiter International Performance Scale, 271
Lexington School for the Deaf, 264, 268
Library of Congress, 292, 336, 341
Lighting, 339
Lip (speech) reading, 41, 93, 241, 257, 259,
260–61, 262, 265, 267, 269, 274, 277–78,
283
Listening, learning through, 315–16, 338–39
Little's disease, 354
Localization theory, 351
Locomotion, 50
Lower-class culture, 399
Low intelligence. See Mentally retarded
children
Lunatic, 162

Major Work Classes, 141–42
Maladjustment. See Emotionally disturbed
children and Socially maladjusted chil-
dren
Malformations, 247, 250
Malingering, 249
Manual method of teaching the deaf, 262,
264–68, 283
Maps for the blind, 341
Marriage, 125, 207
Mass action, theory of, 351
Mass education, 106
Massachusetts, first class for the partially
sighted in, 324
first institution for the mentally retarded
in, 223
Massachusetts Commission for the Blind, 324
Massachusetts Institute of Technology, 144,
342
Massachusetts School for the Blind, 325; see
also Perkins Institute for the Blind
Mastoidectomy, 248
Materials and equipment. See Special ma-
terials and equipment
Mathematics for the blind, 341; see also
Arithmetic
Measles, 175, 247, 248, 354
Memory, 128, 149, 152, 196, 271
auditory, 93
in the blind, 314

Meningitis, 177, 248, 272, 359
Mental health, 125
Mental health clinics, 414–15
Mental imagery, 90
Mental tests. See Psychological tests
Mentally retarded children, 8–13, 28, 30, 32,
33, 35, 41, 44, 55, 57, 75, 91, 161–86
blind, 316
causes of disability, 172–83, 357
with cerebral palsy, 359–62
classified, 163–72
definitions of, 162–63
developmental patterns of, 166–68, 178
educable; see Educable mentally retarded
children
identification of, 164
prevalence of, 183–86
speech difficulties, 73, 81
statistics on, in later life, 178–82, 206–8
teachers of, 201–2, 208–10, 212–17
trainable; see Trainable mentally retarded
children
Merrill-Palmer Scale, 228
Michigan, special education districts in, 428
trainable mentally retarded children in,
222
Michigan Child Guidance Institute, 398
Midcentury White House Conference, 80
Middle ear, 94, 247, 248, 250, 252
Minnesota Mechanical Abilities Test, 308
Minnesota Preschool Scale, 228
Mirrors, use of, in speech correction, 98
in training the deaf, 276
Mobility, aids to for the blind, 336–38, 341
Models, 334, 337
Modified special classes, for the gifted, 141
for the mentally retarded, 231
Mongolism, 174, 182, 186
Monoplegia, 354, 359
Monroe Diagnostic Reading Examination,
310
Moon's phonic symbols, 335
Morons, 161, 224
Motivation, in the crippled, 375–76
curiosity as, 152
loss of, 396
for speech, 99
Motokinesthetic stimulation, 93
Motor coordination of the blind, 307
Motor development and proficiency in the
mentally retarded, 205–6, 232
Motor generalizations, 50
Movigenic curriculum, 51–52
Mueller-Walle Method of lip reading, 261
Multiple handicaps, 18, 23, 33, 316–17, 329
Multiple-sense modality approach, 98–99
Multiple-track plan, 106
Multisensory approaches, learning disabili-
ties, 53–57
Muscular dystrophy, 352, 369–70, 378, 383
Music, 205, 233, 314

Streptomycin, 249
Stuttering, 74, 77, 79, 83, 87–91, 96, 363
  management of, 89–91
  theories of, 88–89
Substitutions, of sound, 82, 83, 96, 261
Success experiences, 216, 217
Superego, 391
Suppressors, 355
Surgery, 94–95, 296, 299, 366
Sweep-check audiometric test, 258
Syphilis, 300
Syracuse Visual Figure-Ground Test, 50

Tactile sense, 15, 262–63, 275, 282, 304
Talking books, 315, 341, 343
Tape recorders, 340, 341, 343
Teachers, attitude of, toward special problems, 365
  of the blind, 293, 311, 329, 333, 343
  of cerebral-palsied children, 354
  certification of, 229, 427
  of crippled children, 379, 380
  of the deaf, 264, 272, 274, 275, 277, 282, 283
  of the gifted, 139–40, 145, 151–54
  itinerant, 30–32, 34, 67, 99, 202, 209, 259, 260, 261, 284, 326, 330, 331, 338, 341, 368, 381, 414
  of maladjusted children, 400, 404, 406, 413–15
  of the mentally retarded, 201–2, 208–10, 212–17
  of the partially seeing, 324, 329, 333, 335, 343
  personal qualifications of, 229–30
  regular, problems faced by, 35
  remedial, 67, 381
  in special education, preparation of, 214–17, 257, 330, 423–24
  speech, 99, 262; see also Speech clinicians who are deaf, 264, 283
Teacher's Guidance Handbook (Kough and DeHaan), 111
Teaching, of the blind, 311, 333–34
  individualized; see Individualized instruction
  of the mentally retarded, 213
  practice, 230
  of reading, 57, 60–62, 203
Team approach, to cerebral palsy, 354, 384
Telescoping grades, 136, 145
Teleteach system, 34
Television, 260
Temper tantrums, 396
Templin-Darley Tests of Articulation, 78
Terman Group Test of Mental Abilities, 123
Tests, achievement, 49, 112–13, 137, 267, 268, 271, 280
  articulation, 78, 261
  audiometric, 241, 258

character, 125
free-association, 313
group, 112–13, 258
for guidance of all children, 4
of hearing loss, 246
intelligence, 4, 7, 49, 63, 109, 110, 112–13, 124, 129, 137, 161, 163, 168, 170, 183, 200, 204, 208, 269, 270–71, 360, 361
of psycholinguistic abilities, 54–55
of reading and arithmetic ability, 63, 280–81, 310
of social maturity, 49
visual, 278, 292, 296, 315
Texas, special education in, 429
Thinking, analysis of, 108–9
  of gifted children, 128–30
Tonsils, infected, 248, 258
Tool subjects, 210
Totally dependent mentally retarded children, 161, 164, 166, 168, 186, 208, 222, 224, 230, 380
Touch. See Tactile sense
"Touch" reading. See Braille
Toxemia, 359
Trainable mentally retarded children, 28, 33, 161, 164–66, 168, 186, 198, 221–35, 380
  community classes for, 227–30
  curriculum for, 230–33
  prevalence of, 222–23
  provisions for, 223–27
  results of training of, 233–35
Transistor hearing aid, 260
Translation, braille, 342
Transportation, 229
Tremor cerebral palsy, 355, 356
Triplegia, 354
Trisomy, 174
Truancy, 397, 408
Tuberculosis, 22, 26, 162, 354, 370, 372
Tutoring, 115, 116, 118, 119, 134, 145, 260, 272
Typewriters, 314, 336, 339, 340
  braille, 314, 336
Typhoid fever, 248, 359

Underachieving gifted child, 108, 110, 121–22, 131–32, 145
UNESCO, 336
Ungraded primary program, 136
Unified instruction, 334
Unit plan for teaching, 281
United Cerebral Palsy Associations, 351, 352
United States, first class for the partially seeing in, 324
  first residential school for the blind in, 325
  mass education in, 106
United States Department of Health, Education, and Welfare. See Department of Health, Education, and Welfare